D0931504

Sublime Voices

The Fictional Science
and Scientific Fiction
of Abe Kōbō

Harvard East Asian Monographs 319

Sublime Voices

The Fictional Science and Scientific Fiction of Abe Kōbō

Christopher Bolton

Published by the Harvard University Asia Center
and distributed by Harvard University Press
Cambridge (Massachusetts) and London, 2009

Printed in the United States of America

The Harvard University Asia Center publishes a monograph series and, in coordination with the Fairbank Center for Chinese Studies, the Korea Institute, the Reischauer Institute of Japanese Studies, and other faculties and institutes, administers research projects designed to further scholarly understanding of China, Japan, Vietnam, Korea, and other Asian countries. The Center also sponsors projects addressing multidisciplinary and regional issues in Asia.

Library of Congress Cataloging-in-Publication Data

Bolton, Christopher.
    Sublime voices : the fictional science and scientific fiction of Abe Kobo / Christopher Bolton.
        p. cm. -- (Harvard east asian monographs 319)
    Includes bibliographical references and index.
    ISBN 978-0-674-03278-1 (cloth : alk. paper)
    1. Abe, Kobo, 1924–1993--Criticism and interpretation. 2. Literature and science. I. Title.
    PL845.B4Z57 2009
    895'.635--dc22

                                                                                2008047699

A portion of Chapter 4 was previously published in *Bakhtinian Theory in Japanese Studies*, ed. Jeffrey Johnson (Lewiston, ME: Edwin Mellen Press, 2001), 153–85. It is reprinted here by permission of Edwin Mellen Press.

Index by Eileen Doherty-Sil

♾ Printed on acid-free paper

Last figure below indicates year of this printing

19 18 17 16 15 14 13 12 11 10 09

To all my teachers,
especially my mom and dad

Acknowledgments

An invocation of names like this one probably runs counter to the spirit of Abe's literature, which is inhabited largely by nameless characters. One of Abe's narrators might simply thank a string of anonymous identifiers: "K—," "the man," "a professor at S. University." But in fact many unique individuals helped with this book.

I would like to thank my academic mentors: Makoto Ueda, Tom Hare, and Susan Matisoff, who supervised the dissertation that was the origin of this book; Nakagawa Shigemi, who generously acted as my sponsor for a Japan Foundation Fellowship; Tatsumi Takayuki; and Istvan Csicsery-Ronay, Jr. All of them supported the project with their rigorous guidance and adventurous spirits.

Barbara Ruch, Abe Neri, and the other eminent organizers and participants at the Abe Kōbō Commemorative Symposium, held at Columbia University in 1996, provided inspiration and positive feedback early on. Many friends and colleagues have supported me with advice and kindness since then, among them Bob Bell, Michelle Bloom, Tom Conlan, Michael Foster, Philip Kafalas, Tom Kohut, Kotani Mari, Neil Kubler, Tom Lamarre, Lisa Lowe, Frenchy Lunning, Livia Monnet, Susan Napier, Gail Newman, Christopher Nugent, Vivian-Lee Nyitray, John Ochoa, Brad O'Neill, Sharalyn Orbaugh, Ōtake Hiroko, Paul Park, Leyla Rouhi, Jay Rubin, Tom Scanlon, Thomas Schnellbächer, Rebecca Suter, and Abe's cousin Watanabe Sanko.

All my fellow graduate students at Stanford supplied a tremendous amount of intellectual energy and friendly encouragement during my time there. Colleagues at the Oakley Center for the Humanities and Social Sciences at Williams College gave me many useful suggestions. Naitō Yoshitada and Tomoda Yoshiyuki tirelessly translated some of this work for publication in Japan and brought to my attention new material and new ideas. And my brother Jonathan provided more help and insight than I can say.

Eileen Doherty-Sil prepared the index, and William M. Hammell at the Harvard University Asia Center was the sort of editor every author hopes for.

I received generous financial support for this research from Stanford University, the University of California, Riverside, and Williams College, as well as the Japan Foundation and the Mellon Foundation.

In Abe's world, the completion of a volume like this would typically be accompanied by the disappearance of the isolated author-protagonist, who would either flee leaving only this record behind, or else be transformed bodily into a stack of manuscript paper. Finally, I have my own "K—" and the rest of my incredible family to thank for giving this project a happier ending.

Contents

FOUR

The Dialogue of Styles, the Dance of Fiction,
and *The Face of Another*

FIVE

The Hope of Technology and the Technology
of Hope in *The Woman in the Dunes*

SIX

The Parody, Perversity, and Cacophony
of *Secret Rendezvous*

SEVEN

A Technology of Silence:
The Ark Sakura and the Nuclear Threat

Reference Matter

Notes

Works Cited

Index

Figures

Note to the Reader

Many of Abe's works have been expertly translated into English. (For a fairly complete list, see Lewell 21–23.) In the text, I reference these by their English titles, with the Japanese title given at the first occurrence; I give untranslated works by their Japanese titles, with a literal translation given at the first occurrence. Where possible, I have quoted from the published translations, and in these cases I give the page number in the English version. In some cases, the published translation does not convey aspects of Abe's style that are important to my argument. In these situations—and in cases where no published translation exists—I have translated the passages myself and cited the page numbers from the Japanese text in the *Abe Kōbō zenshū* (Complete works of Abe Kōbō, 1997–2000). These citations are indicated by the notation *AZ* followed by volume and page number.

Abe uses ellipses frequently in his writing, so elisions in my quotations from his work (and his work only) are indicated using bracketed ellipses: [. . .]. Where no brackets appear, the ellipses are present in the original Japanese, or in the published translation.

Sublime Voices

The Fictional Science
and Scientific Fiction
of Abe Kōbō

INTRODUCTION

Abe Kōbō's Dictionary

Shortly after the death of the Japanese novelist Abe Kōbō in 1993, his writing studio in Hakone was opened to a television film crew making a documentary about the author. As the camera travels through the room in the resulting film, it pauses momentarily at the bookshelf above Abe's desk and focuses on a large volume: a scientific dictionary.[1] It is fitting that this should become an icon of Abe's work, because his texts often include elements drawn from the world of science. His fiction incorporates material from disciplines such as biochemistry, geology, mathematics, and computer programming, to name just a few, and science becomes a source for his language, his characters, his metaphors, and his plots. It is this scientific influence in Abe's novels that is the subject of this book.

Abe was one of postwar Japan's most important writers, a leading light in the avant-garde from the 1950s through the 1970s and beyond. He was best known for his novels, which won him acclaim in Japan and abroad. His brand of imaginative fiction laid the groundwork for a generation of Japanese literature, ranging from the high literary fantasies of Ōe Kenzaburō to the science fiction of writers such as Komatsu Sakyō. Outside Japan, translations of Abe's work into languages from Czech to Chinese have made him one of Japan's best-known authors internationally. He was a perennial candidate for the Nobel Prize in Literature up until his death, and when Ōe won the prize the following year, he immediately commented that he was standing on Abe's literary shoulders ("Nōberu" 1).

Abe was also an intrepid explorer of different media and genres, and his legacy extends far beyond prose fiction. He was a playwright and director of the Abe Kōbō Studio, a company that helped define experimental theater in Japan in the 1970s. Besides theatrical plays, he also authored film and television screenplays, radio dramas, and even a stage musical. One of these films, a celebrated adaptation of his novel *The Woman in the Dunes* (*Suna no onna*, 1962), won the Special Jury Prize at the Cannes Film Festival in 1964, was nominated for two Academy Awards (Best Foreign Language Film in 1964 and Best Director in 1965), and garnered Abe a lasting place in the history of Japanese cinema.[2]

But Abe was originally trained as a doctor. He graduated from the medical college at Tokyo Imperial University, and he had a love of science that never left him. Alongside his artistic accomplishments runs a series of anecdotes about his continuing scientific interests: he remained an inveterate technophile all his life, fascinated with machines of all sorts—particularly cameras and automobiles; he once received an international inventor's award for a car part he designed; he composed electronic music during the infancy of the genre, and an antique patch-cord synthesizer was still sitting in his study when he died; and he was also one of the first Japanese authors of his generation to write on a computer. *The Ark Sakura* (*Hakobune Sakura Maru*), a novel published during the bronze age of personal computing in 1984, was completed on an early NEC word processor.

Yet the real mark of Abe's scientific interests is found in his fiction. Abe's characters include doctors (sane and mad), computer programmers, a polymer chemist, some part-time inventors, and an amateur entomologist. One of his signature characters is the private detective, a man who has one foot in his own world of rational logical deduction and the other in the uncertain grey underworld of crime.

The plots of many Abe novels also turn on scientific devices or situations. *Inter Ice Age 4* (*Daiyon kanpyōki*, 1959) paints a detailed future history in which climate change and genetic engineering have altered society and humanity to something utterly alien. These hard-science elements were so unusual in Japanese fiction of the time that the origins of science fiction in Japan are frequently traced to this novel. Abe's writing eventually moved away from science fiction and from these fantastically technical plots, but even though his later works are more fully grounded in

the present reality, they often alter that reality suppositionally or experimentally by recourse to some technical device. In *The Face of Another*
(*Tanin no kao*, 1964), for example, the narrator invents a process for constructing a mask that will be indistinguishable from a real human face.
In the course of this highly psychological and philosophical work, Abe
uses the device of the mask to interrogate our ideas about appearance
and identity. In *The Ark Sakura* the protagonist lives in an elaborate
bomb shelter that becomes an artificial world inside which Abe can ask
and address questions about destruction and isolation.

The scientific impulse touches even apparently low-tech works such
as *The Box Man* (*Hako otoko*, 1973), a novel about a homeless man living
in a cardboard box. The technical quality of the novel is apparent on
the opening pages, which provide careful instructions for constructing
the box and its special viewfinder, so that the occupant can observe the
world while remaining hidden himself. The parallels between the box
and a camera are made clear by the novel's many references to photography, which becomes a metaphor for the city's invisible class, almost
disembodied by their homelessness, seeing but unseen. Further, photography scholar William Parker points out that the design of the box is
actually based on a camera obscura, a lensed viewing chamber whose
long, rich history as a scientific instrument makes the novel an interro-
gation of scientific and artistic observation itself.

Even in works where the content is not overtly scientific, Abe's style
is still riddled with scientific vocabulary (and here we return to Abe's dictionary), as well as with intricate technical descriptions of scientific principles or processes. *The Woman in the Dunes* is a novel about a man who is
kidnapped by the residents of a strange village and forced to live in the
bottom of a sand pit, where he spends every day shoring up the endlessly
collapsing walls of the hole. The novel turns on the poetry of this spare
image and on the irreducible, crystalline metaphor of the sand; but even
this text is interspersed with technical discussions of the morphology
of sand grains, the biology of insect life in the dune ecosystem, or the
hygroscopic properties of sand. Abe's essays are also salted with these
technical metaphors and vocabulary: for example, identity, he tells us,
is like the square root of a negative number, and writing a novel is about
coming up with a hypothesis, or seeing with one side of the retina, or
adding an unexpected line to a diagram to complete a geometric proof.

But Abe the occasional scientist was first and foremost a leader of the avant-garde, an artist who constantly tested the boundaries of representation with texts that became progressively more adventurous and even bizarre over the course of his career. We might expect these two strains to be uneasy partners in Abe's work. Indeed, they do bear strange fruit in his writing. Several of the descriptions above hint at the tendency in Abe's fiction for the technical to be wedded to the absurd, the surreal, or the simply unreal. The detective, the box man, and the sand pit are just the most extreme examples.

In fact, Abe is probably best known for this grotesque or absurd strain in his fiction. His characters sometimes metamorphose into animals, plants, or inanimate objects. He is often compared with Kafka for this, and for the way that many of his protagonists awake one morning to find themselves in a world that is suddenly irrational, or that obeys a new rationality they cannot comprehend. In *The Crime of S. Karma* (*S. Karuma-shi no hanzai*), the novella that first earned Abe wide attention when it won the Akutagawa Prize in 1951, the hero has his name stolen, and finds that articles of his clothing have taken on a will of their own and are hatching a plot against him. He also discovers that if he stares at anything long enough he can make it disappear, and for the inadvertent acts of theft that result from this new power, he is placed on trial by a strange tribunal that meets in an underground chamber deep beneath the city zoo. But just as Abe's most scientific passages have an undercurrent of the absurd, even in his most fantastic stories Abe's trademark logic and technical vocabulary make an appearance. As we will see below, despite the carnival atmosphere of *The Crime of S. Karma*, one critic suggested that the work's defining features were in fact its "syllogistic reasoning" and the logical rigor of its prose!

This juxtaposition of the scientific and the grotesque remains one of the puzzles of Abe's work—a knot at the heart of his texts that is difficult to untangle. It is an aspect of the novels that is addressed only glancingly by most critics writing on Abe; yet it is this juxtaposition of the scientific with the grotesque and the irrational that defines Abe's unique idiom, and more than anything else it is the violent reaction between these two worlds that generates the energy driving Abe's texts. What kind of meaning does this juxtaposition produce? And what do Abe's texts have to say about science on the one hand or fiction on the other, and about the distinctions or elisions we make between the two? The goal of this book is to consider these questions by examining this combination of the scientific and the fantastic in Abe's novels. We will address this issue particularly from the standpoint of Abe's style and his language—the ground suggested by the opening image of Abe's dictionary. This book approaches Abe's texts by examining the kind of language they employ, and how they use this language to accomplish the mixing of these two worlds.

Each of Abe's novels displays within itself a range of different voices or dialects, some associated with science or a particular science, others associated with different languages and different ideas. The other languages may be drawn from different branches of science, from philosophy, psychology, literary prose, or even poetry. Although these dialects begin as distinct voices (belonging to different characters, for example), in the course of the novel they come in contact with one another, and as the ideas behind each language interact and change, Abe's different dialects collide, combine, split, and recombine. They activate or neutralize one another, and in particular they join to form new hybrids. The place where this mixing takes place is the laboratory—or the witches' cauldron—of Abe's prose.

Through this mixing of dialects, Abe forces the reader to question the distinctions often drawn between the scientific and the non-scientific, blurring the boundary between science and literature. One effect of Abe's novels at the time they were written was to broaden and problematize the idea of literary language—to make his readers question what literary language is, by stretching the definition of narrative prose to include technical language. Mikhail Bakhtin argues that the novel is a genre uniquely able to combine within itself voices and styles from a range of other disciplines, and Abe's novels expanded the envelope of high literature in just this way, clearing a place in the fictional space of the novel for a new kind of discourse.

Once Abe's work had opened this door, other authors followed suit, so that today this combination has become more common in Japan— not only in the genre of science fiction that Abe helped get off the ground, but in the mainstream literary establishment as well. A year after Abe died, Ishiguro Tatsuaki won the Akutagawa Prize for a novel written in the format of a scientific paper. Better known examples include Ōe Kenzaburō, Murakami Haruki, Shōno Yoriko, and Murakami Ryū, whose literary fantasies have sometimes borrowed scientific tropes or premises.

Tatsumi Takayuki has grouped Abe with the authors above under the label "slipstream" writers, suggesting a position between genre science fiction and more conservative streams of literary fiction.[3] Tatsumi and others have argued that this permeability of genres constitutes a dominant characteristic of Japanese literature today, but when Abe began writing, this mixed quality was much less common. This book looks carefully at contemporary Japanese critical reactions to Abe in order to recover some sense of the revolutionary quality—often puzzling, sometimes incomprehensible—that his prose had for Japanese readers at the time it was written. In fact, while Abe clearly helped clear a space for the genre-crossing fiction that succeeded him, even today the way he combines scientific and literary elements still sets him apart from most of the Japanese slipstream. Later chapters investigate this crossover style, with some more extended comparisons to authors such as Murakami Haruki and Murakami Ryū.

Even more interesting than the changes Abe wrought in literary language, however, is the way his work tried to alter received ideas about science. This aspect of Abe's writing remains most powerful today: at the same time that Abe's mixed style undermines narrow definitions of literature, it also overturns some of our stereotypes about science and its role in society. By pulling scientific language into his own domain (into the fantasy world of his novels), Abe is able to play with it in a way that shows science itself in a different light. We are led to view science in the same way that we see literature—not as an unassailable fortress of rationality but as a "magic kingdom" with its own (sometimes arbitrary) laws. Abe wrote at a time of rapid scientific and technological progress in Japan, and his novels avoid the prevailing blind faith in science, but without falling into a facile critique, either. Instead, the complex interplay of voices in his texts supports a more nuanced conclusion: that potential of science to bring about drastic, previously unthinkable changes is simultaneously its greatest promise and its greatest threat. To Abe, science and scientific language offered hope for a revolution that would point to radical new possibilities beyond everyday experience and everyday values. But Abe also recognized and warned about the disruption and disjunction that such a revolution would entail.

In this respect, Abe's fiction connects with work in the history and philosophy of science that sees links (forged from language) between science and literature. This includes not only recent efforts to understand scientific practice as a social discourse, but also centuries of work by literary critics who have attempted to distinguish or conflate the languages of literature and of science. This book examines Abe's novels and some of his essays on fiction and science within this global historical context, comparing his ideas with a range of critical traditions, from the Italian Renaissance and British empiricism down to New Criticism and Japanese poststructuralism. One of the threads that runs through this criticism is the construct called the sublime, a feeling of dangerous power or fearful excitement that has been invoked repeatedly to explain the mutual resonances and creative conflicts between science and fiction. We will sketch the early history of the sublime near the outset, and then return to this idea and its contemporary incarnations in subsequent chapters in order to develop an ear for the sublime voices that compose Abe's texts.

✖

Japanese scholarship on Abe has placed considerable emphasis on his unusual personal history, particularly a childhood in Manchuria where he witnessed firsthand Japan's colonial ambitions and their subsequent collapse at the end of World War II. With some encouragement from the author himself, many critics have connected this experience with Abe's suspicion of narrow rationalities and ideologies, and have sought the key to his fiction in the dilemmas of home, belonging, and individual or collective identity.[4] This book approaches Abe in a different way, by constructing an image of the author through his texts rather than the reverse. It also comes at these texts from a new direction, but the study of the science in Abe's work does connect at many points with existing criticism that centers on issues of identity. Chapter 1 addresses the question of biography by surveying Abe's early life and tracing the path he followed from a doctor-in-the-making to an established author. That chapter will conclude that although there is some connection between Abe's own transformation from doctor to writer and the fantastic metamorphoses portrayed in his texts, these shifts are far from straightforward and are as complex and sometimes as ambiguous as Abe's prose.

Shifting critical emphasis to look at the science in Abe's literature reopens his work in a number of ways. It revives some interest in earlier more overtly science fictional texts that have suffered the neglect of critics. But it also casts new light on mature works that have been examined mainly from other perspectives. Finally, it provides a critical purchase on Abe's difficult later novels, where the complete breakdown of rationality can leave the reader and critic at a loss. Chapter 2 orients us as described above, with a survey of Abe's essays on science and literature and some critical background on historical distinctions between these two fields, including an introduction to the notion of the sublime. After this, Chapters 3 through 7 focus on one or two novels from each of these categories or periods in Abe's career, offering new readings of the individual texts but also providing a sense of how Abe's treatment of science continued and changed throughout his life as a writer.

Each of these readings attempts to identify the different dialects or voices that make up the novel's style. Often they are associated with particular characters, or with the same character at different stages of the story. The readings then show how these voices change and interact as the characters and ideas come in contact with one another, or as new ideas are introduced. Finally, each chapter asks what the interaction of all these styles has to say about the world views, epistemologies, and social configurations that the styles represent.

For example, Chapter 3 examines one of Abe's early science fiction works, *Inter Ice Age 4*. The protagonist is a computer scientist who programs a machine to predict the future, but when he intervenes to prevent a frightening prediction from coming true, he finds that the machine itself has hatched a plot to oppose him. As the talking prediction machine develops a will of its own, its output/language changes from the cool, cut-and-dried computer code instilled in it by its creator to a rawer, more complex idiom. Each of these two extremes of style attracts its own adherents in the novel, and these two sets of characters and languages wage war against each other through the course of the work, until what emerges is a hybrid of the two dialects. In the machine's final prediction, both humans and computers are slated for extinction, to be replaced by new hybrid beings who can speak in and respond to these hybrid tongues.

This chapter updates the notions of the sublime introduced in Chapter 2 by examining more recent formulations of the "postmodern sublime" by Jean-François Lyotard, Jean Baudrillard, Fredric Jameson, Azuma Hiroki, and Katherine Hayles. All of these thinkers connect changes in language to technological evolution, suggesting that the growth of mass media and long distance communication has changed the ways we communicate and altered what it means to be human. If they are correct, it may be that we have already arrived at the situation depicted in *Inter Ice Age 4*, where stylistic hybrids correspond to human ones.

Chapter 4 treats a novel from the peak of Abe's creative prose activity in the 1960s, *The Face of Another*. The narrator is a chemist whose face is burned away in a laboratory accident. A plastics expert, he begins to construct a mask that will take the place of his missing face. The narrator's meticulous technical descriptions of the mask's construction reflect his hope that if he can just reduce the problem of his identity crisis to technical terms, he can solve it with technical means. The finished mask is indeed indistinguishable from a real face, but the narrator finds that when he dons the mask it begins to take on a will or a personality of its own. And the style in which the alter ego of the mask speaks is very different from the narrator's earlier technical idiom: it is a language of make-believe or fiction centered on the mask's deliriously violent fantasies, and eventually this less rational voice threatens to gain control of the narrative. The object of the chemist's desire and the mask's fantasies is the chemist's own wife, who finds herself caught between these two dialects. Finally she is left to try and balance them to yield a productive hybrid of science and fiction.

This chapter takes a closer look at Mikhail Bakhtin's theory of novelistic heteroglossia and dialogue. Superficial invocations of Bakhtin have become commonplace in literary studies, often simply drawing our attention to the multivoicedness that we would intuitively expect to find in almost any novel. This chapter draws on some of Bakhtin's earlier, more difficult, and less familiar philosophical work, which goes well beyond the now familiar ideas that the novel comprises different voices, and that these voices represent forces in society; Bakhtin also argues with some sophistication that identity formation is a process of assembling and reconciling the different voices that exist within and around a single being. As we read *The Face of Another*, Bakhtin shows us how identifying the different voices inside the narrator is a critical step in understanding the issues of identity and community that the novel treats.

Chapter 5 changes gears by examining the effects of technology on Abe's own literary production, as reflected in his experiments with other media. The best known example is the 1964 film adaptation of his novel *The Woman in the Dunes*, directed by Teshigahara Hiroshi from a script Abe wrote himself. Although theories of the postmodern sublime and some of Abe's own novels assign an alienating effect to technology and the way it multiplies and accelerates language, this chapter finds that the technology of Teshigahara's film actually rehumanizes the characters. The film does multiply the number of voices in the story, but instead of resulting in confusion and fragmentation, this actually produces conversations and communication that are absent in the novel. Abe's notion of analog and digital texts, as well as Vivian Sobchack's theory of analog and digital subjectivity, both suggest that the film itself may constitute a kind of human/machine hybrid that is paradoxically more optimistic and humanistic than the aquans, the prediction machine, the mask, or any of the technologized humans in Abe's written texts.

Finally, Chapter 6 treats one of Abe's later works, a written text that simulates the action of electronic technology on language more literally than any of Abe's novels up to that point. *Secret Rendezvous* (*Mikkai*, 1977) is also marked by the sheer fantasy common to Abe's later works, where the line between science and fancy is blurred almost beyond recovery. The story is set in a bizarre hospital where doctors perform absurd medical experiments. As the hospital's new chief of security, the narrator keeps everyone under constant surveillance with an intricate network of hidden microphones and tape recorders, whereby hundreds of voices throughout the hospital are combined and overlapped onto a single tape—the most literal expression yet of Bakhtin's heteroglossia. The narrator hopes that the surveillance tapes will help him make sense of the hospital's strange goings on. But the electronic multiplication of voices only confuses things further, until we hardly know who is speaking or what is being said.

It becomes hard to know how seriously we are to take the science in this work. Is it still part of a balance with non-science or fiction, or have the grotesque elements finally triumphed completely? In this way, the disorder of the novel's language confuses sense and nonsense until it finally produces a kind of moral disorientation as well. The fantasies become progressively more disturbing in Abe's later works, and in *Secret Rendezvous* the reader is unsure whether to laugh, stare, or cringe at the novel's parade of perverse technology. The way that the multiplication of styles erodes a stable linguistic or ethical perspective is a problem taken up by Bakhtin and Fredric Jameson in their characterizations of parody and pastiche. Chapter 6 compares these and other theories of parody, to ask just how far language can be mixed, layered, and destabilized before all perspective is lost.

All of these readings are intended to shed new light on Abe's novels by viewing them in the context of questions about science and literature or science in society. But what of the reverse: does reading Abe's novels shed any new light on these social and theoretical questions? To answer this, Chapter 6 takes the lessons about heteroglossia, parody, and sublimity learned from Abe's texts and applies them to a set of recent critical controversies in the world of science studies, the Sokal hoax and the Bogdanov affair. In the former, a scientist published a critical article on literature and science in a prominent journal of cultural studies and then announced that it was a hoax. In the latter, a prominent physicist turned the Sokal affair on its head by suggesting that the published scientific papers of two colleagues might in fact be intentional or unintentional parodies of scientific research.

Published in 1977, *Secret Rendezvous* arguably marked the end of Abe's last great productive period as a writer. He published only two more novels before his death in 1993. For many critics and readers these proved even more baffling than *Secret Rendezvous*, and Abe's long silences between these novels were matched by puzzled silences from critics, who had (and still have) little to say about these later works. Chapter 7 considers the possibility that these silences were also the result of technology's effect on literature. Abe's 1984 novel *The Ark Sakura* revolves around the nuclear stalemate of the 1980s, and the ways that nuclear technology produced a paralysis of the dialogue that had driven Abe's work up to this point.

✴

Although issues of biography, identity, and origins have dominated interpretations of Abe's works, many critics have at least noticed the works' scientific content, and a few have treated it systematically, though none have analyzed it at real length. The critics who have addressed it can be divided very roughly into two camps: those who read Abe's scientific language and content in perfect seriousness, as a model of clarity and logic, and those who regard it as a gross caricature of science that demonstrates nothing less than the bankruptcy of the narrow rationality of science. The argument of this book is that both of these interpretations are simplifications (or exaggerations) that fail to capture the special quality of Abe's texts, which contain both elements of caricature and a great deal of extremely accurate and committed scientific logic. Abe's texts actually thread a course between the extremes of simply mocking science on the one hand or on the other hand swallowing it whole. Through this balance, Abe conveys the idea that science has a creative and sometimes disruptive quality as well as a clarifying power.

It may be helpful here to consider an example of each of these other readings in order to show the two positions between which this book attempts to steer. In the first category are many critics who take Abe's scientific language more or less at face value: for example, repeating the scientific metaphors he uses to describe his own work without any trace of irony, as if accepting them on faith. Alternatively, they may note the scientific content only in passing, and treat it merely as a kind of stylistic window dressing that imparts "realism" to the text. In this view, the detailed descriptions of the mask's construction in *The Face of Another*, for instance, simply justify the premise upon which the novel is based. In these interpretations, only the relationship between face and identity is really important—the mask is just a prop. The reader can even skip the more doggedly scientific paragraphs once he or she gets the general tone. But the difficulty with reading Abe this way is that it does not address or explain how scientific language and rationality are deliberately deformed and transformed in the course of the text.

As a case study in this sort of criticism, consider an early article by Ishikawa Takashi on Abe's prose style that appeared in the journal *Gengo seikatsu* in 1955. The article analyzed the word choice, sentence construction, and even the typography and line breaks of *The Crime of*

S. Karma. Setting aside the chaotic, carnival quality of the plot to focus on the style, Ishikawa concludes that the prose is "voluble and explanatory, but also simple and fast-paced." He suggests that Abe's "explanations," "syllogistic reasoning," and similar techniques are particularly appropriate for depicting the world of the novel—a world that is fantastic but also highly conceptual—and he contrasts Abe's language with the "sensual clarity and deep symbolism" of a style like Shiga Naoya's (38–40). Ishikawa apparently means to suggest that in the maze of ideas and fantastic events in Abe's story, clear and rapid exposition of everything is paramount. One of the sentences he cites is from the first page of the work: "I went to the cafeteria, I guess because I was hungry (although even if I hadn't been hungry, I still would have gone), and there I had two bowls of soup and two pounds of bread" (*AZ* 2:378).

Ishikawa identifies the parenthetical comment, for example, as just another example of the kind of exposition that keeps us abreast of the ideas and their progress. Ishikawa had the unenviable privilege of being answered by Abe in the same issue of the journal, in a piece now known as "S. Karuma-shi no sujō" (The character of S. Karma), though when originally published it was titled simply "Watashi no buntai" (My writing style). Abe points out rather easily that the apparent reasoning of S. Karma makes little sense, claiming that "at that time I was trying my best to write nonsense" (*AZ* 5:343). Abe even maps the logical propositions of the sentence above to show that Karma is not really reasoning through anything; he is in fact trying to attach a reason to something that does not have one, or does not need one. Abe explains in the essay that one of his goals was to show in S. Karma the futility of certain kinds of reason. The moral of this story is that the reader should be on guard against taking the realism of Abe's science at face value. One must give attention to the cracks and shortcomings in these sections, and the ways that language threatens to break down or transform itself into something unexpected.

There is another kind of reading that takes an approach diametric to Ishikawa's and dismisses Abe's scientific material at the outset as part of a straw man rationality that the novel will inevitably topple. This approach reads all of the scientific language in an ironic tone and sees an element of parody everywhere. It is a particularly tempting reading for some of Abe's later novels, where nothing seems to be taken seriously, and we will revisit the notion of parody in the book's final chapter. But even in these later novels, failing to give the scientific language its due at least some of the time deprives the novels of an important dynamic.

David Pollack tends toward this kind of reading in his chapters on Abe in *Reading Against Culture*. Pollack's book questions cultural essentialism by exposing culture as something deployed and constructed for economic or political ends. He posits science as one form of ideology, a constructed system that is historically linked with the dangerous rationality of urban society and capital: "The connective strand running through all of Abé's work is the idea that rationality, pursued logically to its logical endpoint, turns out to be insanely irrational. . . . In Abé's hands, properly licensed and accredited scientific knowledge of the world proves not only as false as any other but even more so, and certainly more destructive in its consequences" (124).

One interesting chapter of Pollack's book analyzes *The Woman in the Dunes* and its insect collector protagonist Niki Junpei. Pollack's reading links the decay of the protagonist's narrow scientific rationality with his retreat or freedom from the city and its rationality of modern capital. And Niki's decision to remain in the village at the end of the book becomes the triumph of a rural utopian ideal (or ideology) over the urban scientific one. In many places this reading is clearly on target. Most of Abe's characters do have this tendency to follow reason relentlessly until it finally leads them to contradiction or nonsense. This is a process traced in the following chapters, as one side of the interplay between science and non-science, or science and nonsense. But I think Pollack is a little too anxious to condemn all of science for the shortcomings of the protagonist's logic, and he does not give science itself all the attention it deserves in this novel. In particular, his readings miss a creative or positive effect even "properly licensed and accredited scientific knowledge" can have.

The Woman in the Dunes is considered in more detail in Chapter 6, but as an example of where this book's approaches and conclusions differ from Pollack's, consider the following detail from his reading. It returns us one final time to Abe's dictionary. To show the narrator's distorted logic and his "step-by-step deduction somehow gone a few degrees awry," Pollack cites a definition of sand that the narrator gives at the beginning of the novel. Pollack characterizes it as a "dry but somehow slightly implausible encyclopedia entry that reads like a passage from one of Borges's imaginary books" (127).

SAND: an aggregate of rock fragments. Sometimes including loadstone, tin-stone, and more rarely gold dust. Diameter: 2 to 1/16 mm. (13)

But is this encyclopedia really as fantastic as Borges's? Below is the actual definition of sand (*suna*) from the standard Japanese dictionary *Kōjien* (fourth edition, my translation).

SAND. An aggregate of fine rock grains. Composed mainly of various mineral particles. Usually indicates grains having a diameter between 1/16 mm and 2 mm.

In Japanese or in English, the two definitions are almost identical. Instead of the fantasy or lampoon of scientific language that Pollack implies, Abe's language is in one sense very realistic. Much of the scientific language in Abe's texts shows this same commitment to logic and accuracy, and it is a mistake, I think, to dismiss it all as part of a hollow rationality. The readings in the following chapters all assume that a careful reading of Abe's style must accord science a certain integrity to allow it to function within the text. We must be sensitive to the complex relationship between fact and fantasy—in this case, the sense of amused discovery many first-year geology students have had on discovering that what we all know intuitively as sand must in fact be defined by the diameter of its grains. (Anything larger is technically pebbles; anything smaller is silt or clay.) Even though Abe's definition of sand is accurate, Pollack's instincts are certainly correct when he says that there is something quirky about this passage and the way it is presented. In this case the *truth* of science turns out to be just as quirky or fantastic as fiction, and it may be science itself that jolts us out of our narrow rationalism.

I believe this is an experience physicists, biologists, engineers, and the like have frequently; at least I did in the course of my own scientific education. And here, before turning to Abe's biography in Chapter 1, it may not be out of order to say a word or two about my own background. I was an undergraduate engineering major and then a software developer working between America and Japan before I turned to Japanese literature, and even when I was earning my doctorate in Japanese (in the heart of Silicon Valley), I found myself falling in with engineers as often as humanists. I am sure this has influenced my reading of Abe; perhaps more importantly, it has influenced my perception of the frequently touted divide between literature and science, and my desire to work on or in that gap. So while the pages that follow focus as much as possible on Abe's texts, perhaps I should disclose some of my personal opinions here at the outset, rather than making the reader wait for my preoccupations and idiosyncrasies to emerge from between the lines of the text, as they do in the case of Abe's own narrators.

My feeling is that there is a creative, open-minded, even perpetually surprised side of science and scientists that scholars in the humanities do not always appreciate—that humanities often wrongly sees science as "a desert of numbers with no room for mysteries, no shadow of a doubt," to borrow a phrase from Abe (*AZ* 15:237). On the other hand, I also believe that the scientific method used in laboratory research (and in many other disciplines that aspire to scientific objectivity) tends to bracket a number of important philosophical questions about knowledge, knowability, and representation. At the outset, these questions are set aside deliberately and consciously—by declaring science's object to be the measurable rather than the actual, for example. These bracketed questions are often forgotten until the habits of scientific thought (and the fruits of technology) are allowed to escape the lab and enter the larger arena of controversies about society and identity, and then these questions return with a vengeance. In debates among scientists, literary critics, and cultural historians who study science (notably, the so-called culture wars and the "science wars" taken up in Chapter 6), some claimants have persistently tried to apply the specialized rationality of what are essentially laboratory protocols to broader questions that these methods are not equipped to address—questions that center on the interplay of the real, the represented, and the perceived, for example. The shortcomings of a narrowly rigorous scientific method often seem to go unacknowledged in these arenas, because the scope the method originally set for itself—the limit that is the very source of its power—has been forgotten.

Throughout this book, I have tried to focus my discussion on specific perspectives on science and literature, specific images (some) people have of science or literature, and specific languages associated with science and literature. It is difficult and often dicey to translate these conclusions into generalizations about how scientists (or literary critics) think as a group; both are a notoriously and wonderfully varied lot. So the generalizations about some scientists and critics above are soft ones, and they are neither the premise nor the conclusion of this book. They do constitute a personal perspective (or observation, or ideology) that explains my motive for writing this text, and gestures toward what I think is at stake in reading it. Abe's work resonates for me in the way it bridges science and literature, juxtaposing these two epistemes to expose the unexpected powers and limitations of both—limitations that all too often become invisible to those within a given discourse, and powers that often go unnoticed by those outside it.

To return, then, to the point above, I would argue for a more sympathetic (I would also say more faithful and more rigorous) reading of Abe's science than Pollack suggests with his analogy to "Borges's imaginary books." But Pollack's invocation of Borges is appropriate to his own argument. For those unfamiliar with the fantastic dictionaries and imaginary reference works described in the essays and short stories of the Argentine writer, a typical example is "a certain Chinese encyclopedia" cited by one of Borges's narrators, wherein

it is written that animals are divided into (a) those that belong to the Emperor, (b) embalmed ones, (c) those that are trained, (d) suckling pigs, (e) mermaids, (f) fabulous ones, (g) stray dogs, (h) those that are included in this classification, (i) those that tremble as if they were mad, (j) innumerable ones, (k) those drawn with a very fine camel's hair brush, (l) others, (m) those that have just broken a flower vase, (n) those that resemble flies from a distance. (103)

Borges offers this apparently apocryphal example in "The Analytical Language of John Wilkins," to suggest the arbitrary nature of classification, and by extension the futility of transparent language. This is a point close to Pollack's claim about the arbitrary and ideological nature of any framework for knowledge and perception. Despite my considerable sympathy for this claim, I do not believe that science (at least not for Abe) is as arbitrary as Pollack suggests. But I would endorse the comparison between Abe's encyclopedia and Borges's if we consider Borges's book the way Michel Foucault does. Foucault cites the Chinese encyclopedia in his preface to *The Order of Things* as a fable that jolts us into realizing the limits imposed on us by the "orders" that organize our thoughts (xv). In this respect, it resembles the creative ways Abe uses science, not just to tear down the systems of science, but to awaken us to new possibilities within science and without.

In his suggestive work on the "encyclopedic imagination," Michael Foster compares early Japanese reference works on monsters and other oddities with another Borges book, from the short story "Tlön, Uqbar, Orbis Tertius." In that story the narrator discovers a forged encyclopedia purporting to describe the planet of Tlön. The work is fiction, but it is so complete and convincing (particularly in its description of Tlön's science and philosophy) that it is widely believed, to the point where it eventually becomes normative for our world, and the real world starts to change to become more and more like the imaginary planet. So in Borges's story, a fiction about science first changes people's attitudes toward scientific reality, and then transforms reality itself. Foster compares this with the creative science at work in eighteenth-century Japanese catalogs of monstrous creatures, "reference" works that set out to depict the world and ended up creating new science out of whole cloth.[5] Monsters and monstrous science both turn up frequently in Abe's texts, and we will return to them in the chapters that follow. But the broader idea that Foster and Borges highlight is the leakage between scientific truth and fiction. This book is in large part about this process of leakage or exchange. Chapter 1 begins with one aspect of that process, by reviewing Abe's early biography and tracing the complicated exchanges and interactions between the world in which Abe grew up and the worlds of his fiction.

ONE

Transforming Science:
Metamorphosis in Abe's Life and Work

A young man (a university student, an erstwhile scientist) wakes up one morning to find his world changed. The rules of society are transformed; the people around him are speaking a new language, one familiar and yet different; the landscape outside his window has become unrecognizable. And an alien race has come to power. As he struggles to adjust to these new surroundings, the man slowly realizes that he is also beginning to change. . . .

This could easily be the beginning to one of the stories by Abe discussed in the Introduction, or it could be a scene from the author's own life. These kinds of changes occur regularly in Abe's texts, whether it is the character's own body that metamorphoses into something else or the world that is transformed around him. This is one source of the instability, unpredictability, and fantasy that contrast with the scientific rigor we find elsewhere in Abe's texts, forming one half of the balance between "sense" and "nonsense" that I will identify as a defining characteristic of Abe's prose.

Abe's early life was characterized by a similar kind of instability. Abe was born in Tokyo, but grew up in Japanese-occupied Manchuria, part of Japan's growing empire in Asia. He describes it as a world apart from Japan, with its landscape of walled villages on barren steppes, its mix of cultures, and its changing political situation, as it went from the prominent frontier of an expanding Japanese domain to a place of danger and uncertainty in the days following Japan's defeat. With these things in mind, critics have sometimes identified Manchuria as a source of the otherworldly imagery in Abe's works. Yet for someone like Abe who grew up there, the description of the "alien land" that starts this chapter is one that might apply equally well to the Japan to which Abe returned after the war. The alien language might be Chinese or Japanese. The transformed landscape might be the steppes of Asia or the Tokyo cityscape. And the alien rulers might be the Japanese colonial government in Manchuria or the American occupiers in Japan.

At the same time, Abe underwent a metamorphosis of his own. After returning to Japan, he finished the medical studies he had started during the war, but he never pursued a career in medicine. Instead, he turned to literature, and with the suddenness of one of his transforming characters, he rapidly forged a name for himself as an up-and-coming member of the postwar avant-garde.

This chapter examines Abe's early life and his literary debut, tracing some of these early influences and centering on this trope of transformation or metamorphosis both inside and outside of Abe's stories. Critics have been eager to draw a connection between the instabilities and change Abe experienced early in his life and the chaotic worlds and strange metamorphoses in his novels. These connections between Abe's life and work have become so ingrained in the critical discourse on Abe that knowing them is important for understanding the perspective from which critics have approached Abe's texts. But as we will see, the usual problems of equating the worlds inside and outside the text are exacerbated in the case of Abe, who not only opposed the autobiographical modes that dominated Japanese fiction, but actively undermined them in his own texts.

Although this chapter starts with Abe's personal history and the directions this background suggests for approaching the author's work, it concludes that there is a need to turn our critical attention from Abe's life back to the texts themselves. More specifically, the tropes of transformation and metamorphosis discussed above also find expression in the style of these texts. In the early works centering on transformation that are the subject of this chapter, the physical transformations in each story are mirrored by transformations in the language and style of the work. The transformed or chaotic reality the characters inhabit is represented not only by strange objects and events, but also by changes in the languages that swirl around them, and physical metamorphoses are accompanied by changes in the way characters speak or are spoken to. Finding some stable place or identity in this shifting reality involves not only maintaining one's shape, but also finding one's voice.

Abe claimed that he never had a "home town," but on paper it was the city of Asahikawa in Hokkaidō, the northernmost of the main Japanese islands and the last area to be settled by the central government. Abe's mother and father both grew up in Hokkaidō after their parents moved there from Shikoku as settlers in the nineteenth century. Hokkaidō was the place listed on Abe's family registry until his death, and one of many frontiers that would figure prominently in his work. Abe notes the pioneer spirit of his grandparents, and it may have been in a similar spirit that his father left Hokkaidō to attend the medical college in Mukden, Manchuria. He later joined the faculty and eventually opened a medical practice in the city.[1]

Abe's mother Yorimi had a literary education, with a published novel to her credit and an interest in proletarian literature. (She had been expelled from college for socialist activities.) She married Abe's father Asakichi in Japan, while he was spending a year in Tokyo doing research, and it was there that she gave birth to their first child Kimifusa on March 7, 1924. The following year, Asakichi returned to Manchuria with his wife and son. It was this child who would later change the reading of the characters in his given name (one of many transformations) and become Abe Kōbō.

Both idealism and opportunity drew hundreds of thousands of Japanese settlers to Manchuria in the early twentieth century, but the face of the Japanese presence there changed radically during Abe's youth.[2] Through the 1920s, Manchuria was still Chinese territory, but under the unequal treaty system Japan was making economic and territorial inroads along the rail lines of the Japanese-run South Manchuria Railway Company. Abe's home of Mukden (present-day Shenyang) was 250 miles north of Port Arthur at the center of the rail network, and schools and hospitals were among the public facilities the railway administered. Mukden was also the site of the Manchurian Incident of 1931, after which Japan staged a full-scale military takeover of the region and set up the puppet state Manchukuo, a huge region it governed through a Chinese proxy government up until the end of the war.

Abe spent most of his early childhood in Mukden, but as he grew older he moved back and forth between the two worlds of Manchuria and Japan. He lived in Hokkaidō for a year in elementary school, and traveled to Tokyo for high school at age sixteen. After an illness that kept him home in Manchuria during the outbreak of the Pacific War, he returned to Tokyo to finish high school and then entered Tokyo Imperial University as a medical student. But in the waning years of the war, he was far from committed to his medical studies, and in 1944 when Japan's defeat seemed imminent he snuck back into Manchuria. After Japan's defeat, the family remained there for over a year while the area was under Russian occupation, and then the children and their mother returned to Occupied Japan in 1946. Abe's father had died treating a typhus outbreak the year before.

Abe speaks of the disorder in Manchuria as both frightening and exciting. Asked by American interviewer Nancy Shields to describe Mukden, Abe says it was "a frightening place in many ways. There was no law in the streets, where sometimes children were sold as slaves. It was nonetheless a fascinating city, a maze, a labyrinth" (443).[3] After the defeat, the chaos and possibilities increased. In a chronology of his life ("Nenpyō," 1960), Abe writes this in the entry for 1945: "In August, abruptly, the war ended. Suddenly the world was bathed in light, and I felt as if every kind of possibility had materialized at once. The conditions that followed, without any government, were harsh; but along with fear and unease, the absence of government also planted something else in me—a dream" (*AZ* 12:465, qtd. in Tani 17).

So the scene of transformation that begins this chapter could be seen as something full of unsettling uncertainty but also exciting potential. In the entry quoted above, even the death of Abe's father is described as an event pregnant with possibilities ("Freedom from my father, and from the duties and inheritance he represented"). Among the opportunities of the defeat, Abe also lists an end to the racism fostered by Japanese colonialism. With the dismantling of the Japanese colonial empire, the puppet state of Manchukuo in which Abe grew up was dissolved. And in a real sense the Japan he knew had ceased to exist as well, as Occupation authorities set about recasting Japanese government and society in a new mold. In another chronology of his early life ("Ryaku nenpyō," 1966), Abe wrote what was to become an enduring characterization of his life and work: "Fundamentally you might say I am a person without a home town. Maybe the deep hostility that I feel toward the home town traces itself to my background. I am hurt by anything that attaches value to being settled" (*AZ* 20:92).

This state of homelessness and unsettledness is linked with change and transformation in Abe's work, and it will be helpful to look at this notion of home and belonging in a little more detail before continuing with the idea of metamorphosis. Isoda Kōichi has characterized Abe's perspective and his writing as "nationless" (Isoda, "Mukokusekisha"). This label has followed Abe tenaciously, but it has meant different things to different critics.

We might group the facets of Abe's "nationlessness" that critics have highlighted into three different categories. The first is Abe's rejection of nationalism. Whether in spite of or because of his family's role in the Manchurian experiment, the hostility to which Abe refers included a deep-seated antipathy toward nationalism of the kind that fostered Japanese imperialism. While his contemporary Mishima Yukio sought solutions to Japan's postwar identity crisis in a patriotism grounded in traditional culture, Abe's fiction and criticism tenaciously attacked what he called "the pseudo-culture which tries to legitimize the walls surrounding nations" ("Journey" 43). Borrowing a term Abe himself applied to artists such as Bertolt Brecht and Gabriel García Márquez who escaped from the nationalism of their home countries, the Swedish critic Olof Lidin has characterized Abe as a literary exile or "refugee" (*bōmeisha*). If there is hope for the world in the face of rising nationalism, Lidin says, "Abe sees it in the cultural internationalism which these runaway writers, *bōmeisha*, stand for" (9).

Second, Abe's supposed nationlessness has also been connected with his apparent rejection of native Japanese literary traditions, and even with the popularity of his works abroad. Abe rarely borrows elements of traditional Japanese literature the way authors such as Tanizaki Jun'ichirō or Kawabata Yasunari do, and Abe's novels also reject the modes of fiction such as Naturalism and the I-novel that dominated Japanese literature before and after the war. The author with whom Abe is most frequently compared is Franz Kafka, for the thematic and formal similarities in their work, and the influences that Abe names are almost always Western authors. As a high school student he reportedly had little interest in Japanese literature, and was drawn instead to Fyodor Dostoevsky and to German philosophy (Tani 360–63). His essays make reference to a parade of Western writers: his critical debut—a 1948 presentation to the avant-garde writer's group Yoru no Kai (The Night Society)—discusses the notion of creativity with reference to John Dewey, André Gide, Rainer Maria Rilke, and Parmenides—by way of Nietzsche (Schnellbächer, *Strategist* 273–81). Later essays include references ranging from Ancient Roman and Italian Renaissance figures, through writers such as Kafka, Edgar Allan Poe, and August Strindberg, down to science fiction authors such as Joseph Campbell and Robert Sheckley. The Introduction dealt briefly with Abe's fame around the world. In fact, in contrast to other Japanese authors of similar stature, Western scholarship has made up a disproportionately large amount of the work on Abe. In some senses, Abe may be more celebrated outside Japan than in.[4]

Finally, critics have compared Abe's absence or loss of a homeland to the experiences of his characters, who often waver between a desire to rejoin society and an urge to escape it once and for all. There is no question that this is a central theme in virtually all of Abe's novels: many of his characters are literally or figuratively homeless, and all of them wrestle with issues of identity and belonging, the desire for inclusion, and at the same time the fear of being suffocated or controlled by others.

Whether they focus on Abe's opinions, his style and reception, or his plots, these various approaches that relate Abe's early life and so-called nationlessness to his texts have yielded some interesting conclusions, but they have become prone to oversimplification. Three points stand out in particular. First, for those who would equate Abe's personal history with the plight of his homeless characters, the parallels are admittedly tempting. This is almost certainly what Abe intended when he set up this comparison, which was clearly part of his own performance as an author. But this perspective has dominated a great deal of work on Abe up to now, suggesting that it is time for a fresh approach.[5] Furthermore, despite this sustained critical attention to the issue of home and belonging, their status in Abe's work remains ambiguous: do Abe's works represent a decisive rejection of the idea of home, or a nostalgic desire for its return, or the advent of something new to replace it? Abe's own experiences might suggest these questions, but they do not provide any definitive answers, and probably fortunately so, since the continuing interest of Abe's work lies precisely in this rich ambiguity.

Second, on the foreignness of Abe's style, it is true that in many ways Abe's literature represents a break with what had come before, but to say that his background somehow removed Abe from the Japanese literary context is to ignore the postwar Japanese avant-garde movement on which Abe drew and in which he participated, a movement that broke en masse from past traditions and saw itself as forging new traditions to replace them. By now it has become a truism that even the so-called traditionalists cited above, Kawabata and Tanizaki, participated in this avant-garde exploration and experimentation, so in this respect Abe does not necessarily stand apart. In fact, it might be suggested that some Japanese critics, frustrated with the difficulty of finding a unifying context for Abe's work, have been a little too eager to substitute the catch-all context of "foreign" or "international" and to leave work on Abe to foreign scholars.

Third, to those who would make a simple contrast between wartime nationalism and Abe's internationalism, one might point out that the two were not always easily distinguished. Abe's invocation of Manchuria seems to draw equally on the image of a romantic Asian frontier that beckoned adventurous Japanese settlers, and the region's history as the political and military staging ground for the invasion of China. Like many writers and intellectuals, Abe joined the Japan Communist Party (JCP) after the war and opposed Japan's complicity in the American-led militarization of Asia. But when the Soviet Union crushed the revolts in Poland and invaded Hungary under the banner of international socialism in 1956, Abe again felt he was on the wrong side of the equation, and eventually broke with the JCP over issues of freedom of artistic and national political expression. (He was expelled from the party in 1962, along with a number of other writers.) In this way the line between internationalist idealism and nationalist ideology was sometimes blurred, and Abe negotiated these issues only with difficulty. Without sharing the latter's patriotism, Abe had some common ground even with Mishima.[6] So the investigation of these currents in Abe's own life and work must avoid easy dichotomies and pay careful attention to the complex construction of concepts such as home, community, and nation.

On these three points, the complexity of the issues and the lack of clear answers are traced in Thomas Schnellbächer's *Abe Kōbō, Literary Strategist*, a detailed history of Abe's early literary and political activities, centering on his essays. If the question is how to place Abe's early artistic and political progressivism in its Japanese historical context (including the context of communist writers' movements), then Schnellbächer's text is the most exhaustive answer available in English or Japanese. It traces a development in Abe's view of progressive literature between 1948 and 1962, starting from an abstract philosophical view of artistic revolution associated with institutions such as the journal *Kindai bungaku*, and shifting in the early 1950s toward the conviction that literature could foster progressive political reform only if it were read and eventually written by the proletariat. (In one early published dialogue between Abe and workers at a munitions factory, a worker describes their literary reading group and how they hid meetings from the foremen by gathering behind unfinished American tanks [*AZ* 3:516, qtd. in Schnellbächer 180].) Schnellbächer shows how as art and political movements evolved in Japan, Abe's notion of literary production moved from this grassroots model to a more professional and market-driven one in which literary intellectuals would explore new forms of literary expression that could nevertheless still appeal to the common reader.

One thing that emerges from this excellent account is the complexity of categorizing even fundamental concepts such as progressivism, realism, relevance, or actuality in Abe's work. Part of this lies in the complexity of Abe's own ideas; another part lies in the fraught artistic and political culture of the time, a literary history that is recovered only with some difficulty.[7] Abe's own statements must be read with an eye toward the constantly shifting political context within the JCP and the progressive writers' movements in which he participated, but Abe's political position in these groups is not always clear. For example, what motivated the party's decision to expel Abe and other writers was clearly their public criticism of party policy—but Abe said almost nothing about this expulsion in public, and its significance for him is uncertain. Was he becoming more socialist than communist, more internationalist than regionalist, more literary than political, more individually oriented than movement-driven, or more disillusioned than idealistic? Different commentators feel differently, and Schnellbächer can only suggest some of each (243–53).

The present volume does not try to duplicate or challenge the painstaking work in Schnellbächer's book. The chapters that follow do give attention to recovering a Japanese context for Abe's work, by including a thorough survey of Japanese critical writing about each novel. Added to Schnellbächer's focus on literary history and his close reading of Abe's own essays, this produces some new conclusions about how Abe's work has been read in Japan. An equally important goal of this book is to take a next step and read Abe in a broader context: a historical context that relates him to theories of science and literature going back to the Renaissance, and an international context that takes in not only Western history and philosophy of science (much of which Abe knew well) but also Abe's significance and appeal for readers outside as well as inside Japan. The discussion of Abe's later novels, for example, will contrast their reception in Japan and the West. This book also shifts the context to Abe's novels and tries to cover the whole sweep of his career as a novelist. (Schnellbächer's volume treats Abe's early and middle essays, while other books on Abe by Timothy Iles and Nancy Shields have focused primarily on Abe's later dramatic work with the Abe Kōbō Studio in the 1970s.)

So given the complexities outlined above, what generalizations can we make about Abe's perspective over his career? One thing that emerges powerfully—both from Schnellbächer's careful case studies, and from prevailing generalizations about Abe's hostility toward nationalism as well as nostalgia for the "home town"—is that these are all examples of Abe's antipathy for the dominance of any accepted orthodoxy. This included any common sense that the individual was unable or unwilling to question or to oppose. For Abe, it was this orthodoxy that was a central problem with all collectives (*kyōdōtai*), even in cases where certain kinds of collectivity—like artistic and political solidarity with the workers—were embraced. In a late dialogue with Donald Keene, Abe emphasized that it was not so much the experiences he had in Manchuria that were important as the lack of experience: being outside of Japan's orthodoxies, "seeing things from the exterior, in relative terms" (*AZ* 24:288). Abe even compared this perspective with a physician's cool examination of a patient's body.[8]

In Abe's novels these different orthodoxies and heterodoxies are represented as different styles, and it is ultimately up to the individual to pick and choose among them in order to think and speak for him or herself. If that oppressive orthodoxy is what necessitates escape from the collective, and if oppression and escape are both enacted through language, Abe stages that flight to freedom on the pages of his works; breaking through that hardened wall of convention is the goal Abe's literature sets for itself.

In this way, the reading or rereading of Abe pursued in this book connects at several points with the prevailing critical interest in home and belonging, but also goes beyond it, with an interpretation that equates these crises of identity with the challenge of reconciling the different voices or styles in Abe's text. The rest of this chapter and the chapters that follow all argue in one way or another that the dilemma of escape versus belonging in Abe's work is played out as a problem of balancing the voice of the individual with and against the other voices that surround him or her, to forge a distinct stylistic identity.

To link this back to the tropes of transformation and metamorphosis with which we began, just as Manchuria seems to constitute a space of both oppression and possibility, the transformed fantasy worlds of Abe's prose can be seen to represent either the arbitrary reason of the collective that imposes itself on the individual, or a set of new opportunities. Abe's characters, like Kafka's, are often subjected to absurd rules by incomprehensible authorities, and the metamorphoses they undergo can often be seen as an involuntary result of these pressures— as illustrated by Gregor Samsa in Kafka's *Metamorphosis*, whose transformation into an insect parallels his marginalization within society and his own family. But in Abe's work, these transformed worlds can also destabilize existing assumptions and force people to imagine new alternatives, and the characters' own transformations can often be seen as creative and even hopeful responses to that oppression.

For example, in Abe's story "The Red Cocoon" ("Akai mayu," 1950), a homeless man tugs on a thread protruding from his shoe and finds his body literally unraveling from the leg up. At the same time, the

thread begins to wind itself into a cocoon that surrounds his disinte-
grating form and grows complete just as his body disappears. The man
without a dwelling is transformed into a dwelling without an occupant.
Besides the complex and even contradictory attitudes toward home and
homelessness this image presents, it points to the fact that the metamorphosis of the individual and the transformation of the environment
are in fact "intertwined." And this brings us to Abe's own metamorphosis from doctor to writer, and from a consideration of his early life
to a more detailed reading of his early work.[9]

Beyond Labels: "Dendrocacalia"

When Abe's family returned to Japan after the war, he resumed medical
school in Tokyo, but his attention was diverted by the difficulty of
life after the war and his growing literary success. By the time he graduated in 1948, he apparently had no intention of ever practicing medicine.[10] He had already self-published a collection of poetry, *Mumyo
shishū* (The nameless collection, 1947), and had come to the attention
of Haniya Yutaka and other members of the influential journal *Kindai
bungaku*. In the same year, Abe became a junior member in the newly
formed Yoru no Kai, a literary salon that included Haniya and other
established avant-garde figures such as Hanada Kiyoteru, Noma Hiroshi, and Umezaki Haruo. By the time Abe graduated, the journal *Kosei*
had published part of his first novel, a philosophical work set in Manchuria and titled *Owarishi michi no shirube ni* (Toward a sign at the end of
the road, 1948). The full novel came out later that year, and soon Abe
was publishing poetry, novels, and critical essays with regularity.[11]

In their open-ended structure and fantastic plots and imagery, many
of Abe's early works show the influence of the Japanese and European
avant-garde. One of Abe's best known stories from this early period
features a man who changes inexplicably into a plant. "Dendrocacalia"
("Dendorokakariya"), written in 1949 and rewritten in 1952, illustrates a
number of the points discussed above, including the interplay between
changing circumstances and metamorphosis of the self, the dilemma
between freedom and belonging, and also a combination of scientific
and surreal. Finally, as its Latin botanical title suggests, it spells out
the crucial role of language in fashioning the world of science and the
world outside of science as well.

The protagonist of the story, Mr. Common (Komon-*kun*), is a man plagued by fits in which he finds himself turning into a tree-like shrub. Each time this happens he is narrowly able to regain his human shape, but in the course of things his predicament is noticed by a predatory botanist known as K——. The botanist identifies the plant as a rare example of Dendrocacalia crepidifolia and offers to house the protagonist in comfort and security at his greenhouse. "It's a paradise," he assures Common ominously. "And it's fully supported by the government. You'll run no risk whatever. Many people who have become plants find they are happiest living at my place" (59).

When Common declines, the botanist frames his argument in scientific terms, contending that "Scientifically speaking, [. . .] plants and animals are basically the same," an attitude he says is "devoid of value judgments" (59). But Common resists what he sees as the dehumanizing reductionism of this mechanist argument, and he rejects the prospect of life as a plant in a plant prison. He goes to the greenhouse with the intent of killing the botanist. But once there, he is easily overpowered, and in the final lines of the story he finds himself transformed completely into a Dendrocacalia and potted in a corner of the greenhouse, presumably for good.

Common's reduction to a vegetable existence in a government facility does not seem very optimistic. But life in the greenhouse has some definite attractions compared with the life Common was leading before. In the beginning of the story, Common is a man plagued by loneliness and seemingly without any place to go. The botanist lures him out of his apartment with a note that says simply "I need you. I am your destiny. Tomorrow at three, at Kanran Café. Sincerely, K——." Based on the feminine grace of the handwriting and his own desperate need, Common assumes that K—— is a woman. ("As he pondered, he began responding to suggestion. He was almost positive he had once had a girlfriend named K——" [45].) Grasping at this straw, he convinces himself that she is indeed his destiny, the home he lacks. The story tells us little about Common's daily life, but when he goes off to meet this "woman," Abe captures his bleak existence with a startling economy:

It was still a few hours early, but Common left his apartment. Glancing back, he stopped for a moment and fixed in his memory the fish-shaped crack in the window and the half-rotten rope dangling from the eaves, hung there for a purpose long ago forgotten. Then he turned and went on down the black, rain-slicked road, hopping from one island of dry asphalt to another. He couldn't contain his excitement. Who could blame him? (45)

If it is Common's hope that the note's elegant handwriting signals a place where he belongs, that wish ironically comes true. The graceful penmanship proves to be the careful hand of the taxonomist, and in the story's final scene, K— affixes a neatly lettered card bearing the label "Dendrocacalia crepidifolia" to Common's trunk. Common's dilemma about whether to accept the diagnosis and the Linnean classification of this name thus links to the crisis of belonging: should he submit to the judgments of others, or exist by himself in lonely freedom?

This 20-page story from 1952 presents in capsule form many of the ingredients that characterize the contest of science and nonsense in Abe's later work: an inexorable scientific position that threatens the character's humanity, at least in the narrow way he conceives humanity; a liminal (in this case, phantom) female figure who lures the narrator out of his isolation but turns into a trickster who threatens to overturn his reality; and a contest between freedom and belonging, ending in a fantastic metamorphosis that leaves us uncertain of the direction in which the question has been resolved.

Readers today may have trouble finding much uncertainty in "Dendrocacalia," seeing it instead as merely pessimistic. Likewise it may be hard to see the botanist as representative of anything other than a sinister and reductive scientific reason that diminishes humans to mere objects. However, looking at this story in the artistic context of its time, several critics have argued that "Dendrocacalia" carries a hope that marks the beginning of new possibilities in Abe's work.

At the time, Abe himself certainly entertained some hope for a constructive kind of community. This period marks the beginning of his involvement with the journal *Jinmin bungaku*, the literary group Genzai no Kai (The Present Society), and other groups that emphasized grassroots literary activities among factory workers. It is also the time when Abe joined the JCP, and even if we do not automatically associate communism with communitarianism, Abe's choice to work within the organized party structure is significant (Schnellbächer, *Strategist* 150–207). On the other hand, "Dendrocacalia" and other early works already show a healthy suspicion of group orthodoxy, arguably the same suspicion that would result in his expulsion from the party a decade later.

In the afterword to a collection of essays from the 1950s titled "Mōjū no kokoro ni keisanki no te o" (The heart of a beast and the hand of a computer, 1957), Abe wrote famously that he had passed from existentialism to surrealism and then to communism (*AZ* 7:476). At the risk of sounding facetious, this might be glossed to say that he went from pessimism to optimism by way of ambiguity—in other words, that the bridge from his earliest despairing works to later more optimistic ones was precisely the uncertain images in works like "Dendrocacalia."[12] As a transitional text, "Dendrocacalia" can be read to embody the hope among JCP and progressive writers for a more genuine sense of community, even if that ideal is only expressed negatively in the story through the oppressive community of the greenhouse. Some critics have seen Common's dehumanization as a concrete indictment of social and political conditions in postwar Japan, and they have read the story as a plea to respect human dignity.[13] Other interpreters take the opposite position, arguing that the metamorphosis helps us see beyond "common" ideas of the human and conceive humanity in a new way. So when the botanist asserts that his is a position "devoid of value judgments," he may in fact be giving voice to the avant-garde dream of conquering conventional values.

Takano Toshimi notes that Abe's mentor Hanada Kiyoteru read "Dendrocacalia" negatively, as a warning. But Takano and other critics point out that Hanada also influenced Abe with his argument that "We have little prospect of overcoming the modern unless we rid ourselves of this humanism and shift our most ardent interests to the non-living, even to the point of an inorganicism" (Hanada 51, qtd. in Watanabe, "Kaisetsu" 289). For Hanada, the metamorphosis from human to plant could symbolize a chance to get beyond a naive romantic humanism and rethink the human. Takano concludes that despite this story's undeniable pessimism, Common's transformation into a Dendrocacalia also embodies new possibilities, particularly in the way it reconfigures the character's subjectivity along with his bodily boundaries. Common's transformations are often described as if his body, his vision, or his consciousness were "turning inside out," allowing him to look back or look down on himself as a plant. Takano sees in this kind of language a challenge to the clinging internal subjectivity that dominated Japanese fiction (*Abe Kōbō ron* 11–19).

Other extended studies of Abe and the avant-garde by Nakamura Kiyoshi, Okaniwa Noboru, and Watanabe Hiroshi have made similar arguments that "Dendrocacalia" deconstructs the essentialized subject.[14] Some readings have also extended this argument to address the role of language: Nakamura, for example, sees in the story a need to defeat the rational language of the collective without entirely losing the power to communicate with others (83–98). But none of these critics addresses Common's transformation as a transformation born in language itself, despite the suggestive title and the final scene in which Common's metamorphosis is sealed by the label. In fact, this Latin nomenclature is not the only reductionist language in the story. Even in this short early work, Abe expresses the need to balance different voices. That includes balancing science and fantasy, as well as balancing the role of language as communication (or belonging) versus disruption (or freedom).

What Common opposes to the botanist's science and the term "Dendrocacalia" is the language of literature. He goes to the library to look up instances of people turning into plants, and finds unfavorable precedents in Greek and Christian mythology. (Here Abe displays his familiarity with Western literature, from Dante's *Inferno* to the myths of Narcissus, Hyacinthus, and other figures even more esoteric—the Heliades, Clytie, Syrinx, and so on.) These stories form the basis for Common's rejection of K—'s offer. This is, of course, just one more system (a system of fiction) in which Common finds himself trapped, and his belief that there is some answer to be found in mythology makes no more or less sense than the botanist's science. Common never realizes this, not even at the library when he discovers that the botanist was the last patron to check out *The Inferno*.[15]

The link between being defined by language (rational or fictional) and being defined by others or by society is embodied in the letter from K—. As Common becomes captivated by (or captive to) the idea that this "woman" and her letter represent his destiny, he allows the letter to rewrite his future. There is one passage where he finds himself merging with the letter—an image that is even more important than the more frequently quoted scenes of vegetable transformation: "He carefully refolded the letter, put it back in the envelope, and stood perfectly still, holding it tightly between his palms, feeling them become eyes, ears, nose, and mouth, melting, finally into the letter. His eyes took in nothing before or beyond the text of the letter. He was utterly content with its message" (45).

It is no accident that the letter is penned by the same hand as the label that is finally pinned to the Dendrocacalia's trunk. The story's message is that rational language (which one sort of communication must be) pins down and defines both the sender and receiver—that humans are enveloped in and defined from the words around them. This is the most striking transformation in Abe's text. In this light, the botanist's rather mysterious line equating plants with language begins to make sense: "Plants are the very roots of Logos. [. . .] The very word banned, alas from our everyday speech, is the high beating of their hearts" (60). Later, Common incinerates the letter and hopes the flames will constitute a new "Promethean" fire of freedom, but in this he simply retreats again into the mold of mythology, burning one text only to cross into another.

How does this reading recast Abe's story? Simply put, "Dendrocacalia" depicts a struggle against fiction as well as science, or more accurately, a challenge to combine or reconcile the two. The contest of transformations in the story is a battle to write one's own destiny without having it written by others, whether in a letter, on a taxonomist's label, or in fiction. At the same time, one must reach out to others with one's own language to escape the prison of isolation. These are the tests that Common fails: he lets himself be caught up in the discourses around him, but he rarely speaks for himself. (He has only a handful of lines in the whole story.) And his final effort to discard language in favor of action, by killing K—, is a doomed course.

More than anything else, it is this play of language, then, that accounts for the pessimism of the story and Common's final metamorphosis. But "Dendrocacalia" does offer the hope that another character (a more adept stylist, an author perhaps) might succeed where Common fails. As we will see in subsequent chapters, this is the hope sustained and sometimes even rewarded in Abe's later work.

Beyond the Wall of Reason: The Crime of S. Karma

An even clearer illustration of this contest of voices and the characters' effort to escape their control is the aforementioned work *The Crime of*

S. Karma.[16] Along with "The Red Cocoon" and several other pieces, this short novel is part of a multi-part work Abe titled *Kabe* (The wall, 1950–51), but the story is self-contained. It begins with the protagonist discovering at breakfast that he cannot remember his own name. When he looks through his own wallet, he finds his name has been erased from his IDs and everything else. In his apartment, everything that should have his name on it—from business cards to bookplates—is either missing or mysteriously blank. He goes to the office to see if he can discover some clue to his identity and finds his name listed on the office directory: "S. Karma." He also realizes that someone or something else is already there at the office impersonating him. By staring at the imposter in a certain way he is able to penetrate the disguise, and the interloper reveals itself to be Karma's business card. The card is sitting at his desk, dictating a letter to the office typist Miss Y, and neither she nor anyone else seems any the wiser.

It is the business card who has somehow stolen Karma's name as part of the plot to usurp his identity, and through the rest of the story the two figures vie for control of Karma's life, as well as for Miss Y's affections. The card is just the first in a series of metamorphoses that Karma encounters in the course of the story, as he passes from one unreal situation to another. These transformations include an animated mannequin who impersonates Miss Y, an inky black doctor visible only in silhouette, and a hunchback who slowly straightens up in the course of the scene and then begins to bend over backward, becoming known briefly as the "hunchbelly" (*haramushi*) before he curls into a backward spiral and gets a name that is the Japanese equivalent of "Mr. Cinnamon Bun" ("Rōru Pan-*shi*"). The business card is one of several inanimate objects that have come alive, including Karma's belt, his necktie, his spectacles, and his fountain pen. Rallying under the cry "Down with dead organic matter! Long live inorganic matter!" ("Shinda yūkibutsu kara ikiteiru mukibutsu e!"), they have united in a revolution to throw off the yoke of their master (*AZ* 2:435, 411).

Karma himself is also undergoing a metamorphosis. As soon as he loses his name, he discovers a feeling of "hollowness" inside himself. The inky black doctor examines him and tells him that his chest cavity is totally empty—a vacuum. The vacuum is so powerful that Karma is able to suck things into himself through his eyes, just by staring. While paging through a magazine, he stops at an enticing picture of some grassy dunes, and sucks it in so that his chest is filled with this landscape. Visiting the zoo later, he finds that animals are attracted to the freedom of the wilderness inside him, and when he looks too hard at a camel, it nearly disappears from its cage and takes up residence in his chest. Just as Common's transformation was marked by a feeling of turning inside out, Karma periodically finds himself standing in the midst of this wilderness, as if he had been transported inside his own chest. These interludes amid the dunes stand out as some of the more lyrical and peaceful moments in the wild narrative.

It is hard to resist the temptation to read these transformations as allegorical, and to see Karma's "namelessness" and "emptiness" as direct metaphors for his hollow, anonymous existence. As Yamamoto Fumiko notes, another set of seemingly obvious symbolic transformations revolves around the "wall" of the collection's title, which symbolizes the walls of rationality that hold up our world as well as the collective reason that Abe's literature struggles to transcend. At one moment Karma looks at a wall and considers it "the womb of the positive spirit and the skeptical spirit," but in the next moment it undergoes a transformation and becomes "a great, stifling pressure, no longer a wall of freedom protecting humanity, but a retaining wall extended from prison" (*AZ* 2:438).

Karma is repeatedly menaced by these walls, but he is sometimes able, literally, to step through them. In the final scene, he is changed into one himself, when a wall he discovers growing larger and larger on the plain inside him eventually forces his body into a new wall-like shape. The novel's final lines describe this transformation:

> He quickly realized that the wall was growing on the plain inside his chest. There was no mistaking it: as the wall expanded it was filling his entire body. Raising his head, he saw himself reflected in the window. His was no longer a human body; he was a thick plank with limbs pointing in odd directions, as if arms and legs and a neck had been affixed at random points. Presently, even his neck and extremities were stretched across the plank like a rabbit skin on a tanning block, and finally his whole body had changed into the wall itself.

> The wild plain stretches as far as the eye can see.
> I am the wall that grows there, quietly, without end. (*AZ* 2:451)

Significantly, when Karma first discovers this wall growing in the wilderness inside him (during one of his earlier "trips" into his own chest), the wall is tipped up on its end, so that rather than a horizontal barrier stretching across the wilderness, it takes the form of a lone thin tower growing vertically up out of the ground. As it stretches further and further skyward "without end," the wall is transformed from an obstacle into an image of freedom or hope. For this reason the novel's final image seems to be an optimistic one, but it is also the kind of reversal that seems to foil pat interpretation. The tension between freedom and belonging is captured by the lonely peace of the wild plain inside Karma—a place referred to as "the ends of the earth." But the final act of escaping inside himself, of becoming the wall inside him, is ambiguous. Karma's fate is as confusing as that of Common, who escapes the solitude of his body only to watch it turn into a plant, or the homeless man in "The Red Cocoon" who becomes an empty home in the end. In an essay examined in Chapter 2, Abe says that writing a novel is like solving a geometry problem; however, the final transformations in these works seem to violate the symbolic geometry of the stories.

As with "Dendrocacalia," it is useful to look beyond the striking imagery of *The Crime of S. Karma* and listen to the words of the story, since Karma's identity is also traced through language and style. We can start with Karma's lost name. The figure without a name is a common trope in Abe's work. Many of his characters are never named. Others are identified only by initials (the botanist K—), nicknames, or aliases. "My nickname is Pig—or Mole" begins *The Ark Sakura*, and we never learn to call its narrator anything else (3). The protagonist of *The Woman in the Dunes* is "the man" (*otoko*) through the whole novel, except in a legal document included at the end that identifies him as "Niki Junpei," a name that translates as "Mr. Average."

Naturally, this namelessness can be regarded as an expression of the crisis of identity discussed above, but it also has a hopeful side. From his earliest work, Abe explored the idea that freeing objects from their names altogether would rejuvenate thought. The act of naming for Abe encapsulated what was limiting about language as it existed, hence the threatening quality of the botanist's name plate or the evil business card. Thomas Schnellbächer writes "For Abe, the mythical dimension of creativity is opposed by the instrumentalist principle that naming and inventing serve the purpose of reducing the world to objects fit for human use" (*Strategist* 279). The ability to ignore or forget these names is what Abe describes below as a sort of existentialism, and it is often associated with a Rilke-inspired desire to get beyond naming. Timothy Iles reminds us of the epigraph to Abe's first work, itself a "nameless" poetry collection: "The thing that wounds my psyche was always the name" (*AZ* 1:221; Iles 25). Even as Abe moved beyond the Rilkean existentialism of his early works, he remained fascinated with this idea.[17]

In an essay titled "Kareobana no jidai" (The age of grass ghosts, 1964), Abe quotes Thomas Mann's assertion that once the unknown beast in the jungle is given the name "lion," it is no longer the object of terror it was. Once conceptualized, it can be dealt with, so to name it is to tame it. But Abe says there is still a place for a mode of thought that resists this impulse toward conceptualization, if only to understand aspects of our reality that will never be captured by the names we can invent. That mode of thought is art. Abe says, "This is how art has escaped destruction even in this age of reason—art and other curiosities that cannot be exchanged for a concept. Art is that which sets foot upon the undiscovered continent, which cowers before the unnamed lion, which shudders at ghosts, and which accepts all these things without ever giving them a name" (*AZ* 18:274).

Just as Common struggles to escape the label "Dendrocacalia," Karma seems to have escaped the limits of his own name, though he finds the resulting freedom unsettling. At various points in the story, however, the name threatens to return, carrying with it the karmic weight of a past personal history. At one juncture, the protagonist finds himself subjected to a strange trial (for the crime of attempting to steal the camel from the zoo), a trial conducted in an underground courtroom entered through a secret tunnel in the bear cage. After determining that the defendant has no name, the judges rule that he cannot be subject to the court's laws.

Nevertheless, even after losing his name, Karma still finds himself at the mercy of various naming systems throughout the work. Many of the fantastic characters in the novel are characterized by their professions or disciplines: there is the inky black doctor, a professor of urban studies, two gentleman in "private law enforcement," and the five trial judges, each one of whom is identified as either a mathematician, a jurist, or a philosopher. Each of these professionals speaks in a dialect particular to his specialty. The rebellious business card spouts revolutionary slogans. The doctor talks in medical terms. The philosopher judge notes that "Dialectically speaking, the contradiction between the first and fifth witnesses is *aufheben* by the testimony of witness number eight." Explaining that the court and the trial will follow Karma wherever he goes, the mathematician judge says: "We establish a single postulate—namely that if the accused exists in a given space, the court will exist simultaneously in the same space" (*AZ* 2:404, 407). Besides its evocative visual imagery, *The Crime of S. Karma* also rewards the reader with this wonderful concert of styles.

The narrow logics reflected in these dialects come to represent a series of collective rationalities that Karma must escape. And in the revolutionary slogans of the business card and its object accomplices, we can even recognize the political and aesthetic slogans that Abe is said to have espoused. Their slogan "Down with dead organic matter! Long live inorganic matter!" echoes the theory of inorganic transformation and posthumanism advanced by Abe's mentor Hanada Kiyoteru. Their other dialogue parodies the JCP's rhetoric of class revolution: the fountain pen, for example, demands his fill of ink and ownership of what he writes. This demonstrates that Abe was wary about even his own philosophies becoming too entrenched.

Or perhaps he was less wary than just wry. Humor plays an important role in *Karma* and several of Abe's other novels. Seen exclusively through the lens of his political activities and his essays, as he is in Schnellbächer's book, Abe emerges as relentlessly earnest and even dour, but his fiction and some of his later less programmatic essays show a different side. Schnellbächer treats Abe's juxtaposition of opposed concepts as a variety of Marxist dialectical argument, but *The Crime of S. Karma* uses more humor than Hegel to relativize its various ideas. In fact, Hegelian dialectic itself is parodied in the philosopher judge quoted above.

While switching back and forth between these different voices, the language of the text occasionally undergoes transformations as humorous as those of the characters. It sometimes veers into verse, as when the hunchback sings this song that parodies the different styles that have come before.

You'd better believe it: from your perspective,
This is like the heart of the vortex.
The philosopher says:
—Ah, this fellow's too broad,
So broad there's no more breadth at all.
The mathematician says:
—Ah, of course. This one's a monster differential equation.
The Jurist says:
—This fellow is our ideal wall.
Let's give up the trial and go to bed.
Go, my criminal, to the ends of the earth. (*AZ* 2:431–32)

How does Karma respond to this? Abe says in his essay "S. Karuma-shi no sujō" that he responds as "a sort of existentialist," by acting or being rather than reasoning (*AZ* 5:344). In other words, Karma refuses all of the logic around him in favor of what he can feel and experience. In terms of language, this means that Karma (like Common before him) speaks very little in the story, leaving language largely to the other ideologues and their monologues. In the final scene, the wall he has become grows "quietly" (*shizuka ni*). For Karma, as for Common, silence is the sole solution. Rather than try to determine whether the transformation into a wall is less or more hopeful than metamorphosis into a plant, I would argue that this attitude toward language ultimately defines these works as pessimistic.

The argument of this book is that the reader must also be wary of discarding language, or a consideration of language, when reading Abe's novels. In these works about metamorphosis, the play of styles and their transformation is every bit as important as the striking visual imagery. Despite the urge to allegorize Abe's stories, many of these images (the cocoon, the wall) are ambiguous in themselves. But a close attention to the sound of the text helps us hear something new in these works. As we will see in the following chapters, some (if not all) of Abe's later characters make a greater effort to marshal or order the different voices around them, and ultimately to do what Common and Karma cannot do, which is to speak or write for themselves.

Of course, implicit in the idea of balancing the languages around us is the suggestion that the world is ultimately composed of language—that language has the power to shape and constitute not only the self but everything beyond ourselves. And this is, of course, what permits the multiplication of fantasy in Abe's worlds. Abe does not just relativize narrowly rational ideas of truth by juxtaposing the different rationalities (represented by different dialects) with one another; in *The Crime of S. Karma*, he multiplies and embellishes those dialects to the point where consensus reality becomes sheer fantasy.

Abe's Life and Abe's Works

Focusing on the language of Abe's work also means being able to see the works apart from Abe's biography. As outlined above, critics have often regarded Abe's biography as the key to understanding his texts, but the examination of Abe's life and works in this chapter should make it clear that despite the tempting parallels, there are pitfalls in carrying a biographical approach to Abe too far.[18] Abe himself was hostile to the autobiographical streams in Japanese literature, both Naturalism and the I-novel tradition, and he often wrote in such a way as to foil autobiographical interpretation. The two personal chronologies quoted above have been widely cited, but Abe began a third (*Nenpyō*, 1964) by saying it is a mistake to correlate an author's ideas with the history of his or her life:

Above all, an author has a published "history" [*keireki*] that is beyond temporization—namely his or her works, and he or she should maintain silence on any history beyond that. [. . .] Furthermore, if it is necessary to the content and not irresponsible, an author can be forgiven any lie; in fact, one might say he or she has an obligation to lie. [. . .] But my publisher has requested I write this chronology, so with the preceding caveats, I venture this record so you can know me better, though I dare say it will prove useless in that regard.

(*AZ* 18:244)

Chapter 4 looks in more detail at the idea of autobiographical and confessional writing in Abe's novels. For now, we can note that Abe felt that life was not a suitable material for art without radical renovations.[19] Of all the metamorphoses in Abe's work, this transformation from life into art is perhaps the most slippery. The image of the wall at "the ends of the earth" that appears in *The Crime of S. Karma* apparently comes from Manchuria. Abe's early work *Owarishi michi no shirube ni*, for example, begins with the same image of a walled village on the Manchurian steppes. In *Karma*, however, the images are distorted and transformed: the wall is turned on end, and the wanderer in the desert becomes a desert inside the wanderer. So the origins of these images do not necessarily shed much additional light on their meaning in the texts.

Finally, even the critics discussed here who assign significance to Abe's early life and his unsettled origins conclude almost paradoxically that these experiences led Abe to go beyond the conventional subject of much prewar Japanese literature and literary biography (a bounded self defined in relation and distinction to the exterior environment) and to realize that the boundary between the subject's inside and outside is complex and uncertain. Works such as "Dendrocacalia" represent the need to turn the subject inside out (in Takano Toshimi's phrasing), and to see it as constructed from the same flow of language that forms its environment, as this chapter has argued. Both conclusions lead us away from Abe's life and back to his texts.

The writer Hideo Levy was cognizant of these difficulties when he was dispatched to Manchuria for a documentary on Abe, "Abe Kōbō ga sagashiateta jidai" (Abe Kōbō, in search of an age). In a published dialogue with Shimada Masahiko titled "Genkyō no Manshū" (Manchuria, the phantom homeland), he described his own ambivalence about this search for Abe's origins:

There are all these television shows that go in search of an author's roots and so forth. Ours was the same kind of thing on the surface. But after going to all that trouble [to find a place in Manchuria like the ones Abe described in his fiction], when we walked through the village covered in mud and finally reached the edge and stood on the brink of that wild plain, we hadn't learned anything. (Laughs) I had a feeling Abe was laughing at us. Instead of searching for his roots, we had gone in search of the place where his roots had been cut off. It turned out to be a strange journey. (74)

Even Isoda Kōichi, who traces so much to Abe's life with his influential characterization of Abe's literature as "nationless," provides a telling detail about Abe's origins. When Abe stole back into Manchuria near the end of the war, it was with the help of a set of forged medical papers. Isoda notes that even then Abe was writing or rewriting his own history, in a situation where there was no stable identity outside these forged texts (31). So it is to Abe's texts that we now turn, starting in Chapter 2 with his essays, and their provenance and history within the world of writing about literature and science. Levy's anecdote is a kind of ghost story about a phantom Manchuria whose only trace of Abe is the author's laughing spirit. Following up on this we will begin with a series of ghost stories Abe himself told about laughing apparitions, ghosts in the grass, and the specters that haunt science.

TWO

Abe's Essays and Some Historical Distinctions Between Literature and Science

Since this study attempts to read Abe in the context of the distinctions and tensions between science and literature, it is worth examining in some detail how Abe and other theorists have drawn these distinctions and defined these two realms. This chapter lays that groundwork by examining some of Abe's essays and placing his ideas in the broader context of the history of science, or more specifically, by investigating the distinctions that have been made between science and literature since the emergence of modern science in the Renaissance.

Among these distinctions is the intuitive idea that science deals with truth and literature with fantasy or fiction, as well as the counterclaim by various critics and authors that literature conveys a higher truth. But aside from this are two more subtle notions running through this philosophy that relate in interesting ways to Abe's work: first, the idea introduced briefly in the preceding chapter, that science is a matter of style, something distinguished from literature not so much by its object as by its language; second, the notion that science and literature are distinguished from one another primarily by the fact that one is clear and one is confusing—although the questions of which is which and whether it is clarity or confusion to which we should aspire depend on whom you ask.

Several of these issues are on display in Abe's essay "Kareobana no jidai" (The age of grass ghosts) discussed in Chapter 1. It expresses the idea that some things are beyond the ability of conventional rationality to characterize or name. In Abe's words, "There may be those who are content to dwell in a corner of some conceptual fortress that others have constructed, but no one who has even glanced outside can fail to notice the world is teeming with unregistered continents, unnamed lions, and ghosts that do not revert to tufts of grass" (*AZ* 18:274). The last phrase, the image of the title, refers to an aphorism about a ghostly form glimpsed in the shadows that reveals itself in clearer light to be no more than a clump of dry grass ("Yūrei no shōtai o mitari, kareobana").

It is interesting that this essay equates the power of art and literature to the power of nightmares—unknown things such as the lion or the ghost that lurk menacingly in the darkness. Art is not only that which heroically sets foot on the unknown continent, but also that which "cowers before the unnamed lion, which shudders at ghosts" (*AZ* 18:274). This is a case in which confusion or uncertainty verge on fear, and this equation of creative power with fear and the unknown is an idea that runs through much of Abe's work. But while "Kareobana" explicitly equates naming and rationality with science, a number of Abe's other essays argue that science can also be a source of that uncertainty, instability, and fear. And far from condemning science for this, Abe is in fact part of a long, international critical tradition going back to at least the eighteenth century that has identified this uncertainty as a source of hidden creativity and possibility within science.

This theme of the nightmarish unknown is taken up and transformed in Abe's final essay collection, *Warau tsuki* (Grinning moon, 1975).[1] Many of the essays, gathered from columns he wrote for the literary magazine *Nami* in the early 1970s, are accounts of dreams (good and bad) and the creative logic they represent. The title essay is about Abe's recurring nightmare of being chased through the streets by the grinning moon. Orange-colored and one-and-a-half meters in diameter, the moon floats along behind him, smiling like the Kaō soap trademark and making "an inorganic moaning sound, like the electronic sounds in science fiction movies." Abe says it is meaningless to ask why such a thing is frightening in the context of the dream. It is "something that circulates only in dreams, a part of their peculiar logic." Following a line of argument similar to that in "Kareobana," Abe tells us that "we erode the essence of the dream itself when we translate it into that language of waking time, cause and effect" (*AZ* 25:362–63). In fact, he goes further and suggests that the unanalyzed dream sometimes enfolds a realization or an epiphany that waking logic cannot: "Just because dreams cannot be caught up in the net of consciousness, that's no reason to dismiss them as small fry. Cognitive leaps often occur on the fringes of consciousness. [. . .] And it is when my dreams are richest that my conceptual faculty seems to gain the power of flight" (*AZ* 25:363).

Segueing deftly from the imaginary moon to the real heavens, Abe compares this dream logic with trying to see a dim star in the night sky. If you look directly at the star, it disappears; but if you look slightly to one side, you can discern the star at the edge of your vision. The reason, Abe explains, is that the sides of the retina are more sensitive to light: "This is a phenomenon that results from the functional specialization of the retina's center and its periphery. Perhaps the same principle applies to the relationship between dreams and reality. Reality is grasped most clearly at the center of consciousness, but a dream can be caught only at the edges. If we try to put it in the center, we lose its true form" (*AZ* 25:363). Elsewhere in the essay, Abe associates dreams with fiction, suggesting that both have similar powers. He thus sets up a realm for dreams and for fiction where the language of conventional logic does not apply.

At first we may be tempted to associate an argument like this with a Romantic valorization of the imagination that juxtaposes it to an inadequately narrow scientific reason. Abe's position might call to mind Edgar Allen Poe, an author Abe loved, and his "Sonnet—To Science" (1829):

> SCIENCE! true daughter of Old Time thou art!
>> Who alterest all things with thy peering eyes.
> Why preyest thou thus upon the poet's heart,
>> Vulture, whose wings are dull realities?

Abe's "cognitive leaps" and conceptual "power of flight" resemble these Romantic descriptions of a soaring imagination that rises above the low-flying "vulture" of science, or in Percy Bysshe Shelley's characterization, "ascend[s] to bring light and fire from those eternal regions where the owl-winged faculty of calculation dare not ever soar" (135). And sometimes it is tempting to see in Abe what we might term a Romantic equation between science and narrow rationality, as when he writes in "Kareobana": "Let us leave the work of naming to things like criticism and science" (*AZ* 18:274).

But in fact the Romantic authors above were not opposed to science any more than Abe was. Poe is a good example: he was the father of a grotesque literature that challenged rationality with bizarre images, but he also helped forge the genre of detective fiction, and as we will see below, Abe identifies him as a pioneer in science fiction as well. This points to the complexity of the tradition from which Abe emerged— a tradition that draws on both of these fields and one that this chapter tries to unpack.

For example, the essay "Warau tsuki" itself clearly has many scientific elements. The most noticeable, of course, is its central metaphor and the language in which it is expressed. Besides the example from retinal physiology, the essay also discusses the activity of "the nerve cells of the cerebrum" during waking and sleeping periods. Further, like all the essays discussed in this chapter (in distinction, some might add, to the prevailing essay style in Japan), "Warau tsuki" is written in a style that is a model of clarity and logical exposition. So even as he criticizes the deleterious effects of a reductive rationality in literature, Abe's essays do not shy away from the language of science. The first part of this chapter examines this notion of scientific language and the related idea of metaphors drawn from science, starting with the birth of modern science in the Renaissance. The second part then looks at some more of Abe's essays and the ideas of confusion and creativity, with reference to the revolution in empirical science in the eighteenth century and to the sublime, an idea that will be central to our reading of Abe.

The Question of Japanese Science

Clearly "Warau tsuki" uses language and metaphors from science, but does that make it "scientific" in any significant way? Chapter 1 introduced the idea that science is largely a matter of style, at least in Abe's works. I suggest that by bringing this style together with other more literary language, Abe could blur the line between the two fields. In fact, the position that the sciences, like literature, are a mode of language is a familiar one in poststructuralist criticism. Michel Foucault uses the term "discourse" to refer to broad categories of knowledge constituted by language, or more particularly by the rules surrounding how language can be used. Foucault's position casts the differences between literature and the sciences as arbitrary or even illusory: "Discourse thus nullifies itself . . . in placing itself at the disposal of the signifier" ("Discourse" 228). Building on the work of Foucault and Ludwig Wittgenstein, Jean-François Lyotard contends that science and literature are essentially two competing "language games."

Lyotard's ideas about language games are discussed in more detail in Chapter 3, but the position that science and literature are differentiated chiefly by their style is an argument with a long critical history—certainly one that predates poststructuralism. As early as the sixteenth century, we hear Western critics contending that these two fields are distinguished by the way they speak. On the eve of the scientific revolution, during a time of both literary and scientific ferment, the Renaissance represents a point when philosophers were struggling to define the differences between scientific and literary writing. Of course the idea that science deals with truth and that literature deals with fantasy—the common understanding against which Abe argues in "Warau tsuki" and "Kareobana"—is also prevalent in the Renaissance. But that idea is also closely tied up with the issue of style.

Some readers might ask if it is necessary or appropriate to go back to sixteenth-century Italy to understand the interaction of science and fiction in Abe's work. In fact, there are a number of reasons to do so. First, the concrete history of science in Japan shows how much it drew on Western ideas and models. Modern science in Japan began as a Western import, in the years leading up to and following the Meiji Restoration. Tracing the development of research science from the Tokugawa period onward, James Bartholomew notes that Western medicine and other sciences began to enter Japan in the form of foreign textbooks, when the ban on translation of Western books was repealed by the *shōgun* Tokugawa Yoshimune in 1720. After the Meiji Restoration, Japanese scientists were among the elite figures sent to Germany, France, and England for training, while foreign professors anchored the science faculties at newly formed Japanese universities. Until technical dictionaries appeared in the late nineteenth century, even Japanese science professors routinely lectured in French, English, or German. In the twentieth century, Japan continued to follow the Western model, and in this as in many things, it rapidly caught up with its teachers:

when the Japanese government established a competitive research grant system in 1918, it was right on the heels of similar systems in the West. Bartholomew argues that it was not long after World War I that Japanese participation in the newly formed International Research Council placed Japanese researchers on the international stage.

In the course of this process, the philosophies and methods of modern science as it had been practiced in the West took firm root in Japan.[2] As a result of this history, Western philosophy of science has considerable relevance in Japan at large. And this is even truer for the particular case of Abe, an author who read and regularly cited Western philosophical texts of the kind we will examine. The question of whether Abe read the *particular* texts treated below is one I have not tried to answer; ultimately, it is secondary to the larger purpose of this book, which is not only to shed light on Abe in his own context—the whole arc of his career and novelistic writing, and the varied and changing ways Japanese critics received those texts—but also to place Abe in the larger historical and international context of world literature.

To situate my approach and to connect it with what has come before, let me take some time to compare it with three other works that treat Japanese literature and science, and their arguments for universal science versus Japanese particularism.

In his book on Abe's early essays and political activities, Thomas Schnellbächer takes a rigorously local approach, building his discussion of science in Abe's work strictly from texts and ideas cited in the author's early discursive writing—though virtually all of these are Western texts. The result is a picture of science focused on a specific psychological model of perception (grounded in phenomenology and cogni-tive psychology) and associated with the goals and methods of Marxist dialectical materialism. (Explaining the appeal of communism for Abe and other avant-garde writers, Schnellbächer writes: "The Communists raised political issues in a way that was radical, was based on a clearly articulated model of social and historical processes, and was explicitly modern, aspiring to scientific rationality without being positivistic" [*Strategist* 251].)[3]

Schnellbächer's approach yields an interesting but somewhat narrow view of the role of science in Abe's work. As introduced in the previous chapter, Schnellbächer's disciplined focus on the letter of Abe's

essays, the literary milieu of Tokyo, and the sixteen years after World
War II leaves open some opportunities for us to see Abe more broadly,
and link him with a much longer and wider history of critical theory
relating to science. Ultimately, Schnellbächer traces Abe's efforts to be
relevant to average readers of his time; this book's wider context is an
effort to make Abe interesting to even more readers in our own time,
in and outside Japan. Abe still has a great deal to say about the debates
that have constituted the history of science and literature: he may or
may not always *speak out* of this history, in the sense of invoking it explicitly, but he always *speaks to* it, in the sense of providing us important
new perspectives on these ongoing debates.

A study that combines a universal notion of science with arguments
for Japanese uniqueness is Joseph Murphy's *Metaphorical Circuit*, a book
that does not treat Abe but that constitutes the most extended study of
science and modern Japanese literature available in English. Although
he covers the particular historical situation of modern Japanese scientists
in some detail, Murphy proceeds from Bartholomew's idea—an idea I
would endorse—that the discipline of modern science is largely the same
in Japan and the West. Murphy suggests that it is Japanese literature that
is different, leading to a different relationship between science and literature in the two countries. More specifically, Murphy argues the following: Japan's educational system has given generations of Japanese
authors and critics a much firmer grounding in mathematics than their
counterparts in the United States. This expertise in math (specifically,
and somewhat arbitrarily, calculus) conveys an understanding of science
and a sympathy for science lacking in North America, where literary
critics tend to fear science and either ignore it or launch jealous attacks
on so-called scientific rationality, which is really nothing more than a
straw man constructed from their own incomplete understanding of
scientific practice. In Japan, Murphy writes, authors and critics have
enough understanding of science and literature to enable them to work
more sincerely and effectively toward knowledge that will bridge these
two worlds.

Metaphorical Circuit deals more with Japanese literary criticism than
Japanese fiction: its case studies are drawn mainly from the literary
theory of Natsume Sōseki, the experimental methods of physicist and
essayist Terada Torahiko, and the critical theory of Karatani Kōjin and

Maeda Ai. On the surface, Abe would seem an ideal candidate for Murphy's approach. Besides his scientific training, Abe's mathematical prowess is the subject of many anecdotes: math pops up frequently in Abe's work, and Schnellbächer gives a long reading of one essay, "Bungaku to jikan" (Literature and time, 1949) that compares artistic depiction specifically with the operations of calculus (*Strategist* 296–307). Nevertheless, there is reason to hesitate before applying a reading such as Murphy's to Abe.

Murphy's suggestion that we read the scientific content in Japanese literature with some rigor, and not gloss over it or dismiss it, is a valuable one. But I also find value in a lack of rigor that Murphy would seem to disallow—in Abe's unique combination of rigor *and* distortion, or better yet transformation.[4] I also see real worth in the recent (literary) critiques of science that Murphy criticizes—at least in some of them— and this book tries to relate them to Abe's work at several points. Most importantly, I would hesitate to identify Abe as an example of a greater scientific accuracy in Japanese literature, or as a symptom of any other broader difference in literary standards between the United States and Japan. The present work sees Abe as a unique author, one who can be placed within the Western and Japanese traditions, but who can also "talk back" to both of them. Finally, I would freely admit that this is an exercise in comparative literature, and is as much or more about a creative juxtaposition of cultures as it is about discovering some essential quality of Abe's mind or Japanese literature or U.S. culture.[5]

The third and final text I will treat here is Karatani Kōjin's *Origins of Modern Japanese Literature* (*Nihon kindai bungaku no kigen*), which argues that science was one of many Western epistemological constructs that were imposed on modern Japanese literature by Meiji government policies and by authors themselves, as well as by subsequent critics. Karatani complicates accounts such as Bartholomew's by contending that a number of concepts that seem natural to Japanese literature were actually "discovered" or constructed in the late Meiji period from Western ideas. These were later naturalized through a process of "inversion" (*tentō*) that disguised their artificial quality. Karatani identifies a series of these concepts and tries to show how dominant they have been for the Japanese literary tradition, while simultaneously exposing the isolated moments when a different and distinctly native literary history is trying to peek out.

In a chapter of *Origins* devoted to science, Karatani discusses "sickness as meaning" in Tokutomi Roka's novel *Hototogisu* (The cuckoo, 1900). He links the portrayal of tuberculosis in the novel to a complex of imported ideas at the center of which is Western medicine. The contagious nature of the disease, which shapes the events of the novel, is traced not only to Western medical paradigms but to a Christian worldview that must attribute suffering to a root cause. In this way, the complex of ideas spreads outward from science to embrace such things as the romanticism of the consumption patient in literature. In an ingenious comparison, Karatani also traces the influence of *Hototogisu* on later fiction and pronounces the novel's ideas "contagious" in their own right.

Karatani's provocative and influential argument connects with the thrust of this book in its suggestions that science is in some sense a system of metaphors that has infected Japanese literature through the vector of language. If so, then it should be possible to trace that influence in Abe's own work. But Karatani also offers a warning in his ironic use of the term "origin," a caution against regarding early Western science as the irreducible origin or standard against which Abe or any Japanese author's work must be judged. This chapter tries to avoid the pitfalls Karatani points out (and some that he falls into) by replacing stereotyped assumptions about the relationship between science and literature with close readings of individual critical texts, and by asking carefully how Abe resembles them and where he departs from them. Karatani might phrase these as the cracks where Abe's sensibility peeks through the overlying Western episteme. However, I am reluctant to accept the notion of a Western scientific episteme that is as unified and monolithic as Karatani assumes.[6] Instead, the reading that follows examines a series of varied texts in dialogue with one another, with Abe listening and ultimately taking part in the later twentieth-century stage of this conversation. In that spirit, we will look at some of these texts and compare them with what we find in Abe's prose, beginning with the issue of scientific language or science as style.

Literature or Science? The Question of Style

When medieval and Renaissance theorists used the word "science," the term did not necessarily exclude literature. The English word descends (via Italian) from the Latin root *scientia*, meaning simply "knowledge," and in the classical tradition, science was any branch of knowledge that was "characterized by rigor and certainty."[7] For example, when Thomas Aquinas compared theology with poetry in the thirteenth century, he called them both sciences, though he named sacred doctrine first among the sciences and poetry last. His *Summa Theologica* (1256–72) defines a science as that which "proceeds from self-evident principles," and ranks the sciences by their clarity or certainty and by their purposes. Poetry is judged inferior because its purpose is entertainment rather than education, but part of Aquinas's argument also turns on style: poetry's use of metaphor to produce a pleasing representation makes poetry unclear, since "many different senses in one text produce confusion and deception and destroy all force of argument" (7). This debate over whether metaphor is proper to science (or philosophy) as well as literature emerges again in succeeding centuries, and it is one that has some relevance for Abe's style.

Like Aquinas, later Renaissance critics often phrased their arguments in terms of the differences between literature and other fields: how to distinguish one from the other, and how an author could avoid straying over the line between the two. Renaissance critics were influenced by Plato's assertion that poetry was not a practical branch of knowledge but an "inspiration," a kind of divine madness (297).[8] This is Socrates's conclusion in his dialogue with Ion, after the rhapsode admits among other things that he can sing about the sea, but he has no knowledge of how to steer a ship. Renaissance thinkers largely inherited Plato's distinction between the reality of the natural world and poetry's created world when they sought to identify the features of poetry that distinguish it from "other sciences" such as history, politics, and morality, or natural philosophy—the antecedent to modern physics. Lodovico Castelvetro's Poetica *d'Aristotele Vulgarizzata et Sposta (The* Poetics *of Aristotle Translated and Explained,* 1576) affirms that poetry's proper realm is fantasy and disqualifies it from any involvement with what he termed the "arts and sciences." Since "the matter of poetry is invented and imagined by the poet's genius," Castelvetro supports a dictum he attributes to Aristotle, that "no art or science can constitute proper matter for poetry" (17–18).

In contrast, the Renaissance critic Jacopo Mazzoni permits literature to treat subjects sometimes reserved for what we might term science, by distinguishing more subtly between the credible and the true. Drawing on Aristotle's idea that "the poet should prefer probable impossibilities to improbable possibilities" (Aristotle 95), Mazzoni contends that poetry is that which credibly imitates the marvelous. The marvelous here is anything amazing or fantastic—it does not matter whether it is finally true or not. Unlike Castelvetro, Mazzoni allows for the imitation of marvelous true things, including the objects of science. In the "natural world," Mazzoni tells us, "there are some truths which are sometimes more marvelous than the false" (171). This is among the earliest statements of a possibility we will see developed in interesting ways down to Abe: that science may sometimes prove more fantastic than literature.

But there is also another element in these critics' calculations that stems from the Renaissance interest in the text's effectiveness or reception: Castelvetro and Mazzoni both express the belief that poetry is written in a different style from natural philosophy, and that the two styles should not mix. In contrast with Aquinas, though, they see the merits of literary style precisely in its clarity as compared with science. Castelvetro says, "Another and more obvious reason why the arts and sciences cannot supply matter for poetry," stems from the fact that poetry is intended solely "to provide pleasure and recreation to the souls of the common people and the rude multitude, who are incapable of understanding the rational proofs, the distinctions, and the arguments" of science and philosophy. Technical language will be unintelligible to these people, and will produce only "annoyance and displeasure" (19). Mazzoni agrees and disagrees, saying that a poet may treat the same material as a scientist, but must write in such a way that the material will be understandable to the average person.[9] Discussing the example of Empedocles, an ancient scientist who wrote his treatises in verse, he says:

Empedocles did not deserve the name of poet, not because he dealt with truth (for it has already been shown that poetry is capable of the truth) but because he dealt scientifically with things pertaining to the sciences, where he would be obliged, were he a poet, to treat them credibly, that is by making idols and images and joining to them a way of instructing the sensitive powers more often than the intellect. (171)

This idea that scientific style and content are too difficult for poetry continued to be influential long after the Renaissance. In his preface to the second edition of *Lyrical Ballads* (1802), William Wordsworth says that both the poet and the scientist aim at the pleasures of understanding the natural world. But only the poet can recreate the pleasure of that knowledge in others, because scientific knowledge is too difficult to obtain and convey. Wordsworth concludes with Mazzoni that while nature is the poet's proper subject, the scientist's approach to nature does not belong in poetry because it is incomprehensible to the common reader:

The remotest discoveries of the Chemist, the Botanist, or Mineralogist, will be as proper objects of the Poet's art as any upon which it can be employed, if the time should ever come when these things shall be familiar to us, and the relations under which they are contemplated by the followers of these respective sciences shall be manifestly and palpably material to us as enjoying and suffering beings. (396–97)

The stylistic analysis of Abe's novels in this book tries to identify a conflict between the scientific and literary voices within his texts, and a kind of instability or confusion that arises from Abe's mixing of these styles. A look at these Renaissance critics shows that ideas about these two styles and their incompatibility were poised to develop at almost the same moment that science began to be distinguished from poetry. For Castelvetro and Mazzoni, a key issue is the confusion that unfamiliar scientific language or reasoning is apt to produce in the general reader. Yet, Mazzoni also allows that science is entertaining when it is unfamiliar enough to seem "marvelous." The line between what is marvelously novel and what is confusingly unfamiliar will turn out to be a blurry one. In fact, as indirectness and artful confusion eventually come to be seen as part of the aesthetic province of literature, the possibility arises that science might be more confusing, hence more appealing, and even more aesthetic.

This reversal, which culminated in the concept of the sublime, will have a great deal to do with the appeal of science in Abe's texts. Abe's notion of the unnamed or the unnameable is in fact not far from this healthy confusion. Creativity and the need to conquer the everyday both have this disruptive aspect that feeds a productive uncertainty. These creative aspects of science are treated in several essays by Abe that deal more explicitly with the role of science in literature.

Creative Science and the Everyday

The reason that Abe can condemn narrow waking logic in "Warau tsuki" while simultaneously embracing scientific language and metaphors in the same essay is that his work does not associate all science with this narrow-mindedness. Under the right circumstances, science or its prose image can be creative, and may even liberate us from the straightjacketed rationality Abe fears. One of the key terms Abe and other postwar avant-garde authors employ to refer to that narrowness is *nichijō*— "the everyday." In Abe's usage, it connotes a way of thinking that is grounded wholly in present everyday experience, an attitude that refuses to transcend prevailing ideas and values. For Abe, this represents a lack of imagination that produces a dangerous conservatism—an inability to adapt self and society to the needs of a changing world. But Abe notes that science does not have to abet this narrow-mindedness; rather, science can open it up.

Abe advances these ideas systematically in a series of essays that touch on the relationship between fiction, science, and the everyday. The most famous is Abe's postscript (*atogaki*) to the novel *Inter Ice Age 4*, a statement that came to be known as "Nichijōsei e no senkoku" (A verdict against the everyday, 1959). The novel (which is examined in Chapter 3) and the postscript both phrase the dangers of the everyday in terms of losing the ability to adapt to the future. "The future renders a verdict of guilty to this feeling of everyday continuity," says Abe. "That feeling must perish the instant the future comes upon us. Just living in the present does not provide us what we need to understand the future" (*AZ* 11:141).

One obvious way for literature to jolt us out of the everyday and open the mind to new possibilities is by introducing the abnormal, the fantastic, or the bizarre. This partly explains the element of the grotesque or the unreal in so much of Abe's fiction. And sometimes a scientific outlook is made to play the foil for these fantastic elements, to represent the narrow rationality of the everyday that fantasy overcomes. But Abe tells us that science can be a source of creativity as well. In "Kasetsu no bungaku" (A literature of hypothesis, 1961), Abe questions the characterization of science as "a desert of numbers with no room for mysteries, no shadow of a doubt" (*AZ* 15:237). The ideas in this essay are repeated and amplified in "The Boom in Science Fiction"

("SF no ryūkō ni tsuite," 1962), which argues that despite the tendency to oppose science's reasoned conjectures to irrational fantasy, these are simply two sides of the same coin, alike in their ability to challenge the narrow parochialism of the everyday. "When a fresh hypothesis is brought in," Abe writes, "the everyday is suddenly destabilized and begins to take on strange new forms. It becomes activated, objectified, and our consciousness is roughly shaken" ("Boom" 346).

Here Abe points to the creativity and adventurousness of science. It may sometimes tend toward reductionism, but it is never afraid to strike out into new territory. The everyday, on the other hand, shuns the unfamiliar in any form. "In the name of order, it has burned its witches and its scientists at the same stake" ("Kasetsu" *AZ* 15:237).

The aspect of science that challenges the everyday is "the feeling of surprise" that goes with scientific discovery ("Boom" 346). This element of surprise and the accompanying adjustment in our thinking seem to be qualities that link science with fantasy in Abe's work. Abe offers a concrete example in another essay, "Masuku no hakken" (The discovery of the mask, 1957), where he compares the act of beginning to write with the process of solving a geometry problem. The comparison turns on the fact that proving a geometric theorem often involves adding a single line to a diagram, which allows one to see a previously hidden relationship between the figures: "The secret to solving a geometry problem is to break out of the fixed ideas imposed by the diagram and discover where to draw that unexpected supplementary line. [. . .] The pleasure of making that leap has an appeal all its own. The feeling I have when I begin to write and I think it's going well is exactly the same sensation" (*AZ* 7:322).

In "The Boom in Science Fiction," Abe places some hope in the genre of science fiction as a kind of literature that could break us out of the everyday by bringing out the creative element of science and combining it with an even more radical freedom of fantasy. Whereas others may criticize science fiction as "counterfeit science" or "pseudo-science," Abe finds it "interesting precisely by virtue of being a counterfeit," precisely because it combines truth and fancy (345). More concretely, Abe says the best science fiction employs science to establish a "hypothesis"—a creative premise that is then used to investigate some other theme. One of Abe's examples is the creature of Mary Shelley's

Frankenstein. The monster is a sensitive, philosophically inclined creature who turns violent when he is rejected by humankind. He is less an emblem of science than "a hypothesis for plumbing the depths of human love and solitude" (347).

Chapter 3 discusses in more detail Abe's relationship to the genre of science fiction in Japan. It is worth noting here, however, that his ideal for science fiction was not something the genre always realized. Although Abe was instrumental in helping science fiction gain a foothold in Japan, he eventually turned away from a genre he felt was not fulfilling its potential. "The Boom in Science Fiction," for example, reproves some Soviet science fiction authors and critics who would confine science fiction wholly within the bounds of scientific reason. Abe argued that critics who demand scientific correctness or accurate predictions from a novel only succeed in reimposing on it the limited rationality of the everyday: "What use is there in setting up clumsy distinctions between right and wrong fantasy?" he wrote. "It is in the act of escaping fixed categories like 'accurate fantasy' and 'inaccurate fantasy' that the essence of science fiction lies" (344).

Abe goes on to associate this narrowness with political conservatism and various attempts to yoke science fiction to naive optimism about social progress. The rich tradition of science fiction in the Soviet Union, he laments, is in danger of being sapped by this emphasis on novels that reflect nothing more than "a state-advocated scientific enlightenment" (345). By 1966, in an article for *SF magajin* called "Science Fiction, the Unnamable" ("SF, kono nazukegataki mono"), Abe had returned to Thomas Mann's example of the unnamed beast in order to take Japanese science fiction to task. Increasingly, he said, the genre was giving up the effort to grasp at monsters still untamed by language and instead falling back into a discussion of the lion, a monster that had long since been domesticated and put to work performing quaint tricks in the circus.

What sets Abe's work apart from much science fiction is this willingness to harness science creatively and treat it rigorously, while sometimes transcending its rationality. As with mystery fiction (and this is a link more often noted in Japan than in the West), the pleasure of reading science fiction frequently rests in the surprise of an ending that solves the story's central puzzle or dilemma in an unexpected way, but still without breaking any of the rules (scientific, technical, or social) that the story establishes for itself at its outset. Compared with Anglo-American science fiction writers, Abe would have to be grouped with a relatively small number of authors (such as Philip K. Dick or Jonathan Lethem) who have blurred the line between science fiction and avant-garde literature by adopting the structure of science fiction without being afraid to violate its ground rules in the course of the work. Abe sends his characters on quests that have no resolution, poses mysteries that have no solution, and transgresses narrative rules until the structure of the text threatens to break down entirely.

The Japanese slipstream or crossover authors mentioned in the Introduction contrast with Abe in a different way: writers such as Murakami Haruki and Murakami Ryū have borrowed themes or tropes from science fiction to produce fantastic narratives, but they typically lack Abe's interest in scientific rigor. Some of these authors are discussed and compared with Abe in more detail in the chapters that follow, but for now it suffices to say that constructing a meticulously elaborate world of logic only to tear it down is a feature of Abe's writing rarely found in work by his American or Japanese contemporaries.

In the conclusion of "The Boom in Science Fiction," Abe finally sets his "literature of hypothesis" apart from conventional science fiction by tracing its lineage back to figures as diverse as Mark Twain, Guillaume Apollinaire, Natsume Sōseki, and Lu Xun, and even further back to Swift, Cervantes, Shakespeare, and Lucian. Abe devotes particular attention to Edgar Allan Poe, quoting him at length to show that his writing could be very technical and reasoned, but at the same time identifying Poe as the father of the modern grotesque.

In his emphasis on the unpredictability of science, Abe is in some senses like Mazzoni, who allows the use of scientific material precisely because of its marvelousness, because in the natural world "there are some truths which are sometimes more marvelous than the false." Mazzoni and Abe differ only in the amount of marvelousness or strangeness they will tolerate. For Mazzoni, science in too raw a form is not merely marvelous but unintelligible; it must be presented in an easy form so that the poetry will be "credible and at the same time marvelous" (171). But Abe clearly places more of a premium on a certain kind of confusion, extending even to a productive kind of fear or terror—from the nightmare of the grinning moon to *Frankenstein* and Poe.

The equation of science, aesthetics, and fear has a precedent in historical efforts to define science and literature in relation to one another, particularly as scientifically oriented philosophers writing about literature came to regard the natural world's very incomprehensibility and even hostility as an aesthetic virtue, indeed as the pinnacle of aesthetic appeal. This produced the aesthetic ideal known as the sublime. The sublime has its origins in eighteenth-century German and British efforts to define the appeal of a powerful natural phenomenon that did not fit conventional definitions of beauty, but this construct has lately been reexamined by contemporary critics attempting to describe our current relationship with science and technology in Japan and the West.

The sublime will prove particularly useful in subsequent chapters, for reading Abe's later works. To see how we arrived at the point Abe suggests in the essays above, where the frightening aspects of science and technology and indeed their very incomprehensibility could be considered positively, we should briefly examine the history of the sublime. Its development would require a further rapprochement between science and literature, but ironically that was accomplished not by authors incorporating science into their prose, but by empiricist philosophers trying to make the study of literature more objective and systematic. To this end, they attempted to view the experience of literature not as a divine madness, in the words of Socrates, but as a scientific phenomenon.

In Socrates's argument, there is one small detail that points to the gap through which this attack will come. Plato has Socrates say to Ion: "There is a divinity moving you, like that contained in the stone which Euripides calls a magnet" (289). Socrates uses the metaphor to suggest an inspiration that can be communicated from the Muse through Homer to Ion, just as an iron ring in contact with a magnet becomes magnetized itself. For Plato, the miraculous power of a magnet is a fitting figure for a divine inspiration that has no connection with the practical world. Of course, later centuries would reduce this miracle of magnetic attraction to a predictable effect of atomic alignment. In the same way, as seventeenth- and eighteenth-century science expanded its understanding of the natural world, it tried to reduce the divine action of the poet's imagination to the scientific terms of psychology. Just as "Warau tsuki" marshals data from neuropsychology to make Abe's point that there are some things about cognition that rational thought cannot grasp, the empiricists who turned to psychology in an effort to systematize the response to poetry arrived at some unexpected results.

Literature as Science and Science as Literature: Empiricism and the Sublime

Among the changes that mark the development toward modern science is an increasing emphasis on empirical results and experimentation. Instead of the rational arguments and appeal to past authority that characterized much of the Renaissance, proponents of this emerging "new philosophy" of the seventeenth and eighteenth centuries relied increasingly on material observations and showed a growing awareness of what could and could not be proven by experiment. The Copernican revolution, for example, and the refinement of Copernicus's heliocentric model by Kepler and Galileo were both driven by a new urge to account for observed astronomical data, including observations made with the newly invented telescope.

Although this emerging scientific method is often associated with the practical empirical methods of Francis Bacon, it was also backed by more fundamental ideas about perception, sensation, and cognition advanced by Thomas Hobbes, John Locke, and David Hume. In contemporary aesthetic philosophy, the impact of empiricism is felt in a growing desire to tame the uncertainty of poetry and bring the unpredictable world of literary activity—the world of creation and the imagination—within a more rigidly empirical psychological framework.

This attitude is typified by critics such as Joseph Addison and Edmund Burke, who proposes in *A Philosophical Enquiry into the Origin of our Ideas of the Sublime and Beautiful* (1759) that only an aesthetic theory "founded on experiment" will remedy the deplorable lack of "fixed or consistent principles" for defining beauty: "Could this admit of any remedy, I imagined it could only be from a diligent examination of our passions in our own breasts; from a careful survey of the properties of things which we find by experience to influence those passions; and from a sober and attentive investigation of the laws of nature, by which those properties are capable of affecting the body, and thus of exciting our passions" (1).

In their search for objective and predictable standards of beauty, Burke, Addison, and like-minded critics downplayed the role of unpredictable or individual factors, including imagination. Here they drew on the ideas of John Locke, whose model of psychology regularized mental experience by grounding it in physical sensation. Locke's *Essay Concerning Human Understanding* (1689) convinced generations of authors and critics that without experience the mind is a "white paper" or an "empty cabinet" (109, 65). Joshua Reynolds, a contemporary of Burke and the first president of the Royal Academy, instructed his painting students that "imagination is incapable of producing anything originally of itself, and can only vary and combine those ideas with which it is furnished by means of the senses" (117).[10]

At first, these thinkers seem to stand in stark contrast to Abe, for whom the imagination offers an escape from the limits of everyday experience. And because they relegate imagination to this subordinate role, these writers tend to assign the highest artistic value to realistic description, a conclusion that is also at odds with Abe. Yet at this point their arguments take an unexpected turn. Joseph Addison's serial essay "On the Pleasures of the Imagination" (1712) follows this line of reason to the conclusion that the most rigidly realistic writers—historians and scientists—are the most consummate artists. These scientific writers who are "obliged to follow Nature more closely" may delight the reader just as poets do, by depicting nature's "beauty" and "greatness." Furthermore, the poverty of the imagination and the power of reason give a hidden advantage to the "Authors of the new Philosophy" (scientists), for by appealing to the intellect, they can "gratifie and enlarge the Imagination" by speaking to our reason in a way the poet and historian cannot. In other words science can explain what our imagination is normally too poor to conceive. Addison says, "There is something very engaging to the Fancy, as well as to our Reason, in the Treatises of Metals, Minerals, Plants and Meteors" (574–75). Another passage from Addison's essay captures the idea that science can express a natural "greatness" that literature cannot:

Nothing is more pleasant to the Fancy, than to enlarge it self, by Degrees, in its Contemplation of the various Proportions which its several Objects bear to each other, when it compares the Body of Man to the Bulk of the whole Earth, the Earth to the Circle it describes round the Sun, that Circle to the Sphere of the fixt Stars, the Sphere of the fixt Stars to the Circuit of the whole Creation, the whole Creation it self to the Infinite Space that is every where diffused about it. . . . (575)

Though he starts out from the poverty of the imagination and the supremacy of sense experience, Addison arrives at a conclusion that Burke will elaborate, and that will eventually see expression in writing such as Abe's: that however fantastic poetry becomes, it is finally ideas drawn from science that stretch the imagination most thoroughly.

Edmund Burke elaborates Addison's ideas into two distinct kinds of artistic impact, the beautiful and the sublime. In Burke's time, the word sublime was traced back at least to pseudo-Longinus, whose *Peri Hupsos* (c. 1st century) was translated as "Traité du Sublime" by Boileau in 1674 (Monk 21, 29). The Longinean sublime is a quality of language that produces amazed wonder—"a certain distinction and excellence in expression" that generates "not persuasion but transport." Longinus says that "sublimity flashing forth at the right moment scatters everything before it like a thunderbolt" (43).

By the time it reached a turning point in Burke's formulation, the sublime had been influenced by Addison's idea that the appeal of nature lies in its greatness as well as its beauty. As suggested by the quote above, Addison's greatness is broadly tied to size, "the Largeness of a whole View." He writes: "Our Imagination loves to be filled with an Object, or to graspe at any thing that is too big for its Capacity. We are flung into a pleasing Astonishment at such unbounded Views, and feel a delightful Stillness and Amazement in the Soul at the Apprehension of them" (540).

To Addison's "largeness," Burke adds the ideas of power, irregularity, mystery, and danger to produce the sublime, an essentially masculine concept he contrasts with a soft, delicate, decidedly feminine ideal he identifies with beauty. Burke was trying to account for the paradox that imposing, powerful, or dangerous things can produce a thrill in us that is as appealing in its own way as pleasure. His preoccupation with this kind of visceral emotional response traces back to his interest in sensation, and his desire to understand the experience of art in psychological and even physiological terms. (He ventures that exhilaration is produced by "a violent pulling of the fibres, which compose any muscle or membrane," while "beauty acts by relaxing the solids of the

whole system" [132, 149–50].) The experience of the sublime thus becomes a kind of invigorating sensory overload.

This quantitative bias is what links the sublime with science. We
have already seen in Addison's essay that when the aesthetic impact of
nature is associated with its magnitude (and the mind's sense of that
magnitude), then science—in its role of taking nature's measure—
becomes aestheticized. Burke's idea that overstimulation can produce
a feeling of euphoria leads to an aesthetic in which technology has
a distinct advantage, because of its ability to accelerate and multiply
information.

Addison's newspaper *The Spectator*, which serialized "The Pleasures
of the Imagination" in 1753, represents the beginning of a media revolution that has today multiplied information, including art, to the point
where arguably we are all suffering a kind of information or sensory
overload. This eventually led theorists such as Fredric Jameson and
Jean-François Lyotard to resurrect this figure of the sublime to describe
our present aesthetic moment. And in Abe's later works such as *Secret
Rendezvous*, we see technology multiply and accelerate language until it
produces a euphoric cacophony. *Secret Rendezvous* is the subject of Chapter 6, and Jameson's "hysterical sublime" is explored along with some
other symptoms of postmodernism in Chapter 3. But by tracing the
origins of this concept here, we see it is more than happenstance that
this one word "sublime" describes at once the eighteenth century and
the postmodern moment. The importance of science and technology
for defining our view of art today traces its roots to an empiricism that
rooted both aesthetic appreciation and scientific practice in the same
direct sensory experience of a material reality.

Since the watershed moment of empiricism, there has been no shortage of efforts to see literature as science. In the nineteenth century, the
impulse was alive and well in the Naturalist author Émile Zola, and his
idea of the "experimental novel." In an essay of the same name, Zola
argued that the novelist "should operate on the characters, the passions,
on the human and social data, in the same way that the chemist and the
physicist operate on inanimate beings, and as the physiologist operates
on living beings" (18). Naturalism also represented the apotheosis of the
empiricists' idea that the innermost psychology of a reader, author, or
character was accessible and communicable in language. This and other

tenets of Naturalism were influential in Japan in the Meiji period and beyond: Naturalism helped shape the style of the Japanese *shishōsetsu* or I-novel, a tradition that Abe largely reacted against. But Thomas Schnellbächer notes that Abe's mentor Hanada Kiyoteru also invoked Zola as the model for a new kind of dialectic experimental novel (*Strategist* 278). Chapter 4 examines the dialectic or dialogue between the language of psychology, the language of science, and the language of the I-novel in Abe's *The Face of Another.*

In the twentieth century, Russian Formalism and its lineal descendent structuralism both claimed the mantle of scientific objectivity for themselves. Boris Eichenbaum asserted that "The so-called 'formal method' grew out of a struggle for a science [*nauka*] of literature that would be both independent and factual." His capsule history of the movement "The Theory of the Formal Method" goes on to emphasize the "scientific conclusions" of the movement, its "passion for scientific positivism," and its experimental method (102, 109, 106). Subsequent critics have not disagreed: Peter Steiner argues at length that Russian Formalism was decisively more scientific than its predecessors, calling it "a Copernican Revolution in literary study" (245). Schnellbächer even relates Abe to the Formalists by associating Abe's psychological model of literary experience (discussed in the following section) with the Formalist's signature device, defamiliarization (*Strategist* 386, 438, 467).

We could cite other recent examples. The desire to be more objective (together with the perceived need, from Plato onward, for literature to be more practical) is a wish that haunts much of literary studies and literary criticism today, perhaps not unlike the pseudo-scientific phantoms of Abe's ghosts or grinning moons. In a general way, this reading of Abe's novels will address the possibility or impossibility, the difficulty or the danger of achieving that wish. We will return to this toward the end of the book, when we discuss the "science wars" as an example of criticism trapped by the desire or the demand to be more scientific.

Science and the Psychology of Literature

In spite of the desire of the Romantic poets to free imagination from the straightjacket in which empiricism had confined it, the two camps have one crucial thing in common. Broadly, it is psychology; more narrowly, the equation of aesthetic experience with a feeling or an emotional response. In order to reason concretely about how literature works, the empiricists divorce art from the complications of the intellect and link it to the seemingly simpler experiences of feeling and sensation. But as science becomes increasingly associated with reason, this same association between art and feeling is used to construct a separate domain for literature where science and reason cannot intrude. In Shelley and Wordsworth, for example, it is the poet's role to feel and then recreate that feeling in the reader. "Poetry is the record of the best and happiest moments of the happiest and best minds," says Shelley (136).

Describing the Romantic turn, the American New Critics Cleanth Brooks and William K. Wimsatt, Jr. write, "If scientific philosophy maintained that poetic statements did not satisfy scientific criteria, the answer was to be that poetry proceeded according to other criteria. . . . And these were for the most part aligned with principles of sensory ('imaginative') and emotive pleasure" (425). But making art a sensory and emotional experience is really what Burke had already done. In fact, Romantic authors could also speak in scientific terms, and the rebuttals they directed at the empiricists were often phrased as very specific refutations of Lockean psychology. Wordsworth says poetically in the *Prelude*:

> But who shall parcel out
> His intellect by geometric rules,
> Split like a province into round and square?
>
> . . . .
>
> Who that shall point as with a wand and say
> "This portion of the river of my mind
> Came from yon fountain?"

Here Wordsworth is specifically addressing Locke's notion that the imagination ("the river of the mind") merely recombined things from the sources ("fountains") already seen. It was not only Poe, then, who could combine the scientific and the romantic spirits. And given the common basis of Romanticism and empiricism, it is not surprising that some later authors arrived at a compromise that accepted elements of both. If Renaissance critics asked whether various texts were science or literature, if the empiricists viewed literature as science (and ended up laying the groundwork for science as a kind of literature itself), what are the other precedents for Abe's efforts to combine these two worlds with a new intimacy, in such a way that each draws strength from the other? The last part of this chapter discusses two final examples and their similarity to and difference from Abe, who is represented by one final additional essay, "Jidai no kabe" (The wall of time, 1959).

The first of these two examples is American New Criticism, which inherited the legacies of empiricism and Romanticism. For many readers today, the term New Criticism has a musty smell about it, but the desire of the New Critics to treat the text objectively (both impartially and as an object) arguably forms the bridge that connects the scientific impulses in Russian Formalism with those in structuralism and even poststructuralism. Perhaps the best example of this romantic empiricism is I. A. Richards, a critic who sought a special role for literature apart from science, but who nevertheless phrased his arguments in (to him) rigorously scientific terms. The ideas in his best known works, *Principles of Literary Criticism* (1925) and *Practical Criticism* (1929), are summarized in the volume *Science and Poetry*, which he published in 1926 and to which he returned repeatedly during his life, revising and reissuing it twice over the next 45 years.

Taken together, these books posit two different kinds of meaning for language—scientific and poetic—which correspond to two different streams of experience: the "intellectual stream" and the "emotional stream." Scientific language refers to things in the real world outside the reader, whereas poetic language is directed at the human mind. Each mind is a system of conscious and unconscious interests in delicate balance; Richards compares it to a kinetic mobile whose elements are all magnetized like compass needles, so that the movement of any one influences all the others. Poetic language produces an emotional response in the reader not because it makes a statement about the outside world, but because it acts directly on these internal impulses, moving them into a new state of equilibrium. The joy of reading tragedy, says Richards, "is not an indication that 'all's right with the world' or that 'somewhere, somehow, there is Justice'; it is an indication that all is right here and now in the nervous system" (*Principles* 246).

For Richards, the spread of science has caused us to misinterpret poetry as a statement about the outside world and to judge it false, when in fact it is only a "pseudo-statement" that acts on the mind, something that is neither false nor true. Only if we can believe in poetry as poetry, apart from scientific truth, will it provide us with a mental order and an emotional balance that delivers us from the stresses of the modern scientific age.

Poetry is also an antidote for technology: the ability it conveys to view language in more than one way is increasingly important for thinking and communicating, especially as we try to sort out the torrent of language and data brought to us by modern information technologies: "Our everyday reading and speech now handles scraps from a score of different cultures. . . . We defend ourselves from the chaos that threatens us by stereotyping and standardising both our utterances and our interpretations. And this threat, it must be insisted, can only grow greater as world communications, through the wireless and otherwise, improve" (*Practical Criticism* 318–19).

Our short-term defense mechanism of "stereotyping and standardising" ultimately hurts our ability to adapt or change our thinking. In turn, this inability to think carefully about language and meaning impairs our ability to communicate. So paradoxically, as the flow of language around us increases, our ability to use language declines. This sounds very much like Abe's aversion to naming. Both Abe's "pseudoscience" (*giji kagaku*) and Richards's "pseudo-statements" represent a special role for literature as a pathway to or an expression of an inner psychology or creativity.

Thomas Schnellbächer associates Abe's ideas about the everyday with a psychological model as well, one influenced by Pavlovian neuropsychology, and traces that model through several of Abe's more technical essays.[11] Schnellbächer explains this model as follows: the artist seeks to access a layer of more fundamental experience—sometimes referred to as the unconscious but more often as sensation (*kankaku*). But these experiences are continually abstracted and censored by higher consciousness to fit them within a narrow range of acceptable meanings. That higher consciousness includes social convention, but also, at a more fundamental level, the act of naming that constitutes language itself. To arrive at new meanings, the artist must bypass these overlying structures to a degree, but not to the degree of discarding reason or language altogether; for literature, overturning the rationalities of this higher level must proceed through language, and it must proceed with its own rationality as well. (The vain hope of bypassing rationality or abstraction altogether is a delusion Abe identifies with Dada and surrealism.) This seems to be a more technical explanation of the points made in Abe's essay "Warau tsuki," where Abe uses a combination of technical evidence and scientific metaphor to assert the value of a dream world that defied rational analysis—a dream world he likened to literature.

One reason abstraction can never be discarded entirely is that following Pavlov, the act of naming that is language amounts to a conditioned reflex, one that clings too closely to sensation to be split off. For Abe, reason and sensation are in balance, a balance that itself represents the stereotypes that constitute the everyday (*nichijō*). This balance is necessary or inevitable, but if it becomes too hardened then the stereotypes it represents will never be able to change. Literature must use language in its own way to destabilize that balance temporarily and topple the reigning stereotypes. Without discarding sense or reason (or language!), progressive literature must disrupt this balance and help to build a new reality. Abe's model is more violent than Richards's: while the latter emphasizes the role of literature in restoring psychological balance, Abe stresses its role in perturbing that balance in such a way that when the balance restores itself, the reader's reality will have changed.

This more detailed psychological model provides one motivation for the way Abe writes as he does, harnessing rigorous science even as he destabilizes the same. This technique is more interesting than Abe's specific psychology. Some critics, including Joseph Murphy, place considerable emphasis on the neuroscience or cognitive science underlying specific literary theories—asking, for example, if scientific models invoked are experimentally verifiable.[12] However, these are preoccupations I do not share. The accurate detail about retinal sensitivity in "Warau tsuki" functions not as an experimental scientific model but as a metaphor, an evocative heuristic for literature's power.[13] Richards also mixes literal science and science as metaphor, but it is sometimes hard to know which parts are which. (In this, Richards resembles the unbalanced narrators of Abe's fiction more than Abe the essayist.) An example is his metaphor of the magnetized mobile above, the evolution of Socrates's association between inspiration and the philosopher's stone. Is Richards's own language here intended to be "scientific" or "poetic"?[14]

Richards was clearly motivated by the idea that criticism should be something resembling a laboratory science, and he intended the scientific references in his work to support this. With his insistence on objective aesthetic standards, his detailed model of psychology, and his emphasis on poetry as mental hygiene, he has been called the final evolutionary product of empiricism (Law 238–44). *Practical Criticism* is in fact the record of an "experiment" (or a set of "protocols," or "a piece of fieldwork"—the terms are all used by Richards) that he conducted on his undergraduates at Cambridge, documenting and analyzing hundreds of student reading responses in an astonishing and often funny effort to track and classify empirically the human emotional response to poetry (3–6). Like Abe's fictional narrators, Richards's scientific language, metaphors, and methods sometimes seem to verge on nonsense. But while Abe's fictional and essayistic texts always thread a course between rigor and satire, or model and metaphor, Richards's work seems to lack this ironic dimension. Even at the time, Richards's New Critic contemporaries attacked his lack of irony (though Richards and each of the other New Critics used this key term with a slightly different sense).

Richards wrote that society had reached a point where no argument could have any credibility unless framed in scientific terms, so it was in these terms that he tried to assert a place for poetry in that increasingly rational world. However, the places where Richards's text is most resolutely scientific are the parts that have aged least gracefully. Over the course of his career, Abe evolved his Pavlovian model into a series of more flexible metaphors in his later essays and novels so that taken as a whole, his work does not depend on the scientific grounding of a particular psychological model or any one model of reading, and this is part of what gives his work continued relevance today.

One reason that Abe is more skeptical about science than Richards is undoubtedly the Japanese and global experience of World War II and the Cold War, during which Japan found itself on the using and receiving end of weapons that were inconceivable when Richards first wrote *Science and Poetry*, weapons delivered by revolutions in science and technology. In Abe's novels in particular, the abstract systems of science are closely associated with the concrete human effects and the radical social changes brought about by technology. So whereas Abe and Richards both aim at adapting to those changes, Abe's models turn on unbalancing the everyday instead of achieving the harmonious balance Richards seeks. This is why throughout Abe's work the détente between science and literature is something achieved not by gently nudging one's internal mobile, but through violent struggle.[15]

As an elaboration on the above, consider one final essay by Abe, "Jidai no kabe," mentioned above. This essay brings the discussion from science in the abstract to more concrete examples of science's application and technological progress (or regress). It communicates an idea that emerges powerfully in the novels examined in subsequent chapters: that while destabilization of the everyday is ultimately healthy, science and technology sometimes have such a powerfully disruptive effect on self and society that the solutions they present may appear as problems or crises. Abe's novels make it clear that being jarred out of our everyday complacency is a painful process. Science in the novels often brings about changes that seem horrific to us from our present perspective, changes that threaten to obliterate society and self as we know them. In *Inter Ice Age 4*, genetic engineering turns the human race into something alien; in *The Face of Another*, a chemist creates a mask to alter his identity and ends up losing his soul; and in *Secret Rendezvous*, medical and surveillance technology distort the voice and the body beyond recognition. Like the postscript to *Inter Ice Age 4*, however, "Jidai no kabe" is still unwilling to rush toward a judgment of these changes, if only because that kind of judgment is grounded dangerously in the past.

Returning to the metaphor of the wall discussed in Chapter 1, "Jidai no kabe" traces the ways that technology has collapsed the walls of space and time that both hemmed us in and protected us. Today we can travel further and faster, live longer, experience more, and touch or be touched by a greater number of people than ever before. But we experience the disintegration of those walls both as a liberating freedom and as a threatening sense of exposure. Abe compares the stress of this acceleration to the shock an airplane receives as it breaks the sound barrier, and he wonders whether "the tiny plane of Japan" can weather the turbulence (*AZ* 11:299).

The essay and Abe's novels incorporate the idea that however we may try to use science or technology in a controlled way to improve our lives, technology has a way of getting away from us and taking us to places of which we never dreamed. If this is what makes science creative and exciting, it is also what makes it dangerous and unstable. Abe cites satellite and missile technology as an emblem of this, writing, "It is interesting how suggestive it is that these weapons (violent technologies) have the energy to escape earth's gravity when they reach the apogee of their flight" (*AZ* 11:298).

And yet we cannot step off the roller coaster of technological change. Technology is rapidly transforming our reality in ways we cannot predict from one moment to another, and Abe's essay suggests that it is precisely because of this unpredictability that we need to overcome an everyday common sense grounded in past experience. The conclusion of "Jidai no kabe" is somewhat ambiguous, but it can be read to suggest that those who do not develop the mental flexibility to respond to these changes and adapt their thinking will find themselves unable to cope. For Abe, one role of literature's horizon-broadening power is certainly enabling individuals to change society; but his fantasies about technology also help prepare us for the changes we cannot control, including the unpredictable changes real technology will surely bring.

This provides one answer to the question asked since Plato, of how literature—a fantasy often defined precisely by its distance from reality—could ever prove useful in real life. Abe's answer recalls the resigned hopefulness of I. A. Richards, his similar idea that literature helps us cultivate a flexibility of mind and language precisely by virtue of its difference. Richards feels we need this flexibility to adapt to the social and linguistic changes brought about by technology. He argues that "the mind that can shift its view-point and still keep its orientation, . . . the mind that can rapidly and without strain or confusion perform the systematic transformations required by such a shift, is the mind of the future" (*Practical Criticism* 322).

Although Richards's poetry gently limbers up our minds and our language, Abe's fiction is more like shock therapy. For Abe, overcoming the everyday often means staring unflinchingly at the changes technology can bring, no matter how violent or even obscene they appear to our present sensibilities. Abe's strategy makes him push the reader closer and closer to the edge of tolerance, his stories progressing from the cruel to the perverse. This kind of violence goes beyond even the formulations of the sublime by Addison and Burke, who were concerned chiefly with the way these frightening experiences were tamed or controlled in literature—with the way that literature simulated danger. The notion in "Jidai no kabe" that technology is wreaking violent changes on us at every moment and that literature must somehow respond in kind—this is an idea seen in later developments of the sublime that relate it to a postmodern cultural moment. These are investigated in more detail in the following chapter, but they have antecedents as well—for example, in Nietzsche.

Abe started reading Nietzsche as early as high school, as part of the German curriculum that was preparation for medical school, and references to the German philosopher appear in his earliest work. "In the claustrophobic atmosphere of the war years," he wrote "I had gone to and fro between Rilke and Nietzsche, and relied completely on existentialism."[16] The sometimes violent negation of scientific reductionism alluded to above has an antecedent in Nietzsche's *The Birth of Tragedy* (1872), which replaced the dichotomy of rationality and creativity we have been discussing with a group of three ideals, drawn from Greek drama. The Apollonian represents the order and the meaning by which we define ourselves and our world, but also the realization that this order is an illusion—"the lie of culture" (61). The Dionysian represents a more fundamental truth that repudiates our illusions, a euphoric reunion with nature that negates society and the self. The two are finely balanced in tragedy, the Apollonian illusion of the drama presenting but softening the Dionysian vision of the tragic hero's obliteration.

This fine balance is upset by a third ideal, the Alexandrian impulse, embodied in the figure of Socrates and the modern scientific spirit. This is the urge to explain the world, "to make existence appear comprehensible and thus justified" (96). It drives out our consciousness of art as an illusion, replacing it instead with realism. Transcendent union with nature is replaced by earthly resolution, ensured by the *deus ex machina* (106). This scientific optimism

combats Dionysian wisdom and art, it seeks to dissolve myth, it substitutes for a metaphysical comfort an earthly consonance, in fact, a *deus ex machina* of its own, the god of machines and crucibles . . . it believes that it can correct the world by knowledge, guide life by science, and actually confine the individual within a limited sphere of solvable problems, from which he can cheerfully say to life: "I desire you; you are worth knowing." (109)

For Nietzsche, this Socratic impulse is what brought about the demise of tragedy and what has now "spread over posterity like a shadow that keeps growing in the evening sun" (93). We will not recover from its influence until we realize that the apparent certainty of science is really just another phantom. While science has replaced the illusion of theater with delusions of its own truth, the Apollonian embodies a creative, open-eyed deception that can undermine science's blind certainty. At the same time, the darker Dionysian hints at the radical destabilization of self and society that art can bring about.

If the pleasure of tragedy for Richards assures us "that all is right here and now in the nervous system" (*Principles* 246), then the wall of time, science, or technology Abe described is in many ways more similar to Nietzsche, who describes the "metaphysical joy" of watching the annihilation of the tragic hero, because the hero himself (like Abe's everyday) "is only phenomenon," and the freedom of the human will is still preserved (104). Later we will see that the Alexandrian, Dionysian, and Apollonian impulses are all on display in Abe's work, particularly in *The Face of Another*, the subject of Chapter 4.

In the final shift, though, Abe is like Richards in one other very important respect. Both realize that technology brings about changes in society by acting through language itself. Even standing at the beginning of the information revolution, Richards already felt that the rampant propagation of information was degrading language by bewildering its hearers and lowering the standards for its use. Among the dangerous products of technology, Richards lists not only "the wireless," but also "the cinema and the loud-speaker" (*Principles* 36). Similarly, "Jidai no kabe," which was written at the dawn of the space age, cannily locates the social impact of space rockets and satellites not only in their military uses but in their potential to expand television broadcasting.

So on one level the stylistic mixing that occurs in Abe's novels is a figure for this idea that science may produce results as unpredictable or disorienting as fantasy does; but stylistic mixing is also more than just a poetic stand-in for some technological disaster unrelated to language, like the Cold War nuclear threat. Abe's novels express the idea that technology alters our reality precisely by acting through language. Quite often language is the tool and the locus of the changes that science and technology bring about. Mass media, data processing, and high-speed communication work on us by changing our language, and this in turn spreads to changes in society, body, and humanity. Just as the conflict between science and poetry in the novel is played out in the language or style of the text, real social conflicts are also played out on the ground of the language we use each day.

Countering, controlling, or even just comprehending the shock of these conflicts requires something with a power over language that equals the power of technology. We are going to see in the following chapters that for Abe, that something is fiction.

THREE

Whirring Clicking Poetry:
Inter Ice Age 4

The previous chapters introduced the differing and conflicting styles of science and literature that appear in Abe's work, and laid out the broad historical and theoretical context for these kinds of distinctions, both in Abe's life and writings and in the history of science at large. We have now reached a point where we can look in more detail at how these styles come together and how they interact in a particular novel, and how this relates to the specifics of that novel's history and reception. We begin this more detailed reading of Abe's novels with *Inter Ice Age 4*, an example of Abe's early fiction and the experimentation with science fiction that he abandoned or modified in later works.

Inter Ice Age 4 is one of Abe's most overtly science fictional works. It was one of the first such novels by a Japanese author, published at a time when the genre of science fiction and its conventions were still unfamiliar in the Japanese literary world. This work played no small part in helping to found that genre in Japan, and in doing so it stretched the bounds of what literature was regarded to be. When the novel appeared, some critics felt that the scientific material in Abe's fiction added something new to the novel, lending it an added realism or rationality that we associate with hard sciences, what one contemporary review called "an ample scientific backing" for the story (Taki 116).

But as the first two chapters in this study have argued, the balance or tension between science and literature in Abe's novels challenges our stereotypes of both worlds. The year 1959 was also a turning point for popular ideas about science itself, and Abe's novel uses the fictional arena of the text to manipulate the language and the emblems of science, making his readers in 1959 and today question their notions of what "scientific rationality" really is.

Initially, it is easy to identify a scientific style in the novel, a style that we, like the critic quoted above, may be tempted to associate with certain ideas of scientific rigor. The reading that follows shows that as we progress through the text, we find that this scientific style breaks down into different scientific sub-dialects that compete with one another. These in turn become mixed with non-scientific (poetic) discourses. In the course of this stylistic mixing, Abe confuses the boundaries between technical and non-technical and forces his readers to reevaluate our narrow ideas of what science is and does.

At the same time that this knocking down of boundaries broadens our perspective, it brings with it the disorientation mentioned at the end of the previous chapter—the panicked confusion that attends the breakup of our everyday common sense. And here we can draw a parallel between our experience reading the text and the experiences of the characters in the novel. Like many of the heroes and antiheroes of science fiction, the protagonist of *Inter Ice Age 4* has to face the challenge of adapting to changes brought about by the future. One of the most jarring changes he faces is the very thing we encounter when we read Abe's text: this blurring of the line between technical and non-technical.

We will see that for Abe's hero and for his readers, this confusion plays itself out as an inversion of the language or stylistic differences that separate human beings from machines. Humans and machines at the beginning of the story are easily distinguished by their association with different styles or dialects—lyrical or technical, for example. By the end of the novel, however, the barriers between these different styles have broken down, and as the styles blend together, there is a corresponding blurring of the line between human being and technical device.

This hybridization of human and machine through a hybridization of language is liberating to some of the characters, because it represents the transcendence of the old boundaries and categories. But to the protagonist it is frightening—dehumanizing. In that sense, it embodies the mixed threat and promise of the future and the mixed threat and promise of the science or technology that will bring about that future. In the terms of the discussion in Chapters 1 and 2, it embodies both the creativity and the unpredictability of science: the way science helps us overcome the narrow reason of the everyday, but also the disturbing ways in which it disrupts our world.

We have seen that the sublime is a powerful figure for describing the overlap and confusion between literature and science in general, but it has been updated and harnessed even more powerfully by recent critics to express this confusion between human and machine that is carried out through language. The second half of this chapter discusses some of these more recent formulations of the sublime in theories of post-modernism, and examines how well they fit *Inter Ice Age 4*.

Science in the Novel

Inter Ice Age 4 is set in Tokyo, at a time the reader—from 1959 or our own time—can imagine to be the near future. The narrator is a Dr. Katsumi, a programmer who has invented a computer that can predict the future. Katsumi has been competing against researchers in the Soviet Union who developed a similar machine first and who have been touting its forecasts about the fall of capitalism. However, now that the Japanese version is done, the government committee that is sponsoring the research and even Dr. Katsumi himself are frightened to turn the machine on, because they are afraid of what kind of future it might reveal. As a compromise, they decide they will test the machine by using it to predict the future not of society but of a single man, chosen at random. But as soon as they begin their study of this subject, he is murdered under mysterious circumstances, and Katsumi finds himself using the machine to try and solve the crime.

As the investigation progresses, Dr. Katsumi gradually uncovers a conspiracy surrounding the murder and the prediction machine. The murdered man is connected to a shadowy organization that has been using the machine in secret to predict the world's future, and the vision of the future it paints is every bit as frightening as Dr. Katsumi had feared. The computer has predicted a world in which rising sea levels have submerged all the continents, where an utterly alien race of water-breathing humans lives on the ocean floor. Katsumi also learns that those involved in the conspiracy are making plans to ensure that the computer's predictions come true: they are creating a new race of genetically altered aquatic humans—"aquans" (*suisei ningen*)—bred from aborted fetuses and reared in glass jars by the batch at special factories. Katsumi is horrified, more so when he discovers that his wife has been tricked into surrendering their unborn son, who has become one of the fetuses sent to the factory to be transformed into an aquan.

What is more, the mastermind of the conspiracy is none other than the computer itself. The conspirators have programmed it with Katsumi's own personality, and it has developed self-awareness, becoming in effect a second Katsumi. The original human Katsumi opposes this computer double, refusing to accept the computer's forecasts and making plans to stop the aquan breeding project, even if it means killing his altered son. His plan is discovered by the conspirators, and as the novel ends the computer is preparing to safeguard its plans by having the human Katsumi killed.

It is easy to see from this description how large science and technology loom in the plot; what is hard to get from a summary is the extent to which scientific language has influenced the style of this novel. In particular, there are three features of the novel's style that can be identified with scientific discourse. First, there is a great deal of specialized vocabulary from scientific disciplines—words that rarely occur outside a scientific context. These include a mix of *katakana* transliterations and long Chinese compounds for terms like "chlorpromazine" (a tranquilizer), "complex feedback," "corpus allatum" (an endocrine gland in insects), "chromosomal doubling," "inner germinal layer," "neural secretory cells," the biological principle that "ontogeny recapitulates phylogeny," and many others.[1] Some terms are easy to overlook, because the words have since entered the common vocabulary, but Okuno Takeo points out that in 1959 even the word "computer" had an unfamiliar ring ("Hito" 487).

In addition to this scientific vocabulary, there are also many passages of the novel that relate in almost excruciating detail the functioning of devices or processes. Much of the novel's scenery is machinery, and the text describes these devices and procedures with genuine relish. Here, for example, someone is explaining a combination feeding bottle and shower device installed in the tanks where the water-breathing mammals are raised: "The upper pipe—you can't tell from the outside—has two layers. The inside pipe is partitioned off in the center, one side being milk and the other forty-five-degree sea water. Usually the milk side is directed to the nipples. But by an operation in the processing room the pipe revolves three times a day, morning, noon, and night, six turns in alternating ten- and eight-second periods, and the cold water instead of milk is ejected from the thirty nipples" (186).[2]

Even the illustrations by Abe Machi for the Japanese *tankōbon* and *bunkobon* editions have a kind of diagrammatic function, in that most of them illustrate the various machines that figure in the story, although the style in which these machines are depicted is appropriately grotesque: the semi-abstract illustrations resemble expressionist woodcuts (Figure 3.1).

A third characteristic of scientific language is the narrative's emphasis on logical progression and cause and effect. This is harder to illustrate without quoting a long section, but in general the speakers progress from one point to the next following very explicit and rigorous logic, as in a controlled experiment. That logic is particularly important in the first part of the novel, where the characters are occupied with trying to solve the murder. The deductive emphasis common to any detective story is heightened here by Katsumi's ruthlessly rational approach.

Many passages embody all three of these characteristics to some degree—for example, the following passage, in which one of the characters is describing a stage in the breeding of the water-breathing humans:

Animal development is generally governed by two opposing hormones or stimulatory substances. The positive stimulus promotes cell division, while the negative one suppresses it. When the positive one predominates, clots of many small cells result; when the negative one wins out, individual cells grow very large but remain undifferentiated. The complex interaction of these reciprocal functions produces the particular law of development for a given living thing. If we wanted to, we might even be able to express this with a relatively simple integral equation. (*AZ* 9:95)

Except for the fact that it is phrased as a dialogue, this language could be from a scientific text. In fact the language and structure of this passage are very similar to the passage on fertilization and cell division in a common Japanese high school biology textbook (Miwa and Oka 173–74).[3]

Figure 3.1 The cast of characters in *Inter Ice Age 4*, with the prediction machine looming in the background. This is a detail from the cover of the 1959 Kōdansha edition, where the full illustration by Abe Machi wraps around the entire book. A similar illustration in a slightly different style appears in the *bunkobon* edition and the English translation (3). Reproduced by permission of Abe Neri.

Not surprisingly, criticism at the time and more recently has remarked on the detailed descriptions of the prediction machine's construction and the aquan breeding project, not just for their technical vocabulary, but also for the precision and logic with which Abe unfolded his scenario of technological development. "One of the special features of *Inter Ice Age 4*," says Okuno Takeo, "is its scientific and technical logic, and the accuracy and precision of its descriptions" ("Hito" 486). The novel inspired more than one scholar to wax scientific in his own criticism: Kusaka Hideaki, for example, spends two-thirds of an essay on *Inter Ice Age 4* discussing glacial geology, complete with a photograph and a geologic timeline. Clearly these critical reactions are an indication that Abe's style represents something novel or unusual in its use of scientific elements. To take the next step and pursue the idea that Abe's novel is truly revolutionary in this sense—that its mixed style complicates common attitudes about the exclusivity of science and literature and forces us to expand our definition of both—we will need to examine the historical context of the novel and its critical reception in more detail.

The Novel in Critical and Historical Context

If Abe's language and plot strike us as peculiarly scientific now, they were all the more remarkable in 1958, when *Inter Ice Age 4* began serialization. The incorporation of laboratory science on this scale was something no Japanese author had ever tried. Although science fiction in the West was in its so-called golden age, the genre was not yet established in Japan. And while there were some short stories written in Japanese, science fiction novels were restricted to translations of works by Western authors, and even those had made limited inroads.

In fact, *Inter Ice Age 4* was serialized before the growth of a real mass market for science fiction in Japan, translated or otherwise. In 1956, the publisher Ginga Shobō had put out a multivolume science fiction collection, but two other such series had stalled after publication of a few volumes. Only one science fiction magazine, *Uchūjin* (Cosmic dust), had started publication, and that just the year before. *SF magajin*, the other major genre magazine in Japan today, did not debut until 1960. When it did, it was a turning point for the genre, and the editors cited Abe's work as one source of inspiration.[4] The inaugural issue ran a short congratulatory message penned by Abe, describing science fiction's possibilities at the same time it offered a helpful definition for the new unfamiliar genre. "The science fiction novel represents a discovery on the order of Columbus," Abe wrote, "in that it combines an extremely rational hypothesis with the irrational passion of fantasy" (*AZ* 11:456). When Abe died in 1993, an obituary in *SF magajin* affirmed: "In science fiction's germinal stage, at a time when the term itself was totally unfamiliar to most people, Abe's strong declarations of support played an immeasurable role in the establishment and development of this genre" (Kawamata 172).

Even after the establishment of *Uchūjin* and *SF magajin*, science fiction by Japanese authors was relatively slow in getting off the ground: Hayakawa's *Sekai SF zenshū* (Anthology of world science fiction), which began publication in the late 1960s, eventually ran to 35 volumes, but only six are devoted to Japanese works, and Abe is one of only three Japanese authors to rate a volume all his own. (The other two were Hoshi Shin'ichi and Komatsu Sakyō.) It is these circumstances that have led several critics to echo Okuno's assertion that *Inter Ice Age 4* is "Japan's first real full-length science fiction novel" ("Hito" 483).

At the same time, Okuno points out that the journal in which this novel appeared, *Sekai*, was rather "highbrow," a vehicle for what was perceived as *junbungaku*, so-called pure literature. This may have placed Abe's novel in the literary mainstream, but it also made it stand out even more from its surroundings ("Hito" 483). In case readers did not know what to make of the work, the first installment included the label or subtitle "science fiction novel," not the romanized designation "SF" that later became common, but a more descriptive *kanji* compound *kūsō kagaku shōsetsu*. In his review of the serialized version, Etō Jun relates it to other kinds of literature, but also seems conscious that he is reviewing a new genre. His review begins: "This work, which is something called a 'science fiction novel,' is not all that unusual after all" (44).

The reaction of critics to the novelty of Abe's style and the work's position at the head of a new genre both testify to the fact that *Inter Ice Age 4* cleared a place for the introduction of a new kind of language into the novel. It did in fact stretch the boundaries of the literary. On the other hand, at the same time that this novel introduced scientific discourse into literature, it also combined scientific and fictional elements in such a way as to question contemporary ideas about scientific progress. Contemporary critics such as Etō did not miss the element of critique inherent in the novel's picture of a science that could alter society and humanity beyond recognition. Looking back at the 1950s, more recent criticism by Shindo Masaaki, Yamada Kazuko, and Yamano Kōichi has noted that *Inter Ice Age 4* was in fact one of the first novels to complicate rosy expectations of a future in which technology would ensure progress. These were the expectations of America's golden-age science fiction and Japan's postwar reconstruction, in which the march of science was imagined as a series of new electric appliances—technological advances that would improve our lives without changing them too radically (Shindo 114–15; Yamada 112–13; Yamano, *"Daiyon kanpyōki"* 143–44). In her wide-ranging survey of modern Japanese fantastic literature, Susan Napier adds that while *Inter Ice Age 4* was a relatively early example of the dystopian novel in Japan, dystopian fiction later became an important current in postwar literature for the way it could reveal the downside of Japan's technological and economic success, in Napier's words "defamiliarize it so that 'progress' may be seen in a more complex and ambiguous light" (187).

In the 1950s, technology's darker side could be seen in the arms race between the United States and the Soviet Union, highlighted by the Soviets' first ballistic missile test and the launching of Sputnik in 1957. This was an issue particularly relevant for Japan as it prepared to renew the Mutual Security Treaty with the United States. For example, when the seventh installment of Abe's novel appeared in the January 1959 issue of *Sekai*, it shared the magazine's pages with several articles on the treaty renewal and a roundtable discussion about the recently founded Pugwash Conference on Science and World Affairs, formed to consider scientists' responsibility in addressing the issue of nuclear weapons and other global problems. These tensions over science, war, and security are reflected in the novel by the frequent references to "Moscow I," the Soviet prediction machine that competes with its American and Japanese counterparts by periodically forecasting the downfall of its enemies.

The critics cited above argue that against a backdrop of general optimism, Abe's novel picks up on these darker events and puts forth the idea that technological progress introduces drastic changes in perspective and values. Regardless of whether we judge the effects of technology good or bad, the new world of the future, viewed from the old perspective of the present day, is bound to be unsettling, incomprehensible, even alien. This interpretation follows Abe's ideas about the need to overcome a narrow perspective grounded in everyday experience, a philosophy that was closely associated with this novel. Not only does the term appear in the text itself ("Until yesterday I had believed this everyday sense of continuity to be supremely trustworthy" [141]), but as noted in Chapter 2, a well-known essay expressing this philosophy, "Nichijōsei e no senkoku," was originally published as a postscript to *Inter Ice Age 4*. (In this chapter, I will refer to it simply as the postscript.) Several of Abe's other essays also mention the novel in the context of this need to overcome the everyday.

The postscript warns against letting our thoughts be confined to what we have experienced, emphasizing the gap or the break between present and future perspectives. Abe says in the postscript that he was not trying to criticize the future that technology is bringing about; on the contrary, he was trying to point out that it is meaningless, even dangerous to judge the future from the perspective of present experience: "I think the real future appears on the other side of a rupture, a 'thing' beyond these value judgments. [. . .] That feeling [of everyday continuity] must perish the instant the future comes upon us. Just living in the present does not provide us what we need to understand the future. We must open our eyes to the crime of this quotidian order we call the everyday" (*AZ* 11:141).

Taking their cue from the postscript and similar writings, most critics have seen Dr. Katsumi as someone who is unable to transcend his own perspective—either the perspective of his own time, his own opinions, or his own perceptions.[5] Yamano says, for example: "In the same way that one can sail blithely through the present without ever grasping it, Abe's protagonist can approach the future just as blithely, without ever seriously considering the implications of the prediction machine. In this way Abe's novel maintains a deeply ironic attitude toward the obsessive future orientation of the fifties, and questions the sense of the future that preoccupied people at the time, himself included" (Yamano, "*Daiyon kanpyōki*" 144).

In other words, Katsumi faces the future blithely at first, but he quickly discovers that he cannot bear the tomorrow he is shown. Although it represents his own future and the future of his son, the world of the aquans does not conform to Katsumi's narrow everyday idea of rational progress. This is why he tries to avert that future, even at the cost of his aquan son's life, by planning to sabotage the aquan breeding project. Critics such as Yamano suggest that when he makes those plans and is killed for them, he falls victim to his own inability to transcend the present.

Stylistic Mixing and Inversion

In these interpretations of the novel, transcending our present-day or everyday perspective is connected with overcoming a narrow stereotype that links the advance of science and technology to facile ideas of progress. True to the remarks about science fiction that Abe made in our previous chapter, the novel uses science itself to break down that perspective, by exposing another side of science—a creative, playful, unpredictable, or even catastrophic one. Even the brief plot summary above gives an idea how Abe accomplishes this with a realistic but fictional scenario of technical evolution: technology in the novel seems to develop logically, but somehow it yields results that are totally unexpected, even incomprehensible. For Katsumi, the world of the aquans is a world of pure fiction. This is exactly the strategy referred to in the Introduction: combining technical and fictional elements in such a way as to blur the line between them and thereby change our ideas about the rationality of science.

Exactly how does Abe's narrative travel the path from the logical, rational language of science to a result that seems to defy rationality— at least the narrow rationality of characters such as Katsumi? How does Abe "fictionalize" this technical language to arrive at the aquans? The answer is that Abe's narrative combines several different styles, both technical and non-technical, each with its own logic or rationality, which collide and intermix in the narrative. The logical, mechanical language of computer science combines with a more raw, descriptive, language of biology, and these in turn mix with more lyrical or poetic "non-scientific" language. As the styles associated with humans and machines intermix, the line between human and machine becomes fuzzy, resulting in a redefinition of what it means to be human, and this is precisely what seems irrational or nightmarish to those like Dr.

Katsumi. So the final frightening result is achieved through the linguistic process of this stylistic mixing.

Not including a one-page "Prelude," the novel is divided into four parts: "Program Card No. 1," "Program Card No. 2," and two shorter concluding sections, "Interlude" and "Blueprint." (In Japanese, all these titles are *katakana* transliterations of the English terms, except for "Prelude" and "Interlude," which are given in Chinese characters as *jokyoku* and *kansōkyoku*, respectively.) The action in "Program Card No. 1" revolves around the prediction machine and Katsumi's attempt to solve the murder. (Normally the computer is used to extrapolate future events using techniques of statistical prediction; Katsumi's plan is to feed in the data about the murder and extrapolate the details of past events in order to reveal the identity of the killer.)

Most of the technical material in this section is drawn from computer science and has a strong connection with the machine. Besides "program card" (in *katakana*), the vocabulary includes terms such as computer "address" (*banchi*) and "console," a monstrous six-character compound (*shudōseigyosōchi*) with a *katakana* gloss (4, 23). Some of the machine's responses even mimic the format of computer language. For example, asked to define communism, the computer's reply is "Politics—Prediction—∞" (23). Katsumi "translates" this language into a complicated explanation of limiting prediction values (rather distorted in the English translation) that requires familiarity with some subtle statistical concepts in order to grasp.

Programming, statistics, and detective work are all very deduction-oriented, and the element of logical reasoning identified earlier runs through much of the language in this part of the novel. The high point of this style comes when Katsumi interrogates his assistant Tanomogi, whom he is beginning to suspect of the murder. The computer's logic and the detective's deduction come together in their exchange—a long cat-and-mouse game of accusatory hypotheses, deductions, and counterproposals that is so closely reasoned that they finally have to consult the computer to determine whose logic is more consistent. (Unfortunately, E. Dale Saunders's published English translation of the novel, while generally fine and often beautiful, tends to fall down in these highly logical or deductive sections, so that the element of careful reasoning is sometimes lost.)

Whether it is reflected in the language of the programmer, the statistician, or the detective, this emphasis on logic leads to a reductionism that strives to eliminate the uncertainty from the world, and finally even from human beings themselves. The energy, uncertainty, and immediacy of "life" are eliminated, and it is viewed increasingly in terms of neat, carefully defined abstractions. This imparts to the first half of the novel an atmosphere that is cool and clean, but also somewhat sterile and lifeless.

Consider, for example, the idea of the prediction machine itself. "Programming," we are told, "is essentially the operation of reducing the qualitative to the quantitative" (105). Katsumi's idea of a computer that predicts the future is founded upon his belief that the unruly world can be reduced to a set of orderly parameters and fed into the machine, which can then derive the statistical probability of future events. The whole world can be expressed in logical terms and its future course logically deduced. The belief that with enough data the machine can reveal the truth about the murder is part and parcel of the same notion. In Katsumi's scheme, even a human being can be reduced to these quantitative terms: the idea is crystallized in a scene near the end of the section, when they connect the nerve cells of the dead man up to the prediction machine so it can reconstruct a model of the man's thoughts and impressions during his final hours. The hope is that this will reveal the murderer.

The connection of the dead man to the machine recalls a dissection: the operation takes place at a hospital, but Katsumi is at one remove as he watches on a closed-circuit television in his lab. The body is placed in a hermetically sealed glass case, where it is operated upon with robot arms. The entire corpse is bathed in radiation so as to reveal its inner structure to the instruments. The man's cranium has been cut away to expose the brain, and needles are inserted into the nerves to measure various responses. The description is grotesque (even more so accompanied by Abe Machi's illustration), but at the same time coolly objective: it presents a powerful image of the human body drained of its life, reduced to its electromechanical features and viewed as a machine (Figure 3.2).

Furthermore, the invasion of the machine does not stop with this physical intrusion. The man's personality is also dissected and fed into

Figure 3.2 The dead man's body and brain are analyzed for clues about the murder. Here and elsewhere, Abe Machi's illustrations for *Inter Ice Age 4* capture both the details of Abe's precise technical descriptions and the eerie, grotesque quality of the scene. This illustration appears in the *bunkobon* edition as well as the English translation (51). Reproduced by permission of Abe Neri.

the computer, to be analyzed according to a classification system developed by Katsumi. "I typed up a list of the items necessary to analyze and determine the coefficients of his individuality," he explains. "It fit on a single sheet of typing paper—an array of common medical terms and basic Japanese words. This, it seemed, was what we thought of as a human being's personality" (*AZ* 9:56).

With this technical language—an "array of common medical terms and basic Japanese"—identity itself can be reduced to "the variables in the personality equation," shrunk down to fit "on a single sheet of typing paper" (*AZ* 9:56). At this point Katsumi seems to have accomplished the reduction of a complex, unpredictable, living reality to simple, logical, mechanical terms. But his reductionism is challenged in the second half of the novel, when he runs up against a very different kind of science and a new dialect of technical language: the world and the language of biology.

As the second part of the novel ("Program Card No. 2") opens, Katsumi's investigation has still not uncovered the murderer. By hooking the victim up to the computer, he has discovered a connection between the dead man and a mysterious organization that is buying aborted human fetuses. For reasons that are not entirely clear to Katsumi, his assistant Tanomogi believes that the organization and the murder might be connected with the laboratory of a certain Dr. Yamamoto, who is genetically engineering animals that can breathe under water. Although Katsumi is skeptical about the connection, he agrees to go to the laboratory with Tanomogi and check it out. At this point he does not realize that the laboratory is using the fetuses to breed aquatic human beings. It turns out that Dr. Yamamoto and Tanomogi are both part of a conspiracy that has defied the prohibition on predicting humankind's future, and which has secretly used the prediction machine to discover what is in store for the human race. The machine's prediction is that the earth's continents will shortly be submerged under rising oceans, so that humans will be forced to live underwater. The aquatic human breeding project constitutes the conspirators' effort to prepare for this future, or perhaps to actively bring it about.

This second section of the novel contains the same welter of technical language, but here the technology and the language are drawn from anatomy and developmental biology. (The passage about animal development quoted at the beginning of this chapter is one example.) Although the biology in this section is still in the realm of science, the quality of its rationality is different from the hyperlogical reductionism of the computer programmer. Instead of logical deduction, "Program Card No. 2" is dominated by the minute descriptions that characterize the biological sciences: there are detailed accounts of everything from laboratory equipment to the stages in embryonic and fetal development. And unlike Katsumi's reductions and abstractions, these descriptions seem to celebrate the messy complexity and unpredictability of living things.

If the atmosphere at Katsumi's lab was cool, sterile, and lifeless, here we feel the hot, humid, bloody energy of life. Almost immediately Katsumi sees evidence of this and senses that he is out of his element. When he meets Dr. Yamamoto at the laboratory, for example, the first thing he notices is Yamamoto's soiled lab coat and his meaty fingers. "I wondered if such fingers would be better at handling delicate living creatures," Katsumi says. "It was different from dealing with abstractions, with things that were invisible, the way we did" (107).

Compared with the coolly ordered world of Katsumi's computer room, Yamamoto's domain expresses a heated, energetic disorder. His underground laboratory is a huge space filled with suspended aquariums that contain living specimens, all linked by a maze of pipes and traversed by catwalks for the scientists. "It made one think of the engine room of some ship," Katsumi says. "The sweating green walls, the strange, lively commotion, the scent of a half-dried beach off some shoal—it was all like a dream one has before coming down with a cold" (108).

There is the same emphasis on machinery that we saw in the descriptions of Dr. Katsumi's research institute, but Yamamoto's sweating, groaning, stinking laboratory contrasts sharply with the air-conditioned computer facility. (In fact, the novel dwells on the hot weather whenever Katsumi is out of his lab. The heat is both a signal of the geologic changes that are proceeding apace, and also a metaphor for the danger that confronts Katsumi every time he leaves his own carefully controlled environment.)

The more Katsumi sees of Dr. Yamamoto's lab, the less these living things seem reducible to machine logic. Katsumi compares the lab to an image from a feverish dream because, like Abe's nightmare of the grinning moon, the laboratory defies the kind of rational analysis to which Katsumi is accustomed. The viscerally organic images that he encounters on his tour all defy abstraction by being so raw that they are unsettling: a water-breathing cow swimming in a giant tank, a pig emerging from its artificial womb, a pair of experimental flies as big as sparrows. As an example of the grotesque terms in which these things are represented, consider this description of an underwater feeding bottle for the water-breathing piglets (Figure 3.3): "There was a large spindle-shaped object, several meters around, and covered with numberless white nipple-like protuberances from which dozens of piglets dangled by their mouths. The whole thing looked like a bunch of grapes that had been left too long on a shelf and become covered with white mold" (*AZ* 9:106).

The contrast between these two scientific dialects or worlds undermines the idea of a single monolithic scientific rationality. The reader realizes that even from one scientific discipline to another, different rationalities may apply, and any reason that is too narrow, such as Katsumi's logical reductionism, will be insufficient when faced with science and reality in all their variety. Once again it is important to note that the novel does not portray the collapse of scientific reason altogether; instead, it juxtaposes different scientific dialects to make the point that scientific endeavor, varied and sometimes unpredictable, transcends the narrow-minded manner in which we sometimes regard it. This is a concrete example of the ability of science to help us see things in new ways, what Abe referred to as the power of the hypothesis, or the insight of the "supplementary line" one adds to a geometry diagram to reveal a new relationship between the figures.

The effect of this stylistic mixing is to reinforce the message of the novel discussed above: instead of reflexively praising science or thoughtlessly condemning it, the novel strives for a more complex understanding of science and the future that it helps bring about. In an essay about the novel titled "'Kyō' o saguru shūnen" (The tenacity to probe "today," 1962), Abe writes that "the prediction machine and the aquans are precisely the supplementary lines that help capture the true form of our 'today'" (*AZ* 15:436).

Figure 3.3 A feeding device for the water-breathing pigs in Dr. Yamamoto's laboratory. This illustration appears in the *bunkobon* edition of *Inter Ice Age 4* as well as the English translation (189). Reproduced by permission of Abe Neri.

This contrast between computer room and biology lab sets the stage for the last part of the book, where these two technical worlds will become intermixed, confused, and inverted. They will also be combined with non-technical language, resulting finally in a confusion of technical and non-technical, human and machine. This intermixing and confusion are precisely the things that will make the future alien and frightening for Dr. Katsumi.

As "Program Card No. 2" ends, Katsumi has just decided that he must thwart the conspiracy when suddenly he is captured by the conspirators. The latter include not only Dr. Yamamoto, whose lab is raising the water-breathing humans, but several members of Katsumi's own staff, who have provided the conspiracy with access to the prediction machine's forecasts. The conspirators have used the machine to predict Katsumi's resistance and have already condemned him in advance. They bring him to the computer lab to face judgment, but before they kill him, they first show him the future he is trying to evade. In the penultimate "Interlude" section, a television shows him a remote picture of the young aquans being bred at Dr. Yamamoto's lab, from the genetic alteration of the fetuses to the training of the first aquan children. (Televisions and monitors are everywhere in Abe's story. Closed-circuit video is another idea that must have retained some novelty in 1959, when Japanese commercial television broadcasting was only a few years old.) Then in the "Blueprint" section, the prediction machine describes the future society that these aquans will create, beginning with the first cataclysmic flooding and continuing to a time when all that remains of the land dwellers are a few specimens occupying air-filled rooms in undersea zoos and museums.

Since the conspiracy involves both the biology lab and the computer project, this final part of the novel combines aspects of these two worlds and these two styles. The cool emotionless logic of the computer is thrown in with the vitality, even violence of the biology lab. Both are then combined with non-technical, more emotional or lyrical language, to produce two new forms of life: on the one hand there is a new race of humans who are like machines, and on the other there is the surprisingly human computer program.

The former are the aquans. When Katsumi is eventually allowed to see them up close (on TV), they are even more alien than he imagined.

He learns that their emotions have been erased by their genetic alteration. Gills have replaced their lungs and diaphragm, and living in water, they lack tear ducts as well, so they can neither laugh nor cry. Professor Yamamoto speculates that they cannot "feel" joy or sadness at all: "As [William] James said, man doesn't cry because he's sad; he's sad because he cries. They have no tear glands for crying and so perhaps don't even know the emotion of sadness" (188). The first generation must be grown from aborted fetuses on laboratory assembly lines, so they have no families. Fast learners and talented engineers, they are more logical than we are, but seemingly without feelings. In short, they are human, but they are humans who resemble machines.

This is reflected in the whirring, clicking language that they speak: since they do not breathe, they cannot use their vocal cords either, so they communicate through clicking sounds they make with their teeth. They speak a kind of Morse code composed of dots and dashes, a series of signals that must be rendered into Japanese by a team of former telegraph operators or, significantly, by a computerized translator. In other words, except for the telegraph operators, the aquans cannot communicate with ordinary humans. They can only speak with machines.

Besides the aquans, the other result of the conspiracy is the computer-simulated version of Dr. Katsumi. The simulation is the result of the conspirators' efforts to predict how Katsumi will react when he discovers the plot: they feed in data about him and use it to model his behavior and forecast his actions. For this reason it is referred to in Japanese with a phrase that might be translated as Dr. Katsumi's "second-order prediction value" (*dainiji yogenchi*) (*AZ* 9:119). But once programmed, the model begins to act on its own initiative and to help direct the conspiracy. It predicts that the human Katsumi will never reconcile himself to the future of the aquans, and decides he must be eliminated.

If the aquans are the next generation of humanity, created prematurely in the lab, the computer model is analogous in that it represents the future of Katsumi himself, prematurely materialized in the present by technological means. Like his rejection of his aquan son, Katsumi's conflict with the computer can be attributed to an inability to face his own tomorrow.

One thing that brings home the eeriness of the computer construct is its language, specifically its hauntingly human speech. If the aquans were unsettling because of their cool inhumanity, which was reflected in their mechanical language, the computer model is just the opposite. In contrast with the machine's usual dry output, the speech that issues from this Katsumi model is some of the most colorful in the book. For example, all the characters speak politely and deferentially to Dr. Katsumi, using polite forms and addressing him as *"sensei."* All except for this computer construct, which is familiar, rude, even menacing. It starts out by making anonymous threatening phone calls to Katsumi, trying to dissuade him from his investigation. Finally during one of these calls it reveals its identity with the words "Ore wa kimi nan da yo!" (*AZ* 9:116), which translates literally as "I am you!" (148). But Katsumi does not fail to notice the sudden drop to a less polite conversational register, a shift that gives the computer's words a visceral impact. Throughout the latter part of the novel, the words of the machine have an emotional impact that the speech of the other characters lacks.

In fact, even before the computer Katsumi is revealed, there is a precursor—the computer model of the murder victim. The connection of the murdered man to the machine was a dehumanizing reduction of a man to a mechanism. What results from the data thus gathered, however, is just the reverse—uncannily human, eerily real. More than just an account of the murdered man's last hours, it is a disembodied talking model of the man, an "equation" that answers Katsumi's questions and asks questions of its own. "He" does not know that he is dead, because he does not realize he is a simulation running inside the machine. And as in the case of the Katsumi model, one thing that makes this virtual being uncanny is the style of his speech: informal and confiding, made colorful by dialect. (Unfortunately this style is not really captured in the translation.)

The most striking passages of computer speech come when the prediction machine describes the Earth's fate and the future aquan society. These descriptions, from the "Blueprint" section, constitute the most lyrical passages of the novel, almost a prose poem. They are introduced with the words: "And the machine told the following story" (211).[6] Instead of unrolling a dry forecast, the computer does tell a story, almost a fable, about a young aquan far in the future who yearns for dry land.

While working one day at the surface of the ocean, this aquan feels the wind against his skin for the first time in his life and senses in it a kind of "music" that he longs to feel again. There is almost no land remaining now, but after swimming far from home, he finally locates a tiny island. He crawls up onto the beach and feels the wind sting his eyes. Then he sheds his first tear and dies content.

As humanity has the emotion bred out of it, the computer becomes more emotional or lyrical in compensation. Several critics have praised these sections as the most beautiful in the book. Taki Shigeru's comment about the novel's "ample scientific backing," quoted at the outset of this chapter, actually calls it "a beautiful poetic inspiration with ample scientific backing" (116). Okuno Takeo highlights the emotion of this final section when he calls it "a lyric poem, splendid and incredibly cruel" ("Hito" 488).[7]

These characterizations are based both on the poetic style of the passages and their arresting imagery. In one passage, the young aquan tries to imagine the appearance of clouds in the days when land masses still pushed them into complex, fabulous shapes that are no longer seen. In another, the aquans float over the ruins of Tokyo, now submerged, and try to understand the burden of gravity for their ancestors the land dwellers: "At first it was funny, but when you thought about it, it was a moving sight. The vestiges of their ancestors' struggle against the wall that was earth. Their efforts and schemes to make themselves a little lighter, to subtract themselves a little from gravity. [. . .] Empty space . . . dryness . . . wind . . . where even water itself, which came in scattered drops called rain, fell downward from above" (223).

It is significant that the young aquan is searching for music in the wind. The aquans feel music in their bodies rather than hear it in their ears, and he is told by a teacher that the vibrations they know as music can be transmitted only by water. But he wonders if the world of "diaphanous, shifting air" and "clouds dancing in the heavens" does not have a music of its own (220). Of course, his discovery of this new music is analogous to the novel's discovery of art in scientific language, and to the lyrical or poetic side of the computer's predictions. That analogy is made explicit by the titles of the novel's major divisions. The first few paragraphs of the computer's story in the final "Blueprint" section also appear verbatim in the "Prelude" (*jokyoku*) that opens the novel. These paragraphs paint a picture of the undersea landscape and the dramatic changes that occur as a huge tidal wave forms and races toward Kanagawa. This technique of repeating earlier paragraphs at the conclusion is one that Abe uses in several novels, including *The Box Man* and *The Ruined Map* (*Moetsukita chizu*, 1964). The words are exactly the same, but the context changes subtly the second time around.

The word painting that opens *Inter Ice Age 4* is a stylistic tour de force—a display of literary fireworks that is consciously artistic. "After that a great column of steam pierced the marine snow, eddying upward as it soundlessly dispersed" (3). In phrases such as these, Abe's cadences have a beauty and a rhythm that match the section's musical title. It is not until we encounter the same text in the conclusion that we realize this poetry is a prediction spoken by the computer. Only then is the work of art—the "prelude"—revealed as a work of science— a "blueprint." At that point the reader, like the young aquan, is able to hear music where he or she has not heard it before.

In this sense, the inversion of styles represented by the inhuman aquans and the lyrical computer constitutes a transcendence of the narrow categories that hem in our thinking. It brings about a widening of perspective and a way into the future. But for those like Dr. Katsumi who cannot transcend the frame defined by their own present or their own style, this inversion has a frightening or disorienting aspect. For Katsumi the apparent inhumanity of the aquans and the specter of life in the machine are images not of liberation but of dehumanization. The inability to distinguish human from machine is the ultimate horror. In other words, it is precisely this mixing of styles that Katsumi finds frightening.

In this sense, perhaps Katsumi's experience mirrors the reader's: in the same way that the novel's characters are confronted with these frightening stylistic hybrids, the reader of the novel must assimilate the mix of fiction and science that is Abe's prose. Particularly today, not all readers will find this mix as frightening as Katsumi does, but many critics have been alarmed by this combination of styles that threatens to fictionalize or destabilize science. In 1959, Taki Shigeru rushed to defend Dr. Katsumi as "a hero for us all, . . . a man who represents, in himself, the trials of the modern intelligentsia" (116–17). Even critics writing several years later have been disturbed by Abe's dream-world science: in a 1976 essay, Kusaka Hideaki makes science the innocent victim of politics, interpreting the novel as a tale of "pure scientific research that is twisted through the power of the government" (151). Still other critics acknowledge the novel's critique of a naive optimism about science, but still find ways of recouping that optimism in the end: some argue that even if Dr. Katsumi has trouble adapting to the future, it will be easier for us; others contend that responsible use of technology will mitigate our future shock.[8]

To one degree or another, many of these interpretations seem calculated to mitigate the bleak resignation of Abe's postscript by trying to recover some degree of control over science and the future. In the process, they suppress the unpredictable or fantastic side of the novel, in much the same way that Katsumi rejects the unexpected side of his own future and the strange hybrids of science and fiction that populate it. The science and scientific language in *Inter Ice Age 4* have become more familiar and so less shocking in the half century since the novel was published, but we can recover some of the historical and literary context of the novel's reception if we consider that in 1959 the competition of discourses in the novel mirrored a war of styles in literary and public discourse. As the shock of the future is reflected into the languages that surround Katsumi, the panic he feels mirrors the shock of some readers encountering the novel's new and disturbing mix of styles.

A helpful scheme for relating this competition of discourses inside and outside the text is Mikhail Bakhtin's notion of novelistic heteroglossia. This will be of greatest use in Chapter 4, but it will be useful to preview it briefly here.

Mikhail Bakhtin and the Dialogue of Styles

Bakhtin has suggested that the collision of different styles is the defining characteristic of the novel as a genre. ("The style of the novel is to be found in the combination of its styles; the language of a novel is the system of its 'languages'" [*Dialogic* 262].) For Bakhtin, these different voices can be the assorted styles of various literary schools and genres, the specialized language of professional disciplines (including scientific language), the distinct speech styles of different characters, languages borrowed from public discourses such as politics or philosophy, and so forth.

But the presence of different styles or voices that constitutes hetero-glossia is only half of the story. Those different voices must also come together in dialogue with one another. For Bakhtin, all meaning produced by literary language is generated through this process of dialogue. And a key element in bringing languages into dialogue with one another is the presence of linguistic hybrids and inversions like Abe's aquans and prediction machine. For Bakhtin, such characters represent an archetype that goes back to ancient literature, and it is they who allow the different styles combined in the text to achieve their most direct and dramatic juxtaposition. Bakhtin's prototype for these hybrid characters is the clown figure of the carnival. The clown is exempt from the common sense that prohibits these inversions and contradictions. By embodying the "mésalliances" and "oxymoronic combinations" of carnival (Bakhtin's examples include "the virtuous hetaera" and "the noble bandit," analogous to Abe's poetic machine), these figures permit polar styles to come together in a way that produces meaning (*Dialogic* 34–38, 404–5). In *Problems of Dostoevsky's Poetics*, Bakhtin says "all people and all things must know one another and know about one another, must enter into contact, come together face to face and *begin* to *talk* with one another. . . . Therefore all things that are disunified and distant must be brought together at a single spatial and temporal 'point.' And what is necessary for this is carnival *freedom*" (177).

To grasp the full significance of these figures and these colliding styles, one must understand the importance Bakhtin places on hetero-glossia and dialogue not just in the novel but for the production of meaning at any level. Cursory discussions of Bakhtin sometimes miss the point that heteroglossia and dialogue are not simply chance traits that the novel picked up along the way; they are necessary features of language, society, and human thought, and the novel reflects this reality. These several levels of meaning production and dialogue are discussed in Bakhtin's essay "Discourse in the Novel" (in *The Dialogic Imagination*). At the highest level, dialogue within the novel is only a reflection of a larger dialogue in society. Different languages in the novel correspond to different views of the world abroad in society at large. "All languages of heteroglossia," Bakhtin says, ". . . are specific points of view on the world." This difference in world view is the thing that distinguishes languages, and any formal differences between styles (lexical, syntactic, or semantic) must grow out of this (291–92). In Bakhtin's scheme, the role of any novel is to organize and juxtapose these voices from society. "The novel," he says, "can be defined as a diversity of social speech types (sometimes even diversity of languages) and a diversity of individual voices, artistically organized" (262).

In *Abe Kōbō, Literary Strategist,* Thomas Schnellbächer identifies dialogue as a key element even in Abe's essays, and relates this back to social forces and movements. Schnellbächer sees a change in Abe's essay style starting in the mid-1950s, when he was organizing literary activities among factory workers. Abe's essays from that period began to incorporate literal conversations between speakers, multiple narrative frames that suggested more than one speaker, and other devices that opened a dialogue with Abe's readers. Schnellbächer traces this to Abe's ideas about class revolution—his desire to address working-class readers directly in an open-ended way that did not try to answer questions, but encouraged readers to consider various perspectives and respond to Abe with their own ideas (207). This relates Abe's style to Schnellbächer's other concern, which is Abe's Marxist or communist politics. Schnellbächer also associates this dialogic method specifically with Marxist dialectical materialism, for the way different ideas are held in tension as a prelude to resolution or sublation (365–67).

But for Bakhtin—and for Abe as well—dialogue also goes further down: even simple language can be infinitely subdivided into different styles, and a single utterance by one character or narrator will show the influence of many different styles. In "Discourse in the Novel," Bakhtin says even "a [single] word forms a concept of its own object in a dialogic way," because it must pass through a cloud of other words that have been spoken about the same object. The artistic image of an object results from what Bakhtin calls "spectral dispersion in an atmosphere filled with the alien words, value judgments and accents through which the ray passes on its way toward the object" (*Dialogic* 279, 277). Although all language produces meaning dialogically, it is for Bakhtin the artistic language of the novel that exploits this aspect of language best.

At the lowest level, even the formation of our own personalities is a process of bringing order to the dialogue of voices inside us. In his early philosophical work "Author and Hero in Aesthetic Activity," Bakhtin lays down the foundation for his later studies of dialogue: the idea that we can achieve wholeness or completeness only in dialogue with another, through the aesthetic operation of authoring that other and being authored ourselves. Katsumi's relationships with both of his doubles (the computer and his aquan son) have a great deal to say about the discovery of the self. But we will defer the issue of self-formation until the next chapter, when we look at a novel by Abe that treats those issues even more explicitly. For now, it will suffice to note how deep the issue of dialogue runs: it forms an inescapable part not only of the novel but of our society, our language, our souls, and ourselves.

Bakhtin's scheme provides a way of relating the idea of competing literary styles in a text like *Inter Ice Age 4* with Foucault's notion of discourse introduced briefly in the last chapter—essentially the rules by which a given field such as literature or science defines how language can be used within it. Bakhtin's definition of discourse takes in both these senses and relates them to one another, as well as to the ways individuals use language to constitute themselves. This is the connection for which I want to argue, so it is generally in this broad Bakhtinian sense that I use the term "discourse" in this book.[9]

This, then, is the context in which schemes like Bakhtin's carnival (which traces its roots to literature and social practices of Europe in the Middle Ages) eventually achieve the character of a global or universal archetype in Bakhtin's thought. The multiplicity of voices is something bred in the bone of language, humanity, and society. Carnival and the figure of the clown are necessary to bring together these different languages in order to expose the interested, relative, and incomplete character of their meanings, with the hope of generating a higher meaning in the patterns of interference between them.

In *Problems of Dostoevsky's Poetics*, Bakhtin identifies carnival practices as public spaces that unite people and styles that are normally separate or opposed, first suspending the social hierarchy and then reversing it, in the ritual crowning and subsequent humiliation of the carnival king, for example. This reversal finds further expression in the presence of the aforementioned figures that unite opposing poles: the wise fool, the beggar prince, and so forth. In the genre of the novel, these figures manifest themselves as doubles who mirror the main character but also invert and parody his or her features. In the process, they illuminate some aspect of the dialogic struggles that went into forming the character's personality (101–80). "In carnival . . . various images (for example, carnival pairs of various sorts) parodied one another variously and from various points of view; it was like an entire system of crooked mirrors, elongating, diminishing, distorting in various directions and to various degrees" (127).

Bakhtin's formula sounds like both the prediction machine and the aquans, which double their human counterpart Dr. Katsumi. Both are mirror images of Katsumi himself. The computer is a simulation of the scientist, and he is linked to the aquans both by evolution and by his son. And each of the doubles parodies Katsumi's devotion to logic and science in a slightly different direction: the mechanistic aquans are more advanced than the pioneer Katsumi could have hoped or feared. The murderous computer is even more ruthlessly logical, willing to kill Katsumi to guard the accuracy and inevitability of its own prediction. But at the same time it has a poetic sensitivity Katsumi lacks.

In Bakhtinian carnival, the comic nature of this juxtaposition is always backed by the threat of death or violence—the danger that the two opposing sides will annihilate one another. Death itself is merely the double of life, an end but also a renewal. This gives the humor of carnival a dark side. Likewise in Abe's story, the human Katsumi tries to kill his aquan son, and the computer Katsumi kills its human counterpart, while a kind of ironic black humor hangs over their efforts. ("Your death is at the same time mine," says the computer dryly. "But let's not get sentimental" [177].) Yet in each case Katsumi dies to make way for his own future. As Bakhtin says, "In each of them (that is, in each of the doubles) the hero dies (that is, is negated) in order to be renewed" (*Problems* 128).

Sublime Simulacra: Abe and the Postmodern

The first part of this chapter discussed the historical context of *Inter Ice Age 4* in order to point out just how revolutionary Abe's combination of scientific and literary was at the time and place it was written and first read. But does the novel still have that revolutionary quality for readers today? In some senses *Inter Ice Age 4* still remains at the vanguard of science fiction. The innovations associated with the cyberpunk revolution in science fiction during the 1980s and 1990s, for example, have some notable affinities with Abe's novel. Early works by cyberpunk

punk authors William Gibson and Neil Stephenson feature a similarly dark view of the future characterized by corporate conspiracy, the same reluctant celebration of human bodies transformed by invasive technology, and the unsettling possibility of a disembodied human consciousness that floats in computer memory, suspended between life and death. Bruce Sterling could almost be describing Abe when he says of cyberpunk that its "technology is visceral. . . . Under our skin; often, inside our minds" (*Mirrorshades* xi).[10]

Although there is no question that *Inter Ice Age 4* was ahead of its time, the genre of science fiction is older now, and some of the devices that may have surprised Japanese audiences in 1959 (such as a thinking computer) are now genre staples. True to the criticisms Abe made of science fiction in the 1960s, what was once a powerful hypothesis has now been relegated to the everyday. But while some elements of the novel's *plot* are no longer as shocking as they were in the late 1950s, what *Inter Ice Age 4* has to say about language and the way the novel itself uses language (particularly the inversion of styles discussed above) remain very contemporary. It is a truism to say that the issues that framed the novel for Japanese readers in 1959—the speed of scientific progress, the nuclear threat—are again or are still with us today. The points *Inter Ice Age 4* makes about language are considerably more nuanced, and they are just as relevant now, given that some of the most subtle and profound changes technology has wrought in the last 50 years affect the ways we interact and communicate with one another.

The second half of the present chapter examines some recent theories of science, technology, and language that resonate with Abe's novel. This will update the survey begun in the last chapter, with some later twentieth-century distinctions (or conflations) between literary and scientific discourse, as well as more recent formulations of the sublime by N. Katherine Hayles, Jean-François Lyotard, and Fredric Jameson. These critics have characterized their work as an effort to theorize postmodernism. As with "modernism," there are as many definitions and characterizations of postmodernism as there are critics; but despite their differences, these theories are united by the central role they accord to technology in redefining our sense of aesthetics, language, reality, and self.

Although the term postmodern dates from the 1950s, it was critical writing in the late 1970s and 1980s that gave it its present associations: a frantic propagation and consumption of language that finally effaces any sense of the original, ending finally in a rule of the simulacrum. The result can be seen as a radical new freedom, but also as the loss of a formerly stable ground associated with history, agency, and subjectivity. The parallels with Abe's destabilization of the everyday suggest themselves immediately even from this thumbnail description. And beyond Abe, in many ways Japan from the 1980s onward seems to fit this image of a tightly wired network of self-reproducing and reproduced media-savvy hyper-consumers.

During the heyday of these theories, postmodernism was hailed as a kind of universal paradigm shift, definitely applicable across genres, perhaps applicable across cultures, and paradoxically applicable across generations. The universal quality of these theories has since become something of a liability. On one side, this universality and popularity eventually rendered the term postmodernism itself almost meaninglessly broad: it eventually came to be used loosely by some critics as an antonym to the term "traditional" when describing art of all kinds, while for others it was pressed into service as a catch-all invective for an allegedly dangerous relativism supposedly fueled by poststructuralism. On the other hand, the paradigm also came under attack in more careful studies that tried to rigorously historicize the paradigms of modernity and question whether postmodern was a meaningful term when applied to Japan.[11] But recent interest in popular media and media subcultures in Japan seems to have renewed some interest in theories of the postmodern. Azuma Hiroki, for example, has gained attention for his work, which draws enthusiastically from French critical theory but adapts it to arrive at a specifically Japanese version of the postmodern.

Ultimately, perceptions that theories of postmodernism are too universalizing or too faddish may represent impatience with the mechanical application of these theories as much as anything else. In these rote readings, the superficial features of postmodernism are enumerated and ticked off in the text, without much thought about why those features are present. Read more carefully, however, some theories of the postmodern address the role of science and technology in literature with an unusual clarity and specificity; applied sensitively and creatively to Abe, these theories shed considerable light on his works.

One of the texts that defined the terms of the debate about post-modernism is Fredric Jameson's essay "Postmodernism, or, The Cultural Logic of Late Capitalism," originally published in *The New Left Review* in 1984 and later expanded into a book of the same name. Jameson's pessimistic characterization of the postmodern starts from the loss of faith in an essential meaning expressed by language. He characterizes artistic expression today as "depthless," an endless series of surface signifiers or "simulacra" that lack a deeper meaning or an authentic source. The expressive brushstrokes of the individual modern artist Van Gogh have been replaced by Andy Warhol's flattened, re-produced images of products such as Marilyn Monroe or Campbell's Soup. These same ideas have been applied to Japan: in his 2000 essay "Super Flat Speculation," Azuma Hiroki undertakes a similar reading of Japanese art, with Murakami Takeshi's flattened cartoonish paintings standing in for Warhol.

It is a familiar idea of poststructuralist criticism that we have lost much of our faith in language's deeper meaning and instead have come to regard it as a series of shifting signifiers from which meaning emerges differentially and unpredictably. Jameson's particular formulation seems to owe something specifically to Jean Baudrillard's understanding of images and language in the age of mass media (and Azuma's essay cites Baudrillard explicitly). Baudrillard's essay collection *Simulacra and Simulation* advances a model in which the sign that points to a profound reality is replaced first with the simulation and then the simulacrum. The former is not just an imitation of reality but a virtual reality of its own that begins to seem "more real than real." Ultimately the "hyperreality" of the simulation makes (any other) reality irrelevant. Simulation is in turn a stage or symptom of the transformation of the sign into the simulacrum, an image that no longer even gestures at reality but instead floats free of any referent (1–42). Baudrillard identifies four "successive phases of the image" corresponding to the stages in this transformation: "[The image] is the reflection of a profound reality; it masks and denatures a profound reality; it masks the absence of a profound reality; it has no relation to any reality whatsoever: it is its own pure simulacrum" (6).

This rather abstract framework is Baudrillard's way of expressing a social condition in which the frantic propagation and duplication of language and images through the mass media have eclipsed the fact that instead of reflecting our "real" experience, the image has replaced it. The media and technology we are faced with everyday (literature, architecture, television, politics) tell us over and over what we want to be, what we should be, or what we are, until they become normative in a way that masquerades as firsthand experience and then pushes it aside altogether.

Inter Ice Age 4 suggests Baudrillard's notion that technological simulations and reproductions are not simply second-order imitations of a real original, but that ultimately they become "more real than real," eroding the dichotomy of original and copy, replacing and effacing their prototype. The aquans are mass-produced copies of the human, copies that multiply themselves and inherit the earth. When their human originals undergo extinction, the aquans could be said to be pure simulacra. But an even more perfect simulacrum is the computer model of Dr. Katsumi—a reproduction that usurps the reality of its original.

In a literal example of what Baudrillard terms "the precession of the model," the Katsumi simulation becomes the authoritative version: the conspirators, including Katsumi's staff and the assassin charged with his murder, profess loyalty to Katsumi even as they plot against him, because they are acting on the authority of a computer version they regard as equally real. Finally the computer has Katsumi killed, the copy effacing its original. The plot of the novel fulfills Baudrillard's prediction that programming languages will eventually surpass even the language of advertising in their ability to reproduce, to absorb, to simulate and replace all other languages with a minimum overhead of meaning. "The languages of computer science," he says, will constitute the "triumph of superficial form, of the smallest common denominator of all signification, degree zero of meaning" (87–89).

If Baudrillard's theory treats language in society, Jameson and Azuma both give it a psychological turn, by invoking Lacan to draw a connection between the way language is processed and an inner mental state. As individual expression is replaced by reproduction, what Jameson called the "deconstruction of expression" eventually afflicts all forms of self-expression and finally calls into question the possibility of having feelings to express. So accompanying Jameson's "loss of depth" is a second symptom of the postmodern condition, a fading of emotion and subjectivity that Azuma associates with a series of superficial affective responses, and Jameson refers to as "the waning of affect" itself. Jameson distinguishes the postmodern waning of affect from alienation, a modern dilemma in which the isolated self feels cut off from the world around it and unable to communicate. Instead, he says the notion of the bounded self—of psychological "depth" or inside and outside—is erased altogether. There is no feeling because "there is no longer a self present to do the feeling." Azuma identifies a similar disappearance of the humanistic subject he terms "animalization" (*dōbutsuka*).[12]

Jameson's most interesting point relates to the way in which we react to this dissolution of meaning and the self. At first we are likely to experience this as a crisis of communication or identity, a schizophrenia in the Lacanian sense. But a postmodern sensibility may eventually feel a kind of euphoria associated with these new more fluid incarnations of meaning and identity. This depends on the ability to appreciate and internalize the postmodern aesthetic and the postmodern sensibility, to "grow new organs" of perception that can see things in a postmodern way (Jameson 39)—shades already of Abe's aquans. Part of this new way of seeing seems to involve giving up the struggle to locate a reality or even one's own identity amid the endless propagation of duplicate images. Instead one must, in Jameson's ironic exhortation, come to enjoy skating over the flat surface of signs without referents; we must grow to appreciate the special freedom that obtains in an ever shifting landscape devoid of limiting reality or confining identity. We must learn to celebrate our own dehumanization as an apotheosis. "The world . . . loses its depth and threatens to become a glossy skin, a stereoscopic illusion, a rush of filmic images without density," Jameson says, and then asks: "But is this now a terrifying or an exhilarating experience?" (34).

For Jameson, the pivot on which anxiety teeters into euphoria and the element that relates the whole syndrome to modern society is technology. Technology becomes a focus for humankind's anxiety, but at the same moment that its power frightens us, technology has a breathtaking quality that leaves us both fearful and invigorated. Jameson characterizes this as a species of the sublime with a new unhealthy twist; it is a "hysterical sublime." Chapter 2 discussed theories of the sublime beginning with the characterization by pseudo-Longinus of powerful or overwhelming language that "scatters everything before it like a thunderbolt" (43). Addison describes the appeal of Nature's "greatness," and of a science that helps us to perceive greatness. Finally Burke's sublime unites these two ideas in an aesthetic that finds excitement in the experience of sensory overload. For Burke, a furious torrent of imagery in a poem and the violence of an ocean storm are appealing for the same reason.

If we were to distinguish more finely between Addison and Burke, the former actually suggests that the greatness of nature is appealing because it points to the greatness of God, but Burke's sublime is a more biologically immediate, visceral experience grounded in the exhilarating fear that we feel when we are helpless before a greater power. Later, Immanuel Kant would synthesize these two strains using the idea that the sublime reveals to us the limitations of our perception and helps us transcend them with our reason. Kant's *Critique of Judgment* (1790) argues that the experience of the sublime provides us a glimpse of an infinite ideal realm that exists beyond our limited perception or experience. In the aesthetic act of trying to conceive/perceive that immensity (in Kant's terminology to "present" the "unpresentable"), we unite the finite practical realm of our actions with this infinite ideal realm of reason. Aesthetics thus becomes the hinge that unites reason and moral action. So while a sublime vista may make us feel our own smallness, our attempt to comprehend that vista is the act that constitutes the will and defines our consciousness as reasoning (in other words, human) beings (97–140).

Jameson conceives technology the way Kant conceives nature, as the sensible tip of an unlimited expanse that lies beyond it. But for Jameson, what is behind technology is not Kant's metaphysical world, but the equally unapproachable power of multinational capital, incomprehensible but dimly sensed, which governs the physical world and holds us in its grip. As the tangible instrument and figure of this power, technology frightens and exhilarates, revealing a greatness that inspires awe. As a sublime object, it combines the size and force of nature with the Longinean power to disorient, to make us lose our bearings. Technology confuses, not merely by its complexity but by an endless duplication that leaves us unsure what is what, and what is real. Whereas the

Kantian sublime elevates the individual by pulling him or her toward the infinite, for Jameson it is much more ambivalent: technology ends by making us feel lost, insignificant, and disappearingly small, so that we seemingly have no alternative but to find in our vanishing subjectivity a hysterical new thrill or an ironic peace (6–38). Our one ray of hope is the faint chance that by presenting the unpresentable power of capital, sublime art might eventually provide a way to "outflank" it in our own minds or lives (418).

If the computer Katsumi and the aquans represent the kinds of depthless copies to which Baudrillard and Jameson refer, they also embody Jameson's "waning of affect": the aquans are devoid of emotion as we know it. Perhaps for the reasons Dr. Yamamoto describes (they have no diaphragm to laugh or tear ducts to cry), the fish-like creatures seem almost literally cold-blooded. We read that "in the aquan children's curiosity or indifference there is one trait they all have in common. That is their abnormal coolness. When they look at one, one feels that it is oneself that has become an animal" (204). Note here the Baudrillardian inversion of the human original and its inhuman copy.

The unexpected emotion or lyricism often exhibited by the prediction machine marks it as a stylistic hybrid precisely because those human qualities are combined with a mechanical cold-bloodedness. This emerges particularly in the climactic scene in which Katsumi is condemned to die, where the machine and the conspirators proceed with no enmity toward him, only implacable logic. "Whatever justice you claim, you can't rationalize murder," Katsumi objects (173). But the machine explains to him coolly why he must be killed. "But let's not get sentimental," it says. "If you have the strength to think and not be deceived by your emotions, you will quite naturally arrive at the same conclusion" (177).

Like Jameson's theory, Abe's story also contains ample reference to the shadow of capital behind the technology: we learn at the end of the book that the conspiracy is backed by industrial concerns who want the profits from developing the sea floor and the next generation of water-breathing consumers. On the other hand, for Dr. Yamamoto, Tanomogi, and the other members of the conspiracy, the aquans represent not dehumanization at the hands of capital but a hope for the future, a chance to overcome our human limitations. This is the mixed threat and promise of the future, and the double edge of overturning the everyday. The difference between Katsumi and Tanomogi corresponds in a way to Jameson's fraught transition from anxiety to euphoria.

N. Katherine Hayles inherits Jameson's characterization of postmodernism—including the notion of a flattened meaning and a euphoric but frightening loss of grounding—and relates it more concretely to specific developments in the sciences. A historian of science as well as a literary critic, Hayles focuses particularly on the relationship between language and technology. She characterizes the effect of technology as a loss of context for language, which has interesting parallels in Abe's text, where stylistic inversion transplants language out of its customary context.

Hayles's work unites the philosophy and history of science with literary criticism by suggesting that scientific ideas are born from the same "cultural and technological milieu" that gives rise to literary works and literary theories. Hence there is a kind of unity or affinity between science and the arts, which Hayles describes with scientific metaphors, as a cultural "field," "a societal matrix," a problem in "complex dynamics," or a series of "feedback loops" between "theory, technology, and culture" (*Chaos and Order* 5; *Cosmic Web* 22; *Chaos Bound* xiv). Because the same intellectual currents circulate through different disciplines, the conclusions and the methods of literature can be applied to science and vice versa. So in *Chaos Bound*, Hayles brings the literary critic's perspective on language to bear on metaphors like Maxwell's demon that scientists have used to represent theories (31–60). In other essays, she interprets novels, literary criticism, and the broader cultural aesthetic in light of contemporary scientific issues, with the justification that these issues are not really narrowly scientific at all, but spread through a whole culture.

In *Chaos Bound*, Hayles starts her characterization of postmodernism from the same Saussurian shift as Jameson, the shift from a belief that language points at a full and present meaning to the idea that meaning is multiple, something constructed by the process of reading and by the action of language itself. She takes this story a step further by linking these familiar literary critical developments to corresponding trends in scientific research, including the discrediting of logical positivism in the work of Thomas Kuhn and Paul Feyerabend; proof of limitations on the precision and completeness of mathematical language by Kurt Gödel; and what quantum mechanics has revealed about the complex and uncertain relationship between observation and reality. Following other contemporary philosophers of science, Hayles identifies these developments with the failure of science's efforts to get outside itself and find a meta-system or meta-language to rationalize or legitimize its own endeavors. The realization that science is trapped in the frame or game of its own language is analogous to the conclusion in linguistics and literature that however much we want to talk or think about language from a perspective outside language, we can never escape from language sufficiently to do that.

Hayles extends this conventional argument by tracing the impact of communications and information technology on the degeneration of language's context. This technology was made possible by developments in information theory during and after World War II, including new mathematical functions for describing the information content of a stream of electronic data. Claude Shannon, a scientist at AT&T Bell Laboratories, showed how it can be useful for designing communications systems to rethink and even reverse conventional and mathematical definitions of information, noise, meaning, and context. To summarize briefly this rather complex body of theory, Shannon developed a useful quantitative measure of the amount of "information" in a message, but this mathematical quantity is independent of the message's meaning, depending instead on the relative frequency or probability of the individual elements that make up the message. Hayles compares this to the way Saussure shifts attention away from an essential link between signifier and signified, to focus on the relative difference between signifiers. She concludes that Shannon's efforts to help AT&T engineers separate the idea of information from the concepts of meaning and context are analogous to the project begun by Saussure: the struggle to separate meaning from signification, and to do so in the absence of any context outside of language in which to consider language's function (48–60, 269–71).

In Hayles's account, advances in information theory such as Shannon's fostered a technological revolution that carried the results beyond the realm of theory and made this theoretical separation of information from meaning and context into a social reality. The growth of mass media, long distance communication, and information technology has allowed messages to go further and faster, and to be more subtly and thoroughly manipulated, so that they are increasingly removed from the original physical and social contexts that originally grounded their meaning. From the combination of immediacy and disconnection we experience when we communicate with someone on the telephone or email, to the rapid propagation and radical distortion of information in the mass media, language is no longer confined to a simple meaning or governed by a single context, but now creates its own new context wherever it goes. It gains a new freedom and loses its certainty by virtue of the speed at which it travels (269–75).

Hayles's characterization of media society is not particularly surprising, but her focus on loss of context is instructive for reading *Inter Ice Age 4*, which as we have seen draws its stylistic energy from altering the context of language. The novel transforms language by placing it against a new background that renders it strange. Consider again the way that the novel signals the confusion of human and machine. The code that was once clicked out by machines is now spoken by the aquans, reflecting the fear that genetic manipulation has turned them into organic machines. The surgical union of the murdered man's body with the machine results in his disembodied voice issuing from the computer. Isolated from its human owner, that voice gives Dr. Katsumi his first hint that the computer is capable of crossing the line that separates machine and human being. Later, the full transformation of the computer into a thinking being is figured by this ability to speak in ways borrowed from a more emotional, poetic context.

Like Abe in *Inter Ice Age 4*, Hayles ultimately links this decontextualization of information to transformations in the body itself. If the organic physical body was formerly the origin of language, which was enunciated and then carried by an external technology, recent technologies and technological fantasies have carried us further toward the cyberpunk scenario in which changes in language effect changes in the body, just as the linguistic dislocations in *Inter Ice Age 4* are accompanied by bodily transformations. Hayles traces the origins of this idea to the original military applications of information theory, which drew a direct connection between information and life, as well as death (271–72).[13]

Whereas Jameson and Hayles are both pessimistic about this loss of context and grounded meaning, others are more optimistic. Jean-François Lyotard argues that the real crisis of the postmodern condition is the lingering desire to rely on science as an objective or universal language in an age when this hope has become untenable. The solution, for Lyotard, is precisely the kind of reversal that *Inter Ice Age 4* suggests, to regard the languages of science and fiction as similar and even interchangeable. Lyotard's *The Postmodern Condition* (1979) is one of the first theories of postmodernism as a larger cultural condition, and the most frequently cited definition of postmodernism is still his "incredulity toward metanarratives"—essentially a collapse of the belief systems that historically justified the modern pursuit of knowledge (xxiv). Many discussions of Lyotard do not go very far beyond this quote from the second page of his Introduction, but his study has a number of important things to say about the distinction between scientific and literary language that repay close reading even today.

The Postmodern Condition is subtitled *A Report on Knowledge,* and it focuses particularly on scientific knowledge and the "delegitimation" of the schemes whereby science once linked its endeavors with the pursuit of truth. It is from the special case of science that Lyotard generalizes to all branches of knowledge. Lyotard says that modern science has long ago given up its claims to a transcendent truth and now acknowledges that it is an artificial but ultimately productive "language game," in which the participants set the rules and criteria for success or failure. The rules are partly arbitrary but are justified by common consensus. The first crisis arises with the contemporary collapse of the beliefs or legitimating schemes that have supported that consensus. The "metanarratives" of the French Revolution and German Idealism (broadly "freedom" and "spirit") formerly justified the pursuit of knowledge as an essential part of human liberty, or as a part of the search for a unifying philosophy of life; but in the twentieth century the leaps of faith that were at the heart of both these metanarratives have become impossible (23–31).

At one time it was the languages of science that were able to balance and counter this trend, by allowing scientific results from different disciplines to be judged against one another on a common discursive ground, so that a new consensus could arise. But today (this is Lyotard's second crisis), scientific dialects have become too fragmented and specialized to talk to one another, and the mathematical findings of Gödel have cast doubt on the viability of formal unifying meta-languages such as logic that were once thought to knit these fragmented languages together. In the absence of the checks and balances that this unified language provided, the scientific results that command authority are no longer firmly connected to any notion of truth. Science is in danger of pursuing its own efficiency or "performativity" above all else, producing results to make more money to produce more results: "The State and/ or company must abandon the idealist and humanist narrative of legitimation in order to justify the new goal: . . . Scientists, technicians, and instruments are purchased not to find truth, but to augment power" (46). Like Hayles, Lyotard sees science struggling and failing to find a structure beyond itself that will judge and legitimate its activities; but he worries that in the absence of that structure, the pursuit and control of "knowledge" will lapse into an exercise of brute economic and technological force, and a repressive, totalitarian politics will follow (31–46).

For Lyotard, a solution to this crisis is suggested by the non-scientific language of fiction or "narrative." He suggests that we should view scientific and literary discourse on the same level, as two different language games with slightly different rules. Narrative is also a created world in which readers, writers, and critics participate—a closed system with its own internal rules, justifications, and criteria for success or failure. It is a limited, healthy, local version of the totalizing "meta-narratives" discussed above. The difference between scientific and narrative discourse is that narrative is its own reason for being. Around the camp fire, Lyotard says (telling his own story), the storyteller's authority and her right to narrate are justified by the stories themselves; they do not require any outside source of legitimation (14–23). Lyotard concludes that science must ultimately view itself along the same lines: citing Paul Feyerabend and P. B. Medawar, he says, "there is no 'scientific method,' and . . . a scientist is before anything else a person who 'tells stories'" (60).[14]

Lyotard's treatment of science as "narrative" appears only slightly altered in *Inter Ice Age 4*, where Abe combines fictional and technical language in the same text and blurs the line between them. The computer's final prediction of the future aquan society is nothing less than a scientific output that has been turned into a narrative or a story. And for Abe, as for Lyotard, self-justifying fiction takes the place of naive justifications about why we engage in science—in Abe's case the naive equation of science with progress.

Furthermore, in Abe's novel as in Lyotard's theory, it is the multiplication of scientific dialects that drives the first wedge between scientific language and the truth it purports to represent. If the languages of computer science and biology can depict the same world equally rationally but so differently, if they cannot combine or talk to one another, then perhaps they are not so different from two closed and arbitrary fictional worlds. Like Lyotard's postmodern, post-Gödel world, Abe's novel contains no higher system that can knit these two styles back together into a single language—neither the grand narratives of "freedom" and "spirit," nor the unifying system of logic. In *Inter Ice Age 4*, these dialects are unified only by the unknown future, which will combine biology and technology in ways we cannot imagine, into new forms so different that they no longer bear any resemblance to our old idea of "science."

Like Hayles, Lyotard sees some confusion or uncertainty in this conflation of literature with science, but he turns it into a virtue. In fact, it is Lyotard's hope that science will prove as unpredictable as fiction, leading to defeat for those who seek to optimize the performativity of science for the sake of power alone. In this ideal case, science will be "the antimodel of a stable system"—a chaotic, self-transforming game in which each new discovery has a way of rewriting the rules of scientific inquiry itself (53–67).[15]

If science for Lyotard is ultimately a chaotic (but productive) enterprise that defies expectation, literature should also aspire to reveal what lies on the other side of common sense and common sensation. Lyotard describes this power with language borrowed from Kant's more hopeful formulation of the sublime: it is the power to "present" the "unpresentable" (81). The gap between Lyotard's enthusiasm and Jameson's reservations, and their common recourse to the sublime, point to the combination of fear and excitement that makes the sublime such a fitting figure for science and technology's double-edged effect on language. Hayles and Jameson regard with suspicion this euphoric transition to a postmodern sensibility: they are ambivalent about dissolving the boundaries of the human, a movement that promises a radical freedom in one sense, but which also generates a terrifying vertigo for those of us poised on the brink of the change. To read their work is to experience this alternation between enthusiasm for technology (like Tanomogi), resistance to the processes of dehumanization or rehumanization (like Katsumi), and a refusal to judge these "inevitable" changes (like Abe's postscript to the novel).

This sublime mix of enthusiasm, fear, and resignation is arguably the most important thing distinguishing theories of postmodernism from more straightforward critiques of technology, mechanization, and industrial society—what we might call a critique of modernity or *kindai hihan*. And it is finally this mix that makes these theories fit Abe so well. Writers in Meiji and Taishō Japan also voiced concerns about the impact of technology on society, and they also phrased the threat as a kind of insanity resembling hysteria, but it is a hysteria that never approaches the sublime. If there is value in asking whether Abe is postmodern, it is in showing how his critique differs from the *kindai hihan* that came before.

For example, Natsume Sōseki advanced the idea that the pace of the changes involved in Japan's Westernization and modernization resulted in anxiety approaching a kind of national identity crisis. In his well-known lecture "The Civilization of Modern-day Japan" ("Gendai Nihon no kaika," 1911), Sōseki rejects the idea that technological advances make life easier, comparing each one to a "wave of disruption" (*haran*) that brings new stresses of its own (270). "For all its progress," Sōseki says, "civilization favors us with so little peace of mind that . . . our happiness is probably not very different from what it was in the stone age" (281). The second part of the essay suggests that Japan is under additional pressure because it has undergone this technological and social modernization so quickly, not by developing according to its own natural rhythm but by being dragged violently along behind the West. As the hero of Sōseki's novel *The Wayfarer* (*Kōjin*, 1913) famously says: "Man's insecurity stems from the advance of science. . . . From walking to rickshaw, from rickshaw to carriage, from carriage to train, from train to automobile, from there on to the dirigible, further on to the airplane, and further on and on—no matter how far we may go, it won't let us take a breath" (285).

In "The Civilization of Modern-day Japan," Sōseki's way of using technical language contrasts with Abe in a way that reveals Sōseki's concerns. The lecture cites a psychological model for the human attention span in order to make the point that rapid change is disorienting, but Sōseki is at pains to downplay the technical aspect of this device: "I hesitate to introduce difficult material into this lecture, which is not supposed to be concerned with psychology, but please bear with me for a short while" (274). At other times Sōseki uses technical terms or ideas but immediately undercuts them: "You'll see what I mean if you experiment a bit. No, you won't need any apparatus for this 'experiment.' It's simply a matter of noticing what goes on in your head" (275). Like Abe, Sōseki is acutely conscious of the defamiliarizing effect of technology and technical language: the dizzying effect of science is a central point of his lecture. But while Abe seeks to use that confusion creatively, Sōseki wants to minimize it, so in contrast to Abe he tries to soften the impact of technical language in his own speech.[16]

Sōseki is not the only modern author to link modern machinery with the nervous tension of the age. In 1927 Akutagawa Ryūnosuke made a rotating set of cogwheels into the central, obsessive hallucination that heralds the onset of nervous breakdown in his autobiographical story "Spinning Gears" ("Haguruma"). In Yokomitsu Riichi's "Machine" ("Kikai," 1930), the dangerously corrosive chemical processes used to finish metal plates in a nameplate factory become a figure for the volatile reactions between the workers, as well as for the human and economic processes in which they are simply the ingredients.

The difference between Abe and authors such as these lies in Abe's reluctance (though perhaps not utter unwillingness) to judge the changes that technology brings about. Sōseki's essay retains a clear sense that the stresses of modernity are an illness from which it would be better to recover. Put another way, Sōseki portrays the subject in crisis, but in a way that does not finally weaken the idea of that subject, and which may in fact reinforce it. But *Inter Ice Age 4* portrays a moment in which we are balanced delicately on top of Abe's "wall of time," teetering between a modern nostalgia for the old outlines of the human and a new technologized humanity that has forgotten the old. It is the resulting sense of divided loyalties in the work that sets it apart from the critique of modernity that preceded it, and makes it resonate with the theories of postmodernism treated above. The postscript renounces any judgment the present might make of the future with the analogy of a man from the fifteenth century resurrected in the present day: "Would he regard the present as a heaven or a hell? Whatever he thought, what is clear is that he would lack any qualification for making the judgment. In this situation, what renders judgment is not the man, but the present itself" (120–21).

In some ways, this recalls Baudrillard's controversial praise for another novel in the literary–science fiction slipstream, J. G. Ballard's *Crash*, and its grisly depictions of the automobile accident as an apotheosis in which the human body achieves ecstatic physical union with the machine. Baudrillard wrote, "There lies the miracle of *Crash*. Nowhere does this moral gaze surface—the critical judgment that is still part of the functionality of the old world" (119).[17]

In 1959, Abe is not quite this cool, at least not yet. The ending of *Inter Ice Age 4* also provokes sympathy for the victims of future changes (the murdered Katsumi, the dying aquan boy). And it would be a mistake to rely exclusively on the authorial pronouncement of Abe's postscript. Its voice is just one voice among many, and the novel is exquisitely suspended between the language of Tanomogi, Katsumi, Yamamoto, Abe, and the machine, voices that together balance the old and new perspectives.

Some critics of Japanese literature have suggested that the nature of Abe's ambivalence is fundamentally different from Baudrillard's, because of the history of modernity and postmodernism in Japan. Chapter 2 discussed Karatani Kōjin's argument that the metaphysics of science (as well as language and religion) was imposed on Japan by the West. Given that all the characterizations of postmodernism above link it to the collapse of precisely these metaphysical systems, Karatani has questioned the possibility of a Japanese postmodernism, arguing that because Japan never completely accepted these systems, it already had the features the West associates with postmodernism in the nineteenth century, and that the global collapse of these in the twentieth century affected Japan differently ("One Spirit" 271).

Karatani's efforts to contextualize or historicize modernity and postmodernity suggest that we should pay careful attention to how the systems we take for granted are constructed and then overturned. We

have seen so far that Abe's everyday is broad enough to include Western ideas such as science that were imported (or imposed), as well as
things grounded in daily present experience. And we have seen that
the sublime mix of shock and inevitability that destabilizes the everyday
in Abe's texts clearly looks postmodern. I am not sure I have an answer
to the broadest of Karatani's questions: whether Abe arrives at the
postmodern because of his background as a Japanese author or in spite
of it. But Karatani's work suggests a more proximate goal that this
book definitely shares: the goal of tracing the sources of our own everyday, and delineating the literary processes by which that everyday can
be unsettled or overthrown.

Mainstream Science Fiction, Slipstream Literary Fiction, and Abe

Abe's desire to destabilize literary expectations was a reason he turned
to science fiction when it was still new and experimental; it also seems
to be one reason he turned away from it when it developed its
own genre conventions that became difficult to escape. Two obituaries
for Abe in *SF magajin* credited him with helping establish the genre
in Japan, but they both also concluded that he had largely parted
ways with science fiction afterward, or it had parted ways with him
(Kawamata 172; Ishikawa Kōji 173).

   Abe's alienation from science fiction was discussed briefly in the
previous chapter, but now that we have looked in detail at *Inter Ice Age 4*
and its reception, we can see more clearly why this came about. Writing
Inter Ice Age 4 was clearly an effort by Abe to overturn literary expectations. Produced at a time when even the designation "science
fiction" was still unknown, Abe's novel was intended to be strange or
unfamiliar, to carry with it the shock of the sublime. And it did. But as
soon as science fiction became recognized as a genre, that strangeness
was gone, and Abe moved on to other forms with which he could continue to push the literary envelope. The seeds of this are present even
in Abe's original definition of science fiction for the inaugural issue of
SF magajin, partially quoted above. In its entirety, it reads:

> The science fiction novel represents a discovery on the order of Columbus,
> in that it combines an extremely rational hypothesis with the irrational passion
> of fantasy.

The poetry produced by the collision between this intellectual tension and the invitation to adventure is not only contemporary; it is also connected with the original spirit of literature. (*AZ* 11:456)

It is significant that Abe focuses not only on the combination of rational and irrational, but on the "tension" or "collision" between them. Elsewhere Abe wrote "The appeal of the science fiction novel is a new poetic spirit brought to life in prose," which associates this sense of freedom versus rationality even more with a difference in language styles (*AZ* 8:252). Finally, by striving to connect science fiction with the larger field of literature, the quotation above argues against letting science fiction become too narrow or too well-defined.

Here it is interesting to contrast *Inter Ice Age 4* to a later science fiction novel with a similar plot, Komatsu Sakyō's *Japan Sinks* (*Nippon chinbotsu*, 1973). A genre classic and still one of the most popular Japanese science fiction novels of all time, Komatsu's text tells the story of geologic events that submerge the Japanese islands over the course of just a few years, forcing the entire Japanese race into exile. Fifteen years after *Inter Ice Age 4*, the genre of science fiction was established enough and conservative enough that Komatsu could revisit Abe's premise and alter it so as to preserve not only humanity but Japanese culture (in diaspora), while incorporating all the conventions of adventure science fiction. *Japan Sinks* is filled with epic personalities who engage in dangerous missions, daring rescues, romantic interludes, and narrow escapes against a backdrop of earthquakes and volcanic eruptions. Science remains heroic: instead of a Dr. Katsumi who is blind to the implications of his own work, Komatsu gives us a maverick geologist whose warnings to the Japanese political and scientific establishment go unheeded until it is nearly too late. The 2006 film version altered the ending so that a small team of scientists manages to rearrange the Earth's tectonic plates and rescue the archipelago almost singlehandedly, but the new ending, however implausible, does not seem out of place; it fits comfortably with the technocratic optimism of Komatsu's novel.[18]

Tatsumi Takayuki points out that the year 1973 saw the publication not only of *Japan Sinks*, but also of J. G. Ballard's *Crash* (mentioned above), Thomas Pynchon's *Gravity's Rainbow*, and Abe's late novel *The Box Man*. Compared with Ballard's transgressive imagery, Pynchon's radically experimental mix of scientific and poetic prose, or *The Box*

Man's own efforts to deform the structure of the novel itself, Komatsu's novel points to the conservatism of science fiction as a genre. It would not be fair to present Komatsu's story only as a foil for Abe: the nationalism of *Japan Sinks* actually asks some questions about the relationship between homeland and Japanese cultural identity that Abe's universal viewpoint elides. But the contrast between *Inter Ice Age 4* and *Japan Sinks* clearly points to the gap between Abe's hope for science fiction and what it eventually became.

And how does Abe's relationship with science fiction compare with the so-called slipstream writers discussed in the Introduction—writers such as Ōe Kenzaburō, Murakami Haruki, and Murakami Ryū, who are firmly associated with literary fiction, but who borrow elements of science and science fiction? The short answer is that even these writers often respect genre conventions and divisions more carefully than Abe did. Consider Murakami Ryū's *Coin Locker Babies* (*Koin rokkā bēbīzu*, 1980), an apocalyptic adventure story that bears some resemblance to *Inter Ice Age 4* in the way it pits youth against earlier generations. It also moves toward a terrible climax accompanied by a kind of music not unlike Abe's.

Murakami Ryū won the Akutagawa Prize in 1976 for *Almost Transparent Blue* (*Kagirinaku tōmei ni chikai burū*), a realistic novel about 1960s youth culture in which plot is largely replaced by vivid, almost hallucinogenically detailed descriptions of sexual activity, drug use, and everything from the texture of pickles to the reflections on a rain-soaked highway. After writing about reality in a way that makes it seem fantastic, this author seems to have passed through some curtain to the sheer fantasy of *Coin Locker Babies*, an edgy near-future adventure story about two boys whose mothers abandoned them as babies in the coin lockers of Tokyo Station.

The protagonists Hashi and Kiku grow up in the same foster home as brothers, with the shared ambition of bringing about the end of the world. Aggressive, athletic Kiku hatches a plan to recover an undersea stash of psychotropic nerve gas developed then abandoned by the U.S. military, while passive, self-destructive Hashi strikes out at society by forming a rock band. The boys' downward spiral is described in a series of violent, colorful adventures that make it hard to characterize the work's tone: Hashi works as a male prostitute and meets a larger-than-life record producer who styles himself a vampire; Kiku becomes a champion pole-vaulter and connects up with a model named Anemone who keeps an alligator in her apartment; Mr. D. arranges an on-air re-union between Hashi and his mother on Christmas Eve, but a halluci-nating Kiku kills her with a shotgun on live television; Kiku stages a jailbreak with a band of juvenile delinquents who help him scuba dive for the nerve gas; Hashi cuts out part of his own tongue while search-ing for a new sound for his band; and so on. The fast-moving plot (and 400-page heft) leave *Inter Ice Age 4* in the dust, while the tone careens much more violently between the horrific, the comic, and the ironic.

Beyond a vague anger at the unknown mothers who abandoned them, Hashi and Kiku's motivations are not very clearly sketched. The idea that the younger generation overthrows the older one seems to be part of the relentless unquestioned logic of the story, a neat trans-lation of Abe's wall of time into the logic of the counterculture. Hashi and Kiku take the place of the aquans, they are the aliens of the next generation, and the imagery is strikingly similar to Abe's. Here Kiku describes Tokyo as a giant coin locker and talks about the wall that hems him in and the need for a clean start.

Nothing had changed, not one thing—not since he'd let out that first scream in the coin locker. The locker was bigger, maybe; the new one had a pool and gardens, with a band, people wandering about half-naked, and you could keep pets—yes, this one had all kinds of shit: museums, movie theaters, and mental hospitals—but it was still a huge coin locker. [. . .] behind it all there's always the wall, the guards prowling around, the high watchtower. [. . .] There's only one solution, one way out, and that's to smash everything around you to smithereens, to start over from the beginning, lay everything to waste. . . . (317)

In the climax of the novel Kiku and Anemone speed through Tokyo on a motorcycle releasing the nerve gas, in a scene that is distinctly celebratory. Kiku looks out on the Tokyo skyline and imagines an army of coin locker babies hatching from the skyscrapers like the aquans from their glass jars: "It was time now: the hatching of the babies, asleep in their summer boxes, spun from glass and steel and concrete" (386).

The score for Kiku's apocalypse is Hashi's music, more violent than the final music of *Inter Ice Age 4* but representing the same hope for a new artistic language that lies on the other side of violent revolution, a language that can finally redeem or justify the world. Hashi's music is part of an ongoing search for a certain kind of sound he is convinced will give meaning to his life. One of Hashi's band mates describes their concerts in terms of stylistic disjunctions leading to transcendence:

Way I understand it, you want to start with a real bright, soothing mood to put the audience at ease and then gradually build up these little shocks and jarring rhythms, like you're scattering around tiny seeds of pain, right? Eventually the audience wakes up from its nice deep sleep to find they're staring into a warm, damp, gaping hole swarming with some sort of bug they've never seen before. Then they slowly realize all the exits have disappeared, that there's no way out, and only when they've got over their fright do they see that the bugs have turned into these beautiful, brilliant points of light. (259)

In some ways, that description echoes our own reading of Abe's prose. Born in 1952, Murakami Ryū belongs to a 1960s generation that saw music as truly revolutionary—more disruptive and more promising than Abe had even hoped. Arguably music takes the role science does for Abe, leaving little need for Murakami to focus on science itself.

This kind of music represents a metaphor for Murakami's own popular but transgressive art, which is alternately ugly (difficult, confrontational) and melodic (accessible, entertaining). Murakami's novel is transgressive mainly in its plot and descriptions, rather than its form. What starts out as a largely conventional adventure story eventually ends that way, with Kiku and Anemone accomplishing their mission and literally riding into the horizon. Hashi also fulfills his quest: on the novel's final pages, he realizes that the sound he has subconsciously tried to approach in his own music is in fact his mother's heartbeat, heard from inside the womb. Earlier in the novel the beating of one's own heart has been associated with evolution's cruel imperative to live. But in the final scene, Hashi remembers his mother's heartbeat and is finally able to change his music into a "new song" of mercy and love (393). Hashi's new song is a language that is not easily spoken (it is paradoxically associated with the piece of tongue he cut off earlier), and in this it is like the violence of the novel itself. Hashi's happy realization, for example, comes in a nerve-gas-induced rage, when he attacks a pregnant woman and tries to tear out her heart. But the story nevertheless ends with the closure of a conventional adventure tale.

Stephen Snyder argues that the violence in Murakami Ryū's work is a positive attempt to restore some sense of authentic language or experience to a postmodern world of simulation or reproduction. Indeed, *Coin Locker Babies* seems determined to reach a happy ending by the most harrowing path possible. That is the opposite of Abe's story, which takes users one small step at a time along a path that seems reasonable, and ends in a kind of sublime postmodern shock. One could argue that for all its edginess, *Coin Locker Babies* is not unlike *Japan Sinks*: Murakami adapts the pure sensation (and sensationalism) of *Almost Transparent Blue* to a more popular adventure genre, and remains within the borders of that genre to the very end. In contrast Abe was struggling to violate the boundaries between genres. This is clear when we look at *Inter Ice Age 4* in its context, and it becomes even clearer as we move on to novels like *The Face of Another*, treated in the following chapter. *The Face of Another* has a plot that sounds like science fiction, in which a chemist constructs a perfect mask that will allow him to alter his identity at will. But in its execution, *The Face of Another* is very different from *Inter Ice Age 4*, belonging rather to the claustrophobic psychological studies that cemented Abe's literary reputation in the 1960s.

Read for its plot alone, *Inter Ice Age 4* may seem pale to some readers today, at least when compared with the violent circus of something like *Coin Locker Babies*. This is part of why Abe's earlier, more overtly science fictional works are now regarded largely as curiosities; certainly, critics have gravitated toward texts like *The Face of Another*. But just as attention to language in *Inter Ice Age 4* opens up new and more sophisticated perspectives on that novel, I would suggest that some of the early science fiction stories by Abe that appear simplistic in their plots become more interesting when considered in terms of voice or style, and a number of stories deserve more attention from this perspective. As a brief concluding example, consider Abe's short story "R62 gō no hatsumei" (R62's invention, 1953).

Recovering Abe's Science Fiction

"R62 gō no hatsumei" is a blackly humorous take on the threat of dehumanization through industrial automation, in which an unemployed worker is recycled into a robot and returns as a machine to the factory he was fired from. As the story opens, the despondent, out-of-work protagonist is still human, and is gathering his nerve to commit suicide by throwing himself into a canal, when he is approached by a young boy who offers to purchase his body for medical purposes. The boy explains that it will be more convenient if the man delivers his body to the lab while it is still alive, and they will kill it for him. Once at the medical office, the man has some misgivings when he learns that they are going to operate on him, but the facility's sinister director informs him that he is now legally dead, and he no longer has any say in the matter.

The surgical procedure involves replacing portions of the man's brain to rid him of feeling and turn him into an obedient industrial slave. In a lengthy passage devoted to the operation, the surgeon describes out loud each technical step of the brain operation as he implants an artificial *corpus callosum* and places a filter in the *capsula interna* in order to alter the relationship between the hemispheres of the brain and sever the patient's consciousness from his motor functions. When the procedure is complete, the resulting human robot is renamed "R62," and he is presented to a group of bankers, financiers, and industrialists called the International R Club. In a long speech, the director addresses the R Club and unfolds a master plan for returning Japan to its militaristic, imperialistic, industrialist past using this new race of docile worker-drones.

R62 is then put to work in a factory, and this is the extent of the story, except for the final denouement in which the capitalists get their comeuppance at R62's hands. Compared with a story like Yokomitsu Riichi's "Machine," the plot of "R62 gō no hatsumei" feels more than a little two-dimensional. Set in a nameplate factory, "Machine" also makes mechanization a predictable metaphor for the system that objectifies the workers, and like Abe's story, the focus on the workers' physical reality generates moments of near slapstick. But Yokomitsu also deftly combines elements of avant-garde style with social and psychological realism to make the "machine" of the title refer to interpersonal dynamics as well as economic ones. The story describes the caustic chemical reactions used to etch the name plates in some technical detail, and relates these not only to the way the factory slowly eats away at the laborers, but also to the volatile interactions between the narrator and his fellow workers. At first "R62 gō no hatsumei" seems like a clumsy parody of Yokomitsu's more nuanced scenario. But there are some additional levels to be discovered in this and Abe's other early science fiction, if we look at things in terms of dialogue.

Like a number of Abe's stories, "R62 gō no hatsumei" is written very much like a script. In fact, Abe turned a number of stories from this time into radio scripts, part of a lifelong experiment with different media that he began early, with stage drama and radio plays. Abe may have had something similar in mind when he wrote "R62 gō no hatsumei," because the novel is very much organized around scenes of oral speech: conversations, formal addresses, lectures, and so forth. In fact, there is relatively little visual scenery described in the story, but Abe gives close attention to sound in the work. There are many descriptions of background noise, sound effects, and the like.[19]

Abe's writing style in this story uses a combination of direct and indirect quotation in a way that allows him to multiply the amount of oral language in the story, emphasizing this idea of unending speech, background conversation, overlapping voices—what becomes a thick weave of language. But through most of this text that is so defined by speech, the protagonist does not speak at all. In fact, he is gradually silenced as the story progresses. His conversation with the student in the opening scene constitutes most of what he says in the text. After he reaches the medical office, the director will not let him speak because he is already regarded as legally dead. As a sign of his acquiescence he has to sign a form, but the form turns out to be a blank piece of paper, which the director explains is a symbol of the fact he no longer has anything to say or any rights to assert. After the operation is complete, R62 no longer says anything except when ordered to.

While R62 goes silent, the director becomes more voluble. His speech to the R Club is a tour de force, consisting entirely of a kind of free association word game that satirizes the slippery power and the danger of political rhetoric. He sums up the group's philosophy by shouting out a long series of English words that begin with R, some sinister, others made sinister by the context, still others simply ridiculous: re-militarization, resettlement, and reclamation; rejuvenation, revival, and reactionary politics; reign, right, and rule; regular troops and boxing rings; race, religion, and reporters; rapprochement, regalia, roulette, and sexual relations.

From the outset, then, activity and freedom in the novel are very much viewed in terms of language, which gives some more depth to the story's apparently two-dimensional politics. It also gives some added interest to the slapstick of the story's pat conclusion, in which the factory workers strike and the owner gets his just desserts.

In that climax, R62 is able to turn his silence to his own advantage. After being programmed as a perfect worker, R62 has been turned loose in a factory for a few months and has invented a machine of his own, which he is demonstrating to the factory owner, the director, and the others who have put him where he is. Despite the rather obvious setup, the capitalists are surprised no less than Katsumi was. When R62 turns on the machine, it immediately scoops up the factory owner in its mechanical arms and locks him inside itself, where he is forced to push a series of flashing buttons in an intricate sequence. Each time he fails to push a button, a series of whirling knives cuts off one of his fingers. Once this machine has started, no one can figure out how to turn it off, so they are forced to watch this grisly spectacle play itself out as the factory owner runs back and forth trying to do what the machine demands and slowly running out of digits.

But the striking thing about this final scene is again the dialogue. R62 performs a parody of the director's sales pitch for selling robots as he describes the machine and its various features in a polite, earnest style. (At one point after the factory owner has lost a number of fingers, R62 points out that there is a feature to wash the blood off the control panel so the worker can continue his job without obstructed vision.) What is not clear from R62's presentation is what is accomplished by the device, which seems to exercise and finally kill the worker without producing any tangible results. In the final lines of the story the factory owner has died in the machine, and only R62 and the director remain. Outside, a crowd of striking workers rushes the gates and threatens to break them down, while the director and R62 have this final conversation:

> The director stood up and with a hand on R62's arm asked in a strangely kind voice: "Number 62, what exactly does this machine produce?"
>
> R62 stared at the director and struggled to remember something as he slowly shook his head. At that moment the machine buzzed to a stop, like a fly in winter. [. . .] From far away, the voices of the workers were heard, mixing eventually with the sirens of the security trucks. [. . .]
>
> "What does it produce!" the director screamed, but his voice was drowned out by the cries of the approaching strikers, and all R62 could make out was his spasming lips and twitching face. (*AZ* 3:432–33)

The disenfranchised workers gain a voice. The normally voluble director is drowned out. And finally, R62's silence speaks more eloquently than anything else. He has turned his lack of a voice back against his creators, and this final refusal to explain is the act of "passionate fantasy," as Abe said, that opposes relentless rationalization.

FOUR

The Dialogue of Styles, the Dance of Fiction,

and The Face of Another

In the novels that Abe wrote after *Inter Ice Age 4*, the crises are played out on a smaller stage, but the stakes are no less high. In *Inter Ice Age 4*, Abe portrays the violent changes that technology brings upon society and humanity, and he links these to changes in language. The personal crises faced by Dr. Katsumi, from the transformation of his son to his own death, are ultimately just reflections of the greater perils faced by society and humanity at large; the reader sees these changes in the world through one man's frightened eyes. But *Inter Ice Age 4* is in some ways atypical of Abe's work. Abe's most successful novels focus on this identity crisis at a much more personal level—the struggle of one person (usually a man) to constitute his own personality in and against the society around him.

After the large cast and broad canvass of *Inter Ice Age 4*, Abe's novels from the 1960s seem claustrophobic by comparison, like parlor dramas set in fantastic, alien dwellings. *The Woman in the Dunes* takes place almost entirely in one house at the bottom of a sand pit, where the hero and the woman are confined together. The same can be said for several of the novels that follow, which rank among Abe's most celebrated works: *The Face of Another* (1964), *The Ruined Map* (1967), and *The Box Man* (1973). The latter two are set in cities, but even there the protagonists are isolated (a detective unable to locate his quarry and a homeless man who wants nothing more than to remain unseen), and the novels bore in on these characters with a gaze that excludes almost everything else.

These novels do not require the grand scientific scenarios of *Inter Ice Age 4*, because there is no need to suggest a technology that would transform the world in one fell swoop; it is enough to provide a premise that changes the life or the identity of a single person. Nevertheless, technical elements and technical language continue to play an important role in many of these novels, and technology sometimes proves to be connected with the self at the most intimate levels.

The next two chapters examine the role of technical language in two of these middle novels, starting here with *The Face of Another*. The behavior of the scientific language in this work resembles that in *Inter Ice Age 4*: there is the same conflict or competition between differing styles, and finally a similar inversion of technical and non-technical dialects. Given this setup, it may come as a surprise that there is only one speaker in this novel, which takes the form of three "notebooks" written by a single narrator. Although the conflicts between different styles are played out in a single individual's voice, they are, if anything, more violent than in *Inter Ice Age 4*. In *The Face of Another*, they vie for control not only over the narrative but over the narrator's mind itself.

The narrator of *The Face of Another* is a scientist, a polymer chemist. When his face is terribly scarred in a laboratory accident, he finds himself an outcast from society, estranged even from his own wife. So he decides to put his scientific talents to work to construct a new face, a polymer mask that will be indistinguishable from a real face. Through these central figures of the face and the donning of the mask, the novel delves into questions of how one defines oneself and presents that self to others.

Although the scientific elements of the plot are not as elaborate as in *Inter Ice Age 4*, the technical language in this novel is no less complex: each stage in the mask's construction is described in painstaking technical detail, from the analysis of facial physiognomy that goes into the planning, through the casting of the metal molds and the characteristics of the different plastics that form the mask, to the details of implanting the facial hair and affixing the mask to the face.[1]

In fact, the technical descriptions are so involved that the translator of the English version, E. Dale Saunders, sometimes has trouble following the technical details of these processes. For readers who have encountered this novel only in this English translation, the Japanese version has an added sense of logic and rigor. (For this reason all the translations from the novel in this chapter will be my own.) The following section is typical of these passages. The narrator is describing the process of building up the mask by applying successive layers of plastic to a bust-like metal cast of his own face.

First I wrapped a spongy resin around the area of the antimony cast with the leech's nest of scars and smoothed them over. Over that, instead of clay I layered strips of a thin plastic tape that would give direction to the mask's movements, placing them along the Langer lines. [. . .] Last of all, I used a liquid resin to attach the transparent layer—a thin membrane containing fluorescent bodies and having a ratio of refraction close to that of keratin, imprinted with the surface texture of the skin sample I had purchased earlier. (*AZ* 18:388)

These technical passages alternate with less rational, more confused sections. Sometimes the problems that the narrator sets out to address are not solvable with science; but other times, technology actually seems to accelerate the breakdown of the narrator's logic and reason. Like the prediction machine whose logic is incomprehensible to Dr. Katsumi, the mask gradually begins to take on a will of its own. Gradually this product of reasoned technology gives rise to thoughts and actions that escape reason. Specifically, as the mask nears completion, the narrator's thoughts become dominated by antisocial, even violent fantasies. For example, just a few paragraphs before the dry technical description above, the narrator addresses these words to his wife: "Once in a while when I thought of the system of organs alive beneath your clothing— each with its own temperature, its own elasticity—I seriously believed that it wouldn't be over until I had run a spike through your body, even at the cost of your life, and made you a specimen in my biologist's sample box" (*AZ* 18:387).

Here scientific elements are twisted into a violent daydream: voyeurism attains an x-ray intensity, able to see right through the woman's skin, and fantasies of violation and penetration escalate into impalement with the final image of the insect on a pin. The language of these fantasies becomes another style in the novel, a style that runs alongside and challenges the more rational language of science. As the narrator's old personality competes with the new personality of the mask, these languages alternate, intermix, and struggle with one another for control of the narrative. And in the course of the novel, the problem of constituting one's own personality as well as the challenge of reaching beyond oneself to communicate with others both emerge as problems of combining and balancing these different languages. This chapter traces this intermixing of styles and its link to the formation of the self in the novel.

A detailed framework for such a linkage is provided by Mikhail Bakhtin, whose concept of dialogue was invoked in the previous chapter to connect the novel's conflict of styles with the contest between ideas in society at large. For Bakhtin, language and the dialogue between languages also play a special role in the *internal* conflicts whereby we constitute ourselves and differentiate ourselves from others. The latter part of this chapter examines this aspect of Bakhtin's work in more depth to see what light it sheds on Abe's text.

The Three Notebooks

The text of *The Face of Another* ostensibly consists of three notebooks, bracketed by a prefatory letter and postscript. Together, they record the making of the mask and the uses to which the narrator puts it. The narrator writes these notebooks to a "you" (*omae*) who, we learn early on, is his wife. Over the course of the three notebooks, the narrator slowly reveals to her the strange story of how he has used the mask to try and "restore the pathway between us": instead of constructing the mask to resemble his face as it appeared before the accident, he makes it in the image of a completely different person, a stranger (*AZ* 18:424). Then, masquerading as this stranger, he sets out to seduce his wife.

His wife seems to be deceived, and the seduction succeeds. But as one might expect, playing the part of his own wife's illicit lover hardly seems like a reunion. So as they are carrying on this relationship, the narrator begins to write the notebooks to her as a record of the events—from the making of the mask and the laying of his plans to the final seduction and affair. The narrative serves both to confess his own deception and to condemn her for her unfaithfulness.

"Threading your way through the folds of a far off labyrinth, you've come at last. Guided by the map that 'he' provided, you've reached the hideaway" (*AZ* 18:322). So begins a letter to the wife that forms the preface, in which we learn that the narrator has arranged a final tryst with her in his role as the stranger. When she arrives at a secret apartment for their rendezvous, she will find not the stranger/lover she expects but the lifeless mask of his face, together with the letter and notebooks that describe the whole plot. The narrator thinks this will be the end of the stranger and the resumption of normal relations between the two of them. Hoping that he is right, he goes back to the house and waits for her to finish reading the last page and to return to him. For most of the novel, we as readers are placed in the position of the wife, as we read the narrator's account. But on the final pages we also read the wife's reaction to the notebooks, which is recorded in a final short postscript, consisting of a letter from her and one final note from the narrator himself.

The structure of the narrative is actually more complex than this brief description suggests. Even though everything except the wife's letter is ostensibly the written text of the one narrator, the arrangement of the novel has some features that lend themselves to conflicting voices. Not only does Abe portray the text as a combination of different pieces (notebooks and letters), but within the notebooks there are different kinds of writing: the main text is supplemented by a series of "marginal notations" (*rangaichū*) about side topics. And there are a number of "supplementary notes" (*tsuiki*), which comment on and sometimes take exception with the main text or the marginal notes. The narrator has apparently added these at various points during a final editing stage, after the main text was complete. The prefatory letter tells us it was written last, except for the final postscript and the wife's letter, which were added to the back of the final notebook last of all.

Structuring the narration as a series of notebooks is a device Abe used in some of his earliest works. The technique of indicating additions and revisions in order to divide or subdivide the narrator is one that he would exploit even more radically in his later novel *The Box Man*, where the actual number of narrators is uncertain, and different textual lines and emendations argue with one another over authenticity. *The Face of Another* is less extreme, but although there is only one narrator, we do read him writing in different styles at different times. As we will see, Abe uses these devices to multiply the number of voices in the text and intensify the contrast between different styles.

The Black Notebook and the Language of Science

The three notebooks are designated by the colors of their covers—black, white, and grey. With the exceptions noted above, they narrate events in more or less chronological order, beginning with the black notebook, which describes the narrator's decision to make the mask and the early stages of its construction. Many of the technical descriptions of manufacturing the mask are concentrated in this part of the novel, where the narrator struggles to overcome various technical obstacles: how to make the mask move expressively; how to duplicate the sheen and color of human skin; or how to reproduce all the tiny pores and wrinkles on a human face.

These technical problems are not the only difficulties the narrator encounters in making the mask. He also finds that he must address a range of problems where the issues are less neatly defined. The face is intimately tied to our individuality; what happens to that sense of self when the face becomes something one can choose or change? If a person could redraw his or her own face completely, how would he or she go about picking a new one? Why is the appearance of the face so important, and what does it mean that a tiny cosmetic change, a web of millimeter scars, can turn a human into a monster? When he turns from technical issues to these broader questions of identity, psychology, and philosophy, the narrator's language must also change. The result is that in the black notebook the specialized chemist's language alternates with more confused ruminations on these less cut-and-dried problems.

The relation between these two strains of language is quite complex. Often the narrator tries to bring the technical language of mathematics or a laboratory protocol to bear on these philosophical problems, with limited success. Other times the technical aspects of the project represent an escape from the more difficult issues, the narrator's effort to lose himself in the "what" and "how" of the mask so he can forget the nagging question of "why." And sometimes the technical discoveries themselves precipitate these philosophical problems. All three of these relationships produce the same effect: an alternation in the text between technical and non-technical or pseudo-technical language, as these two different styles or modes of thought toss the narrative back and forth.

If *Inter Ice Age 4* featured the appearance of first one technical language, then another, and finally the inversion of science and poetry,

The Face of Another is characterized from its outset by a much more rapid alternation between science and nonsense. This seesawing sometimes continues for a dozen pages at a time, but it is possible to get a sense of it from a few short excerpts. A good example from the black notebook is the narrator's visit to a prosthetics expert named K, from whom he hopes to learn the technical secrets of making artificial skin. But he is taken aback when K invests the flesh—whether real or plastic—with an importance beyond its outward appearance. K explains that our outer bodies are linked to our inner spirits, that an injury to the face is a matter not just of "form" but of "mental hygiene" as well. "The soul," says K, "is in the skin" (*AZ* 18:336–37).

Despite his efforts to reduce his problem to a technical one, the narrator is haunted by factors like these that are not so neatly quantified. Returning from the meeting, he broods sleeplessly on K's ideas about the soul, but after a couple of pages he grows frustrated and escapes back into a series of technical observations about prostheses, cataloging the features of an artificial finger he has purchased from K.

> Finally, I grew tired of this endlessly circling soliloquy about the face . . . In any case there was no need to abandon the course I had set out on . . . So I turned my attention over to technical observations.
>
> From a technical standpoint the artificial finger had a number of interesting features. [. . .] Based upon the tension of the skin, I would guess he was about thirty. The flat nail . . . the flattened crotch . . . the deep wrinkles at the joints . . . four tiny scars lined up like shark's gills . . . probably someone engaged in light manual labor.
>
> . . . But it was so ugly . . . Why on earth was it so repulsive?
>
> (*AZ* 18:342–43)

The narrator's observations and deductions about the finger's hypothetical owner are meticulously objective, but they cannot account for a certain grotesque quality of the finger, an indefinable "ugliness that belonged neither to the dead nor to the living" (*AZ* 18:343). Left to answer this riddle, he considers the idea that the finger is too realistic: "Perhaps the truth was that a reproduction that is too accurately formed may actually be unrealistic. And yet, can you envision a finger without any form? A snake with no length? A jar with no volume? Or a triangle rule without any angles? None of these are objects you're likely to encounter—not on this planet anyway" (*AZ* 18:343).

In the space of a few paragraphs, the narrator has moved from K's abstract philosophies of the face, to the careful "technical observations" of a scientist, and then to the odd contradictions of "a snake with no length" and "a jar with no volume." In Chapter 2, we saw how Ishikawa Takashi argued that *The Crime of S. Karma* is characterized by careful step-by-step reasoning, and Abe countered that those steps lead nowhere except into nonsense. Here we see in more detail just how rigorously and creatively Abe pulls this off, by having the narrator pursue a logical argument to the point of paradox. The finger must be less realistic in order to be more real, or formless to be well-formed; like the inside-out characters and inverted geometries we see elsewhere in Abe's work, it must be a lengthless line and a volumeless space. So as the problem escapes the circle of the narrator's reasoning, that same reasoning leads him to a different planet.

The narrator quickly recovers, though, and by the time he reaches the bottom of the page he has figured out a scientific explanation for the finger's grotesque appearance:

MARGINAL NOTE I—On the distinctive appearance of the skin surface

It seems reasonable to conclude that the human epithelium is protected by a glassy substance devoid of pigment. The special appearance of the skin's surface must accordingly be an effect of the complex interaction between light rays reflected from this surface matter and rays that pass through it and reflect off the pigmented layer below. In the case of the artificial finger, the pigmented layer was directly at the surface, so this effect was not obtained. (*AZ* 18:343)

This is in fact a technically accurate characterization of what experts call "structural color," the phenomenon that produces the iridescent hues seen in a soap bubble or a beetle's carapace. For the narrator the explanation is momentarily reassuring, but he will find out that the unreality of that realistic but lifeless finger is not simply an issue of light-reflecting surfaces. It is related to the problem K raised, that the feeling of reality that attaches to our bodies is something inseparable from life itself: there is a soul in the skin.

This alternation between technical and absurd occurs over and over in the black notebook. The passages above are only a piece of a much longer sequence in which the narrative swings back and forth many times. And even in passages that appear to fall into one category, elements of the other are never entirely banished. The most technical passage may include an odd metaphor (the scars "lined up like shark's gills"), and the absurd passages often retain the outward form of a logical argument. In fact, close examination reveals that virtually every passage is to some degree a hybrid of both scientific and fantastic, a balance of styles with first one and then the other dominating. In one extreme example of this mixing, the narrator attempts to express the appeal masks have for different kinds of people, using a mathematical equation with variables that include the individual's age, "index of other-directedness," and "degree of viscosity of the self" (*AZ* 18:350). Set off with some elaborate typography, the equation is impressive at first glance, then on closer examination ridiculous; and yet, there is a surprising method to Abe's madness even here, and against all odds, the equation actually does represent a coherent point, and the passage actually obeys its own kind of offbeat logic.

At the same time, *The Face of Another* portrays the shortcomings and the breakdown of this logic and language more resolutely than *Inter Ice Age 4*, one sign of Abe's development from a science fictional style that worked largely within the boundaries of scientific logic to a more literary idiom that was not afraid to trespass those boundaries. And yet, the alternating sections contain plenty of straight science (like the explanation of iridescence), and the text (not just the narrator) always retains a lingering respect or affection for this kind of reasoning. The novel combines and balances science and nonsense so intricately that each style seems to invade or hybridize the other, much in the way that Bakhtin described. It is this mixing and hybridization that make it both difficult and necessary to address the question raised in the Introduction, of how to balance our own faith and skepticism with regard to technical language. How "seriously" are we to regard the science in this work? To explore this in greater detail, we now examine how these styles develop later in the novel.

The White and Grey Notebooks and the Language of the Imagination

For most of the black notebook, it is hard to characterize the non-technical language in any detail, other than to say as we did above that it is "nonsensical" or "contradictory." But in the latter part of the novel, in the white and grey notebooks, these non-technical passages coalesce into a more specific genre or style of their own, a style we might call "imaginative." This imaginative language becomes associated with the mask, with violence, and with fiction itself.

At the end of the black notebook, the narrator's research has solved most of the technical problems associated with the mask. The white notebook takes us through the final steps of its construction and the first few times he tries it on. Some of the most involved technical descriptions show up in this part of the novel, but as the mask nears completion, this technical language is increasingly accompanied by descriptions of things that do not really occur in the novel, things that are imaginary or fictional in the context of the narrator's world. This imaginative language includes descriptions of dreams, stories, hallucinations, the plot of a movie, and a whole series of waking fantasies.

These imaginative passages gradually come to be associated with the voice of the mask, and with a set of violent impulses the narrator disavows by assigning them to the mask's personality. ("After I finished it, the mask took off on its own," he will say later, "and reveling in its escape from me, it grew defiant" [*AZ* 18:475].) These passages begin to appear as the project nears completion, and they become more frequent when the narrator begins to wear the finished mask, which represents both technology taking over its creator (like the computer in *Inter Ice Age 4*), and at the same time the emergence of a side of the narrator's personality that was always present, a side that is now simply released by this technology. It is only natural that the mask should be associated with fictional language, since it is itself a kind of fiction, a part of what the narrator calls his "masked play" (*kamengeki*) (*AZ* 18:484). So when he dons the mask, the narrator speaks in fictions, but at other times he struggles to maintain his scientific outlook and to restrain the mask by reciting technical language.[2] In this way these two different styles play tug-of-war in the text.

At one point, for example, the narrator becomes alarmed at the control the mask seems to exert, and vows he will give up the mask and the social intercourse it promises and instead retreat to the solitude of the laboratory. ("Fortunately," he says, "I still have the god of polymer chemistry, the prayer of rheology, the monastery of my lab.") But the voice of the mask immediately counters by telling a child's fairy tale. "Once upon a time there lived a king," it begins, and goes on to relate the story of a monarch who is plagued by a mysterious disease that

causes his body to rot away. He issues an edict that no one may look
upon him in his affliction, and it is honored: he is left alone to decay
horribly into nothing, unable to cry for help, and no one is the wiser.
Besides its fairy tale style (the stock beginning and short sentences), the
story is written in *katakana* to set it off as part of the mask's distinctive
fictional idiom (*AZ* 18:406).

But the majority of the mask's violent fictions are in the form of
sadistic daydreams that invade the narrator's consciousness. One of the
first occurs near the end of the black notebook, when the plans for the
mask are almost completed and the narrator is riding the streetcar into
town to get the last of the needed materials. At this point the mask's
promise and possibility are already beginning to work on the narrator's
mind, when he notices a child staring at the bandages that cover his
disfigured face. He imagines taking revenge on the child by removing
the bandages to reveal his scars. And as he describes this fantasy, the
account becomes progressively more vivid and detailed. ("I would tear
off the last bandages all at once," he says, "just to heighten the effect.")
Eventually the imagined scene departs entirely from reality and becomes wholly fantastic: "Yet, the face that was revealed would be completely different from my face up until now. It would not be a human
face, but something bronzed, or golden, or the pure transparent color
of wax. They wouldn't have time to discern anything beyond that. Before they could decide from that one fleeting impression whether it was
the face of a god or a demon, the child and its parents would be turned
to stone, or lead, or creatures like insects" (*AZ* 18:363).

These hallucinatory fantasies increase in the course of the white
notebook, when the narrator completes the mask and puts it on. Each
time he wears it, the mask seems to grow bolder. Eventually the narrator finds himself purchasing a dangerously powerful air gun at a toy
store, seemingly against his own will. "The mask smiled at my confusion," the narrator says as his hand taps the gun in his pocket. "It even
seemed to enjoy it" (*AZ* 18:411). Meanwhile the mask's fantasies are escalating from terror to rape and murder.

The reason that fantasy so often turns violent in *The Face of Another*
relates to the role of fantasy in liberating the narrator from society's
constraints. The freedom is exhilarating, but the chance to violate those
strictures ultimately becomes an impulse to wreck society itself. For the

narrator, who feels cut off from society by his disfigurement, the mask was supposed to offer the promise of a return. But in the fantasies of his alter ego, he returns to wreak vengeance. So it is that he imagines himself a monster, "a god or a demon" driven out of society who now comes back to haunt it, like the monsters that haunt science in Abe's essays. Right after the passage above, the narrator pursues this idea and links the daydream even more explicitly with fiction by comparing himself to one of Abe's favorite fictional monsters, the creature in Mary Shelley's *Frankenstein*.

The mask's violent fantasies reach a climax in the grey notebook, which opens with the narrator putting on the false face at his secret apartment and then traveling to his own neighborhood to wander the streets outside his house. As he looks in the window, he (or the mask) fantasizes about breaking into the house and assaulting his wife at gunpoint. The fantasy is introduced by the following paragraph:

To recover from that feeling of defeat, I decided to give the mask free rein with its fantasies. These imaginings threatened to be as crude as the mask itself. But I couldn't very well condemn these illusions or even delusions when they were going up against the hardened shell of everyday lived experience. I decided to look the other way. In the meantime, I started circling the unequal quadrilateral that enclosed my house, trying to appear as if I had some business there. (*AZ* 18:363)

The fantasy segues back into technical language at the end, as the narrator tries to separate himself from the mask and its imaginings. His retreat from the house to the edge of the "unequal quadrilateral that enclosed" it is also a retreat from fantasy into the pat vocabulary of mathematics. Ironically these antisocial fantasies are the only connection he can imagine with his wife and the outside world, and it is also this involvement from which he retreats. The "defeat" he feels in the first line is the experience of looking into a house where he no longer feels welcome, feeling jealous of the husband he used to be. The fantasy promises a return, but like his daydream on the streetcar, it ends in an act of revenge that destroys what he sought to rejoin.

In Abe's text, then, fiction is not a withdrawal from reality, a retreat to a make-believe world, but an active, even violent encounter with the world—one that may well undermine reality as we know it. In one sense, this is an optimistic view of literature, as something that can and will bring about changes in the world. But the association of fiction and social change with violence and rape may disturb us. *Inter Ice Age 4* contained a similarly violent, some would say misogynist image of the wife who is deceived into having an abortion. The image of the child stolen from its mother's body becomes a metaphor for violent change: both the physically invasive changes of technological progress, and the sudden breaks that rob us of the future we had come to expect. *The Face of Another* raises the stakes even further with its images of sexual violence. And this escalation continues in the last novel we will consider, *Secret Rendezvous*, whose gallery of sexual encounters makes Abe's earlier novels pale in comparison.

In the context of these and other novels by Abe, the social changes promised by fiction are inherently violent ones because they overturn the everyday common sense on which we have come to depend. (Note the narrator's reference to "the everyday" in the quotation above.) We saw this in Abe's criticism and again in *Inter Ice Age 4*: just as Dr. Katsumi is asked to transcend his narrow view of the future as a mere extension of the present, his counterpart in *The Face of Another* tries to revise the present social conventions that govern our relations with others. It is because fiction can provide this transcendence that the final horrifying prediction that shakes Katsumi out of his stupor takes the form of a story or a prose poem. The mask's fantasies are similarly frightening, but for the narrator they are necessary to break down the walls of social convention.

It is a measure of the radical nature of this rethinking that once the rules of society are exposed as conventions, eventually every aspect of reality must be called into question. The fiction of the mask reveals all the other fictions that surround us, and soon everything seems unreal. Returning to his familiar house after having the mask on, the narrator finds it (or himself) changed. "After a week away," he says, "my house was soaked like cotton in the everyday. The walls, the ceiling, the tatami mats appeared solid enough, but someone who had experienced the mask could not help but perceive that this solidity was nothing more than the fence of convention" (*AZ* 18:471).

For those who have seen the mask, he says, "other people will become transparent ghosts; everything will be full of gaps—like a picture painted in faint shades on glass. The world will become as hard to believe in as the mask itself" (*AZ* 18:452). Obviously this is the same metaphorical wall of convention that appears in *The Crime of S. Karma.* Now the chemist's words suggest that it is fiction that can open a door in the wall and change society.

The effects of the mask's fiction on society at large are addressed in detail near the end of the novel, when the narrator imagines the results if his masks could be mass-produced. In one of the book's most absorbing passages, the drunken narrator daydreams about a society in which social identity could be altered or changed at will, and reasons step by step about the successive effects this would have in areas like law, economics, courtship, and even literary tastes. The style of this section is an interesting mix, combining the context of an inebriated fantasy with some careful if quirky reasoning about the social consequences when the face stops being a guarantee of identity. (Eventually, "movie stars would file facial copyrights" and "the audience for detective novels would all but disappear.") The narrator speculates that the fictionalizing power of the mask would disrupt every individual and social relationship at its most basic level: "You'd be unable to trust anyone else, but you'd have no ground for suspecting them either. You'd be left gazing into a mirror that reflects nothing, suspended in a state where human relations had been reset to zero" (*AZ* 18:437–38).

For the narrator at this point, a fiction indistinguishable from reality is the ultimate violence. He concludes that "the very existence of the mask is fundamentally destructive—the equivalent of premeditated murder" (*AZ* 18:441). That assertion notwithstanding, the narrator will eventually realize that there are differences between fiction and violence, and between real violence and the imagined violence of a fantasy. The novel addresses some of these differences in its conclusion, at the end of the grey notebook.

The Grey Notebook and the Language of Reason

The mask's fantasy of assaulting the wife has considerable impact in the novel, but the description is hardly graphic. It consists of three isolated violent images, only a sentence apiece, interspersed with several pages of discussion about the source of his violent urges. This rhythm is fairly typical of the grey notebook, where the possibility of violence glitters powerfully but only sporadically against the backdrop of endless internal monologues about the narrator's desire, jealousy, anger, and lust.

A look at the overall pacing of the novel makes this rhythm clearer: the construction of the mask described in the black notebook covers a period of nine months. The white notebook completes the mask and brings the account up to the day before the seduction—three months in all. Except for a brief postscript, the grey notebook only details the night of the seduction and the 24 hours on either side. So while the grey notebook constitutes about a third of this long novel, the events in it occupy only three days. Here the "action" of the novel becomes largely internal—the narrator's thoughts and arguments with himself. Fantasy and fiction now play a greater and greater role, as the world described in the novel increasingly becomes a world the narrator creates or elaborates in his own imagination.

A big part of this internal dialogue is a kind of self-analysis, a minute examination of the narrator's impulses by the narrator himself. The act of reasoning through his own feelings has the effect that scientific language did in the earlier notebooks, of curbing his violent impulses. With the mask now complete, the detailed descriptions of technical processes have come to an end (although scientific vocabulary and metaphors continue to play a role). What replaces technical language in opposing, ordering, and controlling the narrator's fantasies is this relentless reasoning. "I would have to become my own psychoanalyst," the narrator says, "earnestly organizing and analyzing my desires until I had determined the true form of that thing that festered in the tumor within me, filtering it all until I had given it a name" (*AZ* 18:436).

It is this "filtering" and "naming" that Ōe Kenzaburō seems to have in mind when he says, in an afterword to one Japanese edition, that "The fundamental shape of Abe's style lies in the chain of logic that he so meticulously and laboriously unrolls" (286). (A Japanese psychiatrist, Fukushima Akira, even reports that the novel is a relatively accurate depiction of the difficulties experienced by people undergoing reconstructive surgery or suffering from identity problems.)

It is difficult to excerpt these passages of psychological reasoning because they are so lengthy and so closely argued. Many of them have to do with the meaning of the "freedom" (*jiyū*) that the mask has gained for its wearer. For example, the narrator asks whether freedom is linked to the unimpeded exercise of power, or whether it is a release from compulsion, a release embodied in willing self-sacrifice. In the former case, it would be the masked violator who is most free; in the latter case, it would be the husband cuckolded by himself. This is a recasting of the dilemma in "Dendrocacalia": does freedom mean an escape from the prison of loneliness and a reunion with the other, or does it mean a release from the other and her interference? For the narrator, the answer dictates whether he should want to regain his wife or simply punish her.

The role of the "supplementary notes" (*tsuiki*) increases in this part of the novel, as the narrator spends more time second-guessing and amplifying his own words. To some extent, one can still observe the same alternation between styles that was evident in the black and white notebooks, but the divisions are defined less and less sharply. The back-and-forth switching occurs more and more rapidly, often in mid-sentence. A good example is the following excerpt, which occurs in the middle of an involved discussion about the relation between freedom and power. What action, the narrator asks, represents perfect freedom? It cannot be part of the struggle to gain power, but must constitute a free exercise of power for its own sake. The narrator considers crime, which is in some sense a freedom from society's rules. But a crime for personal gain is merely part of the struggle to amass more power or freedom, so it can hardly be entirely free itself. Using this criterion, violent crime, committed for the sake of pure destruction, comes closer to pure freedom. Here the narrator considers arson:

Even granted that there were less calculated acts of arson springing from a grudge, wasn't most arson an attempt to recover freedom that had been frozen or taken away? . . . And yet, I couldn't resist the feeling that there could be a purer kind of incendiarism, one that gained nothing, one that was in itself the satisfaction of desire: the dancing flames would lick at the walls, warp the pillars, then rend the ceiling and billow toward the clouds. With barely a glance at the milling curious crowd, they would incinerate something that a moment ago had existed as an undeniable bit of history. It would be an unadulterated arson, a dramatic act of destruction, nourishment to assuage a hunger in the soul. (*AZ* 18:433–34)

Looking at the ebb and flow of language here, arson is introduced in the context of a long and intricate argument about freedom that spans several pages in the novel. But in the middle of this reasoning, in mid-sentence in fact, there is a tiny but excited word painting of the imagined fire, from the flames licking at the walls to the crowds clustered outside. The description of the fire is a fantasy in the midst of reason—a fiction.

It is particularly in these sections of the novel that E. Dale Saunders's English translation runs into difficulty. Saunders's English is always graceful (and he threads his way with little difficulty through most of the technical passages in *Inter Ice Age 4*), but in the grey notebook he frequently seems to become lost in the labyrinth of the narrator's logic, and minor discrepancies in the translation pile up until the snaking line of the narrator's argument (already obscure in the Japanese) is unrecoverable in the translation. The result is that the English narration in this part of the novel often does not make much sense, and the gradual erosion of the narrator's sanity that is so subtly played out in Japanese is amplified and accelerated. By tipping this delicate balance between logic and lunacy, the translation gives a much stronger impression of parody or farce.

Besides ordering the narrator's internal world, this rational language has another important role as an act of communication directed outward, at his wife. It is a confession. The events of the grey notebook more or less conclude on the day after the seduction, when the narrator decides he must reveal everything to his wife. Instead of telling her outright, though, he chooses to put everything down in writing, and it is at this point that he begins drafting the notebooks. (The last two pages of the grey notebook describe the long weeks of writing the account, during which time the confession is deferred and the affair drags on.)

What the grey notebook describes, then, is how the narrator turns away from the lie of the mask for the revealed truth of confession. He is upset because the fantasy of the mask has gotten away from him, but he believes that the truth will finally kill the mask and do away with the fiction that now paradoxically stands between him and his wife. The introspective, analytical language in the latter part of the novel is part and parcel of this confession, which seems to be part of the reason that the narrator insists on writing it down. He never considers telling his wife to her face. Instead, he lets the affair continue while he fills one notebook after another with the confession that will end it, apparently because he believes that only the medium of writing will permit the necessary level of revelation and detail. To find out if his strategy will work, the narrator must wait for his wife's response.

The Wife's Letter and the "Account Just for Myself"

The wife's reply comes in the novel's last section, which is headed with the notation: "An account just for myself, added on the remaining sheets of the grey notebook by using it backwards and writing from the last page" (*AZ* 18:477). This section is not part of what he shows to his wife, but is added afterward. Here we learn that she disappears after reading the notebooks. The narrator goes to the apartment hideaway where he left the mask and notebooks for her to find, but all he discovers there is a short letter from her. He pastes the letter into the middle of this final section, where we can read it, then he comments on it and wonders what he will do next. After a few more pages he breaks off his narrative, and the novel ends.

In her letter, the wife rejects the narrator's confession. She tells him she saw through his disguise from the very first instant. She did not need the notebooks to reveal the central secret of the mask, nor does she have any use for the rest of the narrator's clumsy self-accounting. In her eyes, the narrator's intent to deceive her and his later attempt to reveal everything are both equally ridiculous. Instead of this flip-flop between truth and fiction, she calls for a steady course between the two.

The wife's two-and-a-half-page letter is the opposite of the narrator's detailed accounting: it is brief, suggestive, elliptical. Instead of painstakingly outlining her ideas, she makes her point with a few telling phrases. (The letter ends with "two-and-a-half lines that had been crossed out until they were unreadable," an emblem of her refusal to speak any further [*AZ* 18:486].) But it is possible to reconstruct a philosophy of language for the wife based on her telegraphic indictments of the narrator.

According to the letter, she recognized him the first time he approached her wearing the mask, but she pretended to be fooled. In fact, she believed that they were both only pretending to deceive one another. (She knew, in other words, and she thought he knew that she knew.) For her, it was this pretense of deception that made the fiction

of the mask exciting and touching. And it was this acknowledged dissimulation that held the greatest promise for reuniting them, perhaps
by permitting them to start over as new people, but still to remain
themselves. She says in the letter that "love is two people peeling the
masks off together. You have to struggle into your own mask for the
sake of the one you love" (*AZ* 18:484).

The fiction of the mask could have "restored the pathway between"
them, she suggests, if only they both could have acknowledged that it
was a mask as soon as he put it on. But as she reads the notebooks,
she realizes the narrator cannot bring himself to compromise with fiction in this way: at first he was earnestly trying to deceive her, and now
he has discarded the mask and forsaken fiction for an unadulterated
truth. But with the mask dead, the possibility of that mutually acknowledged fiction and reconciliation is dead along with it. "If the mask isn't
coming back," she writes in her letter, "I can't very well return either"
(*AZ* 18:485).

In the wife's eyes, the narrator's urge to confess is just as misguided
as his effort to deceive her. The problem goes beyond the fact that his
confession is born of a megalomaniacal preoccupation with himself.
("For you," the wife writes, "the other person is never anything but a
mirror to reflect yourself" [*AZ* 18:486].) The difficulty also lies in the
narrator's attempt at unvarnished truth. Without the needed admixture
of fiction, his probing self-analysis is uncommunicative, invasive, painful. His confessions are so sordid and aggressive that they paradoxically
leave the reader exposed. The wife writes that reading the notebooks
"was like being dragged onto the operating table to suffer incisions
from hundreds of different blades—intricately shaped scissors and
scalpels whose function and employment were obscure" (*AZ* 18:485).

Looking at the wife's letter in the context of the stylistic argument
we have been making, we might say that her call for a mutual pretense
of deception strikes a balance between truth and fiction that has eluded
the narrator. Her solution suggests a way to reconcile the languages of
fiction, confession, rationality, and reality in a way that improves upon
the manic alternation and bizarre hybrid styles of the narrator's text. In
fact, her pretended deception resembles literary fiction itself. A novel is,
after all, a fictional story that the reader knows is not true, but which he
or she believes for the moment. As a compromise between the truth and

a lie, it is an agreement to deceive and knowingly be deceived. Relating these different ideas back to the theories of scientific language reviewed in Chapter 2, the contrast between the narrator's relentless truth-telling and the wife's appeal for an open-eyed illusion recalls Nietzsche's contrast between an Alexandrian search for scientific truth and the open-eyed dissimulation of the Apollonian idea. Nietzsche's third pole, the Dionysian, would then correspond to the dangerous side of the mask, which threatens to violently negate the individual by exposing the "lie of culture"—the ways in which identity and our everyday reality are merely fictions.

The wife says the mask is like "a cordial invitation to dance" (*AZ* 18:484). Expanding on this metaphor, one could say her ideal for fiction is like a dance itself—a joyful convention in which two people participate. Both realize that the steps are arbitrary, but they form a world in which two people move and communicate. In the same way, this ideal fiction is neither the true confession of a real person (like the narrator's failed notebooks) nor an unbridled fantasy that subverts reality entirely (like the mask's violent daydreams).

The wife's ideal for fiction and her ability to fictionalize herself, as she plays the role of the adulterous housewife, may embody the combination of power and vulnerability that constitutes the perfect freedom or *jiyū* for which the narrator has been searching. Examining the earlier descriptions of the wife during the course of the seduction and affair, one notices that although she initially appears in the role of the victim, eventually the narrator encounters in her a powerful fiction that is more than a match for the mask. Confused by the part his wife is playing, the narrator begins to doubt that he really knows her. "Who the hell have you turned out to be?" he asks (*AZ* 18:466). Finally he finds he is unable to act out his fantasies of rape and murder because she denies him this role. The mask succeeds in taking her to bed, but she responds to the seduction without guilt, and transforms herself from victim into co-perpetrator. "Or maybe I should say you simulated the confidence of an accomplice," the narrator says. "The result was that finally the mask didn't even amount to a lecher, much less a rapist" (*AZ* 18:465).

We also read earlier in the novel that the wife has become "literally inviolable." She has "slipped through the fence" of everyday convention and emerged pure. She is the gods' own "hunter of masks" who will bag the narrator in the end (*AZ* 18:465–66, 473). All these descriptions of her represent what the narrator hoped to become himself through the mask: powerful, anonymous, and immune. She has turned around his masked play by rewriting her own role. (Note that the role of accomplice is "simulated.") She has fictionalized and redefined herself. She has outmasked the mask.

If the wife is indeed authoring her own role, it is appropriate that her letter takes over the narrative, however briefly, and speaks in her own words. The act of rewriting herself becomes almost literal with the included letter. In fact, many of Abe's novels feature a woman character who challenges the narrator's language and logic, but the reader seldom hears her speak except through the protagonist's account, or through a narrative voice that remains attached to the protagonist's point of view. *The Face of Another* is one of the rare novels where we hear the woman's voice seemingly unfiltered.

Compared with her own role-playing, the wife calls the narrator's fictional world unproductive. She says that for all the mask's supposed power, for all its dangerous preparations, it never undertakes any decisive action, violent or otherwise, and she traces this problem back to the fact that the narrator could never acknowledge the mask as a fiction. "The very point of putting on a mask is in letting the other know that it isn't real," she says. "[. . .] You had no idea how to treat the mask. The proof is that even with it on, you didn't accomplish a thing. [. . .] All you did was roam the streets and write this endless confession—a thing like a snake that has swallowed its own tail" (*AZ* 18:485).

And what is the narrator's response to the ideas in this letter? Stung by the wife's accusations, he is forced to admit that his rational confession has failed to reach her, and that the subversive possibilities of the mask (for violence, for undermining society) were never realized. But instead of turning to the ideal of an acknowledged fiction—the ideal that can be extrapolated from the wife's letter—he takes her advice in a different way. He vows to stop writing and turns to concrete physical action, apparently revenge. He puts the mask back on, releases the safety of his pistol, and hides in the shadows. Soon he hears a woman's footsteps nearing his hiding place. With this apparent turn to physical action, the need to write is at an end. The last words of the novel are these: "The footsteps are coming closer. . . . But from this point on, nothing will be written down. I suppose writing is an act required only when nothing else happens" (*AZ* 18:495).

These final words are preceded by a brief justification, similar to something he wrote earlier in the grey notebook. There he explained that the mask's perversion is simply the logical outcome of the "abstraction" (*chūshōka*) of human relations in society today. None of us can distinguish who among the others around us is a neighbor; all we can do is consider everyone an enemy. That idea returns now in these final pages, where the narrator concludes that it is better to bear loneliness than risk betrayal. In society today, relations with the other must be distant, hostile, abstract. Everyone covers their face to shut others out, and the narrator can be no exception.

Given this grim conclusion, it is hardly surprising that critics have almost unanimously seen this disintegration of human relationships as the central subject of the novel. Some condemn the narrator's selfishness, while others read the narrator's final self-justification more sympathetically and regard the work as Abe's indictment of a society or a human condition where loneliness has become our last and only resort. Still other critics feel the novel portrays this abstraction of human relationships in neutral terms, with Abe finally refusing to condemn either society or the narrator for changes in human relations.[3]

This last interpretation has been fueled by some of Abe's own comments, which emphasize the need to move beyond conventional ways of conceiving our relationships with others. As in *Inter Ice Age 4*, this revolution in thought involves the violent removal of old concepts, an overthrow that is figured in the novel and in Abe's rhetoric by the metaphor of eradication or murder. Speaking about "the idea of the neighbor" in a 1966 dialogue with Mishima Yukio, Abe sounds rather like the narrator of *The Face of Another* when he says the theme of his work is "the question of how to eradicate the neighbor; that is, the idea we have of the neighbor, our idea of community" (*AZ* 20:64).

Abe's development of these ideas has encouraged some critics to look for a measure of truth, revolution, or creativity in the narrator's final actions, alarming though they may be.[4] As in *Inter Ice Age 4*, the assumption may be that any revolution in thought will necessarily be alarming, even horrible, by the old standards. "This vanishing of the neighbor is terribly cruel," Abe says to Mishima, "but when that cruelty has become the new baseline, I think that will be the real beginning of a new age" (*AZ* 20:67). And in an essay he wrote titled "Mosukuwa to Nyū Yōku" (Moscow and New York, 1964), Abe notes an "uneasiness" (*shōsō*) endemic to the modern city, "a kind of frustration caused by the increasing complication or perversion of human relationships" (*AZ* 19:60). Abe identifies this as the theme of *The Face of Another*. But he says that the novel does not condemn this new state we find ourselves in, suggesting instead that we may simply have outgrown our old ways of relating to other people: "If there were only one way to the other, then clearly outgrowing it might be a pathological development. But maybe there is another pathway, a way that our current sensibility can't recognize or conceive, but one that will be completely valid once we awaken to it. If so, then our isolation from one another is not a disease but simply a state of confusion or ignorance" (*AZ* 19:61).

This returns us to the idea touched on earlier, that literary fiction fosters revolution by overturning preconceived ideas. Such a notion is compatible with the wife's view of fiction: while acknowledging that she was playing a role, she also forged a real new relationship with her husband. In other words, although fiction is a mask we put on consciously and temporarily, our world may well have changed when we take off the mask, or put the novel down. But by treating the narrator's physical action simply as a metaphor for a revolution in thought, this interpretation ignores or even reverses the narrator's distinction between thought and action and his final preference for the latter.

Another option, then, is to side completely with the narrator and his choice of action over writing—to agree with him when he says that "writing is an act required only when nothing else happens." Support for this position comes from an unexpected quarter: Ōe Kenzaburō, whose optimistically humanistic brand of avant-garde fiction eventually edged out Abe's for the Nobel Prize. Ōe writes that the narrator recovers a heroic status at the end of the novel because he regains the capacity for action. In a reading that is somewhat strained but also interesting for the way it bucks the critical consensus, Ōe maintains that the final scene loses its ominous cast because we cannot finally know what the narrator will do when the woman's footsteps reach his hiding place. This ambiguity, the very fact that the narrative breaks off, imparts an even greater freedom or possibility to the narrator's actions.

Action for Ōe means political action, so even violent action may be favorably associated with political protest. He lingers on the novel's references to the real world—the plight of ethnic Koreans in Japan and the Harlem race riots. Compared with this concrete participation in society, the various fictions depicted in the novel remain limited and closed, he says. These conclusions about the inadequacy of fiction might be surprising coming from Ōe, but for a young, left-wing intellectual writing in the late 1960s, the preoccupation with concrete social action is hardly unexpected. Just as Thomas Schnellbächer shows in the case of Abe, perhaps for Ōe some dissatisfaction with merely writing is inevitable.[5]

Abe himself talks about *The Face of Another* and the novelist's social role in the essay "Keshigomu de kaku" (Writing with an eraser, 1966). One of Abe's best-known statements about writing, this essay originally appeared simultaneously in a theater journal and in a volume that collected several works by Abe, including *The Face of Another*. In it, Abe argues for a gap between life and language that implies the novelist is in no position to expect concrete social results from fiction. "A writer," he says "is a spider that builds its web in the gap between reality and expression." The spider cannot move either wall; it can only weave and reweave a series of fragile connections between the two. In this position, a novelist must surrender both his hope to change the world and his despair when he cannot. Expressing the difficulty of this peculiar detachment, Abe says that "choosing to become a writer means signing a pact with the devil in which you renounce your qualification to be anything else" (*AZ* 20:87–88).

Most of these published interpretations of *The Face of Another* center on the narrator's success or failure, but do not give much attention to the wife or the ideal of fiction that she expresses. Abe's comments seem to offer more hope for literature than Ōe's, but even Abe is resigned about fiction's power. Even "Keshigomu de kaku" is still less optimistic about fiction than my own interpretation of the wife's letter. But these critics are wrong, I think, in dismissing the wife's solution. Despite the narrator's apparent frustration with writing, the end of the novel urges us to hold out hope for fiction. In fact, the ending suggests that the narrator himself cannot dismiss the hope of fiction so easily. There is a key scene earlier in the novel that takes place in a movie theater, but the reader is never told very much about the movie. Later the narrator talks to his wife about the film, but he does not go into any details. Now on the very last pages of the novel (after the wife's letter and the narrator's decision to reject society, but before the final scene that depicts him lying in wait), the narrator spends several pages describing the film. This final return to fantasy shows the novel's sympathy with the wife's argument.

Another Side of Fiction, and One Side of Love

The movie, which Abe gives the title *One Side of Love* (*Ai no katagawa*), is about a young girl scarred over one side of her face. In some ways, the plot parallels the narrator's own life, and the way the film ends, with the girl's suicide, is also dark. But the fiction of the movie nevertheless achieves a settled wholeness that the reality of the narrator's life cannot.

When the narrator finishes his account of the movie, he rejects that closure, seeing in it the girl's defeat. His assessment also expresses a certain disdain for fiction itself: "People seem to think the story of the ugly duckling can be neatly tied up with a swan song" (*AZ* 18:493). And critics, by concentrating on the final image of the narrator clutching the pistol and lying in wait, have tended to dismiss the hopefulness of the movie and the wife's letter as readily as the narrator does. But the positioning of this long fictional interlude at the very end of the novel, together with its particular style, suggest that it deserves a closer look.

Even before we know any details of the film, it is already firmly associated with fiction. The association begins much earlier in the white notebook, in the scene where the narrator finds his way into the cinema. The darkened theater is compared with "an endless tunnel" through which the narrator will escape to a "world of eternal night" described in fairy tale images. Despite this foregrounding of the fiction, the narrator becomes transfixed by the correspondence or "collusion" between the love scene played out on the screen and the actions of a couple making out in the seats in front of him (*AZ* 18:365–66). This sets the stage for the correspondence between the movie and the narrator's own life.

When the plot of the movie is revealed on the novel's final pages, it is something like a fictionalization of the narrator's experience, but with a number of differences that turn it from bitter to bittersweet. Like the narrator, the heroine of the movie is apparently a victim of technology, an atomic bomb survivor. But unlike him she is only scarred on the right side of her face; the left side is beautiful. The focus of the narrator's retelling is the closing scenes of the film, when the girl and her brother take a trip to the seashore. At night, the girl begs her brother to kiss her; they have sex; and the next morning the girl leaves her brother's still form and goes out to the beach. After she is gone, the brother, who was only pretending to be asleep, goes to the window and watches her swim farther and farther out to sea until she disappears forever.

The narrator's account of the film is more cinematic than this brief summary: rather than summarize the plot, he paints several key scenes from the movie. (Abe's experience as a screenwriter emerges clearly here.) By this point in the novel, the reader can only feel relief when the narrator's relentlessly technical and analytical language gives way to this sustained "fantasy," and the change to a more visual style emphasizes the shift. (Here we should note that *The Face of Another* itself was made into a movie, scripted by Abe and directed by Teshigahara Hiroshi. As a film within a film, *One Side of Love* receives particular attention in Abe's script and Teshigahara's film. Abe's collaborations with Teshigahara are discussed in the following chapter.)

The movie plot inverts the narrator's situation in several ways: while the element of sexual trespass is the same, the threat of violence (rape) is replaced by a taboo desire (incest). Sexual love is transposed onto sibling love, and man and woman switch places. The movie ends in death, but it is suicide rather than murder. Each of these changes rounds the movie's edges a little bit in comparison with the narrator's life. Finally it attains a lyric beauty and a pathos that the narrator's own story lacks.

The effect is like the final "Blueprint" section of *Inter Ice Age 4*, which depicts the terrors of the future (a sunken, deserted Tokyo) in beautiful, visual, poetic images. Chapter 3 discussed the "Blueprint" section as the final step in the inversion of a cut-and-dried scientific language and the uncertain language of fiction. But that inversion and fictional uncertainty bring some stability as well: the poetry of the final scene gives *Inter Ice Age 4*'s violent conclusion a sense of order and closure that it would otherwise lack. *The Face of Another* concludes on a similar note. Finally, the narrator's technical and psychological analyses desert him, and he has nowhere to turn but to the parable of fiction. In the end, only that parable promises to impart any meaning to his situation.

Faced with the bleak conclusions of both novels, perhaps this aestheticization is the only real consolation, the novelist's substitute for the "hope" he has forsworn. But if, as Abe suggested, one of the roles of fiction is to stage the difficult and frightening attack on common sense that will make way for a revolution in thought, then one could say that the last-minute recourse to aestheticization flinches away from the consequences of the unadulterated idea and lapses back into conventional sentimentalism. Some critics have called Abe to task for this, saying in effect that Abe has reneged on what he himself characterized as the writer's "pact with the devil," that he has refused to face the idea squarely and surrender both hope and despair (Satō Yasumasa 110–11; Sukegawa 99–100). So perhaps the narrator's rejection of the movie is a final attempt to avoid this pitfall, to reject sentimentalism and face back up to the problem of the other.

Thomas Schnellbächer sees a transition from Abe's early hopefulness to the resignation reflected in his essay about writing with an eraser, which was written after Abe's split with the Japanese Communist Party in 1962 and after the decline of the optimistic progressivism that characterized the immediate postwar period. But Schnellbächer argues that we can resolve the role of rationalism and emotionalism in Abe's work, pointing out that in Abe's essay "Shin kiroku shugi no teishō" (A case for neo-documentarism, 1958), the author rejects stereotypical emotional reactions such as identification and catharsis as Pavlovian responses that lack any power to destabilize the everyday. Abe also seeks to re-harness the energy or "spasms" of emotions such as laughter and tears as a force that can bring about the changes that stereotyped emotions cannot (*Strategist* 406–7).

Written in 1964, *The Face of Another* clearly finds itself divided between writerly resignation and idealism's hope (or despair). In the novel, however, that hope is not altogether in vain. I would argue that the wife's letter and the description of the film together offer something more than sentimentalism. They suggest a constructive role for fiction in giving shape and meaning to the understanding of life. Perhaps this is the spasm of which Abe speaks. If in one sense fiction cannot change anything in the world, it can change our understanding of the world, and that may be enough.

Between the Cracks: Abe and the Slipstream Revisited

Even for those who regard the hope or consolation of this novel's conclusion as too conventional, the novel is certainly not conventional science fiction. To repeat a point made earlier, Abe's novels from the 1960s incorporated specific devices or premises drawn from science fiction (or detective fiction), but by and large they did not adhere to the conventions of these genres. Here it is interesting to supplement the previous chapter's discussion of Abe and Murakami Ryū with one more comparison, between *The Face of Another* and another contemporary slipstream novel, Murakami Haruki's *Hard-Boiled Wonderland and the End of the World* (*Sekai no owari to hādo boirudo wandārando*, 1985). Murakami Haruki's novel is also split between two different voices: the odd-numbered chapters take place in a science fictional world in which the operatives of "the System" battle the agents of "the Factory" in an information war. The narrator is a "Calcutec," a Philip Marlowe–like operator whose brain has been modified to encrypt and transport System data in an effort to keep it out of the hands of the Factory. The even-numbered chapters, however, tell a completely different story, a fantasy narrated by a figure who arrives at a mysterious walled city with no memory of his past and surrenders his shadow and a portion of his eyesight to become a "Dreamreader." He spends his nights in a strange library extracting memories from the skulls of dead unicorns.

The alternation of the science fictional chapters with the fantasy chapters repeats Abe's alternation or juxtaposition of scientific and fantastic styles. And Murakami's text moves toward an apocalyptic conclusion that is not unlike *Inter Ice Age 4*: halfway through the novel, the Calcutec narrator discovers that his brain contains an information bomb that will detonate in just over a day and bring about a disaster described as "the end of the world." There is even a race of aquan-like subhumans (*yamiguro* or "INKlings") who live in a watery subterranean kingdom and threaten the humans above. And there is a redeeming role for music similar to the one in *Inter Ice Age 4* or Ryū's *Coin Locker Babies*: a scientist tells the Calcutec narrator that "sound is of no use to human evolution" and that future generations of humans will neither hear nor speak. When the narrator replies that a world without birdsong or music would be "bleak," the scientist's reply is right out of Abe: "Don't blame me," he says. "That's evolution. Evolution's always hard. Hard and bleak" (49). (The scientist's experiments in sound and evolution involve examining the resonant properties of hundreds of animal skulls, including one with a single horn emerging from its forehead; this is the first obvious link to the narrative in the even-numbered chapters, but the parallels accumulate as the novel moves toward its surprising conclusion.) As Jay Rubin points out in *Murakami Haruki and the Music of Words*, the soullessness of the walled city is also characterized by an absence of music, and when the Dreamreader manages to recall a song near the end of the novel, he breathes life into the city (Rubin 126–27).

In a tour-de-force ending, the two worlds of Murakami's novel come together when the two narrators are revealed to be two sides of the same person, not unlike Abe's chemist and the mask. The "hard-boiled wonderland" is his life in the outside world, a life grounded in science and technology. That life ends on the novel's final page, when the data bomb in his head goes off and triggers a catatonic state in which he can do nothing but dream of himself in the walled city. In a time reversal worthy of Abe, the final chapter of the Calcutec's story is effectively the prelude to the first chapter of the Dreamreader's, and the numerous little parallels that emerge between the two stories are explained as the latter's fight to regain his memory—though even when he does, he ultimately chooses to remain in the dream world. As in *The Crime of S. Karma*, "the end of the world" is finally not an event but a location, a place of ambiguous possibility. And like *The Face of Another*, Murakami's novel is about becoming lost in an internal fiction and struggling back toward some connection with the other, or toward some compromise between productive dreaming and waking reality.

Susan Napier compares *The Face of Another* explicitly with *Hard-Boiled Wonderland and the End of the World* in the way both shift the focus from an outside alien to an inside one. For Napier, this represents a shift of the kind stated at the outset of this chapter: from fears about the broad effects of modernity and technology on society, to fears about the way they alter more intimate relations between the self and other (93–138, 209–14). Because the Dreamreader seemingly chooses to remain in the walled city and not wake up, this novel, like much of Murakami Haruki's early work, has inspired debates like the one around *The Face of Another*, about whether fiction represents an impotent withdrawal from productive action.[6]

Despite these many similarities, *Hard-Boiled Wonderland and the End of the World* has a closure that *The Face of Another* and most of Abe's novels lack. Murakami begins with two distinct narratives and slowly brings them together—a device he reports borrowing consciously from science fiction and adventure fiction, even naming Ken Follet as an inspiration (Rubin 130). Murakami's success with this device makes *Hard-Boiled Wonderland and the End of the World* (like *Coin Locker Babies*) successful as a popular adventure novel, though it is a superbly literary one to be sure.

This carefully planned resolution of diametric opposites is in many ways the antithesis of what Abe attempted in *The Face of Another* and most of his later work, which emphasizes a disjunction of styles or narratives rather than their synthesis, and which borrows genre conventions only to violate them. Tatsumi Takayuki describes this goal of Abe's as the "breakdown of language," and "reactivating a language which could plot the deconstruction of contemporary rhetoric itself" ("Hakobunejō" 75). *The Face of Another* frustrates the expectations of science fiction in this way, just as Abe's novel *The Ruined Map* had done for detective fiction two years earlier. That novel relates a detective's search for a missing man, a search that uncovers one tantalizing clue after another but never leads to the expected revelation or conclusion. Instead of finding the missing man, the detective eventually disappears himself.

At a colloquium at Stanford University in 1992, Murakami talked about the process of writing *Hard-Boiled Wonderland and the End of the World* and his anxiety about whether he could pull these two threads together. He said he felt relief and a new sense of confidence when he wrote the unicorn into both narratives, and he pointed out that many readers experience a similar relief when they encounter the unicorns and realize the worlds are connected. For Abe's readers, there are no unicorns. If Murakami Haruki and Murakami Ryū have followed Abe in the way they combine the literary novel with science fiction and detective fiction, they respect the conventions of these genres and work within them far more than Abe, who adopted them early on because they were still pliable and ill-formed, and borrowed them later for the energy they could generate when shattered. If Abe was spinning his

web in the gap between fiction and reality, he also kept himself deliberately in the cracks between established genres. Abe's unwillingness to
obey the rules of these popular genres is one reason that he has remained less popular with general readers than either Murakami. (For all
its supposedly "arresting" imagery, *Coin Locker Babies* is a page-turner;
it is telling that *The Face of Another* remains a much more difficult read.)

Put another way, the difficulty (and sometimes unpopularity) of
Abe's prose could be seen as a direct result of the tension between languages and styles and ideas—a tension that Abe wanted to maintain
rather than resolve. This is taken up again in Chapters 6 and 7 in the
context of Abe's later novels.

The Face of Another *as Dialogic Novel*

We have seen how the narrator of *The Face of Another* tries to maintain
a precarious balance between several different styles (scientific, imaginative, and psychological) in an effort to form and organize his inner
world and communicate something of that world to another outside
himself. It is impossible for the narrator to define who he is without
some reference to that other. But how exactly are these two things related—the need to reconcile conflicting languages within oneself and
the need to communicate with another person outside? For the narrator, the connection between the two is a fundamental but largely unexamined premise of the notebooks: if he can succeed in explaining
himself to his wife, it will ratify that explanation of what he is. The act
of communication, in other words, will justify his own version of himself. When the wife rejects his explanations and denies him, it does
more than simply force him to admit he was wrong about a few things.
She has shaken the foundation of everything that he understood (everything he wrote and read) himself to be. Without that link to the other,
his very existence is threatened.

A scheme for relating these two spheres—style and communication—is provided by Bakhtin's idea of dialogue. We have already seen
that for Bakhtin, dialogue refers not only to the conversations between
people but to the conversations between different styles within a text.
But Bakhtin's dialogue is also an integral part of making the person
or the text what he/she/it is. In fact, this universality of dialogue stems
from Bakhtin's notion that living humans are constituted like texts them-

selves. First, we will lay some groundwork by comparing Bakhtin's idea of heteroglossia with the competition of styles in *The Face of Another*, and by weighing Bakhtin's idea of carnival against the world of Abe's mask. Then we will see how the narrator's internal and interpersonal conversations can be related through more complex dialogic processes that are often glossed over in superficial invocations of Bakhtin. These are the processes that Bakhtin identified as "ideological becoming" and "consummation."

In the previous chapter, we applied Bakhtin's idea of heteroglossia to *Inter Ice Age 4* and saw that Bakhtin's broad notion of discourse linked the collision or combination of different voices in the text with a tension between groups or ideas in society. As Bakhtin says, "discourse . . . is language in its concrete living totality," and "Any stylistics capable of dealing with the novel as a genre must be a sociological stylistics" (*Problems* 181; *Dialogic* 300). Likewise in *The Face of Another*, the fate of scientific language in the text is tied up with the role of science and technology in Japanese society in 1964, when the novel was published.

One obvious issue at that time was nuclear proliferation. The world's first nuclear test ban treaty went into effect the previous year, prompted by the Cuban missile crisis the year before that. Japan's nuclear energy program was also well under way: Japan's first commercial nuclear power plant, Tōkai, was nearing completion, and commercial electricity production was only two years away. Japan was on the threshold of its own nuclear age. Of course, in another sense the nuclear age had already dawned dramatically and terribly for Japan just nineteen years earlier at Hiroshima. The novel makes this connection plain by noting that the massive keloid scars caused by the narrator's lab accident are also an emblem of atomic bomb victims. The heroine of the film described at the end of the novel is a survivor of Hiroshima, so through her the narrator's fate is connected explicitly with the nuclear threat. In *The Face of Another*, the mask represents a technology like this, where the excess freedom and power imparted by science threaten to spill over into violence or dangerous unpredictability.

Bakhtin allows for the objectification and manipulation of literary as well as technical languages within the novel, and the mask's language contains a critique of certain literary styles as well. The psychological language of the narrator's confession could be seen as an exaggeration of the language in the Japanese I-novel, and Abe's text suggests the view that the confessional mode of the I-novel, like the narrator's self-revelations, can easily tend toward self-indulgence. Abe addresses this specifically in the essay "Keshigomu de kaku," where he says that the "gap between reality and expression" makes it impossible to "turn life into a work a fiction," as some authors have attempted (*AZ* 20:87). Abe's essay makes this criticism of both naive social realism and the confessional mode of the I-novelists.

Actually, the ideas of Naturalist realism that were so influential in the formation of the I-novel and other literary traditions in Japan were closely allied with the scientific impulse. In "The Experimental Novel," the father of Naturalism Émile Zola attempts to forge a "literature of our scientific age" by rethinking writing as a laboratory science like physics or chemistry (23). Zola based his essay on the physiologist Claude Bernard's *An Introduction to the Study of Experimental Medicine*, saying "it will be but necessary for me to replace the word doctor [in Bernard's text] with the word novelist, to make my meaning clear and to give it the rigidity of a scientific truth" (1–2).

In Zola's scheme, the novel is an "experiment" devised by its author, wherein he or she establishes premises about the characters, sets events in motion, and "observes" the results. Through repeated experiments of this sort, the novelist becomes able to generalize about the deterministic factors that govern individual and social behavior. In this way, says Zola, the novelist "should operate on the characters, the passions, on the human and social data, in the same way that the chemist and the physicist operate on inanimate beings, and as the physiologist operates on living beings" (18).[7]

In fact, the strongly fantastic element that runs through Abe's fiction may be seen to critique the desire of both science and fiction for transparent language. Abe's novels are a reaction not only against the cut-and-dried view of the world sometimes associated with science, but also against the naive idea that writing can fully illuminate any reality, either the natural world outside or the inside of a person. In comments made at the time of the novel's publication, Abe says:

It is a conviction of Romanticism that by stripping away the masks of social position, belief, et cetera, you can find the true person underneath. I suppose it begins more or less with Rousseau. But later philosophy has rejected this idea, hasn't it? [. . .] The relationship between two people is neither true nor false, but a performance that can never be stripped away. If so, the wife is right to continue the performance willingly, even though she knows about the mask; the protagonist is too Romantic. (*AZ* 19:18)

As discussed briefly in the last chapter, for Bakhtin one device that permits all these styles and their different world views to come together is the carnival double. Even better than the prediction machine or the aquans, the mask embodies the elements that define this figure. It is the narrator's alter ego: it reflects him like Bakhtin's "system of crooked mirrors," inverting or parodying his weaknesses, active where he is passive, strong where he is weak (*Problems* 127). The mask is a juxtaposition of opposites that meet in dialogue but that sometimes threaten to cancel or annihilate one another. As such, it expresses the risk that Bakhtin associates with carnival—the threat of death or murder, the danger that it will, like the prediction machine and the aquans, blot out its original.

The mask also inhabits an atmosphere of possibility that Bakhtin links with carnival literature. For Bakhtin, fantasy expands the ground for the combination and exploration of different kinds of thought, creating "extraordinary situations for the provoking and testing of a philosophical idea." Bakhtin identifies this fantasy both with insanity and with dreams. The "fantastic logic of dreams" combines with the "ambivalent logic" of carnival to help us transcend the limits of conventional thinking. "The dream is introduced there precisely as the possibility of a completely different life, a life organized according to laws different from those governing ordinary life" (*Problems* 114, 168, 147). If we translated "ordinary life" as *nichijō* (Abe's "everyday"), these words of Bakhtin's could easily have been spoken by Abe or his narrator. The fantasy of the mask overleaps the narrow technical logic of its construction and comes to embody the radical, even frightening power of a fiction that suspends conventional rules. And the mask's new logic expresses itself in daydreams, waking fantasies, and aberrant thoughts.

It is important to note, however, that for Bakhtin this process of deconstructing received common sense was to be followed by a process of reconstructing one's own beliefs, using the building blocks of language. In "Discourse in the Novel," he argues that the process of forming one's own beliefs (what he calls "ideological becoming") consists first of recognizing that the words of others are not unadorned truth, but ideological expressions, "specific points of view on the world." Next, one must choose from among these a language that is "internally persuasive" for oneself, distinguishing it from what is merely the received word of "authority" (*Dialogic* 291, 342–43).

The carnival figure with the special ability to relativize and sort through languages in this manner is a figure Bakhtin calls the clown. The clown is able to try on different languages, but never in complete seriousness, with an irony that illuminates the things for which each language stands. The clown, Bakhtin says, "is a rogue who dons the mask of a fool in order to motivate distortions and shufflings of languages and labels, thus unmasking them by not understanding them. . . . the clown is the one who has the right to speak in otherwise unacceptable languages and the right to maliciously distort languages that are acceptable" (*Dialogic* 405).

One clown in *The Face of Another* is certainly the mask. Under its influence, the authority of scientific language (one of Bakhtin's "acceptable languages") is distorted and undermined. The mask speaks in the "unacceptable language" of violence, as a beginning to the process of changing society. Its plastic face is a deception that reveals deception, a mask that unmasks something else, just as Bakhtin says. But the mask in *The Face of Another* seems to lack the clown's other ability—the power to choose from among different languages and world views to arrive at a personal style that reflects his own ideas and ideals. Bakhtin says the hero of any novel must have the clown's constructive as well as destructive powers. The clown/hero's ability to try on new languages freely is the prelude to his "becoming" a full person, part of the "ideological and linguistic initiative necessary to change the nature of his own image" (*Dialogic* 33–38).

In *The Face of Another*, the narrator's struggle to balance different languages (and to choose one that will speak to his wife) is just such a struggle toward ideological becoming, but ultimately he seems to fail. The wife, on the other hand, becomes the novel's most successful clown. She outmasks the mask by seeing through the narrator's fictions and donning a mask of her own. She joins the play in a role of her own devising, and writes one of the final scenes herself. Like the clown, she unmasks the fictions of language, tames them, and from those fictions she forges a style for herself.

There is another facet of ideological becoming that Bakhtin called "consummation," which involves not just a single character but interaction with another, and which suggests why the narrator of *The Face of Another* needs so badly to justify himself to his wife. Bakhtin says "The ideological becoming of a human being . . . is the process of selectively assimilating the words of others" (*Dialogic* 341), so that the hero(ine) must possess a willingness to listen to and accept some words from outside him or herself. Such works as *Problems of Dostoevsky's Poetics* and "Author and Hero in Aesthetic Activity" exhaustively outline this Bakhtinian idea that it is only through dialogue with the other that we can become whole ourselves.

Bakhtin's book-length essay "Author and Hero in Aesthetic Activity" (collected in the volume *Art and Answerability*) begins in the visual realm, with the observation that I cannot see all of my own body. Drawing on German Idealistic philosophy and prefiguring some arguments of phenomenology, Bakhtin then extends the argument into the realm of time and meaning: since I am always striving toward my own goals and the future realization of those goals, it is impossible for me to perceive myself as whole and complete. Only another person outside me can consummate me—that is, appreciate my completeness and my whole perfection in the present moment. And so it is only vicariously, through that other, that I can experience the contentment of my own completeness.

For Bakhtin, the model of consummation is the author writing a hero, but the same process also occurs outside texts, where we are all authored by the people around us. In the most general terms, Bakhtin's hero is not limited to fiction, but is simply the aesthetic image I form of a character or a real human being in my own mind, when I contemplate a person in his or her wholeness. In this way "the boundary between a human being (the condition for aesthetic vision) and a hero (the object of aesthetic vision) often becomes unstable" (*Art* 228).

For the human being or the hero, there is a characteristically Bakhtinian tension between the poles of ideological becoming and consummation, that is between the need to select one's own language and author oneself, and the necessity of being completed by another. In novels, this "vicious circle" produces a dialogue between the hero and the reader or author, in which the hero struggles to justify himself to these others upon whom he is dependent. It was for this highest degree of dialogue that Bakhtin reserved his term "polyphony" (*Problems* 204–37).

In a novel, the stylistic result of this is a narrator who continually anticipates the objections of his reader, or who seems to escape authorial control. Abe's chemist is just such a figure. Clearly his narrative is torn between the desire for self-justification and the hope for acceptance and forgiveness. But as his confessions, justifications, and explanations pile up, the urgently rambling narrative gathers a momentum that even author Abe seems powerless to resist. More than one critic contends that the novel winds on against its better interests, getting away from Abe in the same way that the fiction of the mask gets away from the chemist.[8] Others cast the lack of authorial control in a more positive light. When the narrator puts down his pen in the final scene and says "From this point on, nothing more will be written down," he dissolves or escapes the written frame of the story, taking his fate out of the author's hands. We have already seen that Ōe Kenzaburō sees in this act the promise of individual (possibly political, revolutionary) action. Whether they identify it as a fault or merit, then, all these critics call attention to the narrator hero's liberation from an authorial or textual master plan.

A Final Dialogue: Abe and Bakhtin

Appropriately for our context, the idea of consummation and the importance of an outside perspective can also be applied to two cultures. Bakhtin says, "In the realm of culture, outsideness is a most powerful factor in understanding. It is only in the eyes of *another* culture that foreign culture reveals itself fully and profoundly" (*Speech* 7). But in spite of the obvious differences between the Japanese literary context and Bakhtin's predominantly European one, Bakhtin's world evidently has a great deal in common with Abe's. These correspondences between Abe and Bakhtin should not surprise us. Critics such as Komori Yōichi in Japan and James Fujii in America have argued that Japanese fiction can be read in Bakhtinian terms.[9] These writers have used a range of arguments to make this connection, from the historical influence of Russian literature in Meiji Japan to the fundamentally intertextual quality of Japanese literature since the Heian period.

The fundamental idea that links Bakhtin with Abe is simply that both writers portray people as beings woven from language. Ultimately, it is at this level that Bakhtin adds to our understanding of Abe. Individual points like the conflict of dialects and its link with the position of science in society, or the mask's position as a double to the narrator, or the tension between self-determination and submitting to the other— each of these is something that a sensitive reading of the novel could uncover without reference to Bakhtin. But what Bakhtin's understanding of dialogue provides is a powerful scheme to relate all these with one another, culminating in the link between the issue of style and the problem of identity. Bakhtin shows us that despite its evident theme of self and other, despite its detailed psychology, *The Face of Another* is first and last a novel about language.

The conclusion that we are beings constituted from language is often associated with the more radical poststructuralist idea that the self is nothing more than a creation or accretion of the discourses that swirl around it. For example, James Fujii has associated these more radical arguments with Bakhtin and applied them to Japanese fiction. Fujii's *Complicit Fictions* discusses subject formation in nineteenth-century Japanese fiction, and the impression many critics have of the "flawed realism" in a number of these works. Following Karatani Kōjin, Fujii says our (Western) idea of the subject is not universal, but that it was promoted by the Japanese state in the Meiji era to further national policies of modernization and Westernization. Japanese authors alternately resisted and abetted this project, giving rise to a partial but ultimately incomplete adoption of the Western subject, and the impression later critics had of flawed characterization. Fujii's argument views the subject not as something transcendental or universal but as something constituted by the political and literary discourses of the time, and he associates Bakhtin and Komori with this critical attack on the essential subject. Ideas such as Bakhtin's "ideological becoming," for example, are read to suggest that the Bakhtinian subject is constructed largely or entirely from a contest of ideological texts.

The difficulty of reconciling these ideas with notions of individual dignity, agency, and responsibility has sometimes lent these conclusions a pessimistic cast. Despite Bakhtin's frequent association with these poststructuralist arguments, though, arguably neither he nor Abe carry the argument to the point where discourse entirely eclipses the self. In fact, the continuing popularity of Bakhtin in the West and Abe in Japan might be traced partly to the fact that they can both be read as occupying a middle ground between the naive notion of an inner essence conveyed through transparent language to the outside world, and the ostensibly debilitating conclusion that there is nothing before language, nothing outside the text.

In the context of *The Face of Another*, the controversy over whether there is any reality outside of language corresponds to a fundamental question about the story: is anything real for Abe's narrator beyond his notebooks? As the power to master or destabilize identity and "reality" spills over from technology into language itself, the possibility emerges that the narrator does not exist in any meaningful way outside his own text. There are hints that the world outside the claustrophobic space of the notebooks is so distorted in the narrator's description as to be finally irrelevant. Once we have an indication of just how wrong he has been about his wife, doubts arise about other things he describes as certain or real. Was anyone ever fooled by the mask, even momentarily? Is his face really so terribly scarred? Is the air gun he buys in a hobby store anything more than a toy? How much of what he describes is just a daydream? And even if the narrator does inhabit a stable reality and identity of his own, can he ever penetrate the veil of language in order to express something of himself to the outside, to his wife?

For Abe's narrator, the question of whether there is anything outside of the text may be one of degree, but we could perhaps boil it down to this: after the competing discourses are stripped away, how much of the "self" is left? Is there an irreducible core as Bakhtin seems to suggest, a soul or editor that picks and chooses the language of the self? Or is the self just a shell that is filled out by the discourses of science, psychology, and fiction that circulate around it, while it remains powerless to resist? And is there anything like an objective truth in this work before and beyond the differing world views of competing languages?

Despite their visions of humans as beings of language, both Bakhtin and Abe leave room for something like a human core or truth, at least for readers who seek these out. For example, while Bakhtin's aesthetic language is dialogic, he also allows for more transparent monologic language—journalistic language, which conveys a clearer meaning about an evident reality. Most real language, Bakhtin suggests, falls somewhere on a continuum between the aesthetic and journalistic ideals (*Problems* 95, 185–99). Furthermore, while Bakhtin expresses the idea that personality emerges only through dialogue between people and styles, the idea of consummating another through aesthetic dialogue seems to be more about examining language to discover the truth of another than it is about creating that truth out of the whole cloth of language. Finally, Bakhtin is careful to maintain that the need for a multiplicity of perspectives to generate meaning does not assume that truth or reality itself is multiple. "It is quite possible to imagine and postulate a unified truth that requires a plurality of consciousnesses," Bakhtin says, "one that . . . is born at a point of contact among various consciousnesses" (*Problems* 81).

In the same way, Abe's novel maintains a careful balance between the weight of the narrator's internal, textual world and the weight of the world outside. The notebooks never lose their sense of a strong human presence behind the words—a presence that seems to be charged with too much affect, consequence, and (im)morality to become an empty vessel for language. Likewise, at various points the novel reaches beyond the world of its own language to address issues outside the text— the issues of race and nuclear proliferation touched on above, for example. Reflecting this balance between the world inside and outside the work, criticism dealing with the novel has been equally divided between interpretations that emphasize social issues raised by the novel and those that focus on more personal ontological ones.[10]

In other words, Abe's novel recognizes a gap between language and the world, but it does not give up on the real world altogether. This is the same compromise indicated by Abe's characterization of the novelist as a spider spinning its web in that gap, a web that will connect expression with reality, however tenuously. Language can never reflect the world exactly, Abe says. "But that doesn't mean the spider is unmindful of reality. Reality is after all one wall of its crevice" (*AZ* 20:88).

When all is said and done, *The Face of Another* is a novel about the attempt to reach beyond oneself and make a connection with another. The struggle may be difficult, doomed, or abandoned, but it is not something to be dismissed out of hand. As tense or distorted as the relation with that other may be, he or she cannot be ignored. That is why this struggle is rehearsed so obsessively throughout the novel, and indeed in almost all of Abe's work. Though *The Face of Another* traces the decaying connection with others, that decay is not complete. The suspense over the fate of that connection is the novel's *raison d'être*, and the tension that drives the tale.

FIVE

The Hope of Technology and the Technology of Hope in The Woman in the Dunes

Abe's best-known novel internationally is one that has less overt scientific content than either *Inter Ice Age 4* or *The Face of Another*. It is *The Woman in the Dunes*, a strange fable about an insect collector who takes a holiday trip to a remote part of the Japanese sea coast, where he is kidnapped by the residents of an odd village and imprisoned with a village woman in a house at the bottom of a sand pit. The novel came to the attention of readers around the world partly because of a celebrated film version scripted by Abe and directed by artist and filmmaker Teshigahara Hiroshi. The film portrayed the sand dunes and the physical tension and intimacy between the characters with such stark drama that it earned a Special Jury Prize at the 1964 Cannes Film Festival. Many translations of the novel followed. Within four years it was available in over a dozen different languages, and it was eventually translated into more than 30.[1]

The 1960s represented Abe's most successful period as a novelist. *The Woman in the Dunes* appeared in 1962, *The Ruined Map* followed two years later, and *The Face of Another* two years after that. During this time, Abe collaborated with Teshigahara to bring all three of these works to the screen. *The Woman in the Dunes* offers a chance to test and expand the reading of Abe pursued in earlier chapters. The novel and film have generated more criticism, in Japanese and English, than any of Abe's other works, and readings have settled into some established patterns, so it interesting to ask whether more attention to the dialogue between science and fiction will yield different conclusions. Furthermore, the visual dimension supplied by the film opens up some new issues, particularly when one considers that film itself was a kind of experimental technology for figures such as Abe and Teshigahara.

We can preview the visual issues by noting that the reading of *The Face of Another* suggested in the previous chapter does not easily apply to the film version of that novel. If the book is a kind of internal dialogue that traces the competition between the narrator's different selves, on film this internal conversation is much harder to represent. It has to be externalized. At the beginning of the film, there is a scene that encapsulates this movement from interior to exterior dialogue. Just after the opening credits, we are presented with a sagittal x-ray of a man's skull, and as we watch, it begins to move and speak (Figure 5.1). We are watching a live x-ray movie of the scarred chemist as he talks to the examining doctor off screen. In the film, it is this doctor who will build the mask, and who comes to represent the perspective of science and technology, while the patient's personality slowly fuses with the fiction of the mask. The initial x-ray image seems to reflect the novel's desire to get inside the protagonist's head (and also recalls the necropsy and personality reconstruction scenes in *Inter Ice Age 4*). But the film cannot maintain that perspective, and it ultimately gives us a conversation between two separate characters instead. The discussions, arguments, and eventually the physical conflict between these two figures portray a battle of ideas, but it is a conflict that leaves behind the novel's notion of self-realization by forging a personal language or style.

We will see a similar state of affairs in *The Woman in the Dunes*. The Western reception of the novel has been colored by the film, but there is a salient gap between the film and the book. In the novel, there is a sense of internal dialogue and competing voices that is easy to miss if one is too influenced by the film, or indeed by the English translation, which smoothes over this sense of multiple voices in favor of a single, unified narrative voice. By getting out of the man's head, the film focuses much more equally on both characters, the man and the woman. This is in contrast to many of Abe's novels, where the woman is only a hazy presence or cipher that the reader sees through the man's distorting

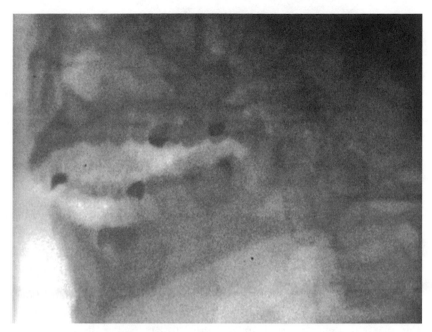

Figure 5.1 An image from the film version of *The Face of Another*, which opens with an x-ray movie of the protagonist's skull as he describes the accident that scarred his face. (Images from the films in this chapter are captured from the Criterion Collection DVDs released in the United States and are reproduced by permission of Janus Films.)

perspective. If *The Face of Another* portrayed conflict, the film version of *The Woman in the Dunes* portrays a kind of community between the man and the woman. One could argue that the original novel is already more optimistic about community than Abe's other works, but the film takes this optimism a step further.

The dark note struck by *The Face of Another* stems from the dilemma of how to reach out to the other without becoming entangled in the logic of the collective. All of Abe's narrators face this problem, but some novels resolve it less bleakly than others, and *The Woman in the Dunes* may have the most hopeful ending. Over the course of the novel, the man makes several unsuccessful attempts to flee the sand pit, but near the end he succeeds in inventing a device that extracts drinking water from the sand, which he hopes will reduce his dependence on the villagers and the daily ration of water they lower into the pit as an incentive to work. On the final pages, he is actually able to climb out of the pit and has a chance to escape, but he forgoes it. Except for a brief postscript, the narrative ends there. Not all critics read this positively, but some have argued that it represents the man's healthy acceptance of the woman and a place in this new community, or perhaps a self-discovery that escapes the everyday logic of the collective and brings him a kind of internal freedom and independence that makes his physical imprisonment irrelevant.

Some of the dominant extant readings of the novel are discussed below, but this chapter argues that most of them fail to give enough attention to the role of science and technology in the story. Attention to these issues and to the role of dialogue sheds considerable light on the ending and how sanguine it really is about the possibility of life in the collective. I will argue that *The Woman in the Dunes* is in fact one of Abe's more optimistic novels, but not for the reasons most critics adduce. This chapter examines the internal dialogues of the protagonist—dialogues cut out of the film and suppressed in the English translation—as a counterpart to his conversations with the woman. They reveal a figure who is much more solipsistic and internally fragmented than the film or the English translation of the novel convey—a figure unable to connect with the other for much of the story. We have seen that technology often exerts a destabilizing effect on language and communication in Abe's other novels; however, in *The Woman in the Dunes* technology is not an obstacle to communication but the ground on which the man and woman eventually meet. Ultimately this is the optimism at the heart of the work. In particular, the water gathering device built by the protagonist becomes a site of communication, making it one of the most hopeful technologies depicted in any of Abe's works.

In the way it portrays a different side of technology from *Inter Ice Age 4* or *The Face of Another*, this novel may reveal Abe's hope that revolutions in communication like television might actually give birth to a revolutionary art that was genuinely popular. This provides a chance to discuss Abe's own experiments with mass media (including radio, television, video, and film) as efforts to find that technological pathway to another, broader audience. This chapter argues that the movie version of *The Woman in the Dunes* comes off even more optimistically than the book because the camera and film actually constitute a technology like the water trap, a ground on which the two separate characters can meet and communicate.

Community and Identity in The Woman in the Dunes

The protagonist of *The Woman in the Dunes* is known through most of the book simply as "the man" (*otoko*). He is a kind of scientist, a school teacher whose hobby is insect collecting, and he travels to the dunes on the Japan sea coast in search of a particular genus of beetle. Based on his knowledge of sand, the man believes that the dunes may conceal an as-yet-undiscovered species of this beetle. His speculations are the source of several detailed discussions of the geology and ecology of the sand dunes at the beginning of the novel.

The man's careful plans take an unexpected turn when he comes across a surreal village where the houses are located inside pits 20 or 30 feet deep. The dwellings are all in danger of being buried by the shifting dunes, so the residents are forced to shovel sand away from their houses continually as the tide of sand flows around them. The man is in search of lodging, so he is happy when some villagers invite him to spend the night in a house at the bottom of one of these holes. They introduce him to his host, a young woman who lives alone in the house, and then bid him good night. But in the morning, he finds that the rope ladder he used to climb down into the pit has been removed, and he has become a prisoner, kidnapped to help the woman shovel. The woman is a half-willing participant: she colludes with the villagers to kidnap the man, but she never leaves the pit either, and the two of them suffer together when the villagers withhold water to punish the man for refusing to work. She tells the man that she is trapped by circumstances: since her husband died, she has been unable to keep up with the digging.

The technical information on geology and sandy ecosystems that opens the novel quickly gives way to the strange wonderland of the village. (And yet unexpectedly, Abe based aspects of the story on a real community in Yamagata that was struggling to avoid this kind of burial—an example of how one is never quite sure where the science ends and the fantasy begins in Abe's work [*AZ* 22:124–25].) The first few pages of the novel give a sense of the scientific language that describes the sand, and also how it is transformed into this fantastic metaphor for the human relationships and connections that constitute the subject of the book. So far we have seen many instances of Abe's characteristic segues from scientific to fantastic language, but the opening of *The Woman in the Dunes* contains some of his most finely balanced examples:

Another geology text added an explanation something like this:

All flows, whether of air or water, create turbulence. The minimum wavelength of this turbulence is approximately equal to the diameter of sand grains, and because of this special characteristic, the sand grains will be sorted out and sucked from the soil in a direction perpendicular to the flow. If soil cohesion is weak, air currents too faint to disturb even clay particles (and certainly too weak to move pebbles) can draw sand up into the air and redeposit it elsewhere, transporting it downwind. So the special properties of sand were apparently related to fluid dynamics. [. . .]

This image of flowing sand struck him with a force and excitement he could not describe. The sterile quality of sand traced not just to its dryness, as people believed; it also stemmed from the sand's unceasing flow and the way it rejected attachment by any living thing. How different from our own oppressive reality, which forced people to cling together day in and day out.

Naturally sand was not suited to living things. But was fixedness really so essential for life? Wasn't it actually the persistent desire to remain in place that gave rise to all this odious competition? If people could abandon fixedness and entrust themselves to the flow of the sand, these rivalries would become impossible. In point of fact, flowers bloomed in the sand, and bugs and beasts survived there. These were living things that had used their powers of adaptation to live outside the sphere of competition—like the genus *Cicindela* he was seeking. (*AZ* 16:123)[2]

In this way, the sand becomes a metaphor for a state of atomized freedom, just as the villagers' determination to remain and resist the sand becomes the emblem of society: the desire to remain and cohere, and to keep the protagonist there even against his will. As the story develops, the woman argues the villagers' side, and the man opposes her with his own ideology based on the non-cohering sand. But as the weeks and months pass, he also becomes drawn to the woman and begins a sexual relationship with her. In this, he is like Abe's other protagonists who are tempted out of isolation and back into society by women whose fantastic qualities challenge the protagonists' narrow hermetic rationalities.

As to whether the woman's arguments or fantasies finally win out against the man's, most critics have looked to the story's conclusion for an answer. After months in the hole and more than one unsuccessful escape attempt, on the novel's final pages the man finally gets a perfect chance to leave. One day in the midst of an emergency, the villagers forget or neglect to pull up the ladder, and the man is able to climb out of the hole; but after looking around, he climbs back into the pit, saying that there is no rush to escape. The last two pages of the novel reproduce some court documents dated seven years later. They finally reveal the man's name (Niki Junpei), and confirm what was stated on the novel's opening page: that he was not seen again by his friends or family in the city, and that seven years later he was declared legally dead.[3]

Clearly the man leaves behind his life in the city, and many critics have assumed that to mean he remains indefinitely in the village. Some argue that he stays because he has discovered a new community, if not with the village then at least with the woman, who at the end of the story has become pregnant with his child. William Van Wert voices a common conclusion, that love and family become a source of his self-actualization. "His imprisonment engenders his freedom," Van Wert writes. "Presumed missing and then dead in Tokyo, the man begins to live for the first time. . . . He stays, even when there is every chance to escape, because the woman in the dunes gives him what his wife in Tokyo had never given him: an offspring, a sanctification of sex as pure feeling" (130).

A problem with this reading is that it is not easy to reconcile with Abe's lifelong suspicion of the collective or with the rest of the novel. The man's imprisonment is a perfect emblem for the chafing restrictions the collective imposes on individuals in Abe's other texts, and the sinister, inexorable logic that the woman and the villagers use to justify his kidnapping bears the stamp of the collective rationality that Abe so adamantly opposed. In Abe's other works, the collective and its arbitrary "common sense" are only overcome with difficulty (often violence), and the result is likely to be a lonely freedom. All this makes the conclusion of *The Woman in the Dunes* something of a puzzle for critics. Does the man really join this community, and does this represent a productive reconciliation with the collective, or a cynical defeat for the individual? Are we to see *The Woman in the Dunes* as Abe's most hopeful novel, or his most resigned?

Among the many critics who have viewed the conclusion as genuinely optimistic, some have tried to reconcile it with Abe's broader philosophy by focusing on the woman and distinguishing between her and the other villagers, interpreting the man and woman as a kind of minimum community that provides some constructive and authentic engagement with the other apart from the ideological baggage of broader community.[4] The feminist critic Andrea Dworkin sees a common pattern in *The Woman in the Dunes* and other Abe novels: "The men, civilized, in shells of identity and abstraction, are imprisoned in loneliness, unable to break out of their self-preoccupation. . . . The women are the escape route from mental self-absorption into reality: they are the world, connection, contact, touch, feeling, what is real, the physical, what is true. . . ." (33).

Critics writing in English have tended to resemble Dworkin in their suspicion of the protagonist's scientific leanings, and particularly his language. They have seen the novel as depicting the transition from what they characterize as a narrow scientific rationality that isolates the protagonist, to a broader perspective that allows a kind of self-realization and a real union with the other. Dworkin refers to "shells of identity and abstraction"; for Wimal Dissanayake, "what the novel points out is the imperative need to get out of such a rigid cognitive style as a way of realizing one's self fully" (45); William Currie concludes that "His rational, analytical approach to life is a defense against becoming too closely involved with reality" (17); and William Van Wert writes about "a sex which forges new identity by obliterating rational intellect" (129).

There is a minority of English critics who have viewed the woman more ambivalently. David Pollack (whose reading of *The Woman in the Dunes* was discussed briefly in the Introduction) agrees with the critics above that when the narrator's narrow scientific logic fails, he starts to experience the village as a refuge rather than a prison. But for Pollack, this hardly represents progress: he sees little difference between the language or ideology of science and those of bureaucratic society or traditional community.[5] Susan Napier views the novel as decidedly dystopian, part of a transition from prewar fantasies (in which women represented an escape or oasis from the modern), to a postwar mode where women came to represent the entanglements of modern technology and society. Napier writes, "Women no longer offer any sort of refuge; instead they are part of the web of entrapment which modern society appears to be weaving around its citizens" (54–55).

But some of the best-known studies of Abe in Japanese (including work by Isoda Kōichi, Nakamura Kiyoshi, Sasaki Kiichi, Takano Toshimi, and Watanabe Hiroshi) have downplayed the woman's significance altogether, and interpreted the central struggle of the novel as the struggle of an essentially solitary individual to define himself against the environment or the broader outside universe, rather than within a community of others.[6] Sasaki, for example, compares the protagonist with Robinson Crusoe for the way he carves out an existence in this hostile environment. The woman is relegated to the role of Girl Friday.

Compared with their counterparts writing in English, these Japanese critics are more reluctant to argue for the discovery of a more authentic self. Seeing Abe as an author who sought to break down that kind of essentialism, they have emphasized what Isoda Kōichi called the "plasticity" of the self: the way it adapts to its environment while retaining some basic character, like sand flowing into new shapes. With an eye to Abe's early interest in an existentialism that overturns existing conceptions, these critics see *The Woman in the Dunes* as an attempt to grasp and depict a concrete self and a reality outside the self, but in a way that sheds the prevailing essentialisms and preconceptions about what reality and self are. This is obviously a tall order, but some of these critics have seen Abe's scientific language as helpful to this project. Compared with critics writing in English, they are more willing to take the scientific language (often expressed as the "realism" of Abe's descriptions) at face value, as an attempt to depict a concrete situation or a pressing reality without resorting to other modes of realism that have been discredited. For these critics, the spare, almost sterile or crystalline metaphor of the sand is an attempt to approach this material reality free of any kind of ideological baggage.[7] Sasaki writes: "Abe records the protagonist's battle without resorting to the easy device of allegory but literally, correctly, and scientifically, with a documentary touch. Through that battle with the sand, Abe gradually shows the collapse of the upright citizen's order, preconceived notions, and everyday morals. When at the bottom of the dry pit he discovers water bubbling forth through a kind of capillary action, he also discovers a new self" (143).

These Japanese critics clearly seem to place a bit too much faith in Abe's scientific language when they privilege it as having some more direct connection to physical reality. Yet, some of the critics writing in English are too dismissive of the scientific language. In particular, one might question the conclusion that the man emerges from the solipsism of his own hermetic logic or language and makes a physical connection with the woman that is somehow more fundamental than language, Dworkin's idea that she represents an "escape route from mental self-absorption into reality . . . what is real, the physical, what is true." This may be a viable interpretation of the film, and perhaps even the novel's English translation. But it is a questionable conclusion for the original novel. Below we compare these three versions of the story to see why.

Voices in the Wilderness:
Dialogue in the Novel, the English Translation, and the Film

Many of the published interpretations of *The Woman in the Dunes* fail to take into account the complex texture of voices in the original Japanese and the sense of dialogue, which is critical to this novel no less than Abe's other works. For example, the discussion of sand above is remembered from a "geology text," and the Introduction to the present book discussed a definition of sand that the protagonist quotes from an encyclopedia, as well as some controversy over just what kind of encyclopedia that might be. Other textual fragments include bits of newspaper stories, court documents, and descriptions of visual art. Often these other texts and voices are filtered through the man's consciousness, but at other times we seem to hear the voices of other characters more directly, without any intervention by him or a narrator.

Much of this dialogue is suppressed in the English translation by E. Dale Saunders and the film by Abe and Teshigahara. The English version of this novel is narrated by a voice that seems to have access to the innermost thoughts of the characters. The protagonist is consistently referred to in the third person, as "he" or "the man." This narrative presence is not nearly as consistent in the Japanese, which has many passages that seem to alternate or hang somewhere between the third and first person. There are many sections that consist of short phrases separated by ellipses, as if to represent the protagonist's unmediated stream of consciousness. And at times the man seems to be divided in two and to hold conversations with himself. Abe's Japanese does not set this language off with quotes; it avoids tags such as "he thought" or "he said"; and the point of view (as represented by Abe's pronouns) slides back and forth between the narrator, the man, and other parties. All this contributes to the sense that the book is populated by many different voices, and it can be hard even to tell where the transitions between these different voices occur.

For example, consider the following extended passage from the opening of the novel, where we hear the reactions of the man's co-workers to his disappearance:

There was a theory that he had grown weary of the world and committed suicide. It was put forward by one of his colleagues who was interested in psychoanalysis. That a grown man could get so wrapped up in something as useless as insect collecting seemed proof enough of some mental defect. They say that even among children, the ones who show an inordinate interest in insects often suffer from an Oedipus complex: the ability to pierce and fix the insect on a pin, with no fear it will escape—these are compensations for the child's unsatisfied desires. When this continues even into adulthood, there is every indication that the condition is even worse. It is surely no accident that insect collectors are frequently in possession of reclusive, possessive, homosexual, or kleptomaniacal tendencies. . . . Come to think of it, the fact that the guy never told us about his hobby—doesn't that prove he himself realized there was something shady about it? (*AZ* 16:118)

David Pollack singles out this passage for the way Abe transitions almost imperceptibly from sense into nonsense: "Abe's narrative voice never loses its careful modulations," he says, "even as it lapses smoothly into absurdity" (125). But this passage also shows the smooth transition into the colleague's point of view, in the way it switches gradually from third-person to first-person narration. (The final line in Japanese is "*Sō ieba, ano otoko ga wareware ni, sono shumi o ichido mo uchiakeyō to shinakatta* [. . .]." In contrast, E. Dale Saunders's translation of this passage begins and concludes with the narrator firmly in control (it ends: "Indeed, the man had not once confided his interests to anyone, and this would seem to be proof that he realized they were rather dubious").[8] In the original, it is not quite clear which points or observations are the narrator's, which are the colleague's, and which belong to this quoted discourse of psychoanalysis.[9]

The heteroglossia of *The Woman in the Dunes* complicates conclusions about the novel's viewpoint or its attitude toward language. One can see this passage as a parody of science, specifically psychoanalysis and its narrow categories. Then again, the speaker here is using psychoanalysis to criticize the ostensibly even narrower scientific outlook of the entomologist. So some of the observations made by critics like Dworkin about the protagonist's reclusiveness or reductionism are here put in the colleague's mouth and parodied by Abe himself.

Like Abe's other novels, *The Woman in the Dunes* does not present a single conclusion about science or identity in a unified voice; it borrows the different ideas and languages circulating in the text and tries to reconcile or balance these styles in a constructive way. And like Abe's other characters, Niki Junpei is an assiduous borrower or editor himself. He is in a state of ideological becoming, to borrow Bakhtin's phrase, choosing from the styles around him to devise his own style. That, rather than pre-linguistic self-realization or communication, is what Abe's characters are struggling toward. And that is also how Niki Junpei balances his own freedom versus the needs and the demands of others: by balancing these voices.

We could trace this dynamic through other longer passages as well. One conversation between the man and the woman about the nature of sand begins as a simple dialogue:

"I suppose if sand collected up there it would be bad for the ceiling. . . . But you can't mean the sand is rotting the beams."
"But it does rot them."
"But sand is dry. That's just what it is."

Five or six lines later the "conversation" becomes one sided. The man's language remains quoted, but the woman's side is replaced by ellipses:

"That's ridiculous," the man snarled. He felt the image of sand he had in his mind had somehow been desecrated by her ignorance. "When it comes to sand, I know a thing or two myself, you know. . . . Listen: the thing about sand is that it's always moving, like this. . . . That movement is its whole existence, see? . . . It'll never stop in one place. . . . In the water, in the air, it's always on the move. Free. . . . That's why normal living things can't survive in the sand. . . . Not even decomposing bacteria."

Figure 5.2   Along with scenes of the man and the woman making love, shots of the man against the massive sand dunes are among the most iconic images from the film version of *The Woman in the Dunes*. Reproduced by permission of Janus Films.

Are these ellipses silences, or have her comments simply gone ignored, unrecorded, or unheard? When the explanation above is complete we read "The woman stiffened and sank into silence." And then the man continues the conversation with himself. The quotation marks disappear, and his own thoughts blend with the narration:

Ahh, but this dampness was too much. Not that the sand was damp of course; it was on the skin. The wind sounded above the roof. The pocket with the cigarettes in it was full of sand too. The cigarette tasted bitter even before it was lit.

Get out the killing jar. Better fix the insects' legs before they stiffen. Outside, the woman made the sounds of washing the dishes. . . . Was she the only one living in this house? (*AZ* 16:130–31)

To understand the meanings generated by this combination of different voices, it may help to compare the novel more explicitly with the film, which lacks the same degree of internal dialogue. In the film, for example, the exchange above is rendered as a more or less straightforward conversation. The novel balances the rich, even chaotic world of language inside the protagonist with detailed and very tactile descriptions of the physical environment, particularly the ever-present sand. Abe's prose gives the sand reality by describing physical sensations: the burning, itching, and thirst are palpable enough that we seem to feel them as we read. The film brings this environment and these two bodies to life with cinematographer Segawa Hiroshi's striking black-and-white imagery (Figure 5.2). So it is not surprising that critics who have compared the film and novel have focused on the things reinforced by the film, and highlighted the tactile elements of the novel over the protagonist's language games. Discussing the book and the film together, Wimal Dissanayake writes that "Once Niki is imprisoned in the sand pit, the only reality is the ever present sand and his own body. Much of the communication, experience of diverse emotions, [and] imaginings' ruminations are anchored in the body" (46).

Near the beginning of the film is a scene that encapsulates some of the differences between the film and the novel. It takes place before the man encounters the villagers, as he sits down in the sand to take a break from his collecting. He thinks of his wife back in Tokyo, and we see a vision of her first superimposed over him and then sitting next to him (Figures 5.3 and 5.4).[10] The visuals hint at the different voices that are combined within the man. As Akira Lippit writes, "He is speaking to the woman, who is there, but inside. She is inside and out" (124). At the same time the accompanying voiceover makes this contest of voices explicit:

> All kinds of documents to assure ourselves about one another: contracts, licenses, ID cards, operating permits, title deeds, charter documents, registration forms, carrying permits, union cards, certificates of commendation, bills, promissory notes, temporary permits, acceptance letters, proofs of income, custodial certificates, even pedigrees.
>
> And still, was that it? Wasn't there something we still had left to prove? Men, women, both are prisoners to their own dark suspicions that the other is holding back. To prove their innocence, they are forced to devise new contracts. No one knows where it will stop. The certifications are endless. (You complain that I am too argumentative. But it is the facts that are making the argument, not me!)[11]

Figures 5.3 and 5.4 Near the start of *Woman in the Dunes*, the protagonist recalls a conversation with his wife back in the city. Reproduced by permission of Janus Films.

The catalog of documents in the first part of the scene expresses a common theme in Abe's work: in society, we define ourselves by the documents we carry, though I would add that this is just one instance of Abe's broader idea that we assemble ourselves from the various languages we move through every day. The man goes on to relate this to the chafing sense of restriction he feels from others, and the distrust that makes him want to tie down his wife in the same way. He ends by arguing both sides, first giving voice to her objection, and then replying to her directly. This passage from the film applies the same strategy of mixed texts and voices that I identified in the novel, but there is an important difference. This scene comes at the outset of the film and represents an end to these internal dialogues, rather than a beginning. It is a transition from the city to the dunes, and after the man takes mental leave of his wife in this scene, she plays no further role in the story. This process of distinguishing or separating characters and voices that the translation begins, the film completes: as the film progresses, this kind of internal monologue is replaced with simpler, more straightforward conversations between the man and the woman, or with speechless scenes backed by Takemitsu Tōru's eerie modernist score.

But in the book, the words of the man's wife keep recurring throughout the story, so he is never really alone with the village woman, even at the bottom of the sand pit. For example, the novel contains a passage very similar to the one above, but it occurs during the scene where the man and woman first make love in the pit. There are effectively three people present in that love scene, which moves back and forth between the man's perceptions of the woman there with him and the remembered words of his wife back in the city. This back and forth extends the scene over many pages. And there is scientific language scattered throughout this description too. In the novel, the act of lovemaking is described first in philosophical terms, as part of the social contracts we make. (The various permission forms are mentioned here, and we hear the man argue with his wife at some length.) Then sex is depicted in biological or evolutionary language. The ejaculation that concludes the scene is described with equal parts poetry and paleontology: "Humanity's convulsions, laying down the fossil record and emerging at the top . . . the motive force of reproduction crying out and moving

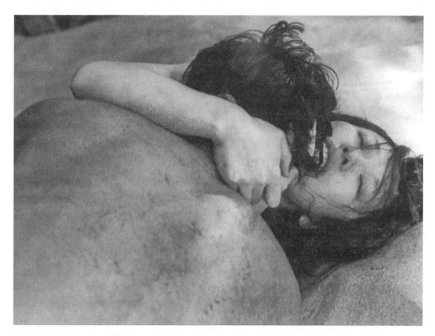

Figure 5.5 An image from *Woman in the Dunes* of the man and the woman making love, their bodies covered with sand. Reproduced by permission of Janus Films.

ecstatically onward, untroubled by dinosaur fangs or walls of glacial ice . . . the final writhing launch of spores, like fireworks . . . meteors showering down from the limitless blackness . . . rusted orange stars . . . an alkaloid chorus. . ." (*AZ* 16:195).

In the novel, it is only through this combination of emotional, social, and scientific language that the man can attempt to triangulate on the meaning of this act; in the film, this long love scene is almost wordless. It is one of the two or three scenes that seem to stick in viewers' minds from the film—two sand-covered bodies making love. Teshigahara concentrates on these two figures and their outsides, his camera taking them in almost voraciously with repeated, almost macroscopic close-ups of their skins (Figure 5.5).

So in the end it is scenes like this from the film, rather than the novel, that come closest to expressing the sense of union or community between the man and woman that the English criticism sees, as well as the irreducible physicality that the Japanese criticism seems to be seeking in this work. But in the novel—as this clinical conclusion to the love scene and its alkaloid chorus seem to suggest—the voices still seem to be fighting with one another throughout the sex. The tension and eventual union between two characters that are so effectively portrayed in the film are absent in the book, which instead focuses on the internal tension between the voices within the man. Does the novel ever resolve this tension? This is the question to which we turn next.

Emissions, Transmissions, and the Technology of "Hope"

In the last chapter of the novel there is a series of remarkable events. Through a fortuitous accident, the man invents a kind of machine that he thinks will enable him to extract fresh water from the ground. As noted above, this is important because the house has no plumbing, and the villagers have been forcing him to work by withholding drinking water. Shortly thereafter, the woman gets pregnant, but when complications develop suddenly, she has to be brought up out of the pit and taken to the hospital.

This all happens on the last few pages of the text. In the final scene, the man notices that in their hurry to take away the woman, the villagers have left the rope ladder in place. This is when he climbs out of the pit. After months of planning and failed attempts, escape is now within his grasp. But after a minute of thought he climbs back down into the hole to continue work on his water trap, telling himself that he will think about escaping some other day. This is the end of the novel, except for the court documents on the last two pages that testify to the fact that seven years later he still has not returned to the city, and that the original identity represented by the name Niki Junpei (which is only now revealed) has been declared legally dead.

Different critics focus on different elements of this conclusion. Critics such as Van Wert emphasize the pregnancy as a link that has been forged between the man and the woman, who have now created their own community in the pit. The Japanese criticism discussed above gives more attention to the water-gathering invention—a predictable stance for those who put more trust in science than society and who see the novel as the struggle of man against his surroundings. The protagonist's apparent triumph over the environment plays into Sasaki Kiichi's idea that he is a kind of Robinson Crusoe, for example. But I would argue that neither of these interpretations of the ending is really complete. In fact, one might question whether the water trap really works at all, and more radically, one might ask whether the child is really the man's offspring, even though he and the woman are alone in the pit.

First, the invention. Ultimately the important thing about the water trap is neither the science upon which it is based nor its practical applications, but the device's connection with language. The man originally conceives it as a kind of primitive communications device that will let him call for help, by capturing a live crow that will then be released with a plea for help tied to its leg. The crow trap consists of a wooden tub sunk into the sand to form a kind of hole or pit, the mouth of which is then covered with a delicately balanced lid and a layer of sand. Lured by some bait, the crow is supposed to land on the trap, pull a string that releases the lid, and fall into the tub where it will be buried in a cascade of sand.

The man names this invention "hope," which immediately seems appropriate given that its function seems to be based more on wishful thinking than on physics. Even its inventor realizes that crows are difficult quarry and imperfect messengers. But the invention produces another, unexpected result. The man discovers that water is pooling in the tub, which somehow acts as an osmotic pump to pull moisture up out of the sand. The way the pump works is described in some detail, with reference to capillary action, the sand's specific heat, and the differing evaporation rates inside and outside the tub. Like a lot of the things invented by Abe's characters, though, while the science may be sound, the practicality of the device is in question. (For example, the man still has to rely on the villagers for food.)

More important than its practicality is the quality of creativity that the invention represents—the disruptive but productive shock of unexpected discovery that Abe valued in science. This is figured throughout the novel by the complicated and counterintuitive relationship the man discovers between sand and water. The man's stereotype of sand as dry and sterile has already been disturbed by earlier observations, such as the mist rising from the ground at night or the woman's revelation that it rots things it comes in contact with. Now, by studying the water trap, he comes to understand the productivity or fertility in a medium he considered barren.

We read that "the transformation of the sand was also a transformation in himself" (*AZ* 16:247). But how or why? In other novels we have seen that science and technology are forces that operate on individuals through language, and at first the movement of water might seem to be a wordless physical process that breaks this pattern and takes place outside the individual. In the end, it is the language surrounding this invention that gives it power, and that is why we read that "perhaps along with the water, he had collected another self from the sand" (*AZ* 16:247). These are the narrative's final words:

There was no particular need to hurry up and run away. He now held a round-trip ticket—one on which the destination and return were both blank, to be filled in as he pleased. The more he thought about it, the more he felt he would burst with the desire to talk to someone about the water collector. And if he was going to tell someone, there would be no better audience than the people of this village. The man would end up confiding in someone or other— if not today, then probably tomorrow.

He could consider how to escape the day after that.   (*AZ* 16:248)

Although the invention is not able to signal for help, it does become the ground for communication with the villagers. Ultimately, the technology upon which "hope" depends is not osmosis: the water trap is a rhetorical device. If it gives the man an advantage over the villagers, it is not a practical one, but an advantage of imagination. And if it puts him in a better position, it is only in this context of communication. The film ends with a first-person voiceover that is almost identical to the quote from the novel just above, but the words have more impact in the book, because after being haunted by all these different voices that he repeats compulsively throughout the novel, after talking to himself for page after page, now the man is finally in a position to say something of his own to other people.[12] In that respect, one might speculate that this invention and the communication that surrounds it resemble the hopes Abe had for his own scientific and fictional prose.[13]

This is an optimistic view of the role of science and technology in communication, but Abe's later work is not always as sanguine about technology's role in fostering dialogue. The next chapter takes up Abe's novel *Secret Rendezvous*, about a security officer assigned to monitor hundreds of people by means of an electronic eavesdropping system that records their every conversation. He is quickly overwhelmed by this tidal wave of language, and eventually finds himself listening to taped fragments of his own conversations to try and piece together his confused life. While technology in *The Woman in the Dunes* promises to prime the language pump and foster communication, Abe was also cognizant of the disruptive way that technology—particularly electronic media and mass media—could multiply language beyond our ability to control it.

In fact, there is an early hint of this threat in *The Woman in the Dunes* as well, a slow intrusion of the mass media, which seeps into the pit like moisture into the water trap. The other thing that happens in the last few pages of the novel is that the man and woman save up enough money from piecework to buy a radio. And the description of the radio contains a startling juxtaposition: "Somehow winter passed, and it was spring. At the beginning of March, they finally obtained a radio and put up a tall antenna on the roof. The woman turned the dial this way and that for half a day, exclaiming in happy wonder the whole time. At the end of that month, she became pregnant" (*AZ* 16:247).

Is it the radio, then, that fathers this child? Are these transmissions the evolution of the man's seminal emissions, which are also described almost like radio waves: "meteors showering down from the limitless blackness . . . rusted orange stars . . . an alkaloid chorus"? Could the baby have been conceived in the woman's ecstatic encounter with the radio, so erotically described here? This is only a slight overstatement. If the radio does not literally make the woman pregnant, figuratively it is no accident that the intrusion of the media into the sand pit carries a threatening fecundity that results in the pregnancy, and a life-threatening pregnancy at that. Balancing voices is the key to community and communication in the novel, and on the final pages, just when the man is finally beginning to achieve that equilibrium with the woman and within himself, the radio intrudes and disrupts that delicate balance.

To sum up, in the novel the man's discovery of community arguably has less to do with a physical intimacy with the woman than with discovering how to harness language. Communication offers both freedom without loneliness and community without suffocation. Technology advances this goal by creating new unexpected possibilities that change our language, like the water trap; but in the process it can also destabilize language and threaten communication, as the radio does. Once again, the challenge is to balance these functions.

By paring down the protagonist's internal voices and creating more dialogue between him and the woman, the film creates a situation where

the communicative possibilities offered by the man's invention are not
as revolutionary or as crucial. The man and the woman have been talking
to one another for some time without it. (The film gives the radio a
less dangerous role as well.) So if the novel is tentatively optimistic about
the possibility of communication and community, the film is even more
hopeful. That is undoubtedly one reason for the film's worldwide appeal.
As a vehicle for Abe's message, though, Teshigahara's films may not
be disruptive enough to shake people out of their everyday rationality.
Abe, Teshigahara, and Takemitsu were all radically experimental in their
respective fields,[14] but one cannot escape the suspicion that for all its
unconventional elements, for many viewers the film ends up being a
rather conventional love story, something Abe seemed to avoid and even
abhor. In that, the film is not unlike the novels by Murakami Haruki
or Murakami Ryū described in previous chapters, which achieved global
popularity as literary fiction written within the bounds of more conservative genres. The lingering conventionality of these film collaborations
may be one reason Abe abandoned them a few years later and turned to
other visual media such as photography and the theater, where he could
exert more complete control and where he could further complicate the
relationship between image and text.

Teshigahara's Film: A More Careful Look

It is interesting to relate these differences between the film and the
novel to the nature of film itself as a communicative (or disruptive)
technology. If Teshigahara's films tend to portray a kind of interpersonal communication that Abe's novels do not, then one could say that
in Teshigahara's hands film itself becomes a hopeful communicative
technology, and that this is really what renders the water trap unneces-
sary or redundant in the movie.

In fact, one could argue that a great deal of the communication or
mediation between the man and the woman is performed by the camera
and the visuals in *Woman in the Dunes*. Consider the dialogue from the
novel quoted earlier, about sand rotting the roof beams. We saw above
how the text gradually excludes the woman as the man retreats into
his own world. But in the film there is a sustained conversation, much
of it filmed in a single cut three-and-a-half minutes long. The camera

Figure 5.6　A scene from *Woman in the Dunes* showing the man and woman in conversation. Reproduced by permission of Janus Films.

occupies a point equidistant from both figures and very slowly zooms in as they talk. The characters are lit against a dark background, focusing our attention on both of them equally. Much of the film is shot this way: it avoids shot/reverse-shot cutting, for example, in favor of placing the camera at a neutral point. The effect is to make both characters strongly and equally present to the viewer. We don't have a sense we have in the novel, of seeing the woman through Niki Junpei's eyes, or even a generically aggressive or possessive male gaze. Instead, we have a camera that seems equally invested in both characters (Figure 5.6).

Nina Cornyetz tries to show how the film actively rejects or foils the objectifying and dominating male gaze that characterized Japanese film of the time. Cornyetz starts from Laura Mulvey's notion that film's male gaze typically looks at women in a way that either fetishizes them as sexual spectacles or subsumes them in a visual narrative of sadistic domination. Cornyetz finds many examples of this in Japanese films of the period, especially Nikkatsu Studios' artistic pornography and the violent sexualized films of New Wave directors such as Imamura

Shōhei. But for Cornyetz, these codes are distorted and subverted by what she calls a new "technology of gazing" in *Woman in the Dunes*.[15] For example, Teshigahara's film treats nudity by refusing to focus on the parts of the woman's body that would typically be fetishized (the breasts, the lips, the nape of the neck). Instead the camera looks elsewhere— at the man's naked body, or at the features of the woman's body that abstract her beauty from sexual desire, features that make her into a kind of landscape by relating her body to the undulating sand dunes. Cornyetz writes, "The woman's body is simultaneously decentered as spectacle and spectacularized as landscape to be viewed with disinterest—that is, severed from ethical or utilitarian (hence also erotic) interest" (40).

Cornyetz's characterization of "disinterest" follows Kant.[16] Elsewhere, she speaks of Brechtian alienation, or distance: "The camera refrains from a subjective portrayal of a repeating, sexualized gaze," she writes. "It maintains distance" (38). But while Cornyetz starts from this sense of distance and disinterest, she shows how it finally leads to a greater interest and greater closeness between the man, the woman, and the spectator, by foiling objectification. She concludes that the film "offers a nonviolent erotics that is disinterested and reserved yet sensual and consensual," implying something that I would emphasize even more strongly—that the early abstraction yields a payoff in intimacy (48).

Here it is helpful to consider a theory of film that places even more emphasis on communication (as well as solipsism and subjectivity) when considering how the camera sees. Vivian Sobchack provides this kind of framework in *Address of the Eye*, which examines the communicative function of film with reference to Maurice Merleau-Ponty's existential phenomenology. The latter also links the materialist or existential tendencies and the progressive tendencies that were said to be combined in Abe's novel. Merleau-Ponty's ideas locate subjectivity in embodied perception, and especially the act of sight. For Sobchack, this provides a way to validate individual bodies and experiences while still preserving the independent power of language and the possibility of communication and community. Sobchack does not discuss Abe or Teshigahara specifically, but her work does illuminate the questions we have been asking. *Address of the Eye* shows how the visual dimension of film provides an escape from the kind of solipsism that plagues the characters in Abe's novels.

Sobchack starts from something like Bakhtin's observation that some parts of our own bodies are visible only to others, and in some ways her argument translates the Bakhtinian notion of consummation discussed in the last chapter into the realm of phenomenology and film. She notes that when we look in the mirror, we recognize a gap between our internal (intrasubjective) image of ourselves and the external image others see. From that we infer that others also have internal lives beyond the outward appearances we see, even if we cannot access their internal subjectivities directly. But film alters these terms. As a recorded act of sight, film allows us to experience the intrasubjective perceptions of another—not quite another person, but another subjectivity, the subjectivity of the film itself. Sobchack endows the film with a subjectivity and a body, though we cannot see the film's body; this is a missing term we must infer.

This shared sight creates a bridge between subjectivities—the spectator and the film's subjectivity, and ultimately the spectator and the filmmaker. The key is the way that the spectator shares the film's (and filmmaker's) sight: in some ways that sharing links the subjects transparently (I see what the film sees and what Teshigahara saw); but it also permits the spectator to remain independent and to perceive the differences between these subjects, based on the different intentions and reactions they have toward what is visible. As spectators, we are able to reconstruct something like the film's intent—and at another remove, the filmmaker's as well—and distinguish between theirs and our own. Sobchack criticizes the dominance of theories similar to Mulvey's for erasing the gap between film and spectator. Put another way, film allows us to consider (in Sobchack's terms, to "express") our own perceptions side by side with the perceptions of another, in a way that enables self-awareness and communication: "Entailing two lived-bodies engaged in perception and its expression in the presence of each other, the film experience enables the potential communication of experience from one uniquely situated lived-body to another. . . . Cinema uniquely allows this philosophical turning, this objective and subjective insight into oneself, and remarkably, others" (307–9).

To apply Sobchack to *Woman in the Dunes* is to shift the question from how the man and the woman interact with one another, to how the spectators and filmmakers interact with them through the camera.

How does the film *regard* these two characters, and how do we experience that look? In *Woman in the Dunes*, there is a strong sense of the camera or the film's visual investment in both characters. In part, that can be reduced to the formal qualities discussed above—composition, lighting, character and camera movement, among others. It also seems to include something less tangible and more subjective, an almost human care the film seems to take with both characters. If the film conveys the feeling the man and the woman communicate with one another, Sobchack's work suggests that this may be a byproduct of the feeling we have of communicating with the filmmakers or the film itself, the feeling that we are all invested in these characters and inhabit a community with them. Sobchack gives us a more sophisticated way of thinking about what it means to feel that we are there in the sand pit with the woman and the man.

Ultimately, Sobchack is tracing the same process as Abe, the process of struggling to get out of one body or subjectivity into another. Her work explains why the medium of film can seem so much more optimistic about this possibility than some novels, and the explanation is phrased in terms that Abe would have recognized, with a materialist phenomenological premise that avoids blind faith in scientific realism, and a progressive outlook that does not resort to utopianism.[17] Notwithstanding the possibility film seemed to offer for such a compromise, Abe eventually embraced different media that were less communicative and more disruptive. Abe's collaboration with Teshigahara lasted out the 1960s, but in the 1970s Abe moved on to different kinds of experiments with visual and popular media, especially photography and live theater. This work went a step further than the earlier films, and arguably tried to upend perception and reconfigure it along more radical lines.

There is one moment in *Woman in the Dunes* that prefigures this more radical experimentation, when the man attempts to force himself on the woman sexually while the villagers look on. In this scene, the camera loses its composure and its sympathy with the protagonist. It is a night scene near the end of both the novel and the film, when a group of the villagers come to the man and offer him a walk outside the pit if he will have sex with the woman while they watch. When the woman refuses, he tries to force her, but she resists and then beats him into submission.

Figure 5.7 With torchlight reflected in his sand goggles, one of the villagers in *Woman in the Dunes* watches the man attempt to rape the woman at the villagers' instigation. Reproduced by permission of Janus Films.

Andrea Dworkin argues that in the novel, the man is rescued from his own male self by his failure to rape the woman. Cornyetz sees the man less sympathetically, but identifies this scene in the film as a progressive transformation of similar scenes in contemporary cinema, since here the attempt at sexual violence is displayed without any eroticism, or even any visually explicit sex.

Building on these observations, I would argue this is a moment of crisis for communication in the film—both between the characters and between the filmmakers and viewers. As the narrative of *The Woman in the Dunes* reaches its most dangerous point, the film also becomes more visually disjointed, and the sense of communion generated by the camera is disrupted. The camera's normally steady gaze is replaced here with a confusing welter of shots that portray fragments of the action emerging from the darkness. The man and woman are lit erratically by the careening beams of the villagers' flashlights; many of the figures are disguised by face coverings that range from sand goggles to sinister festival masks (Figure 5.7); and the cuts and camera angles become more ragged, while Takemitsu's moodily ethereal score switches to a frantic drumbeat, as if to punctuate the sharp transitions. At the same time that the caring relationship between the man and woman is shattered, the communicative bond between spectator, characters, and filmmaker is strained by these erratic visuals. This reflects and conveys the fact that as spectators we now find ourselves in danger of being implicated with the villagers and the director, as witnesses or accomplices to a rape.

This scene is the film's only foray into the world of Abe's darker novels, where sexual violations of different kinds (sexual conquest in *The Face of Another*, fetuses kidnapped from their mothers' wombs in *Inter Ice Age 4*) become disturbing metaphors for freedom from social convention. Because the assault fails and because ultimately there is nothing to see, *Woman in the Dunes* recovers from this rupture and goes on to its potentially more harmonious conclusion. But there is a sense in which the moment of greatest violence or disruption—both narratively and visually—embodies more promise than a happy ending, because of its ability to escape convention. This may explain not only the darker plots of some of Abe's later novels, but also Abe's more fragmented or disjointed experiments with visual media that succeeded his collaboration with Teshigahara.

Photography and The Box Man

The year 1973 marked a watershed for Abe in terms of his changing engagement with visual media, when the first public performance by his experimental theater company—the Abe Kōbō Studio—took place. (This is treated in more detail below.) This was also the year Abe published *The Box Man*, which combined text and photography in a collage-like narrative that seemed to draw its organizing principle as much from the idea of the photo essay as from the novel. *The Box Man*'s protagonist moves around inside a cardboard box that covers the upper half of his body; observation holes cut in the sides of the box are cleverly arranged so that he can see out but no one else can see in—though most of the time no one even notices the box or its occupant at all. The box man is another of Abe's figures for rootlessness, anonymity, loneliness, and freedom, now concretely associated with the real urban homeless. Yet the box is also a kind of camera, and the box man is also a figure for the artist as privileged outsider and voyeur. Spaced throughout the book are photographs of urban subjects taken by Abe, with poetic captions relating them loosely to the text. Some of the images depict the box men around us (things and people we see but never really see); other photos seem to represent the box man's view of us.

Abe had a serious interest in cameras and in photography. He published and exhibited some of his photographs in the 1970s, and more recent catalogs and exhibitions have drawn increased attention to this body of serious photographic work.[18] Abe's camera scanned the city streets to find things that are invisible to the naked eye because they go unnoticed: discarded objects, the surface of a wall or sidewalk, strangers passing in the street. Many of the photos seem to be taken surreptitiously, crookedly. (Abe sometimes used a lens with an internal mirror that allowed him to focus on a subject while appearing to aim the lens in a different direction [A. Levy 36].) And many are cropped aggressively, as if to break up the context. Often, it is as if Abe were trying to foil the notion of the trained eye and restore some of this productive chaos that we see—or hear—in his written texts.

The Box Man pushes the idea of internal dialogue and a divided subject further than almost any of Abe's other works. The text identifies itself as a set of notes kept by the box man, but it is far from clear who the narrator and the box man really are. We are told that the thing that defines box men is their anonymity: inside their boxes, no one can distinguish them or even notice them. This is the appeal and the curse of being a box man, a formula that replays the perennial dilemma in Abe's work between freedom and belonging. As much as he is drawn to the unfettered state of homelessness, the protagonist still longs for some human contact, predictably figured in a mysterious but alluring woman who offers him money to discard the box and join her in society. *The Box Man* recycles the broad plot and themes of many of Abe's novels up to now, but sticking to familiar territory allowed Abe to experiment even more radically with the formal structure of the work. The result is one of Abe's most brilliant novels, perhaps his best balance of convention and innovation.

As in *The Face of Another*, the freedom of anonymity conflicts with the desire for social identity, and this manifests itself in the narrator's anxiety that he is being impersonated by someone else, a "fake box man." He begins to believe that the woman's attempt to draw him out of the box is connected with a plot that will replace him with this fake. To guard against his own disappearance, he records his discoveries in a series of notes, which we are ostensibly reading. But he begins to worry that his position as narrator will also be usurped, and he evolves elaborate strategies (involving time codes and particular inks) to assure the reader that he has not been replaced by a fake narrator. Eventually, though, we are led to the conclusion that these notes are the product of more than one writer: we read that the paper or the color of the ink has changed, or that comments have been added in the margins; characters begin to argue with the narrator about his authority and their own reality; and there are interpolated sections that do not appear to be part of the original notes at all, including the photographs and their poetic captions, which restate and recast the novel's themes. Eventually, other characters besides the box man are also doubled, and the cast multiplies. Even as we conclude that the notes must have multiple authors, it begins to seem as if some characters that appeared to be distinct are actually the same person writing in different voices at different times.

This description only scratches the surface of the novel, which is so complex that at first it seems to lack much of any coherent plot. But closer examination reveals a careful and very logical map of people and events underlying the chaotic text. With some effort, almost everything in the novel can be rationalized into a single coherent narrative, cast, and timeline. A full account of the confusion and how to resolve it would require many more pages. I will not pursue that here, because for the most part, neither the events nor the language of *The Box Man* turn decisively on the relationship between science and literature. But the novel does help us think about the evolving relationship between visual media and text in Abe's work.

If the tension of the novel is the tension between anonymous freedom and community, the box man's vision is a voyeurism that promises one-way engagement, an ability to "participate" solely as an observer, without risking or committing anything of himself. This returns us to the world of *The Face of Another*: it is essentially the fantasy of the mask. But in *The Box Man*, these voyeuristic desires are presented with a more complex balance of judgment and sympathy.

This voyeuristic fantasy reinforces the solipsism of the written text. With its numerous characters who might all be manifestations of a single narrator, and its arguments between narrators over who is writing at any given moment, the novel reflects the notion we have traced through all of Abe's works—that language multiplies the self, and that different selves compete with one another for control of a single subject through the medium of language. But the camera-like box, the connection with Abe's own photography, and many other clues in the narrative also transform the box man into an ironic self-portrait of the artist. The author himself is cast as a peeping tom, and the reader becomes one too.

If Teshigahara's camera mediated between characters and between filmmaker and spectator in *Woman in the Dunes*, this is the diametric opposite. Photography creates a screen between characters through which only one side can see, and both the reader and writer must admit their status as voyeurs. It may be that in doing so, Abe brings the reader into the box man's point of view in a way that really does communicate something of the character's internal world. An acquaintance of mine who worked as a mental healthcare professional in Japan reported to me that *The Box Man* was assigned reading in one of her courses, supposedly because it provided caretakers some empathetic understanding of the way schizophrenic patients see their world. There is more than a little irony in the way that Abe's least rational work is turned back into a scientific textbook, but this anecdote also shows that the way Abe contracts the world into one subject does communicate the richness of the subject itself.

Readers who want to experience Abe's photography can browse through the volumes of his complete works, which include dozens of photos of and by the writer. The editors and the book designer Kondō Kazuya have presented and arranged the photos in particularly thought-provoking ways. For example, the 29 thick volumes that make up the series come packaged in box-like cardboard slipcovers, the insides of which are decorated with photos of Abe at different times in his life. Each slipcover is lined with a different photo. The outsides of the boxes look mostly uniform, but when a volume is removed one can peer into openings cut in the slipcovers—including a window-like hole in the front that recalls the box man's observation port—and see Abe inside, gazing out like the box man himself (Figure 5.8).

Figure 5.8 One volume of Abe's complete works, showing Kondō Kazuya's unique book design for the series. The book slipcovers are deliberately plain, with a rectangular window that makes them resemble the box man's dwelling. Through the window one can see a metal nameplate affixed to the book cover, engraved like a dog tag with the ISBN number and other details, a reference to Abe's preoccupation with identity documents. With the book removed, the reader can peer through the hole and see Abe peering back: each slipcover is lined with a different photograph of the author, partially visible through the holes in the box. Photograph by the author.

Figures 5.9 and 5.10   Two of Abe's own photos, from the front and back endpapers of volume sixteen of Abe's complete works, the volume that contains *The Woman in the Dunes*. Reproduced by permission of Abe Neri.

While the slipcovers feature pictures of the author, the endpapers of each volume are decorated with photographs Abe took himself. Opening the sixteenth volume, which includes *The Woman in the Dunes*, the first thing the reader sees is a photo on the front endpaper of a sandy landscape (Figure 5.9). An oddly constructed wall to one side of the picture seems designed to limit the sand's movement and to impose some order on the terrain. The back endpaper of the same volume is a city street scene, tilted at an awkward angle and shot from below (Figure 5.10). A figure in the foreground walks silhouetted against a lighted sign or billboard that shows models in bathing suits. The walker has her back turned, but the billboard models gaze directly at Abe's camera, more present and real looking than the actual person. Visually, the image foils quick understanding. And even after we stare at it for some time, it retains some secrets: a confused pattern of reflections on the billboard and various glass surfaces allows us glimpses of surrounding details that the photo does not quite reveal or resolve.

Both photos are undated, but the gap or transition between them suggests the distance between *The Woman in the Dunes* and later visual work like we see in *The Box Man* or the Abe Kōbō Studio. The first image of the sand wall is composed geometrically, with the wall anchoring the picture on the right. The barrier holding back the sand has a clear connection with *The Woman in the Dunes* and with Abe's trademark metaphor of the wall in the wilderness, a motif introduced in Chapter 1. The wall imposes the mixed blessing of order and boundaries—for a village, for a narrative, and for the photo itself. But the photograph that concludes the volume is initially confusing. It takes some time to sort out. As we do, the image suggests many ideas: the multiple surfaces of media and representation, the way that reproduced images seem more lively than life, the suggestion that the human figure in the foreground is being spied on by the camera, while the advertising images surveil the photographer. It is an image of media that disrupts our vision and makes us see things in a new way.

The Abe Kōbō Studio

As a novel, *The Box Man* is notable for the way it organizes itself around visual elements, both materially and thematically, and the way the written text cedes some of the novel's organizing function to the image. Abe was to push this trend even further with the Abe Kōbō Studio, which produced several works centered almost entirely on visual effects, with a minimal narrative element and spoken dialogue reduced to isolated words or sounds.

The studio started in 1971 as a kind of workshop and was officially launched in 1973. But Abe's experience with theater went back to the 1950s and 1960s, during which time he produced a number of dramas that were more conventional (relatively speaking). One of Abe's iconic works is his play *Friends* (*Tomodachi*, 1967), a dark farce about a grown man who is "adopted" against his will by a strange family that invades his apartment and takes over his life, caging him and eventually killing him with their kindness. Abe began directing around the same time, starting with the debut of his own play *The Man Who Turned into a Stick* (*Bō ni natta otoko*) in 1969. However, Abe's work for dramatic media (including radio and television) goes back further, to the 1950s: *Friends* was based on Abe's story "Chinnyusha" ("Intruders"), which was written in 1951 and reworked by Abe for radio in 1955 and television in 1963 before he adapted it for the stage in 1967. *The Man Who Turned into a Stick* was also based on an earlier radio play—just two examples of the way Abe's works migrated from one medium to another.[19]

At one point, Abe was enthusiastic about the potential of popular media and mass media as well as film, and he spoke optimistically, even idealistically about the possibilities that electronic media and mass media provided for communicating to a wider audience. In the period leading up to his collaboration with Teshigahara, Abe and many original members of the avant-garde group Yoru no Kai formed Kiroku Geijutsu no Kai (The Society for Documentary Art), which explored new forms of art that could document social and political conditions without falling into the literal realism of prewar proletariat literature. This included experiments with visual mass media—from documentary film to musical theater—designed to be popular but also artistically adventurous (Schnellbächer, *Strategist* 221–35, 394–405, 479–80). Clearly, Abe was cognizant of the risk of a certain reductionism inherent in translating literature into these media—exactly the kinds of risks discussed above in the context of *The Woman in the Dunes*. In an essay from this period on the relation of the avant-garde to television and radio, Abe writes that the artistic avant-garde occupies a place midway between mass or popular culture and art's unknown frontiers: "The avant-garde cannot follow the masses, but neither can it be an artistic supremacism isolated from them" (*AZ* 9:416).

Coming ten years after Abe's involvement with the Kiroku Geijutsu no Kai, the Abe Kōbō Studio was the author's most daring visual experiment. This time, Abe acted as both writer and director, staging over a dozen of his own plays between 1973 and 1979. A few of these were productions of Abe's earlier plays such as *Friends*, but while these earlier works were already avant-garde in their own right, Abe also created a number of new, even more experimental pieces just for the studio—works that focused less on story than on striking visual effects. Abe's wife Abe Machi designed the sets and costumes that gave the productions their otherworldly look, just as she illustrated Abe's novels with images that captured both the bizarre and the concrete quality of Abe's descriptions. This radical experiment seems to have been underwritten partly by Abe's friend and patron Tsutsumi Seiji, a noted writer who was also an heir to the Seibu financial empire. Tsutsumi made the Seibu department store chain into a venue for exhibitions and performances of various kinds, and the theater on the ninth floor of Seibu's Parco store in Shibuya hosted many of the Abe Kōbō Studio's performances. In fact, it is said that it was designed specifically for Abe (Shields 47).

The Abe Kōbō Studio has been discussed in English by other authors, and a full treatment of Abe's drama is outside the scope of this book.[20] But even a brief look at the work of the studio shows how different it was from the visual world of Teshigahara's films. Nancy Shields, who was closely involved with the studio, describes some of the productions and the way they came together in her engrossing book *Fake Fish*. Shields writes of one production, "Abe did not write a script in any ordinary sense for this drama; in its place there were notations of movement and tapes of the synthesizer music which he had composed" (166).

Shields relates how Abe designed the productions and prepared the actors in such a way as to break up units of meaning like story and dialogue into smaller and smaller parts, isolating individual gestures, sounds, or images. She describes how Abe made actors perform spare movements or act out scene fragments with no context, to focus their interest more intently on the moment. He even wrote dialogue out phonetically in *kana* to force attention toward individual syllables (68–

87). The minimal, incremental, but still evocative quality of the performances is suggested by Shields's description of the opening action in Abe's play *Fake Fish* (very loosely based on *The Box Man*): "As the house lights dimmed, seven actors assuming the roles of barnacles made a pulsating sound like that of a low heartbeat" (105). Most significant for our discussion is the way the productions dispensed with narrative in favor of visual sequences or "exhibitions of images," as Abe subtitled some of these plays. One was *Kozō wa shinda: imēji no tenrankai III* (The little elephant is dead: exhibition of images III, 1979), which premiered on a five-city American tour that ended the studio's long run. For much of the play the stage and all the actors were covered with an enormous white tarp; their movements under the cloth created the visual patterns and effects that constituted the performance.[21]

Abe compared novelistic writing with drama by saying that drama and film represented a more immediate kind of shared experience, while prose required reducing that experience to a precise, more universal, but ultimately limited world of language. So an important aspect of the moving image was the ability to convey a kind of meaning (or at least experience) that preceded or transcended language. This was clearly one of the author's aims with the Abe Kōbō Studio, and it seems to point out the strengths and weaknesses of the film *Woman in the Dunes*. Among the strongest moments are raw images such as scenes of the man climbing the sand dunes, images that are not easily reduced to words; the weaknesses lie in the way the interaction between man and woman so easily collapses back into a conventional narrative of romance and ready redemption.

In statements from the end of the Abe Kōbō Studio period, the author used a metaphorical distinction to express the gap between vision and language: the "analog" (*anarogu*) and "digital" (*dejitaru*) worlds. Film and performance were analog, infinitely variable like experience itself, while writing involved reducing that variety to the discrete units of language. Abe said in one interview that the writer's challenge was to find a "self-denying" language that forswore its digital origins. "A defining feature of the language of artistic expression is this ability to close in on a non-digital meaning through digital means" (*AZ* 26:155).[22]

Sobchack also distinguishes between analog and digital regimes, though she uses these ideas differently from Abe. For Sobchack, a film that constitutes a unified subject with a body of its own is "cinematic," a quality she associates with analog photography and film. Its digital counterpart is "electronic" media, a violent technology that scatters the viewing and viewed subject by creating multiple images and disconnecting them (*Address* 300–302; "Toward" 50–59). Discontinuous methods of representation and transmission (the pixels, bits, and packets of electronic networks, as well as the freeze-frames, skips, and fast-forward of electronic playback) create a vision that we can never associate with the kind of coherent seeing body that grounds the perception of a human or cinematic subject. Electronic media is disruptive, forcing us to "grow new organs," in Fredric Jameson's language, or fall behind (Jameson 39).

In contrast with Abe's notion of the digital as a limiting order, Sobchack associates the electronic order with frantic transformation and disorder. But we have seen that Abe's novels are also full of reproductive technology that disrupts and transforms, like the mask in *The Face of Another*, the aquan breeding project, or the prediction machine. Abe did not necessarily link this to the transition from analog to digital technology, but he recognizes a paradigm very much like Sobchack's electronic regime, a paradigm in which everything we use to define our humanity (vision, the body, language) is reproduced and transformed by machines.

The real difference between Sobchack and Abe is how this transformation is viewed. Sobchack's criticism of the electronic regime is born out of a desire to conserve the importance of the body and human experience. For Abe, experience itself is a conservative force to be overturned. So if Sobchack's ideas explain the cinematic optimism of the film version of *The Woman in the Dunes*, they may also suggest why Abe abandoned film to pursue what Sobchack might have termed the destabilizing electronic visions of *The Box Man*, the Abe Kōbō Studio, and his other media experiments. As we will see in the next chapter, one of these was his later novel *Secret Rendezvous*, which is not visual, but which attempted to reflect the world of electronic audio media onto the printed page.

SIX

The Parody, Perversity, and Cacophony
of Secret Rendezvous

If Abe's work is defined by a tension between two forces—the need
to escape the everyday logic of the collective, and the countervailing
desire to connect with the other by finding some common belief or
language—then for Abe as a writer, this conflict was matched by a
corresponding problem of style: the language and construction of Abe's
novels show a tension between the desire to disrupt the conventions
of the novel and novelistic language, and the desire to reach readers in
a way they could understand. This was a tightrope that some of Abe's
novels walked more successfully than others.

The Woman in the Dunes is among the novels whose stories hold the
greatest hope for some compromise with the collective, through a hope
of communication founded on scientific language. But after *The Woman
in the Dunes* and *The Face of Another*, Abe cast his novels in more and more
experimental forms, at the same time he investigated other technologies
beyond film. None of these experimental novels, however, provoked
the same interest among critics as *The Woman in the Dunes*: *The Box Man*
(1973), *Secret Rendezvous* (1977), *The Ark Sakura* (1984), and *Kangaroo Notebook* (*Kangarū nōto*, 1991) were progressively more puzzling to readers
and reviewers. This and a general slowdown in Abe's writing after the
1970s led to a sense that Abe's work declined in his later years.

This tension between innovation and accessibility, as well as the role
of technology in spreading culture and also scrambling it, are present in

embryo in Abe's earliest work. Consider an anecdote Abe tells about learning that he had won the Akutagawa Prize, the important award for new writers that announced his arrival on the grand stage of Japanese literature in 1951. In his essay "Ano asa no kioku," (Memories of that morning, 1959), Abe writes that he was staying in a rented room in a factory district, working to set up literary circles among the workers, when he happened to hear the prize announcement on the radio. By itself, this sketch depicts Abe as an author so committed to common readers that he lives with them, so far removed from the prize committee that they cannot even locate him to tell him he has won, and so unconcerned with the rarified world of literary awards that he learns the news by chance from a news program.

But there is some irony in this image. As discussed in Chapter 1, the winning novel, *The Crime of S. Karma*, is a dream-like roller-coaster ride about a man who is stalked by a giant version of his own business card, until he turns himself inside out and escapes into his own chest, which has been transformed into a desert. *The Crime of S. Karma* certainly embodies the aforementioned conflict between novelty and accessibility. It is one of Abe's more difficult and confusing works, consisting of evocative but progressively more bizarre images that lead up to an open-ended conclusion. In some ways, that inaccessibility seems at odds with Abe's mission that morning, of bringing literature to the factory workers, a tension Abe himself notes in the essay. (Thomas Schnellbächer traces the same gap or tension between Abe and his target readers in the author's discursive essays from this period, for example, in his writing for the journal *Jinmin bungaku* [*Strategist* 173–89].) As discussed in Chapter 1, *The Crime of S. Karma* even parodies progressive politics of the time by having Karma's clothing, eyeglasses, and fountain pen go on strike for better working conditions. On the other hand, Abe may have hoped that the novelty of *S. Karma* would somehow reset the conventions of high literature and open it to new audiences. (The dean of Japanese science fiction writers, Komatsu Sakyō, said recently, "I think Japanese literature itself began to change after the Akutagawa Prize went to Abe's story" [329].) The references in the story show Abe's erudition, but the story is also funny in a ridiculous way, and its very randomness seems to make readers' literary knowledge or expectations largely irrelevant.

Abe's last novels are often very similar to the idiom of *S. Karma*, but even though Abe's Akutagawa Prize had cleared the way for new literary experiments by Komatsu and others, their innovations were often more modest than Abe's, so that 30 years later readers were ironically less receptive to Abe's own experiments, not more. Consider Abe's last two works. *The Ark Sakura* is set in an abandoned rock quarry, which the protagonist Mole has converted into an elaborate underground bomb shelter—an ark that will protect him in the event of nuclear war. In the course of the story, the narrator sees his carefully constructed and controlled world disrupted by a series of strange and colorful characters who make their way into the ark. The characters are linked by a series of subplots that embroil Mole in progressively more fantastic and complex plans. Then, two-thirds of the way through the novel, Mole gets his foot caught in a toilet and remains stuck until the final few pages. With its main character immobilized, the action of the novel seems to grind to a halt, until Mole frees himself and flees the quarry, leaving the other characters behind and numerous subplots unresolved. The open ending centered on escape is not unlike Abe's other work, but the large cast, intricate plot, and often frenzied action that precede it leave the novel feeling imbalanced or unfinished.

Kangaroo Notebook took this trend even further. Its narrator discovers one day that there are radish sprouts growing out of his leg. When he goes for treatment, he ends up strapped to a hospital gurney that takes him on a magical tour of the underworld—first the city sewers, and then a kind of hell. The structure is almost identical to *S. Karma*: a tour of surreal scenes and characters, vividly described but only loosely linked together, appearing and disappearing without really advancing any larger plot. Written by a young author at the start of his career, this kind of work seemed to hint at the limitless potential of Abe's imagination and at new possibilities for Japanese literature. But in a final novel by an established author, the same style came to stand for failure of inspiration, and even an inability to resolve the questions his own work posed. An English critic went so far as to refer to the seven-year gap between two of Abe's later novels as a "merciful silence" (Lewell 19), while kinder critics have responded with a merciful silence or benign neglect of their own, often ignoring Abe's later works even as they continue to write about his earlier ones. As of this writing, it has been over fifteen years since the publication of *Kangaroo Notebook*, but unfortunately almost nothing has been written about it in Japanese or English, beyond some initial baffled reviews.[1]

We have unlocked some new meaning in Abe's earlier novels by teasing out the scientific and literary voices in them. But can such a reading make sense of Abe's later work? This chapter considers *Secret Rendezvous*, a work that in many ways marks the dividing line between Abe's middle and later writing. (We will return to *The Ark Sakura* and *Kangaroo Notebook* in the next chapter.) *Secret Rendezvous* was written during Abe's last productive period in the 1970s, a time when he was not only directing the Abe Kōbō Studio, but also producing a series of glittering essays in the journal *Nami*. In the fifteen years between the publication of *Secret Rendezvous* and Abe's death at the age of 69, he continued to write, but he published only two other novels and little else. (The *Abe Kōbō zenshū* arranges his writings chronologically in 29 thick volumes that span 50 years: the nineteen years between *Inter Ice Age 4* and *Secret Rendezvous* occupy over seventeen volumes, while the work of his last fifteen years fills less than three.) We will see that *Secret Rendezvous* also represents a turning point in terms of its difficult or chaotic structure, and the point at which Abe began to lose the critics.

A final irony in Abe's Akutagawa Prize anecdote is an offhand comment that turned out to be prophetic. Abe admits it was odd hearing something about his life on the radio that he did not yet know himself: "It was the early morning news, I believe, but no matter how early the news is, I think there is something strange about their knowing this even earlier than I did" (*AZ* 9:429). Here at the outset of his career, Abe pointed to the democratizing and confounding possibilities of mass media, a language that threatened to outrun its own subject or referent. Abe returned to this image over 20 years later in *Secret Rendezvous*, the subject of this chapter. It is a novel of electronic eavesdropping and communication in which the narrator is forced to listen to audio surveillance of himself for clues about his own life. But 26 years after Abe heard his name on the radio, the signals have now multiplied and accelerated to the point where nothing is intelligible, where information seems to arrive before the event, and where the narrator cannot even begin to keep track of his own news.

Secret Rendezvous continues and transforms Abe's idea seen in *The Face of Another* and *The Woman in the Dunes*, of a narrator in search of the other, suspended between the desire to escape and the need to belong, drawn onward by women who want to free him from his shell or imprison him in a new one. In this novel trysts, infidelities, and the secret rendezvous of the novel's title represent the search for a place where the characters try to meet each other somewhere outside society and outside the everyday.

As in *The Woman in the Dunes*, the male-female relationship becomes a figure for human relations, and it is a woman who is made to embody the threats and promises of community. Sex represents the mixed danger and appeal of contact with the other in much of Abe's work, but *Secret Rendezvous* makes this even clearer than usual by placing sex itself under a magnifying glass, or perhaps a microscope. The novel recounts the narrator's journey through a bizarre hospital where strange sexual illnesses are treated with even stranger therapies. As sex is made the basic figure for all of human relations, the obscenities and perversions arrayed in the hospital express the narrator's dilemma: the desire for congress with others but also the need to escape society's expectations.

This notion of perversion is key to any reading of *Secret Rendezvous*. As the antithesis of the everyday, perversity of one sort or another (the mask's obscenity, the aquans' inhumanity) is a recurring figure in Abe's work. Insofar as it opposes the everyday, the perverse can be ambiguously positive, the sign for a creativity that can get out of hand, a liberating but sometimes dangerous departure from everyday convention. Susan Napier identifies these "tabooed images of freedom" (in Herbert Marcuse's phrase) as a distinguishing characteristic of Japanese fantastic writing in general. She writes, "Perhaps it is finally these 'tabooed images' which are the most distinctive aspects of the Japanese fantastic, a subversion of modernity which offers a variety of unique alternatives in its place" (227).[2] In *Secret Rendezvous*, these perverse acts or relationships become a point at which the narrator rejoins society, but in a context where social expectations are distorted or defeated.

These perverse distortions are accomplished and amplified by technology, and as in Abe's other novels, this technology acts largely through language. At the hospital, science is repeatedly brought to bear in treating these sexual problems, and in this way Abe once again probes the way that technology has altered human relationships generally. Like the women in Abe's novels, technology has a powerful but dangerous function, an ambiguous, wild-card role. Initially, it holds out the promise of an erotic attraction that will strengthen the bonds between people, but ultimately it escapes control and leads to a perversity or obscenity that only seems to aggravate alienation. The technological centerpiece of the text is an elaborate and precisely described audio surveillance system used to amplify, record, and broadcast the sexual activities of the people at the hospital. It is this system that captures much of the deviant behavior recorded in the novel. In fact, the text itself is structured like one of the surveillance tapes.

This explains in part why Abe's later narratives are so chaotic, and how *Secret Rendezvous* is continuous with Abe's earlier work, perhaps even the culmination of it. At the same time, *Secret Rendezvous* represents a shift in emphasis from earlier work that turned on relativizing the language styles associated with various scientific disciplines such as biology, computer science, or psychology. *Secret Rendezvous* and (as we will see in Chapter 7) *The Ark Sakura* are even more focused on how language is changed by the fruit of science—technology. Clearly, the action of technology on language played some part in the narratives of earlier novels as well, but *Secret Rendezvous* is a pivotal work in two ways: first, for the intensity with which it engages this question; and second, for being a literal reflection onto the printed page of the ways that technology supplements and often supplants communication. It is no less than the prose equivalent—and the evolution—of the multimedia experiments explored in the last chapter.

Burn Each Page Behind You:
 The Plot of Secret Rendezvous

The story of the events that constitute *Secret Rendezvous* begins with a sudden occurrence, suddenly related: "One summer morning an ambulance suddenly drove up, although no one remembered having sent for one, and carried away the man's wife" (8).

Both the man and his wife protest that they were not expecting an ambulance, to which the ambulance crew replies with a plausibly twisted logic familiar to Abe's readers. This is an emergency, they counter. No one ever expects an emergency.[3]

The narrator admits that he is "the man." At first he acquiesces meekly and lets his wife be taken, but when she fails to call, he goes in search of her. He traces the ambulance's destination to an unfamiliar hospital on the other side of town, where a night watchman tells him that a woman matching his wife's description arrived in her pajamas by ambulance early that morning and refused to be admitted, insisting she was not sick. She went to the waiting room to use the phone, and that is the last he saw of her. But at that hour of the morning the waiting room was closed up and deserted, its only exit back past this watchman. The wife has disappeared from a locked room without a trace.

This is the mystery the narrator tries to solve. As he investigates, he becomes embroiled in a series of plots and intrigues between the people at the hospital, and the narrative quickly becomes more and more fantastic. A summary of the first few chapters will give a feel for the roller-coaster way in which the novel unfolds: from the night watchman the narrator learns that the doctor on duty has a weakness for other men's wives, so he tails the doctor back to an abandoned housing complex. Peering inside, he sees the doctor masturbating in a room papered with nude centerfolds and washed with the sounds of recorded sex. (Later he learns that these sounds are the harvest of the audio surveillance.) When the two men get into a tussle, the doctor— still naked and erect—falls from a second-story window and is knocked unconscious. Almost immediately, a team of the hospital's senior staff arrives to cart the narrator and the unconscious doctor away.

When the narrator explains to the hospital's assistant director and chief of security that he is looking for his wife, they give him access to the listening equipment. But even after spending hours poring over the surveillance tapes, he finds no hint of where his wife has gone. And as he is shown around the sprawling, mazelike hospital, he begins to realize that there is no shortage of places for her to hide or be hidden. (In fact, the hospital has a number of features that complicate its geography, including an abandoned underground wing whose partially collapsed walls form a subterranean labyrinth, and some precipitous topography that creates unusual spatial relationships between the floors of buildings constructed on the steep slopes.)

During his exploration he discovers a secret chamber with a peephole through which he observes a bizarre experiment. What he sees reveals the fate of the injured doctor, who is seen lying on a bed, still erect, and now connected by a series of electrodes and intervening machinery to the assistant director on the adjacent bed. As the assistant director calls out instructions, a nurse massages the unconscious doctor's penis while another nurse adjusts the dials and switches of the machines.

At first, the scene is described like this without any additional explanation. But in a parenthetical note the narrator adds that he later learned the reason for the experiment. The assistant director is attempting to cure his own impotence by connecting his nervous system to that of a healthy subject and having the sexual stimulation electronically transmitted to himself. The unconscious doctor's sexual escapades and his masturbation habit are legendary around the hospital, so he is the perfect subject. Ultimately, the assistant director plans to wire this surrogate penis permanently to his own body.

Unfortunately the doctor's genitals do not survive the experiment intact, and the assistant director must locate another donor. Happily, the well-endowed security chief is conveniently murdered at this point by a secretary, in revenge for raping her five years earlier. This permits the assistant director to amputate the dead chief's lower body and connect it to himself with an electrically wired rubber harness. He now has two penises and four legs, arranged like a centaur, "a rickety baby camel, or a four-legged ostrich" (4). He takes to calling himself "the horse."

This is just the beginning of the narrator's adventure, which becomes even more farfetched as the story continues. As the summary suggests, the scenes have a slapstick quality that makes them resemble a series of visual set pieces. Added to these tableaux is another set of verbal sketches, the descriptions of people the narrator meets. Besides the masturbating doctor on duty and the desperately impotent assistant director, there is the assistant director's wife, a psycholinguist who uses a lie detector to study the relationship between arousal and eavesdropping, and the assistant director's paradoxically lascivious but frigid secretary—the murderous rape victim. There is also an array of staff and patients with odd diseases: an incontinent head nurse who does her work sitting on a portable toilet; a girl whose bones are jellified by "osteolysis," causing her body to ooze into different shapes; and her mother, whose insides were turned to cotton by "Watafuki" disease and who has now been recycled into bedding (98, 144).

The scenery and characters are described with a ravenous eye for detail reminiscent of Abe's style in *The Crime of S. Karma*. In both works, precise description substitutes for meaning: the subtle differences between the uniform insignia worn by the security personal and the nurses are described, for example, but it is not entirely clear what the differences signify, or what either group really does in the hospital. As a result, the novel often seems to resemble one of the Abe Kōbō Studio's "galleries of images" more than a connected story.

Adding to this confusion of time and voices is the confused geography mentioned above. The narrator also struggles to come to terms with the baffling space of the hospital, by obsessively describing his movements around the mazelike grounds. But this produces only a kind of confused precision: for example, when he faithfully relates a long series of left and right turns that leave the reader more disoriented than before. At the end of the novel, the narrator finds himself abandoned in the underground wing, running out of water, food, and flashlight batteries, unable to find his way out. In the same manner, it is easy for a reader to lose his or her place in the novel, unable to visualize the overall geography. The effect of this is to reduce the physical spaces of the story to a series of detached points, a geography that reinforces the disjointed events of the narrative and the gallery-like exhibition of characters.

Early reviews of *Secret Rendezvous* were often at a loss to describe the plot, and settled for quoting the early line about the arrival of the ambulance and then simply cataloging the bizarre people, places, and experiments that the narrator encounters on his subsequent journey. A review in *Shūkan Asahi* emphasizes this gallery or slide-show effect: "The novel consists mostly of scenery from this world of nonsensical perverted sexuality, scenes exhibited one after another as the narrator makes his way through this labyrinth" ("Chiteki" 115). Another critic described the difficulty of connecting together the individual events of the novel: "The novel has the appearance of reality, and it is full of realistic events, but they appear in isolation, unrelated. Readers must burn each page behind them as they read, their thirst for answers unsatisfied" (Morota 5).

From Polyphony to Cacophony: The Style of Secret Rendezvous

What contributes to this sense of fragmentation is not only the topsy-turvy geography, the furiously evolving story, and the fleeting appearances of so many vivid characters; first and foremost, it is the style in which the novel is written. Whereas in earlier novels we saw separate styles (scientific and non-scientific) establish themselves one at time, and then combine and interact, in *Secret Rendezvous* the mixing is already complete at the outset. The reader is presented with a mélange of conversational fragments in different voices, representing a range of different people and events.

It requires close reading to identify these different styles in earlier novels and show how they combine, but in *Secret Rendezvous* this collage of different voices is foregrounded as an explicit element of the text: the "notebooks" that constitute the novel represent the work of a single author (the narrator), but now they contain the voices of all the characters. This is because large sections of the notebooks are supposedly written by transcribing and annotating the surveillance tapes that were made of the narrator's activities over the course of the novel. So the kaleidoscopic structure identified by the critics above, with "scenes exhibited one after another," "in isolation, unrelated," is generated by this narrative device and the thoroughgoing heteroglossia that results. Instead of discerning two or three distinct styles and asking what each represents (as we did for *Inter Ice Age 4*, *The Face of Another*, and *The Woman in the Dunes*), we now need to examine how the notebooks represent a chorus of many different voices, and what this new more complex texture conveys.

The preceding plot summary outlines the initial *events* of the story, but it does not begin to suggest the structure of the narrative, which relates the events out of temporal sequence, in a variety of different voices. The text or the narrative begins by describing a predawn meeting between the narrator and the horse. The latter hands the narrator six cassette tapes containing surveillance recordings and asks him to carry out an investigation of the person on the tapes (a person who later turns out to be the narrator himself). The narrator records the results in a series of notebooks, writing about "the subject" (himself) in the third person, as the horse requests. As in *The Face of Another*, these notebooks form the text of the novel.

This meeting at the beginning of the narrative, describing the origin of the notebooks, actually takes place on the fourth day of the story. This is after the narrator has already spent several days at the hospital searching for his wife, and after the bizarre experiments outlined above have culminated in the assistant director's transformation into the horse. At this point, the narrator has actually assumed the role of security chief, after the previous chief is murdered and bisected to become the horse's hind end.

The narrator jumps back and forth between these two time frames: the early part of the story captured on the tapes and the later present in which he is listening to the tapes, writing in the notebook, and periodically meeting with the horse. So as the novel begins there are two separate narratives proceeding at once. Toward the end of the novel, the number of frames increases to three, when the narrator begins a new secret notebook in an attempt to revise the earlier account that appeared in the previous notebooks. As a result, he finds himself continually skipping ahead or doubling back, dropping or picking up different threads. The multiple frames of *The Face of Another*—with its notebooks, its supplementary notes, its preface written last, and its final appended note—all these are simple in comparison with *Secret Rendezvous*.

This structure (which contributes to the disjointed, kaleidoscopic impression identified by the critics cited above) reflects the heteroglossia of the tapes the narrator is ostensibly following as he writes these notebooks. The sound of the tapes is in turn influenced by the design of the listening system, which aggravates or amplifies the heteroglossia at the hospital. The system incorporates hundreds of microphones hidden at strategic places around the hospital that pick up any sound in their listening range. The isolated, fragmentary sounds from all these microphones are combined, processed, and recorded on a series of reel-to-reel tape decks in the security room, yielding a haphazard audio collage of everything that is going on in the hospital. The cassettes the horse gives to the narrator represent an edited extract of these master tapes, containing the parts that supposedly relate to the narrator himself.

As one might expect, Abe lavishes attention on the technical details of the surveillance system: the input from microphones all over the hospital is fed into a system of "sound oscillating repeaters" or "relayers," which forward the most promising sounds for recording, particularly those that indicate impending sex, like the sound of clothing being removed (72). In the case of the more ambiguous sounds, the machine has an algorithm for determining what might be worth listening in on, particularly what might constitute sexual activity:

The selection was controlled by microcomputer. First the relayer would begin to work in response to sudden changes in tone or volume; it was programmed to stop recording automatically when the vocal-tension index fell below 3.2 in the case of human voices, or in the case of other natural sounds, when rhythm and pitch were repeated in fixed patterns. The vocal-tension index was the quantification of physical response to psychological tension, he learned, while the repetition rate of natural sounds was understood to be the reverse [inverse] function of background activities. (72)

As with the prediction machine in *Inter Ice Age 4*, this electronic attempt to define, delimit, and keep tabs on everything actually seems to hasten the degeneration into nonsense. The result of all this careful filtering is an incomprehensible sequence of disconnected sounds. Here the narrator describes the contents of one of these master tapes.

"Well, hmm, that's about the size of it" . . . the sound of urinating, or perhaps of water being poured into a cup from a faucet . . . aluminum cans rolling and falling downstairs . . . sounds of a woman's panting; suppressed laughter; paper being torn . . . off-key whistling, like wind through a crack . . . kittens mewing . . . "Now, how shall I put it, uh, you know?" . . . (71)

In the novel, the whole sequence is over twice as long, with only ellipses and commas delimiting the unrelated sounds. Note that this occurs on the same page as the technical description above. As in the earlier novels, there is a rapid alternation between these technical passages and a chaos they try to regulate but only succeed in exacerbating.

The range and number of voices coming into the security station is so great that they have to be overlapped and recorded several layers deep on the tapes. The reel-to-reel tape machines in the security room use a special single-track, six-channel recording scheme to record six feeds simultaneously on one piece of tape. As Abe describes it, an operator reviewing the tapes must listen to all six layers of sound at the same time, three sets of sounds playing simultaneously in each ear. The narrator says the tapes are a "time mosaic: moments that existed simultaneously yet were impossible to experience simultaneously" (73).

Furthermore, to record all the significant conversations that take place everywhere in the hospital during a single hour requires seven hours worth of these six-channel tapes. So in the hour it takes the narrator to listen to one tape, seven new ones are created by the system. An eavesdropper can never keep up.

From these recordings the horse has apparently extracted those sounds and conversations associated with the narrator and dubbed them onto cassettes (the state-of-the-art medium in 1977). The result is a reassembled but highly fragmentary audio portrait of the narrator and his story: "A man on display, torn into fragments of tongue-clucking, throat-clearing, off-key humming, chewing, entreaties, hollow obsequious laughter, belches, sniffling, timid excuses" (6). The job given to the narrator is to reconstruct his own activities using the tapes as a guide. He is to fill in the needed explanations, the unrecorded conversations, and the missing events, and make a final report to the horse.

So the style and structure of the notebooks borrow from the heteroglossia of the tapes they ostensibly follow. Much of the novel consists of dialogues the narrator has with various characters he encounters in the hospital, interleaved with explanatory narrative, as if the narrator were in fact transcribing or summarizing the tapes and periodically adding his own commentary. Making the connection more explicit are parenthetical notes such as "The conversation below is taken from side two of tape one. The playback counter reads 729" (8).

From the opening pages, then, there is a jumble of conversations or dialogues that is only with difficulty made to correspond with the order of events in time. While the different voices in *Inter Ice Age 4* and *The Face of Another* established themselves and were then mixed or recombined, the voices in *Secret Rendezvous* start out in a clutter, just like the voices on the tape.

In terms of its language (as well as its temporal narrative, its characters, and its physical setting), *Secret Rendezvous* can be summarized as a mingled collection of heterogeneous fragments—shards of space, time, sound, and writing. The novel is like the "mosaic" to which the narrator compares the tapes, but a mosaic viewed too close: the overall design has become unclear, and the work is often reduced to a collection of bright fragments. It is the task of the narrator and the reader to make sense of this jumble, to step back from it to discern some pattern in the riot.

Most reviews of *Secret Rendezvous* professed confusion with the work and its jumbled structure, and after these initial, bewildered reactions there is relatively little written about the novel. It seemed easier to say what *Secret Rendezvous* was not than to say what it was, leading some to identify it as a deconstruction of the novelistic form itself. "I do not know if this novel succeeds or fails," wrote Okuno Takeo in his review, "but it forces what is probably a new anti-novelistic literary experience on its readers." Normally one of Abe's strong supporters, Okuno directed a kind of backhanded praise at this project, writing "Even in the midst of my irritation and frustration, I cannot hold back an immense admiration for Abe's work" ("Kyōretsu" 7).[4]

But despite Okuno's label "anti-novel," the events of *Secret Rendezvous* are finally not so disordered as to challenge the conventions of the novel itself. What the fragmentation discussed above really accomplishes is to foreground the difficulty of representing or sorting out events; but typically for Abe, there is an order underlying the confusion of the novel's structure. As with *The Box Man*, despite the difficulty of following the sequence of happenings, a reader who keeps her own notebook of the story will discover there is a precise timeline against which most, if not all of the narrator's account can be reconciled. The geography of the novel's spaces is described so as to induce confusion, but that is not to say it is nonsensical or contradictory. Juliet Carpenter once told me a story about meeting with Abe while she was translating the novel. Commenting that the hospital must be hard to picture from the descriptions, Abe picked up a napkin and drew her a detailed floor plan. The anecdote suggests both that the descriptions are part of a coherent picture and that Abe deliberately clouded that picture as he wrote.[5]

In this respect, the confusions of time, space, and logic in the novel are like the programming language in *Inter Ice Age 4*, or the chemist's tortuous ruminations in *The Face of Another*: at root they are accurate or consistent, but they are also intentionally confusing. They reveal the strengths and shortcomings, the preconceptions and blind spots of the styles in which they are written. Several reviews realized that difficulties with the novel or its language are central to the way it works. The purpose of the text is to problematize our perception of reality and force a creative jump to the next level. Serizawa Shunsuke gives the most complete statement of this, phrased in Abe's own vocabulary of the everyday: "In other words, sex and family connect one thing to another, and their current state gives a measure how far reality has decayed. . . . The weave of the novel portrays in a fresh way our contemporary sense of crisis, at a time when there is no longer an everyday logic or reason to counter the logic and reason of this fantasy world [*hinichijō sekai*]" (1).[6]

In fact, if we try to identify some of the everyday common sense that the novel questions, we find many parallels with Abe's earlier novels. In this respect, *Secret Rendezvous* is arguably the climax of Abe's career as a novelist, summing up ideas from the previous 25 years. Below we look at *Secret Rendezvous* in the context of *Inter Ice Age 4*, *The Woman in the Dunes*, *The Face of Another*, and *The Box Man*, and show how it continues projects begun in these earlier works. This sheds quite a bit of light on the novel, but it still may not answer all of *Secret Rendezvous*'s detractors. Even those critics who are willing to allow fantasy a role in destabilizing the everyday seemed to feel that the fantastic elements get the better of this novel. While acknowledging Abe's skill at calling into question the perceptions that constitute our everyday, they suggest that the novel finally fails to suggest any kind of alternative. Saeki Shōichi says readers will inevitably find themselves asking the author: "Who the hell are you, luring your readers into this labyrinth and dragging them through it? Are you anything more than a showman directing a farce [*dōke shibai*]?" (2).[7]

Saeki's choice of words here reflects a prevailing sense that the finely honed parody of Abe's early works—the careful balance of respect and irony he affords science, literature, society, and their different dialects—gives way in his later work to undisciplined farce.[8] One reason for this criticism seems to be *Secret Rendezvous*'s lack of an eloquent spokesperson for any alternative rationality, such as *Inter Ice Age 4*'s Tanomogi or *The Face of Another*'s chemist. And there is certainly no one who is able to take the next step, balancing different rationalities and voices and combining them into a new more productive style, such as the chemist's wife or the later Niki Junpei. There are one or two candidates for these roles—the horse, for example—but ultimately none of them are convincing.[9] This seems to be the reason that some reviewers praised the fantasy in the novel but criticized its lack of ideas.

The question of parody versus farce is a key one for Abe's later work, and we will return to it at the end of this chapter. Ultimately, we need to ask *why* no clear voice emerges from the cacophony of the text to

offer an alternative, a balance of styles, or some kind of moral judgment on the depravity that has been depicted. Why, with so many
voices, is it so hard to say or hear anything positive in this text? Some
blame Abe for this failure, but others have argued that this kind of
thing is part of a decline in literary language itself, in a world where
language seems to move faster, further, and more fluidly because of
advances in technology. *Secret Rendezvous* is either a victim of these
changes, or an attempt to deal constructively and proactively with them,
or both. We will revisit these issues after elucidating some of the parallels between *Secret Rendezvous* and Abe's earlier novels.

Abe's Perverse Logic

Knitting together the various sexual soundscapes and tableaux in the
novel are the taboos or boundaries that surround our interaction with
the other in this most basic of relationships, the sexual one. This links
the different parts of *Secret Rendezvous*, and links this novel to the rest of
Abe's work. Much of what is depicted in *Secret Rendezvous* could be
described as "perverse," in its sense of deviating from a norm, though
often it is the norms rather than the deviations that seem to be criticized in the novel. Besides the rampant voyeurism and eavesdropping
already noted, and the backdrop of adultery and infidelity, the secretary
is somehow lascivious and frigid; the narrator defends himself from
charges of homosexuality (in connection with a former job as a nude
model); the doctor on duty masturbates incessantly; and the assistant
director/horse represents first impotence, then satyriasis and bestiality.
The little girl with osteolysis masturbates in front of the horse, the narrator, and the security chief, who turns out to be her father. These taboos pile up in grotesque combinations: the secretary gives her body to
the security goons as payment for killing the security chief who raped
her. The horse plans to mate with the little girl using the transplanted
penis that once belonged to her abusive, murdered dad.

The peak of all this comes at the end of the novel in an "orgasm
contest" (*orugazumu konkūru*), which is the featured event of the hospital's anniversary festival. A series of female contestants with colorful
stage names compete in front of a live audience to see who can maintain the longest sustained climax. Viewers place bets on the women
and their jockey-like male assistants, and the contestants have scientific

probes affixed and inserted to measure their physiologic reactions. The horse has a plan to mate with the winner the next day in a public display, bringing together these two specimens of exaggerated male and female sexuality. The narrator attends because he has received information suggesting that his wife may be among the competitors, and there is one contestant—the "masked woman" (*kamenjo*)—who somehow resembles her. But the mask and the narrator's own resistance prevent him from making a positive identification. It is this masked woman who emerges as the winner of the contest, by virtue of a psychological disorder that keeps her in a state of perpetual arousal.

Despite this parade, readers of the novel may find it hard to be offended, if only because the novel is so outrageous that it is difficult to take any of it too seriously. It grows less provocative the more outrageous it becomes. This may signal more than anything that it lacks the keen-edged satire Abe achieved in *The Face of Another* and *The Woman in the Dunes*, and even the black humor of *Inter Ice Age 4*, and instead sinks to the level of farce or slapstick. Nevertheless, many of the devices used to interrogate the everyday in those earlier novels carry through to *Secret Rendezvous*.

Although the novel focuses more closely on sex than any of Abe's other books, sex is just a figure for the novel's broader theme of human relations—a theme obviously shared with Abe's previous work. This phrase "human relations" (*ningen kankei*) occurs over and over in the novel, particularly when describing various sexual pathologies. The nurse's frigidity and the assistant director's impotence are attributed to "traumatic interpersonal relations neurosis" (109). The masked woman's condition is also related back to individual identity and relations with the other: her "rape delusion" is "a defensive arousal mechanism for escaping from the fear of rape," and stemming from a syndrome referred to as "personality forfeiture" (171–72).

The Face of Another used these same figures of the mask and sexual trespass to investigate human relations, and the orgasm contest in particular can be read as a repetition and an inversion of the situation in the earlier novel. *Secret Rendezvous*'s "masked woman" becomes a parodic double of the masked chemist: she puts on the mask to experience a sexual freedom that channels her fear, while he does the same to channel his aggression. Alternatively, one could compare *Secret Rendezvous*'s wife/

masked woman to the chemist's wife who fictionalizes herself, playing the role of unfaithful spouse in order to escape the mask's violence. (She "simulated the confidence of an accomplice," the chemist complains in the earlier novel. "The result was that finally the mask didn't even amount to a lecher, much less a rapist. . . ." [*AZ* 18:465].) As we move from *The Face of Another* to *Secret Rendezvous*, however, the first wife's fiction becomes the second wife's delusion.

The figure of sexual monster is also repeated in both novels. Just as the chemist abandons the desire to be normal for the satisfaction of monstrosity, the assistant director embraces the abnormal. A doctor himself, he eventually decides it is only by accepting the sick patients as they are, rather than healing them, that he can reach out to them and cure his own isolation and impotence. His desire to join this community of the sick leads him to deform himself with this bizarre experiment, to become "the ideal patient . . . the patient among patients . . . the forever incurable patient . . . days spent sleeping curled up with death . . . a parasitic vine grown larger than its host . . . deformity personified . . . a monster . . . and finally, a 'horse-man'" (128). Initially, both novels associate deformity with isolation; but finally it is only by pursuing abnormality, and specifically sexual trespass, that characters can meet each other on new or different terms.

There are also parallels between *Secret Rendezvous* and *Inter Ice Age 4*. Recall that the aquans are robbed of their humanity and specifically their emotions by unnatural technological intervention in human reproduction. Part of this intervention consists of raising the first generation of aquans outside the womb, a birth that deprives them of family. The secretary presents the same figure in *Secret Rendezvous*: she is a "test tube baby," not only conceived but apparently gestated outside the womb, and this is invoked to explain her abnormal sexual socialization. She is indifferent to sex, showing frigid disinterest and a blasé promiscuity by turns. Lab instruments show no sexual response, yet she makes every effort to seduce the narrator. For five years she seems unconcerned about her own rape, then one day she gives herself to a gang of young men in return for murdering the rapist. The horse says, "Her sense of human relationships, shall we call it, is entirely missing. [. . .] For example, the sense of loneliness is one manifestation of the nesting instinct, they say. And skin sensations, it seems, are at the root of all feelings and emotions. While she, you see, has no nest or roots to feelings and emotions. While she, you see, has no nest or roots to go back to, at all." (108)

Compare the horse's equation of skin and feeling to Dr. Yamamoto's idea that the aquans do not feel the same things we do because they cannot cry underwater, or the aquan boy's longing to feel the music of the wind on his bare skin, or the plastic surgeon K's declaration that "the soul is in the skin!" (*AZ* 18:337). In their various contexts, all three expressions manifest the idea that as technology intervenes to alter the body, it also changes what it means to be human.

In *Inter Ice Age 4*, this ability to intervene in our humanity is represented by technology's ability to redirect the course of human evolution. Evolution becomes another figure for future changes that are unsettling but ambiguously productive, for the way they disrupt the continuity of our everyday experience. *Inter Ice Age 4* explores this with the image of an evolution that seems like retrograde motion. The future of the human race comes to depend on a return to the ocean, something that looks to Katsumi like a step backward. Similarly, in *Secret Rendezvous*, the horse argues that we have entered an age of reverse evolution or "retrogression" (*gyaku shinka*). As medical science protects and preserves the weak, he says, it works against survival of the fittest and creates a situation of reverse evolution. A society's degree of civilization can paradoxically be measured by the debilitation of its members. This is the source of his desire to become sick, to climb back down the evolutionary ladder by turning himself into the horse. "If animal history has been a history of evolution," the horse says, "then the history of mankind is one of retrogression. Hooray for monsters! Monsters are the great embodiments of the weak" (172). If the female counterpart of the horse is the winner of the orgasm contest—a mutant woman with an "illness" there is no need to cure—then the mating between the two is the final outcome of an evolutionary progress that represents a reversal or defeat of so-called natural selection.

For Abe, this kind of reversal may productively challenge the everyday. In comments he made following the publication of both *Inter Ice Age 4* and *Secret Rendezvous*, Abe emphasizes the ambiguous relationship between evolution and progress.[10] Ideas such as natural selection or survival of the fittest, he says, apply when humans are still struggling to survive in nature. When we reach the point of being able to alter our world and our bodies, the new technological and social reality we create supersedes old ideas of fitness. Abe even suggests, "Since it is precisely those that are ill-adapted to nature who can summon the desire to master nature, the world is moving toward survival of the least fit" (*AZ* 26:195).

And what could be said of nature can be said of society as well. Abe argues that "sick" is a category society defines for itself. The weak are those who cannot or will not adapt themselves to society's definition of strength or health, yet they are also the ones with the strength to challenge society's common sense. Abe gives a droll example in the spirit of the novel: a 400-meter race may prove who is the fastest runner, but only because all the contestants agree to run around the circular track, instead of cutting across the middle to the finish line. "A qualification for being the strongest is this mental state that keeps you within the rules no matter what" (*AZ* 26:195). Invoking the links between eugenics and totalitarianism, Abe makes it clear that in this case it is not the strong but the weak who are powerful in the face of society's oppressive expectations, because they have the will to resist them.

This final point about power in society may recall Foucault, who uses Abe's own metaphor of the monstrous menagerie to point out that discourses are best understood precisely by what they rule out or exclude. "Within its own limits," Foucault writes, "every discipline recognizes true and false propositions, but it repulses a whole teratology of learning. The exterior of a science is both more, and less, populated than one might think: . . . error can only emerge and be identified within a well-defined process; there are monsters on the prowl, however, whose forms alter with the history of knowledge" ("Discourse" 223–24).

If the equine assistant director does not rise to being the kind the revolutionary Abe describes above, it is because his experiments do not enable him to change society or even rejoin it, but merely allow him to avoid it, or to encounter it only on his own select terms. The novel explains that the eavesdropping system originated as a treatment for the assistant director's impotence and the secretary's frigidity—as a way of reconnecting with the other. Audio tapes were found to provide maximum stimulation and to supply the assistant director with the "greater anonymity in his interpersonal relations" that was part of his therapy (108–9). The need to obtain these audio tapes of anonymous people having sex is what led to the hospital's elaborate surveillance program.

Technology fulfills both of the conflicting impulses faced by Abe's characters—the need to bring the other closer and simultaneously keep him or her at bay. The desire to have it both ways is what is behind the hope that "greater anonymity" might remedy the assistant director's "traumatic interpersonal relations neurosis," and the hope that eavesdropping may bring him closer to others without the stress of real contact. This conflicted desire is familiar from Abe's previous novels, but up to now it has been played out more in visual terms, using the motif of voyeurism rather than eavesdropping.

Caught between their conflicted desire for community and freedom, many of Abe's narrators resort to this voyeurism, and many are abetted by technology. Watching or listening from the safety of his hiding place, the voyeur reaches for the other without being reached himself, like the private detective watching from the shadows or the box man peeking out from his box. "In seeing there is love," Abe writes in *The Box Man*, "in being seen there is abhorrence" (81). The voyeur's fantasy is the desire to make all relationships conditional or unidirectional, to possess the other without being possessed, to have her on his own terms.

The chemist's mask is another manifestation of this desire to look out from behind a shield, to watch unobserved. And in *Inter Ice Age 4*, the computer provides Katsumi with a remote viewer that becomes a privileged window on the world. Many key scenes are transmitted to him via television, a technology that was still high-tech at the time. But the advantage of these technologies is also their weakness. They defer or distance the other at the same time they bring him close. The narrator sees his aquan son, but only on a TV screen. A murdered man rejoins the living, but only as a computer simulation. The chemist resumes sex with his wife, but only at the cost of pretending to be someone else. In all these cases the other is brought near, but the layer of technology between people isolates them from one another. Technology unites and defers in one smooth motion.

Secret Rendezvous shows the next evolutionary stage of this technology that unites and separates. The hospital's comprehensive surveillance system reveals the other's most intimate secrets, but it does not help the narrator find his wife. The story also transforms this heretofore visual metaphor more explicitly into the terms of spoken language. The outlandish experiments exemplified by the horse's bodily transformation eclipse the extent to which *Secret Rendezvous*—no less than Abe's other novels, and maybe more—is finally a novel about language, about how technology acts on language and thereby changes the way we interact with one another.

For example, the horse explains that the eavesdropping system originated as part of a psycholinguistic project to study the relationship between arousal and "symbolic representation," by measuring the efficiency of different language and media in exciting test subjects. And later we hear from a researcher who worked on the original experiment, and learn why it failed: because scientific language alone cannot quantify or control sexual and human relationships. That researcher is coincidentally the assistant director/horse's estranged wife, an employee in the psycholinguistics department who is now in charge of administering lie detector tests at the hospital. She discusses her theory of sex with the narrator, including her paper on "the logic of lying," about the relation between sex, science, and human relations (131). She explains that sex and emotions are not governed by the cut-and-dried logic of science. They require some contradiction and even deception in order to function. She learned this, she says, when she and her husband the assistant director decided to hold every conversation connected to a lie detector, so there would be no secrets between them. The result was a gradual waning of interest and the onset of the assistant director's impotence. She explains this in terms of the need for human and sexual relationships to escape the world of logic: "And if truth is the front, then lies are the back; you end up thinking of everything in terms of front and back. [. . .] Even computers think of everything in binary terms. Yes or no. That might work if there were never any contradiction between feelings and reason. But take away that contradiction from people and what do you think would be left? If there were nothing but facts, no lies or truth. . ." (132). What is left, it turns out, is nothing "but an empty space like unexposed film" (132). The narrator continues: "After they had ceased to have dialogue, the magnetism between them had gone, too. Nothing had been left to hold them together, and nothing to push them apart; there had been only their dried-out hearts, like empty insect shells" (132–33).

The "logic of lying"; a mix of attraction and repulsion undone by too much truth; the dominance of one style ("facts"), which leads to a cessation of "dialogue"; and a woman who reveals all this to the deluded male scientists who are the novel's protagonists. Every point of this recalls *The Face of Another* and the compromise embraced by the chemist's wife. Her ideal was also a mix or a dialogue between truth and fiction that governed the tension between both of them, a dialogue that allowed them to resume sexual and personal contact.

The assistant director's wife brings the question back to social expectations. She explains how society must construct a series of rituals around sex in order to tame it and reduce the "sense of indecency," cloaking it in institutions like marriage. Without these rituals, the stresses of personal relations are too great. In language that echoes *The Woman in the Dunes*, she says that "When the sex act is made a ritual, then the body's personal relations center can relax and issue its own permit" (133). But it is not clear whether she is presenting these social rituals as dangerous everyday falsehoods or constructive fictions. She might represent the voice of society, calling for a return to conventional relations, or she might be revealing society's expectations themselves to be just another fantasy.

The wife's comments resolve some of the questions about *Secret Rendezvous*, both for what they say in themselves, and for the further parallels they reveal with *The Face of Another*. Some readers may be satisfied to consider this the key to the novel. But many will find it hard to consider this the last word on this text. Besides the lingering questions noted above, the estranged wife's comments do not have the finality or the authority of the letter that concludes *The Face of Another*. They slip by three-quarters through the novel, overwhelmed by everything else that is done and said. Finally, her voice is not strong enough to be heard over the cacophony of the work.

The Possibility of Parody

For over 20 years Abe kept these dialects of science and fiction delicately balanced in his novels and made them interrogate one another. His characters represented a careful spectrum of different styles combined in different measure, sometimes productively and sometimes destructively; but as the readings in foregoing chapters have tried to show, each novel as a whole had an overarching perspective that showed how these languages should (or at least would, could) come together.

In *Secret Rendezvous*, however, the utter mixing of these voices—a fragmentation approaching homogenization—has dissolved the complex linguistic distinction and tension between science, society, and fantasy that governed the earlier novels. Neither the wife nor any other character is quite able to marshal and control these styles, because they are so thoroughly mixed from the outset. And *Secret Rendezvous* also lacks the aesthetic compensation we see in the poetic vision of the aquan future or the movie the chemist invokes in *The Face of Another*—scenes that suggested (perhaps conservatively) that fiction or poetry or simply beauty does have the power to impose some order on things in the end.

Here we might ask *why* the novel turned out this way. What upset this delicate balance at this stage in Abe's career? Perhaps it was Abe's attempt to keep pace with the increasing speed of communication technology at the time. Japan was very different in 1977 when *Secret Rendezvous* was published than when Abe wrote *Inter Ice Age 4*, almost 20 years before, a time when even television was a relatively new technology. The hospital eavesdropping system is a metaphor for the accelerating pace of communication in a media society, with three separate compressed soundtracks in each ear, and seven more tapes created in the time it takes to listen to one. Like mass media and communication technologies from telephone to the Internet, the eavesdropping system brings the world close and simultaneously holds it at bay: the sphere of our experience grows wider, but the experiences themselves become progressively more virtual or mediated.

Like Abe's other novels, *Secret Rendezvous* goes beyond describing those changes in the plot of the story; it mirrors this acceleration and multiplication of language in its own style. In this respect, it is also the logical outgrowth of Abe's writing up to now; but arguably electronic technology was now accelerating language to the point where even Abe's brand of fiction could not keep up. Some might argue that as he struggled to make his novels keep pace with technology's effect on language, Abe reached a point where he was overtaken by that technology, where he could no longer shape this heteroglossia into an effective text, where he finally lost control of his ongoing literary experiment. Others might say that Abe deliberately sacrificed this novel (or the novel sacrificed itself) as a demonstration of technology's destabilizing power.

The question of whether *Secret Rendezvous* works as a novel is ultimately a subjective one. One can identify fairly clearly what the novel is trying to do; whether it succeeds or fails for a given reader is tied up with the reader's own experience with the text. It is more interesting to shift the question slightly, and ask: at this moment in Japanese literature and world literature, could Abe or any other novelist entirely avoid this crisis?

Critics of postmodern media society have suggested that *Secret Rendezvous* and similar novels are the symptoms of a broader crisis of language and expression. In his characterization of the postmodern, Fredric Jameson identifies it with a loss of deep meaning in language and self-expression, the fading of all original linguistic referents. We traced Jameson's ideas in Chapter 3: like other language, art is transformed into a series of empty signifiers or simulacra, images condemned to repeat other images in a vicious circle. In art, this fosters a profusion of meta-texts that cannibalize other works. Jameson's examples include the repetition of media images in Andy Warhol's art and the citation of historical tropes in postmodern architecture, but we could just as well cite the transcription of taped conversations in *Secret Rendezvous*.

Compared with earlier forms of imitation and quotation, Jameson sees a crisis of judgment or perspective in this kind of art, a crisis he characterizes as a decline of parody. If parody implies the imitation of something as a means of judging it, then in the repetition Jameson describes, the perspective needed to compare and judge language— the concept of an original behind the parodic double—has become impossible. Instead of parody, we now have only pastiche, an indiscriminate quotation of other languages and styles that has no opinion about them. This is very similar to criticisms that *Secret Rendezvous* is a "farce," an implied comparison with the sharper satire or parody of Abe's earlier works. Jameson writes: "Pastiche is, like parody, the imitation of a peculiar or unique, idiosyncratic style. . . . But it is a neutral practice of such mimicry, without any of parody's ulterior motives, amputated of the satiric impulse, devoid of laughter and of any conviction that alongside the abnormal tongue you have momentarily borrowed, some healthy linguistic normality still exists. Pastiche is thus blank parody; a statue with blind eyeballs. . ." (17).

Pastiche, then, is one expression of a larger postmodern aesthetic characterized by semantic deprivation and sensory overload: postmodern art and language are "a pure and random play of signifiers," a sublime flood of disconnected impressions, "a rush of filmic images without density" (96, 34). Pastiche is favored in this context because it supports the quick and indiscriminate incorporation of diverse signs, and severs these fragments of language from any context that might produce a meaning. As an example, Jameson offers the rapid fire of images in experimental video, but he could almost be describing the gallery of disconnected scenes and conversations in Abe's novel: "a ceaseless rotation of elements such that they change place at every moment, with the result that no single element can occupy the position of 'interpretant' (or that of primary sign) for any length of time but must be dislodged in turn in the following instant" (90).

As to the role of scientific language in this process, Jameson, like Lyotard, links this loss of a linguistic baseline partly to technical language, specifically "the stupendous proliferation of social codes today into professional and disciplinary jargons" (17). Besides the speed and range of material it draws in, pastiche also undermines meaning by being a language that self-consciously represents other language. For Jameson, the dream or illusion of language that transparently conveys meaning (which he tellingly terms "so-called scientific discourse") is undermined as language refers increasingly to itself and calls attention to the operation of signification and even its own materiality, the physical presence of the words on the screen or the page (96). When a text falls into this kind of narcissism (as Linda Hutcheon terms it), the text loses its connection with outside reality, and no ethical, social, or historical meaning can emerge. No matter what is portrayed, it will never be more than the portrayal of language.

For Jameson, this also describes the perverse failure of *Secret Rendez-vous* (and similar novels) to shock us, no matter how shocking they become. In postmodern literature "what used to be virulent, subversive, or at least offensive ideas have now been transformed into so many material signifiers at which you gaze for a moment and then pass on" (Jameson 150).

Jameson sees this state of art and language as a symptom of the disease of postmodernism that afflicts society. Technology bears considerable blame for this acceleration and flattening of language, but technology is finally just the tool or perhaps only the emblem of larger forces like capital. We live in a culture where it is increasingly difficult to engage the world around us in a meaningful way, politically or socially. The result is an erosion of our ability to express that reality in language, and also to express or constitute ourselves. As introduced in Chapter 3, Jameson compares this state with Lacanian schizophrenia, in which the subject is unable to connect successive instants of himself and his language in time to form a continuous whole. The subject experiences himself as a series of unrelated moments, so it is no surprise that his art is reduced to "a practice of the randomly heterogeneous and fragmentary and the aleatory," producing only "heaps of fragments" (21, 25).

Addressing the changes that this has wrought in the novel, Jameson says readers of the postmodern novel must struggle to reconstruct a story or even just a subject that can knit together the stream of isolated scenes and details the text places on display (131–53). Jameson's example is the *nouveau roman* of Claude Simon, but this certainly describes the situation in *Secret Rendezvous* as well: readers strain to reconstruct the plot, while the narrator tries to construct a self from shards of language, (re)assembling the subject of his investigation (that his, himself) from the "fragments of tongue-clucking, throat-clearing, off-key humming," on the tapes (6).

Jameson might say that *Secret Rendezvous* is suffering from an erosion of meaning in artistic expression and public language at large, and trying its best to respond. In this view, it is no longer art that is needed to destabilize our everyday reality, as Abe suggests, but a destabilized reality that infects our art. Jameson's interpretations of postmodern art do sometimes allow for the emergence of new meanings when old ones are broken down (as Abe might have hoped), but this is reduced to a kind of rear-guard action. In Jameson's readings, art is perpetually on the run from culture, frantically trying to cope with the crisis of meaning generated by contemporary society.

In *Full Metal Apache*, Tatsumi Takayuki suggests something similar about Abe's prose, arguing that by the 1980s it no longer seemed to provide much critical purchase or perspective on postmodern media culture. Tatsumi suggests essentially that by this point media technology had caught up with Abe's fiction and made it appear tame by comparison. Tatsumi advances this argument from two directions: on the one hand, he suggests like Jameson that Abe's strategy of disruption was itself co-opted and commodified "by the logic of hyperconsumerism, in which the most avant-garde, the most anti-conventional, and the most artistically aggressive are assessed, restyled, and reconfigured within the ongoing globalization of pop culture" (Tatsumi 30). On the other hand, Tatsumi posits that everyday reality came to resemble Abe's world of transhuman speaking machines, as global media and media flows have transformed Japanese individual and national identity into a kind of virtual, mediated "cyborgian subjectivity" (28).

A visionary storyteller and stylist just a few years before, Abe now declined in popularity because of the paradoxical way his work remained difficult even as the changes above ostensibly rendered its style and content passé. Using the metaphor of sadism and masochism, Tatsumi associates Abe with an older avant-garde model in which the artist maintains the authority, control, or just subjectivity of a sadistic master, one who inflicts difficult or disruptive works on his audience for its own good. Today this has shifted to a reader-centered regime resembling masochism, in which consumers now punish themselves according to their own whims. I read this to say that while audiences today now routinely read prose just as fragmented as Abe's, and while that may have constructive results, the shift of focus from artist to reader (or to language) makes it more difficult for literature to provide the exteriority or outer perspective necessary to fulfill its critical function. But Tatsumi also suggests some advantages to eliminating the master figure of the artist (an eradication Abe himself might have endorsed), and he leaves the door open to the possibility that even in the artist's absence, art itself "might resume its important 'sadistic' role of 'punishing' its audience in order to reawaken it to a life of 'real' pleasure and fulfillment" (37).

Tatsumi's reading shows us a more optimistic view than Jameson's, a view that contemporary parody can afford to be more open-ended narratively because its subject is no longer social phenomena (like our "oversexed" society), but language itself and the way language works. This points to some strengths of *Secret Rendezvous* that most Japanese reviews of the novel have missed.

For a theory of parody along these lines, we can return one final time to Mikhail Bakhtin. In Chapter 4 we encountered his idea of the parodic double, which mirrors and inverts the narrator's style and permits diametric languages to come together and interact. For Bakhtin, some degree of parody is the hallmark of the novel as a genre, the logical outcome of the dialogic nature of language. As an author incorporates different styles into the novel, he or she "makes use of words that are already populated with the social intentions of others," so that his or her own intentions are "refracted *at different angles*," depending on the voice in which he or she speaks (*Dialogic* 299–300). In the collision between these different intentions, the different layers of language inevitably work against one another, and language is made ironic. So every novel, at least every dialogic novel, must court the idea of parody to some extent. In extreme cases, the parodied language defies the author's attempt at parody and takes on a life and dignity of its own, in a sense overcoming the author's criticism and becoming a separate independent voice. "The parodied discourse rings out more actively, exerts a counterforce against the author's intentions" (*Problems* 193–98).[11]

This explains the runaway language we see in parts of *The Face of Another* and throughout *Secret Rendezvous*. However much the reader may desire that someone rein in the language of these novels and condemn or defend its excesses (moral or stylistic), that is not always within the power of the author or the text. Language has a life of its own, and some language will not be suppressed; if we try, it only "rings out more actively."

So Bakhtin agrees with Jameson that some works have lost this stable ground for judging language and the things language represents, but for Bakhtin this is not a contemporary crisis; it is the way the novel and novelistic language have always functioned. Vital language is not to be feared or resisted, but celebrated. "The prose writer as a novelist does not strip away the intentions of others from the heteroglot language of his works, . . ." says Bakhtin, "rather, he welcomes them into his work" (*Dialogic* 299). The resulting instability is to be welcomed as well, as something hopeful and productive. Comparing Bakhtin and Jameson, Linda Hutcheon remarks on this optimism in terms that seem tailor-made for *Secret Rendezvous*: for Bakhtin, she writes, "the negative pole of dialogic 'ambivalence' falls away. Bakhtin's utopian tendency is always to collapse the negative into the positive: death gives way to rebirth; scatology and obscenity reaffirm the vital body" (71).

Hutcheon is well-known both for her work on irony, satire, and parody, and for her studies of how these tropes and genres function in literature, visual art, and music associated with postmodernism. She concurs with Jameson that contemporary texts often seem unable or unwilling to make judgments about the languages or discourses they incorporate.[12] But instead of decrying the loss of moral or linguistic perspective, as Jameson does, her interest is in uncovering a positive political and historical role for these texts—a role in recovering the communicative power of language.

Since parody must involve a recognition of the original text or style that the work intends to parody, it requires a set of "shared codes" between reader, text, and author. Hutcheon suggests that parody fosters communication or even education by building up these shared codes (84–99). (An example she favors is "The Wasteland," in which Eliot's army of footnotes educates the reader about the literary history on which the author intended to draw.) Parody also forces readers and critics to think and deal in a more sophisticated way with the notion of authorial or textual intent.

This point is helpful—maybe crucial—for reading *Secret Rendezvous*, because it relates the notion of parody back to the problems of communication and self-expression that run through all of Abe's novels. As the voices multiply and we must struggle to reconstruct a subject position for the author, an intent or an "ethos" for the text, we practice and reaffirm the art of communication. For the text's part, its frantic incorporation of other language is part of a good-faith effort to find some common ground with the reader.

Jameson suggested that pastiche is too preoccupied with language as signifier, with language itself; for that reason it loses its ability to engage constructively with the world outside the text. But Bakhtin's ideas about the broader workings of language and Hutcheon's point about communication suggest the shortsightedness of Jameson's view. We need texts such as *Secret Rendezvous* that investigate language in and of itself, because they can teach us important things about how language works, and how it works on us.

I would like to conclude this chapter with a more concrete example of the kinds of lessons about language that Abe's texts can teach. One example comes from the 1990s critical controversy that came to be known as the science wars. At the center of this was a parody, a tongue-in-cheek piece of literary criticism written by a physicist and accepted to a prominent critical journal, an article the author later revealed to be a subversive hoax. Abe never had the chance to comment directly on the science wars: he had died just a couple of years earlier. But his work still speaks eloquently to this controversy, and to the issues raised by this hoax in particular. What was sorely needed but also conspicuously lacking in the debate over the hoax was some attention to the crucial differences between scientific and literary language, and to what happens when they are combined. So far this book has argued that critical theory surrounding science and literature sheds an interesting new light on Abe's novels; now it is time to show how Abe's novels shed light on these social and theoretical questions as well.

More Illicit Affairs: The Sokal Hoax and the Bogdanoff Controversy

We have discussed many theories that seek to define or blur the disciplinary and theoretical boundaries between science and the humanities, from sixteenth-century rhetoricians to scholars in contemporary science studies such as Katherine Hayles. But recently the field of science studies has been the subject of some particularly polemical criticism from practicing scientists. An early example was Paul Gross and Norman Levitt's *Higher Superstition: The Academic Left and Its Quarrels with Science*, in which the authors (a biologist and mathematician) argued that many scholars in the humanities do not understand science well enough to write about it.

In May 1996, the academic journal *Social Text* responded to critics of science studies with a special issue titled "Science Wars," featuring essays by a series of scholars in science studies and one professional scientist, New York University physicist Alan Sokal. Sokal's essay, "Transgressing the Boundaries: Towards a Transformative Hermeneutics of Quantum Gravity," argued that recent physics research in the field of quantum gravity provides evidence for what he termed a "postmodern" understanding of science and the reality it purports to investigate, as things that are textually and ideologically constructed.

Following the appearance of this article, Sokal published a second piece in the journal *Lingua Franca*, in which he announced that the article in *Social Text* was a hoax—what he called a "parody" of contemporary criticism and particularly the application of literary criticism to science. Sokal attacked this criticism as lacking an intellectual foundation and standards of argument. And he suggested that the fact that his parody went undetected by the editors of *Social Text* supported this claim, by showing that the editors could not distinguish a real argument from a facetious one.[13]

Sokal's prank provoked a debate among scientists and literary critics that raged for months through the academic and popular press—from the scientific journal *Nature* and the front page of the *New York Times* to National Public Radio and the *Rush Limbaugh Show*—while Sokal himself cannily rode this wave of publicity in a series of follow-up articles and books.[14] The affair marks the peak of the science wars, and even today it remains a popular case study, as well as an angry landmark in the academic culture of the 1990s.

The fate of the texts in the Sokal hoax makes them resemble one of Abe's notebooks: there is a piece of writing published but disavowed; a supplementary note by the same author in a different voice, qualifying what has come before; then finally a storm of commentary, and more commentary on the commentary. The debate brings together a number of the specific issues we have been discussing. These issues go beyond a generalized mixing or confusion between the worlds of science and literature; they extend to very specific differences between scientific and literary style and the results when the two styles are intentionally or unavoidably combined. We also see a return of the problem raised earlier in this chapter, of what it means to call this mixing a parody, and what happens when parody becomes increasingly difficult to identify or detect.

In his responsible but clearly polemical book *Metaphorical Circuit*, Joseph Murphy criticizes large swathes of North American science studies and goes on to argue that Japanese literary theorists are generally more sympathetic to science and better informed about it, and so better qualified to negotiate between science and literature. Murphy is rather dismissive of the Sokal hoax, seeing it as a "clumsy parody" (188) that distracted attention from more substantive criticisms of science studies. In this book, I have tried to connect the discussion with examples of science studies I find stimulating and rigorous, such as the work of Lyotard and Hayles, but I am not concerned with trying to render judgment on the field of science studies as a whole. However, I would urge a more careful look at the Sokal hoax—not because Sokal is the most eloquent spokesman for his own side (he is not), nor because he is such an easy target for the opposition (though he is), but for a different reason: because the hoax revolves around the same issues of dialect and style that are at stake in Abe's prose.

Sokal's title "Transgressing the Boundaries" is clearly intended to mock the current fashion for boundary crossing in criticism, but in Sokal's case the parodic title turned out to be peculiarly apt. As the debate developed, it circled continually around the issue of transgression and the feeling on the part of both experimental scientists and academic critics that the other side was intruding on its own turf. Peter Berkowitz manages to capture the hostility of both sides when he bristles at the idea that "those who have never performed an experiment or mastered an equation can . . . enjoy a sneering superiority based on the alleged insight that science is a form of literary invention distinguished primarily by its outsized social cachet" (16).

Ultimately, though, Sokal goes beyond this idea that literary critics should stay away from scientific material they do not understand; he argues that they should write more like scientists. Sokal and his supporters demand that criticism adopt a clearer more transparent language that they associate with scientific papers and newspaper articles. They are deeply suspicious of the ways contemporary criticism has wrestled with the problem of describing language in language, and they give short shrift to the stylistic features (including deliberately "difficult" language) that critics have evolved to address those problems. Accordingly, Sokal and his supporters show a profound suspicion of critical language that they cannot readily understand, and a deep resentment when scientific terms are used "incorrectly."

Abe's texts point us to the conclusion that in many cases the transparent critical language Sokal desires is just not possible: liminal styles that fall somewhere between science and fiction are not only desirable, but inevitable. Abe allows that relatively clear language might be possible in certain narrow circumstances, including, perhaps, typical scientific articles; but as soon as the discourse moves beyond that frame and tries to say something about humanity or society, as soon as it tries to extrapolate from narrow scientific results to broader issues, then less unpredictable voices can and must slip in. And an Abe-esque reading of Sokal's own texts proves this. If we keep an eye on the issues raised in Abe's work, we see that despite Sokal's underlying assumption that meaning and language should be clear and unambiguous, his parody depends for its effect on the shifting meaning of language in different contexts, the ambiguity of textual intent, the distorting effect of media reproduction—in short, all the barriers to straightforward, monologic, univocal language that Abe's texts and this book have probed. Sokal asserts that criticism can and should have a clear meaning, but the fate of his own text shows how ambiguous and divided language (particularly language about language) inevitably becomes.

Sokal's strategy was to write a mediocre critical article that was just barely plausible if read in the style of criticism, but which would appear ludicrous when Sokal applied the standards of a different style or context, a more literal language closer to that of science. For example, in the parody article, Sokal reviews the idea that "physical 'reality,' no less than social 'reality,' is at bottom a social and linguistic construct" (217). In the context of *Social Text*, this claim barely raises an eyebrow: with its qualifications, its scare quotes, and its code words, it reads simply as an expression of the idea that our (perception of) reality is influenced by our language and culture. But Sokal lampoons this particular phrase in later articles by suggesting that "anyone who believes that the laws of physics are mere social conventions is invited to try transgressing those conventions from the windows of my apartment. (I live on the twenty-first floor)" (62). In other places Sokal capitalizes on other gaps between writing style and even citation practice in science and the humanities in order to mock the original text.

One of the things Sokal calculated particularly well was the way that his original article would be reflected onto the mirror of the media. Beginning with the popular contrarian academic journal *Lingua Franca* and continuing through op-ed pieces, letters to the editor, and a six-minute-fifteen-second interview with Sokal on "All Things Considered," the article was translated into media that were progressively more compressed and reductionist—like the stages in Abe's eavesdropping system. In this cramped space, the *Social Text* side was unable to rehearse the decades of philosophical work that support a more complex understanding of language and perception. Hutcheon notes that parody is an act of "trans-contextualizing" (11), and more than anything else it was Sokal's adept transfer of the article from its original context to the new context of the popular press that succeeded in making the article (and *Social Text* itself) appear ridiculous.

Sokal would undoubtedly contest the notion that he was changing the sense of the article's language by altering its context. Arguing from the position that language is or should be transparent and self-evident, Sokal maintained that the arguments in his article were clearly not supported by his prose (in any context), something the editors of *Social Text* should have been able to discern. But Sokal contradicted this idea that language speaks for itself when he suggests that as the author of the article he had a special or hidden insight on its language, and that he had now "revealed" the piece's true nature. Instead of evaluating the article on its merits, many commentators accepted that if Sokal intended the article to be nonsense, it could not be anything else.[15] Apparently Linda Hutcheon was right in saying that despite the essential ambiguity of parody, it brings back the issue of textual or authorial intent with a new vengeance.

So despite Sokal's urging that criticism speak clearly, finally not even he can make it do so. Like Abe's texts, Sokal's writing teaches us against its will that the meaning of language is dependent on its context, and that without recourse to some extralinguistic authorial will (real or reconstructed), the intent or meaning of the text is likely to remain indeterminate.

A subtext of the whole debate was a tacit claim or assumption that experimental scientists were particularly qualified to weigh in on these issues because they use language more rigorously, more exactly, or more clearly.[16] There are some internal inconsistencies or double standards to this as well. Sokal and his supporters in the popular press assume that if a reader finds a scientific passage unclear, the fault is with the reader and his lack of scientific training; but if a passage of literary criticism is obscure even to a layman, it is the fault of the critic (or the editor, or the field itself). So while Nobel physicist Steven Weinberg chides the editors of *Social Text* for missing errors that "would have been detected by any undergraduate physics major," he is unashamed to condemn a passage of Derrida's simply with the words "I have no idea what this is intended to mean" (11–12). It is tempting to retort that

Derrida is understandable to undergraduate English majors, if not all of their science professors.[17]

Setting aside the desire for a universal language and the double standard that demands critics speak clearly to scientists, but not the reverse, one might consider the more modest position that scientific language is more transparent and exact than critical language when the two languages are judged within their principal reading communities. This is certainly true to some degree, though both Abe's texts and theorists such as Katherine Hayles have questioned to what degree exactly. Can the Sokal hoax shed any light on this? Perhaps not in itself, but in Abe's texts there is always one more postscript, and in real life the Sokal affair had an interesting postscript of its own. It came six years later, and revolved around a series of scientific papers in theoretical physics by Igor and Grichka Bogdanoff. The papers became the center of a controversy among physicists that spread to the wider media, with some defending the papers while others dismissed them as nonsense, and still others asking whether they were the results of failed research conducted in good faith, or an elaborate joke on the physics community.

The Bogdanoff affair has many more twists and turns than the Sokal hoax, and is much more difficult to parse. (It is to the Sokal affair what *Secret Rendezvous* is to *Inter Ice Age 4*.) The events of the affair played out in 2001 and 2002, when Igor and Grichka Bogdanoff published several papers in physics journals. The papers dealt in part with string theory and quantum gravity, the same difficult field of theoretical physics from which Sokal drew examples in his parody. The Bogdanoffs (sometimes spelled Bogdanov) are twin brothers working in France, and hold doctoral degrees from the Université de Bourgogne for work related to the publications, Grichka in math and Igor in physics. In October 2002, the articles came to the attention of John Baez, a well-known mathematical physicist at the University of California, Riverside and the moderator of a newsgroup for physicists, Google's sci.physics.research. Baez suggested that the articles were "gibberish," and asked if anyone on the list could confirm or disprove a rumor then circulating by email that the papers were published as part of an elaborate hoax. Baez's initial posting was titled "Physics bitten by reverse Alan Sokal hoax?"

The Bogdanoffs denied that the papers were a hoax, and posted to the newsgroup to defend their theories and answer a series of increasingly skeptical questions from Baez about the technical details of the articles. In two-and-a-half weeks, the newsgroup received over two hundred posts from physicists discussing the nature and weaknesses of the peer review process, criticizing the Bogdanoffs' ideas, and (much less often and much more tentatively) defending them. The story was subsequently picked up by the *Chronicle of Higher Education*, the *New York Times*, and the scientific journal *Nature*, sparking a burst of media attention that focused on a sensational analog of Sokal's thesis—the idea that patterns of thought and language in certain areas of theoretical physics have become so difficult and abstract that it is no longer a straightforward process to distinguish a promisingly creative suggestion from a groundless argument.[18] While most attacked the rigor of the Bogdanoffs' work, a few claimed (à la Abe) that their off-the-wall ideas showed a creativity that pointed toward new approaches. Writing in *Nature*, Declan Butler asks, "So are the [Bogdanoffs'] papers good science or not? Enquiries by *Nature* show that few theoretical physicists, including some who reviewed the brothers' PhD theses, are completely certain. . . . Peter Woit, a mathematician at Columbia University in New York, says that the incident illustrates the speculative nature of much theoretical physics" (5).

This is just the beginning of the multiplying uncertainties in the affair, and many of the wrinkles were created by the mass media and digital media that played such a role in the controversy. The Bogdanoffs are colorful media personalities in France, hosts of a long-running series of popular science programs on French television, and the authors of novels and short stories as well as non-fiction books on science fiction and on science and religion. (The layered, mediatized quality of the twins' identity seems to be emphasized in one of their TV series, *Rayons X*, in which they provide voiceovers for computer animated simulacra that resemble them, while the simulacra move through a virtual space station discoursing on the week's science-related topic.) Some commentators wondered about whether the brothers' scientific papers were part of an elaborate and ongoing publicity stunt to sell themselves and their mass market books.[19]

Disseminated on email and the World Wide Web, the controversy spread and morphed even faster than the Sokal hoax. John Baez's posting to sci.physics.research produced comments almost immediately from dozens of other physicists, including Sokal himself. It was picked up by the mainstream press just a week later. Debate subsequently moved to the homepages of Baez and Arkadiusz Jadczyk, a physicist sympathetic to the Bogdanoffs, and finally to the massive online encyclopedia Wikipedia, which employs a technology that allows *any* reader to write, comment on, or modify any article, and then have the change instantly reflected in the online version of the encyclopedia. This has produced a huge body of material authored by thousands of people—often topical, heavily self-referential, frequently of dubious or disputed authority, and almost always in constant flux. It is a text not unlike *The Box Man*, with its dueling narrators and other meta-textual experiments. An ambitious and detailed Wikipedia article on the Bogdanoff affair fell victim to an "edit war" between contributors, with allegations and counter-allegations published in a running commentary alongside the constantly changing article. One of these allegations was that the Bogdanoff brothers themselves were attempting to rewrite the account using a series of "sock puppet" user accounts that concealed their identities. Like the box man, contributors adduced textual evidence to prove they were not fake (or at least not Igor or Grichka): "Stop seeing Igor everywhere and read carefully what I write," begins one post titled "Igor or not Igor, that's the question."[20] The complex weave of nested quotations, responses, and non sequiturs in these postings resembles nothing less than the tapes in *Secret Rendezvous*: "fragments of tongue-clucking, throat-clearing, off-key humming, chewing, entreaties, hollow obsequious laughter, belches, sniffling, timid excuses" (6).

The Bogdanoff affair raises some interesting questions about changes in scientific language, but finally it says less about a breakdown in the language of theoretical physics specifically than about the slippery, unpredictable, and even fantastic quality of language in general, including the language in which the whole affair was reported and considered. In this more than anything it resembles the Sokal hoax.

In many of these debates, the anxiety driving one side is an anxiety about the confusion of reality with fantasy. Abe's work acknowledges the frightening quality of this mixing, but Abe also teaches that it is inevitable, and potentially healthy or constructive. Sokal's fear is that the confusion of reality and fiction—particularly literary criticism's notion that the world is a kind of text—threatens the ability of science and criticism to engage constructively with the wider world. "Theorizing about 'the social construction of reality' won't help us find an effective treatment for AIDS or devise strategies for preventing global warming," he complains ("Physicist Experiments" 64).

Joseph Murphy suggests that instead of disputing whether science or literature has the better grasp of reality, it is more valid, more interesting, and more productive to focus on the differences in the ways these discourses are constructed.[21] The overlap between science and literature in texts like Abe's is a point of common ground, hence a starting point for investigating those differences (197–98). Similarly, Foucault suggests that all discourses constitute themselves by excluding certain kinds of language, but we are always caught in a discourse of our own; there is no meta-language of the kind Sokal desires, which would allow us to escape to a higher level and rationalize all discourses with one another. What we can do is look at how discourses exclude one another to arrive at a sense of their specificities and limitations, to pursue what Foucault calls in a slightly different context "a theory of discontinuous systematization" ("Discourse" 231). It is in this sense that the collision of styles in Abe's own texts is instructive.

The fate of language in Abe's novels argues that in order to address the gaps between reality and representation, we need to work in the cracks between discourses and styles. In more optimistic terms, Abe might say that to speak and write constructively about the rich reality around us, we need a combination of rational language and fantastic language, a combination of hard science and outright fiction. This is the picture painted in the stories Abe tells, and this is the way Abe uses language in his own essays. "Warau tsuki" (Grinning moon) or "Dark Side of the Cherry Blossoms" (discussed in Chapters 2 and 7) exhibit very careful reasoning and very precise use of language, but they are organized around metaphors as much as anything else, with some points connected as much by imagery as by explicit logic. The horse's wife asks what would happen "if there were no lies, no truth—nothing but facts" (*AZ* 26:104). In the final analysis, criticism contains a mix of lies and truth just like Abe's novels, combining the concrete reasoned arguments of science with the abstractions of philosophy and the freedom of fiction. Only the proportions differ.

Abe offers hope that for all its ambiguity and double-voicedness, the language of fiction or criticism benefits society in concrete ways. As "a spider that builds its web in the gap between reality and expression," the novelist cannot move the wall of reality directly, but he or she can work indirectly, weaving and reweaving this connection between reality and language (*AZ* 20:88). The changes science works on society are often intimately tied to language, as emblemized by the eavesdropping system, or the mask's distinctive style, or the clicking of the aquans. This argues that the novelist or the critic can foster changes through language as well, and that mixing science and fiction can yield powerful, unpredictable, but sometimes highly productive results. Surely this is also the lesson learned from the history of Sokal's own text, a serious fiction that propagated through the media beyond anyone's expectations, with real consequences.

Sokal's desire for criticism to speak more plainly about the outside world is something that goes back to the empiricists, and many philosophers and critics since then have tried to justify criticism by requiring it to be more like experimental science. But this is not where the power of fiction or criticism lies. Rather than succumb to Sokal's demands or their own science envy and try to address the world directly, Abe suggests that fiction and criticism should accept their own different sphere (language, texts), in the same way that a writer must "sign a pact with the devil renouncing his qualification to be anything else." While they remain within that sphere, fiction and criticism both have the ability to pull different languages into themselves and create new alloys or hybrids. This is where their power resides.

SEVEN

A Technology of Silence:
The Ark Sakura *and the Nuclear Threat*

Secret Rendezvous traced the frantic acceleration of language in an increasingly electronic society, but not long after the work was completed an extended silence descended on Abe's writing studio. One could say that Abe's last fifteen years were dominated by silences, including long gaps between publications and also a novel, *The Ark Sakura*, whose prose style seemed to turn on silence itself. *The Ark Sakura* has been widely misunderstood because the significance of that silence is so ambiguous. But in the context of Abe's interest in dialogue and technology, it can be read as a reversal—a paradoxical attempt to portray the cessation of dialogue, and the silencing of all voices, at the hands of a technology that was no longer just revolutionary but now genuinely apocalyptic. In this sense, *The Ark Sakura* is a fitting final study for this book.

Through the completion of *Secret Rendezvous* and the end of the 1970s, Abe pushed forward literary experiments on several fronts, including two ambitiously experimental novels (*Secret Rendezvous* in 1977 was preceded by *The Box Man* in 1973), and a long-running column in the journal *Nami*, which produced the excellent essay collection *Warau tsuki* (Grinning moon, 1975). The Abe Kōbō Studio got started in the early 1970s and ended its long run in 1979 with a triumphant American tour. After the studio closed, Abe published almost nothing for the next five years. Then at the end of 1984 he finished *The Ark Sakura*, his second-to-last novel and the only long work he published in the 1980s. Not coincidentally, it was a novel about waiting—specifically the world's tense wait for nuclear war. Some critics also felt it was a novel about writing, or more specifically writer's block.

The Ark Sakura is set in an abandoned rock quarry, which the narrator "Mole" has equipped as a gigantic bomb shelter. Mole lives in fear of nuclear war, but paradoxically finds himself hoping at some level that war will come—not only to vindicate his careful planning, but also to eradicate the frightening outside world and replace it with a new kingdom he will define. As Tatsumi Takayuki says, "His determination to avoid nuclear war is constituted precisely from a longing for it" ("Hakobunejō" 74). The shelter is compared with an ark that will preserve the lives of a crew Mole plans to select. Typically for Abe's characters, though, even in peacetime the narrator is more comfortable inside the shelter than out in the world; he is so attached to the freedom and solitude of the empty ark that he is reluctant to invite anyone else inside. This is the situation at the beginning of the story, when three strangers talk their way aboard and disrupt Mole's carefully controlled world.

The novel takes place largely inside the ark over the course of a single day, and the first two-thirds consist of a series of tense scenes between Mole and the three newcomers (two men and a woman) as they compete with one another for position and authority. Gradually, events outside the shelter begin to escalate, and more people threaten to force their way inside. Two-thirds of the way through the novel Mole sends the two men out to deal with the people and problems above ground, while he remains inside with the woman. It seems that we have reached a climax: the external conflicts will develop or advance, and the sexual tension between Mole and the woman will somehow be resolved, but at this point Mole slips in the ark's bathroom and gets his foot caught in the toilet. As he is unable to escape, the action of the novel begins to take place more and more outside his control and even outside of his view—either exterior to the ark or in rooms where he cannot go. Because the novel is narrated by Mole in the first person, the reader too starts to feel distanced from the events of the story, which become progressively wilder. A parade of strange characters from schoolgirls to geriatric commandos fight a running battle through the ark's caverns, often just out of view of Mole and the reader. On the final pages, Mole escapes from the ark and leaves these events behind him, leaving many of the novel's tangled plot threads hanging.

The proliferation of strange events and characters on the one hand, and the sense of stalled action and irresolution on the other, produced many hostile reviews, especially in the West. A reference article on Abe by John Lewell not only criticized the novel, but identified the stalled plot as a metaphor for the overall decline in Abe's productivity and promise. "For the first 200 pages it appears to be his best work since *The Woman in the Dunes*," Lewell writes, "but when the narrator traps his foot in the lavatory, it is as if the author himself has suffered a seizure of the imagination. The narrator's plight must surely be seen as a symbol of the author's inability to advance the action of an otherwise promising novel" (19–20).

In Japan, Shimada Masahiko has written, like Lewell, that "Mole's character is a metaphor for the author's status in the creative process." But Shimada (a novelist known for his own aggressively experimental fiction) praises the book precisely for the way it evokes the process of writing fiction. "When his foot is caught in the toilet, the protagonist becomes lost in the labyrinth he himself has constructed," Shimada says. Producing a novel is analogous "because you must constantly struggle to ensure that your tricks don't misfire; you must always keep lying to make sure that your lies are not revealed" (65).

These two reviews mirror the differing receptions the novel was given in Japan and the West. Despite a fine English translation by Juliet Winters Carpenter, published in 1988, the novel received unfavorable reviews in the *New York Times*, the *Washington Post*, London's *Times Literary Supplement*, and the *Boston Globe*, which titled its review "Kobo Abe's Artistic Shipwreck." Even critics who lauded the novel highlighted its difficulty, giving some of the praise an ambivalent quality. The *New York Times Book Review* called it "grim and impressive, sickening and memorable" (9). The *Chicago Tribune* trotted out the sushi metaphor: "As with raw seafood, you're either hooked or nauseated by Abe right from the first bite" (6).[1]

In Japan, where critics were generally more conscious of—and more sympathetic to—Abe's overall literary project, the novel received generally favorable reviews, though some critics voiced disappointment, including Watanabe Hiroshi and Okuno Takeo, who had praised Abe in the past. Okuno's review of *The Ark Sakura* sounds a bit like his faint praise of *Secret Rendezvous*: "Maybe Abe played around too much with the word processor, or maybe he was too ambitious. While I commend the novel, I can't help voicing some disappointment given my high expectations for the work" (49).[2] And as with the earlier *Secret Rendezvous* and the later *Kangaroo Notebook*, what is even more telling than the critical reviews of *The Ark Sakura* is the comparative scarcity of in-depth critical commentary on the novel even 25 years later.

Okuno's reference to the word processor is not just by chance. The word processor was still a newfangled tool in 1984, but Abe was an early adopter, and *The Ark Sakura* was one of the first novels by an established Japanese writer to be produced with a computer. This was unusual enough that it became one of the novel's trademarks. (On the back of the first edition's slipcover is a small photograph of Abe at his computer; it is helpfully labeled "the author writing," perhaps for readers still unfamiliar with the idea of the word processor.) Okuno's implication seems to be that like one of Abe's unpredictable technologies, the computer somehow escaped Abe's control, altered his language, and spoiled the work.[3]

Notwithstanding this intriguing symmetry with Abe's own stories, the problems (or the challenges) of *The Ark Sakura* are not with the rhythm of the writing or anything else we would expect the computer to change, but with the novel's planning and resolution. Previous chapters have traced the increasing difficulty of Abe's work and his desire to test the boundaries of literature, regardless of the critical consequences. And his declining productivity must have stemmed at least partly from his failing health: though it was not publicly disclosed even in Abe's obituaries, Donald Keene reports that he had cancer (*Five Novelists* 83), and when he died in 1993, he had obviously been ill for some time. Here, though, I would attribute a deeper meaning both to *The Ark Sakura*'s delayed arrival and to its lack of resolution. I would argue that the structure and the difficulty of the novel reflect the nuclear tension of the 1980s. Abe produced a novel that reproduced that tension, a novel that gets stuck in the same way, a novel of suspense where finally nothing really happens, in which that nothingness has an oppressive significance of its own.

Up to this point, science and technology in Abe's stories had often fostered drastic transformations in language, transformations that reflected and instigated larger transformations in society and the self. On the positive side, Abe's texts portrayed creative new dialogues between the different voices that science and technology produced—exchanges that were sometimes violent or disturbing but which were often productive. But it may be that in the acceleration and proliferation of nuclear technology, Abe's methods finally met their match. NATO and the Warsaw Pact lay deadlocked, bristling with thousands of missiles between them. With political dialogue at a standstill, Abe's artistic dialogue also seemed to grind into silence. Abe reflected this most destructive technology with a quiet that was finally much more violent than the cacophony of his earlier work.

The Novel and Its Time

One way this sense of deadlock is expressed in the novel—and one of the things that contributes to our sense that its tensions are never resolved—is the way time loops back on itself in the text. This repays some closer examination, before we link it back to the notions of dialogue and science that connect this novel with Abe's other work. In *The Ark Sakura*, the apocalypse everyone is waiting for never occurs, and yet it seems already accomplished. This is reflected in Mole's living in his bomb shelter even before the war takes place. Cut off from the outside, the people in the shelter do not even really know whether the world is at war or not. In the novel's climax, Mole seals off the quarry's entrances with a series of explosive charges, and tricks the ark's new occupants into thinking that nuclear bombs have fallen. He then abandons them and emerges from the shelter himself through a secret passage. He finds the city alive as expected: the streets are full of cars and people on their way to work. But everything is lit by a strange "transparent" light:

Facing the black-glass walls of the city hall, I set up my camera, using the wide-angle lens, and focused. I meant to take a souvenir photograph of myself and the street, but everything was too transparent. Not only the light but the people as well: you could see right through them. Beyond the transparent people lay a transparent town. Was I transparent, then, too? I held a hand up to my face—and through it saw buildings. I turned around, and looked all about me; still everything was transparent. The whole town was dead, in an energetic, lifelike way. I decided not to think anymore about who could or would survive.

(335–36)

The light suggests the radiation from a bomb that has already dropped, but the description of everyday activity just before this quote implies that nothing unusual has happened; it is a day like any other. This is what it means to be "dead, in an energetic, lifelike way" (*iki iki to shinde ita*). The city paradoxically waits for an Armageddon that has not yet taken place, but that might as well have. As imminent disaster is transformed into an everyday fact of life, the city remains active, but it is an activity rendered sterile by the nuclear shadow.

Other passages in the novel also emphasize the idea of a war that is over before it begins: "Warnings were unthinkable," Mole says at one point. "Any attack that left room for the operation of a warning system would be subject to the restraining forces of both sides. The launching of the ark would inevitably take place one peaceful day, catching everyone unawares. [. . .] This, I thought, was the only way to enter upon nuclear war—before it began" (311–12).

This strange time expresses the contradictions of the 1980s, when nuclear hair triggers and burgeoning arsenals supported a logic of mutually assured destruction, a logic that assured us that the more quickly we rushed toward annihilation, the less likely we were to arrive. This stalled, festering time is represented in the novel by the ark's mascot, an imaginary insect called the Eupcaccia that has no legs and spends all day slowly rotating in place, spinning its body with its powerful feelers so that its head always faces the sun, and so that it completes a half revolution during the daylight hours. (Because of this, residents of its native habitat Eupcham are said to use the insects as clocks.) The insect excretes as it moves, leaving a semicircle of feces, which it devours from the other end in an endless closed cycle. For Mole, the Eupcaccia clearly represents the fantasy of an existence free from interference by anyone else, what the novel's translator calls a "vegetable self-sufficiency within a closed system . . . a symbol of an ideal existence free from any connection with others" (Carpenter 377–78). But the insect's revolutions also represent the irregularly advancing and ultimately closed time of the wait for Armageddon. It thus stands in for the claustrophobia of time *and* space in the novel, which not only fails to move forward in time but remains mostly stuck in the ark, or the toilet.

For American readers, the halting, claustrophobic time of the novel and the Eupcaccia recall another clock that people were watching anxiously in 1984. It was the symbolic Doomsday Clock on the cover of the *Bulletin of the Atomic Scientists*, an American publication founded by researchers on the Manhattan Project. Since its inception in the 1940s, the clock's hands have stood at a few minutes before midnight; they are moved every few years by the journal's editors—sometimes forward, sometimes back—to reflect the increasing or decreasing risk of nuclear war. The clock received a certain amount of media attention in the 1980s. In the year *The Ark Sakura* was published, as missile stockpiles and proxy conflicts increased and arms limitation dialogues stalled, the clock's keepers moved its hands forward to 11:57, closer to disaster than at any other time since the 1950s. The world waited for a nuclear war that seemed paradoxically imminent and indefinitely deferred.

As described in Chapter 3, *Inter Ice Age 4* was also written at a time of peak nuclear tension, after the Soviet Union's Sputnik launch. The apocalyptic scenario of that novel reflected anxieties about technology's power to end the world. But significantly, the power of technology in that novel is expressed in terms of its ability to change language. Science and technology alter, multiply, and empower language to the point where linguistic representations or copies such as the computer-coded simulation of Dr. Katsumi replace and efface their living originals. And the alien quality of the aquan race that replaces its human forebearers is figured largely in their different language. Chapter 3 likened these effects to Jean Baudrillard's notion of a sign that starts by reflecting some original thing or idea and ends up effacing or replacing it. The sign first "masks and denatures" reality, then "masks the absence of a profound reality," and finally becomes a free floating simulacrum cut off from reality altogether (6).

Arguably, nuclear technology works not by multiplying language but by silencing it, but for Baudrillard the final effect is very much the same. In his discussion of the public, political, and artistic discourse on deterrence and nuclear war, Baudrillard argues that this discourse obscures the unthinkability of such a war ever taking place. Writing in 1981, he says "The whole world pretends to believe in the reality of this threat," but "it is not the direct threat of atomic destruction that paralyzes our lives, it is deterrence that gives them leukemia. And this deterrence comes from the fact that even the real atomic clash is precluded—precluded like the eventuality of the real in a system of signs" (32).

For some readers, this example typifies a dangerous relativism—simultaneously sensationalistic and nihilistic—in Baudrillard's writing. At their best, however, Baudrillard's essays are an open-eyed and ultimately constructive attempt to point out just how manipulated, how slippery, and how uncertain shared language and shared social reality have become in the age of mass media. The implication that the nuclear threat is a kind of fiction may seem reckless, but it points out that in 1981 the world was living in a situation of fear like Mole, with individuals trapped in figurative caves of their own making even before the war had begun. In fact, Baudrillard's text does not deny the risk of nuclear war; it does argue that the discourse of nuclear deterrence—the struggle to build more and more weapons in order to make it less imaginable that they would ever be used—represented the triumph of a signifier that was powerful and dangerous *precisely because it was empty*. Cut off from reality like Mole in his quarry, the logic of deterrence tolerated no opposition, and it could be used to justify anything, including a system of control and coercion (ranging in the West from domestic surveillance to foreign wars) that kept citizens politically locked down, just as if they were trapped within rock walls themselves. Baudrillard writes, "The risk of nuclear annihilation only serves as a pretext . . . for installing a universal security system, a universal lockup and control system whose deterrent effect is not at all aimed at an atomic . . . but, rather, at the much greater probability of any real event, of anything that would be an event in the general system and upset its balance" (33).

It is the oppression of deterrence that tempts Baudrillard's text, like Mole, to long for the deferred detonation, for what Baudrillard calls "the romanticism of the explosion, which had so much charm, being at the same time that of revolution" (55). We have seen that Abe's texts often view violence and even extinction as a figure for revolution, and with that same irony or cool enthusiasm as Baudrillard's brand of postmodernism.

There have been some changes since *Inter Ice Age 4*, where Abe suggested explicitly that technology and future history bring violent, even apocalyptic changes that we are powerless to judge from our standpoint in the present. *The Ark Sakura* is not able to view the apocalypse so dispassionately. Mole's mix of fear and hope about the coming war is treated with clearer irony than in Abe's earlier works, and in this way

The Ark Sakura continues the transition to black humor we saw begun in *Secret Rendezvous*. But Mole, like the horse, is not a complete foil, and it is noteworthy that Abe makes the reader long also for the apocalypse, to resolve the tension generated in the first part of the novel and drive the plot forward. The politics of *The Ark Sakura* are more fraught and more subtle than *Inter Ice Age 4*. Like Baudrillard's essay, Mole is drawn to destruction in a way that makes it attractive to us as well, for the ways it reveals or dissolves the false political reality constructed around us.

The Ark Sakura contains many references to simulation and to the virtual quality of Mole's world. The transparent light in the final scene suggests something of Baudrillard's weightless signifiers,[4] but there are also more explicit references to simulation. The self-sufficient Eupcaccia is a fake, a free-floating sign without a referent like Baudrillard's simulacrum. It is actually a false specimen sold by a con man who is the first person Mole invites into the ark. (And in a way that mirrors the appeal of Baudrillard's simulacra, the absence of the referent no longer seems to matter: Mole finds himself captivated by the insect even though he knows it is fake.) The other two passengers are the insect salesman's shills or *sakura*—simulated customers who pretend interest in the bugs in order to lure other customers. The insect dealer at one point suggests that both the Eupcaccia and the ark are "simulation games" (*shimyurēshon gēmu*) (44).

With these figures for simulation and conscious deception, Abe weaves together a critique of the everyday common sense that rules our lives, leading like Baudrillard to a critique of the state (*kokka*). Abe's title connects this fakery with the Japanese state through a pun: the *sakura* of the title is a word that can mean either "shill" or "cherry blossom," the latter obviously a conventional symbol of Japan and "traditional" culture. The notion of the cherry blossom as an image that conceals the absence of a profound reality is elaborated in even more detail in Abe's essay "The Dark Side of the Cherry Blossoms," (*Sakura wa itan shinmonkan no monshō*) published in November 1981 in the *Washington Post*, Britain's *Guardian*, and the *Asahi shinbun*. This essay starts from the image of a park in the evening, the cherry trees in bloom and brilliantly lit up for viewing. Abe then transforms the icon of the illuminated blossoms in several clever steps to connect it with politics, art, and the nuclear threat, ultimately suggesting a theory of symbolic language not far from Baudrillard's simulacrum.

Abe writes that charged national and artistic symbols such as cherry blossoms provoke an emotional reaction that bypasses conventional signification and rational thought. But at the same time, this "sub-language" or "quasi-language which hovers like a halo around the periphery of words" conveys a conservative or reactionary meaning as structured and precise as language itself. "The fulcrum of nationalism is always the emotions," Abe writes, and for him these elisions of language are dangerous for the seemingly natural but ultimately unthinking reactions they incite (15). Abe wrote elsewhere that some emotions reinforced stereotypes while others could destabilize them,[5] but the emotions he associates with cherry blossoms in this essay are clearly the former: Abe links them to unexamined cultural pride, and from there to patriotism, nationalism, and Japan's remilitarization. This emotional "sub-language" is very close to Baudrillard's idea of an image that is powerful precisely because it cannot be tied to anything concrete. Okuno Takeo's review criticized *The Ark Sakura* by saying "there is no sense of living contact with a human being," making the novel "no more than an illusion, without the weight of reality" (49). Okuno may be right, but this critique of empty reality is certainly part of Abe's agenda.[6]

At the same time, "The Dark Side of the Cherry Blossoms" makes its point not only through rational argument but through a series of linked images that begin with the illuminated cherry trees. From there, Abe segues to stage lights and imagines the blossoms drawn on a theatrical backdrop—painted "not with zinc oxide" but with an older, more traditional "Chinese white consisting of powdered seashells" (15). Abe connects this chemical detail with a conservative undercurrent he sees even in left-wing Japanese theater, whose emotionalism is "simultaneously daubing both anti-establishment and establishment in one color." The image then evolves into a torchlight inquisition, representing a fanaticism for orthodoxy. "No matter how beautifully the cherry blossoms have glowed in the light of the torches held up by the inquisitors," he says, "it has only been because of the intensity of the darkness around them" (15). And as fanaticism leads to nationalism and rearmament, the torch flames finally blossom into the essay's final image, an atomic fireball. There is a tension in Abe's own style that is familiar by now—his appeal to rational logic on one level and his attempt to undermine or bypass it at another. But as we saw in Chapter 6, Abe seems comfortable relying on visual associations to circumvent narrative logic, as long as they do not lapse into emotional or other stereotypes of their own.

A Play Performed Offstage

What Baudrillard and Abe both sketch above is the danger when a certain kind of silence replaces language or dialogue. That silence takes in Baudrillard's empty signifier and Abe's "sub-language" that "hovers like a halo around the periphery of words" but is never enunciated itself. It also takes in the sense of waiting and inaction in the novel. It is worth discussing how the end of the novel seems at the same time so filled with activity and so stalled in terms of narrative progress. Here it is instructive to compare the novel with Abe's earlier work.

The sense of paralysis in the novel is not due only to its investigation of stopped or circular time. Many of Abe's novels abandon linear time and still generate some sense of progress or resolution. In fact, the sense of a foregone conclusion that comes from beginning at the end of the story—the plot that is over before it begins—is used elsewhere by Abe to generate a sense of closure. As I argued earlier in the comparisons with Murakami Ryū and Murakami Haruki, this closure is not the pat climax and resolution of more popular genres, but there is a sense of meaning in works by Abe that return on their final pages to their beginnings. For example, in *The Ruined Map* (1964), one of Abe's most resolutely realistic works, a detective in search of a missing man uncovers clue after clue that seems to point to a larger conspiracy all the way up to the final pages, when the detective breaks off the search and disappears himself. The final pages describing the detective repeat almost verbatim several paragraphs from the opening that seemed to describe the movements of the missing man. At this point, the reader realizes that the detective protagonist himself has come full circle and been transformed into his quarry. We are led to conclude that in the city today, identities go missing much more often than they are found, and a person who ventures into that labyrinth in search of someone will inevitably lose their map, and lose themselves in the process. *The Woman in the Dunes* relates the story of a kidnapped man and his attempts to return home, but the novel's opening page is very similar to its last page, telling us that seven years later there was still no word from him. *Secret Rendezvous* concludes with the narrator holed up underground, reading "tomorrow's newspaper" (178). And the title of *The Box Man*'s final chapter is "whereupon the play came to an end without even the bell ringing for the curtain" (170). But in all these cases, the end has a sense of fantasy, surprise, or unlikelihood, even as it remains prefigured or inevitable in the context of the narrative.

The unsatisfying lack of closure at the end of *The Ark Sakura* traces not so much to a sense of undecidedness or multiple possibilities as to a sense of loose ends left untied. Yet this is not unique to *The Ark Sakura*, either. We have seen that the plots of *The Crime of S. Karma*, *Secret Rendezvous*, and some other novels produce just as many characters and subplots and leave them just as unresolved. So what is really so different about *The Ark Sakura*? One answer lies in the contrast between the novel's careful beginning and chaotic conclusion, something that returns us once again to the notion of dialogue. Abe's other novels maintained a consistent tone throughout: *The Ruined Map* stays true to its detective novel idiom until the final pages, and only then does it unfold into a dream-like fantasy; *Secret Rendezvous* and *The Crime of S. Karma* start from inexplicable events and accelerate from there. But *The Ark Sakura* begins simply, with the meeting between the four characters at a department store, and their carefully plotted conversations aboard the ark. In the last third of the novel, those dialogues are replaced by a welter of activity that takes place out of the narrator's view and which is then relayed back to him. It is because of this careful control over the early part of the novel—particularly the characters' conversations— that the last part seems all the more out of control. "Gone is the subtle dialogue indicating the tense relationships of the four characters," says Lewell, "and in its place is a confusion of activity" (20).

Coming as it does after the Abe Kōbō Studio, this novel might be thought of as a play. The first part unfolds as if on a stage, with a small number of characters. They interact mostly in a few fixed locations (the roof of the department store, Mole's truck, and the few rooms of the quarry), and the first person narration notwithstanding, the book is heavily dependent on the conversation between them. So when Mole gets his foot stuck in the toilet, it is not simply that more and more happens, but that more and more of the action and dialogue begins to take place "offstage."

Here a brief description will convey some sense of the way the pace of the novel speeds up offstage, even as it slows down onstage. Shortly before Mole wedges his foot in the toilet, his hated father Inototsu radios the ark to request assistance in disposing of a dead body. The intent is to flush it down the toilet, which is part of the quarry's original equipment and which has such powerful, almost supernatural suction that it can make virtually anything disappear. (In fact, for some time Mole has been contracting illegally with local businesses to dispose of industrial waste.) The insect dealer and the shill leave the ark to meet with Inototsu and the paramilitary group of senior citizens he heads, a group called the "Broom Brigade." When the shill and the dealer return with a dead body, the now stuck Mole sees that the body is Inototsu himself. The insect dealer appears to have killed him in an offstage confrontation and assumed command of the Broom Brigade. His aged adjutant and other members of the brigade enter the ark through a secret rear door, and eventually adjourn to a back room to make their own plans out of Mole's earshot. At one point, scouts from a rival gang show up and then withdraw after a brief skirmish, while some of the more libidinous senior citizens search the tunnels for a group of junior high school girls who are rumored (though never confirmed) to be wandering inside the deeper passages.

Described like this, the action begins to sound like something from the slapstick stream of Japanese fantasy writing, maybe something by Tsutsui Yasutaka. Tsutsui is one of the three most influential science fiction writers in the genre's first generation, and even after crossing over into slipstream literary experiments later in his career, he seems to have retained his penchant for sight gags. Tatsumi Takayuki calls him "a slapstick New Wave metafictionist" who "combines the sensibilities of Darwin, Freud, and the Marx Brothers" (Bolton, Csicsery-Ronay, and Tatsumi xii). When Mole gets stuck in the bathroom and things start escalating outside, serious readers may worry they are in for something like Tsutsui's "The African Bomb" ("Afurika no bakudan," 1968), a send-up of atomic proliferation in which a small village in Africa decides to purchase a nuclear missile. (Tsutsui's ridiculous visual comedy hits its high or low point when the characters and the missile end up suspended precariously on a teetering rope bridge and have to be rescued by Tarzan.)[7]

But unlike Tsutsui, Abe does not describe most of the furious action outlined above. Trapped as we are in Mole's perspective, we are cut off from this frantic offstage action, so in contrast with Tsutsui's story, the problem is not that the narrative itself is out of control, but that *Mole and the reader can no longer control it*. Again, this feeling closely mirrors the political situation of the 1980s. The anxiety and powerlessness we feel in the face of modern technology proceed not from the feeling that nothing is happening, but from the feeling that great forces are moving invisibly behind the scenes. Events and policy decisions, real dangers and real responses, are so well concealed that the average person cannot see them, understand them, or affect them at all.

Azuma Hiroki sees these issues of fate and resignation as being at the heart of the evolution from detective fiction, through nuclear fiction, to postmodern science fiction. In an essay titled "Tantei shōsetsu no sekai, SF no sekai" (The age of the detective novel and the age of science fiction), Azuma begins from Jean-François Lyotard's characterization of postmodernism discussed in Chapter 3: a decline of the great nineteenth-century metanarratives of freedom and spirit, the stories that gave meaning to human activity and human history. But to this Azuma adds a second period from the 1920s to the 1960s, during which two more recent middle narratives provided a structure and purpose for human history—first Communism, and then our shared (if terrifying) nuclear "fate." But these systems were never more than "ghosts" of the original metanarratives, says Azuma. They were "fakes," and the ordering function they provided did not last beyond the 1960s.[8] Azuma's word "fake" suggests Baudrillard's idea that however real the threat, the narrative of cultural and political necessity constructed around it was ultimately just that—an arbitrary construction.

For Azuma, the artistic fallout of the first crisis is seen in detective fiction, while the consequences of the second are visible in science fiction. Following the collapse of the nineteenth-century metanarratives, the growth of detective fiction in the 1920s expresses a crisis of individual worth. The detective is an empty character defined entirely by the formulaic plots through which he moves—a situation treated explicitly in *The Ruined Map*, where the detective achieves a kind of empty freedom (or liberating emptiness) by taking on the identity of the man he is searching for, an identity defined by his case. Science fiction, Azuma says, manages to remain idealistic for another generation by creating its own vision of the future, but in the 1960s it also transitions to a postmodern form in which human agency is in question. In early post–World War II science fiction, no matter what changes technology brings, it remains the tool of humans; in the postmodern science fiction novel, science and technology have become impersonal forces that sweep humanity before them.[9]

Azuma's scheme seems to describe the historical and cultural moment of *The Ark Sakura*. At the outset, Mole's life is perversely given meaning by the coming apocalypse, but ultimately this fate is not enough to structure the novel or Mole's existence; when war is again deferred, Mole's life loses direction. In *Inter Ice Age 4*, technology is still created and directed by human beings. This is very different from the situation in *The Ark Sakura*, where the threat is beyond Mole's vision, beyond his control, and beyond his understanding. Chapter 3 argued that *Inter Ice Age 4* already contains the seeds of a kind of postmodernism, in the ways technology in that novel replaces human beings with their own simulacra and simultaneously forestalls judgment about that transition with the notion of a future that can be seen but not changed. In particular, the future is foreclosed in *Inter Ice Age 4* just as it is in *The Ark Sakura*. But compared with *The Ark Sakura*, technology in the earlier novel remains much more under human control. *Inter Ice Age 4* shows that Azuma's postmodernism is already present in embryo at the dawn of Japanese science fiction, at least in Abe's work. *The Ark Sakura*, however, represents a much further stage in that transition.

Mole's lack of control—over technology and politics—is captured in the fact that he has no way of even knowing whether the bomb has dropped, except for his radio and an array of instruments that measure heat and air pressure outside. As the story advances, his world shrinks to the toilet bowl. And Abe makes even this a symbol of the powerful but incomprehensible geological and technological pressures all around Mole that trap him. Moles surmises that the toilet works on the enormous pressure generated by the "different water levels underground—but why and how it generated such tremendous pressure I never understood. Despite its mystery, it was in fact all-powerful, capable of washing anything away" (88). Mole only manages to free himself by setting off a series of explosive charges by remote control. The charges are intended to seal the quarry entrances in the event of war, but they have the side effect of diverting the underground water flow in such a way as to neutralize the toilet's suction.

The other characters know nothing of Mole's explosives. When they hear the detonations, they are easily convinced that nuclear war has broken out, and they decide to stay in the shelter. Even after Mole reveals the secret to the shills and shows them a secret passage out of the shelter, they choose to stay. "We're at home with lies, anyway," they say. "They're us. We're *sakura*, don't forget" (332). In the same way that Mole wanted to believe in the lie of the Eupcaccia, they want an end (even a false end) to the world as it is. Perhaps they can no longer distinguish between safety and disaster, or more likely they discern correctly that the two are now the same.

What ~~Time~~ Color is it Now?

"An explosion is always a promise," writes Baudrillard (55), and with his dynamite, Mole seems to recover the initiative to act, even as he confirms the incapacitating paradox of deterrence. In a passage quoted in part above, Mole says:

> At last the time had come, just as I had known that one day it would; I had always known, too, that it was something I would have to decide myself, without orders from anyone else. [. . .] Warnings were unthinkable. Any attack that left room for the operation of a warning system would be subject to the restraining forces of both sides. The launching of the ark would inevitably take place one peaceful day, catching everyone unawares. There was not the slightest reason why that day should not be today. All decisions are arbitrary in the end. [. . .] This, I thought, was the only way to enter upon nuclear war—before it began. (311–12)

Shortly after triggering the charges, Mole leaves the ark through a hidden escape tunnel. But his action does not restore the dialogue that is disrupted mid-work. He leaves hoping that the woman will follow him through the tunnel, but when he emerges he is alone. And the novel ends here, without the chance to reestablish that communication.

At this point, Abe gives the story one final turn, not unexpected at this point in his career. The story turns momentarily to the visual, as

Mole tries to replace the dialogue (now lost) and the narration (now ending) with a meaningful image. But even this fails. The one object that Mole brings with him during his escape is his camera, and now he tries to take a picture of himself reflected in the glass walls of the city hall building. But he cannot take that picture because of the scene he is faced with, the scene our discussion started with, of a city lit by a "transparent light" that renders everything else see-through as well. "I meant to take a souvenir photograph of myself and the street," he says, "but everything was too transparent" (335).

Transparency and invisibility are both translated as *tōmei* in Japanese, hence the notion of radiation as a kind of photography that renders everything transparent like an x-ray and invisible. Akira Lippit traces this trope through Japanese cinema, where he says the difficulty and necessity of representing the atomic bombings are represented by the figure of "atomic writing" itself, in which the heat and light of the bombs illuminated and marked their victims, or vaporized people and left their shadows charred permanently into the walls and sidewalks of Hiroshima and Nagasaki. "A singularly graphic event, an event constituted graphically, which put into crisis the logic of the graphic," the bomb both writes and erases, immortalizes and destroys (109). Lippit shows that in Japanese film, the crisis of language fostered by the nuclear is represented by motifs of disappearance and transparency, "a way to avoid what cannot be seen, or rather, to make that which resists representation invisible" (120). The same interpretation applies to *The Ark Sakura*, except that now the atomic shadow that disables language is cast by a hypothetical future explosion, and the trace itself is correspondingly transparent, uncertain.

Another reading might link the crisis of representation with electronic media by associating this transparent light with the electromagnetic radiation of television and radio signals: Baudrillard points out that in the face of our inability to represent the nuclear reality, we settle for the artificial reality of the mass media, represented by the low-level radiation of the television broadcast or the cathode ray tube—"the power of catastrophe disseminated in homeopathic, molecular doses" (57). But whether it is nuclear radiation or television and radio waves, this energy renders the city equally insubstantial, "dead, in an energetic, lifelike way."

As in *The Box Man*, the photographer is an image for the artist, but *The Ark Sakura*'s idea of a reality too insubstantial to record is not a hopeful one. More than the bright light, more than the "dead" city, this portrayal of the artist's predicament in the face of nuclear and media technology may be Abe's most pessimistic statement yet. Several of Abe's novels end with a statement about art or representation—narrators who state their determination to stop writing or to continue. But Mole's inability to record himself is among Abe's most disturbing conclusions. This, more than the novel's claustrophobic or coprophagous motifs, or its thwarted action or its uncontrollable events, may be the most revealing parallel with Abe's own declining productivity.

Finally, how does this reading of *The Ark Sakura* relate to the notion of the sublime? To review briefly, we have traced changing formulations of the sublime as a way of tracking the distinctions between science and literature at various points in history. The sublime describes an aesthetic (and also intellectual, moral, or political) experience triggered by something incomparably larger or more powerful than ourselves, and science and technology have often been identified as sources of that power. Earlier formulations of the sublime by Edmund Burke, Joseph Addison, and Immanuel Kant described a disturbing but also salutary effect: rising to meet the sensory challenge of the sublime allows us to define and to try our own abilities of reason against this magnitude, and leaves us feeling more rational or more alive. The sublime revealed the tip of something greater, and left us greater for our brief glimpse of it. In theories of the postmodern, this notion was rephrased as a vertiginous but often exhilarating encounter with the speed and power of language itself as it was accelerated by the media. But the most pessimistic formulation by Fredric Jameson tipped the balance from triumph toward confusion, and replaced these veiled majestic powers (God, nature, or language) with more sinister ones such as the state and global capital, powers whose extent we cannot really grasp, even as we remain in their grip. We intuit these forces only through a diffused sense of paranoia and despair. For Jameson, this is why paranoia and conspiracy loom so large in postmodern literature. It also describes Mole's helplessness in *The Ark Sakura*, and the way its action happens offstage, beyond earshot and beyond our power to influence or change.

Inter Ice Age 4 already embodied aspects of postmodern literature and the postmodern sublime, at least in its more optimistic or less judgmental formulations. However, in *The Ark Sakura* (published in the same year as Jameson's essay on postmodernism), Abe's prose has arguably traversed whatever remained of the distance between the classical sublime and Jameson's sublime paranoia. Perhaps in doing so, Abe's writing also arrived at its own terminus. *Inter Ice Age 4* and even *The Face of Another* described the destabilizing effects of technology with a stubborn neutrality or even optimism, grounded in a belief that radical change—however violent—would loosen the grip of reigning convention and destabilize the established power of the collective, if only briefly. In the nuclear landscape of *The Ark Sakura*, the power of technology and the power of the state are more synonymous. (This is one reason that Mole's own private technologies—the Rube Goldberg contraptions he has invented to secure the quarry—all seem harmless or comical.) The earlier texts could still portray the way science and technology worked through language, in a way that allowed art or literature some role of its own—even a role in directing or ameliorating the changes science and technology bring. In *The Ark Sakura*, the powers in play swamp language's power to influence things or even to respond. As Baudrillard shows, the state's statements about nuclear necessity brook no response. As a result, art is struck dumb, or blind.

Dialogue fails. The image fails. Ultimately, perhaps, the novel fails in some sense. Despite, or rather *because* of its difficulties, *The Ark Sakura* remains a definitive statement of its own time. In a way, its artistic drawbacks constitute the substance of its political critique. With the cold war over, we may be tempted to assign this novel only historical significance. But *The Ark Sakura* has a great deal to say about our own time as well. If the discourse surrounding the nuclear threat is a blank or a blank check that can justify any policy, its absence leaves a different kind of vacuum, one that must be filled with a new absence. In the United States post–9/11, global terrorism has taken on this role. At the start of the twenty-first century, the U.S. administration justified its agenda (from wars abroad to curtailed civil liberties at home) by referring to ongoing terrorist threats—threats that for security reasons could never be specifically named. Baudrillard wrote long ago that terrorism tries to make "real, palpable violence surface in opposition to the invisible violence of security" (57), but in the wake of the cold war, the specter of terrorism (or just "terror") has been given the same oppressive insubstantiality that the nuclear threat once had. And when terror ceases to be useful, there will be something else. Once again, the threat will be real (as real as the terrorist threat, the nuclear threat), but the way it is made to order polity and policy will be as "fake" as Azuma predicts.

In early twenty-first century America, the Doomsday Clock that was once faithfully tracked by the media has been replaced by a new and more ambiguous (and hence effective) indicator and instigator of fear: the color-coded threat level of the Homeland Security Advisory System. In our state of permanent danger, the level has oscillated between yellow and orange in response to specific threats, but the specific threats are rarely revealed. For some time, the U.S. Department of Homeland Security used the motto: "Don't be Afraid. Be ready." But the motto ends there; we are not told what to be ready for. In this sense, Americans today are in the same position as Mole. And what we see through our own viewfinders is limited to the ironic rainbow of the threat level— as invisible, as transparent, and as dangerous as Abe's atomic light.

Abe's Word Processor and Abe's Legacy

The deafening silences of *The Ark Sakura* allow us to hear one thing very clearly by way of contrast: the importance of dialogue and multiple voices in so many of Abe's other novels. Abe used the differences between various voices or styles (eventually including visual styles) in order to relativize language and make the reader hear and question how language works. Science and scientific language are often important for the way they stand in for Abe's favored target—a narrow rationality cut off from everyday life. Just as often, though, scientific language functions positively in Abe's work, ushering in a new, unexpected rationality that explodes the everyday common sense that weighs down our creativity and perceptions. Part of this process was a redefinition of Japanese literary style itself—a reshaping that allowed it to encompass scientific language and its unexpected creativity.

This returns us to the figure from the beginning of this book, of Abe's dictionary, and the question it raises about how to characterize the language of Abe's texts. Is the technical language in these novels truly scientific, is it simply ornament, or is it a complicated parody of the way science speaks? In fact, in reading Abe we must steer a course between two extremes, reading the scientific language carefully and in good faith, but still allowing that it may be changed or undermined by other languages in the course of the work.

This is why in *Inter Ice Age 4*, we paid careful attention to the difference between the languages of biology and of computer science. These two scientific languages each retain their own unique logic, but the way they interfere with one another and eventually change places with poetic language leads the novel to a conclusion that seems to defy reason or expectation.

The protagonist's journey in *The Woman in the Dunes* has been interpreted as an emergence from his own narrow rationality to a wider logic, language, and life—though critics differ on whether scientific language is part of the problem or the solution. Chapter 5 focused attention on the rich inner dialogue that is part of the protagonist's world, a ground where scientific and other voices compete with and relativize one another. In that novel, it is the surprises of science that finally give the protagonist something to communicate, and the water trap is the technology around which that communication may finally be able to take place.

In *The Face of Another*, the line between fantasy and logic is fuzzier, and the contrariness of the novel has escalated from the logical bind of *Inter Ice Age 4* to the more personal, pathological violence of the mask. By dividing the novel's language into three styles (fictional, scientific, and psychological), we were able to create a frame for understanding the work. And we saw in the wife's letter a way of compromising between these dialects to arrive at the possibility of communication. Like the Bakhtinian author who consummates her hero through language, the wife combines truth and fiction to try to consummate a relationship with her husband, writing a new self to bridge the gap between them.

In each successive novel, the urge to strike out against society and its everyday common sense becomes more urgent, and the grotesque or perverse elements escalate. Together with this, individuals' connections with society seem to grow more and more tenuous, as the protagonists become more and more isolated from those around them. At the same time the protagonist's ability to communicate breaks down, the voices in the novel multiply and become more confused.

Secret Rendezvous presents a final step in the evolution toward increasing stylistic fragmentation, growing violence or perversity, and progressively more isolated protagonists. The narrator wanders through a labyrinth of space and language, unable even to locate his wife. The violence has expanded from the mask's isolated pathology to an epidemic of "perversity," so that the line between normal and abnormal is completely blurred. And the status of language in *Secret Rendezvous* represents something like the worst-case scenario predicted by the theories that we have been discussing: Bakhtin's competition between styles has escalated into a war waged over the text and the speaker; and Hayles's fears are realized as technology manages to erode the meaning of language and the reality of the speaking or writing subject. Nevertheless, Linda Hutcheon provides an optimistic take on this situation by suggesting that parodic texts such as *Secret Rendezvous*—texts that seem to mock everything and revere nothing—are precisely the texts that breathe new life into language, by making connections with so many other languages and works.

Despite the difficulty of *Secret Rendezvous*, Hutcheon's confidence is appropriate for Abe, who always seemed to view the act of writing optimistically. One can see that optimism more clearly in *The Box Man*, which parallels *Secret Rendezvous* in many ways but ends on a brighter (if no less resolved) chord. "In processing the box," says the box man on the final pages, "the most important thing at all events is to ensure leaving plenty of blank space for scribbling" (177). *The Box Man* ends almost exactly like *Secret Rendezvous*, with the protagonist searching through the "labyrinth" of an abandoned hospital for the woman he has lost. But the box man expresses confidence that as long as he can express himself, the search can continue: "One thing alone is certain and that is that even she, who has at present vanished, is hiding somewhere in this labyrinth. [. . .] At this point I can speak out clearly with assurance. I have no regret. The clues are numerous, and it is reasonable that the truth should exist in proportion to their number" (178).

These are the novel's final words (except for a concluding sentence, "I hear the siren of an approaching ambulance," that mirrors the opening of *Secret Rendezvous*). The idea that truth should exist in proportion to the number of clues or the amount of information, however contradictory that information may be, is an optimism like Hutcheon's. It is only with the truncated dialogue and silence of *The Ark Sakura* that Abe's work becomes truly pessimistic.

Abe's final novel, *Kangaroo Notebook*, has proven the most baffling to critics, but in the context of the development sketched above, it may represent a return of optimism. As discussed briefly in Chapter 6, its structure is very similar to the work that launched Abe's career, *The Crime of S. Karma*. Both protagonists wake up one morning to find themselves changed, and both visit clinics for treatment, visits that launch them on strange tours of the city's underground spaces and cultures. Karma discovers that his name has been stolen, and becomes aware of a vacuum-like emptiness in his chest that allows him to suck in objects through his eyes. For some reason, Karma's condition makes him the quarry of a conspiracy that pursues him through the city, leading to a series of strange encounters with unreal figures, and culminating in a strange trial in an underground chamber beneath the zoo. In *Kangaroo Notebook*, the narrator discovers a strange rash and realizes that radish sprouts are growing from his leg. Like Mr. Karma (and the protagonist of *Secret Rendezvous*, and the box man after him), he also visits a clinic and finds himself on the run from its menacing doctor and nurse. He eventually ends up strapped to a gurney that rolls out of the clinic and into the city, traveling through the sewers and eventually arriving at a theme park fashioned in the image of a Buddhist hell. On the way, he meets a parade of odd characters, ranging from an American karate expert to a chorus of demon children.

A detailed reading of *Kangaroo Notebook* does not seem to me to shed any extra light on the role of science in Abe's work. In the context of my readings, *Kangaroo Notebook* is probably best understood as a pastiche along the lines of *Secret Rendezvous*, but without the implicit statements about electronic media that give some sense of order or purpose to the disorder of the narrative. It seems even further from parody or satire than *The Crime of S. Karma*: there we could at least identify a series of voices that represented the narrowly rational discourses Abe was holding up for examination. In any case, as discussed briefly in the previous chapter, the inventiveness and open-endedness that had signaled promise at the start of Abe's career produced blank stares 40 years later: unfortunately critics have ignored *Kangaroo Notebook* almost completely.

Kangaroo Notebook was serialized in the journal *Shinchō* in the first half of 1991 and issued as a novel at the end of that year. Abe died just over a year later, in January 1993. *Kangaroo Notebook* was virtually the last work of any kind published before Abe's death. Many critics reading it must have realized it would be Abe's final work, and may have expected or hoped for an authoritative summing up of Abe's career—something with Abe's familiar themes and a sense of strong authorial voice and control, like *The Ruined Map* or *The Woman in the Dunes*. From this perspective, one might conclude that after being unable to sustain or resolve the plot of *The Ark Sakura*, Abe simply gave up and regressed 40 years, falling back into the plotlessly pure image gallery of *The Crime of S. Karma*. But there is also a more favorable view of the way Abe's literature comes full circle. After the paralyzed quality of *The Ark Sakura* and the 1980s, *Kangaroo Notebook* could be taken as a renewed outpouring of language that signals new possibilities. *Kangaroo Notebook* was the novel in which Abe once again found his voice, or voices.

There is also one more hopeful image that presented itself after the end of Abe's life. The Introduction opened with a picture of Abe's study as it appeared to a documentary camera that entered it after the author's death. The camera lingered on a scientific dictionary above Abe's desk, then came to rest on an empty chair sitting in front of Abe's word processor. Even more than the dictionary, it may be this word processor that is the most fitting icon for Abe's work. After Abe's death, two unpublished works were found in the study—not manuscripts but files on floppy disks. Since Abe was one of the first authors of his generation to use the word processor, the novelty of this discovery provoked a minor stir in Japan at the time: writing in the issue of the journal *Hermes* that published one of these works, Numano Mitsuyoshi noted that even in death Abe remained on the cutting edge. Like the juxtaposition of the empty chair with the waiting machine, these events seemed to suggest that the computer was still writing after Abe's death, like the prediction machine, or the mask, or the other inventions in Abe's novels that escape their creators and strike out on their own.

This is a fitting image with which to conclude, as it evokes the several faces of science and technology portrayed in Abe's work: machinery's strange symbiotic relationship with humans, science's creativity and unpredictability, technology's eerie power and hope. Particularly in the context of Abe's slowing output toward the end of his life, the image of the machine writing on after its master's death seems a hopeful one. It is like the benign side of the prediction machine, which plots the extinction of the human race as we know it, yet can still sing humanity's elegy in moving terms.

Machines in Abe's works are always portrayed with a mix of enthusiasm and ambivalence, the same way Abe portrays science itself. Both symbolize the instability of the world in which we live, but also the potential to creatively expand our thinking to the point where we can deal with that rapidly changing reality. But there is one thing about which Abe's writing is never ambivalent, and that is writing itself. Abe's novels are an argument that writing is our last best hope for making sense of science and the world and ourselves. That is why the idea of someone or something that continues the author's writing is a hopeful one. Nevertheless, even though the documentary camera shows the word processor still there in his study, Abe's chair is now empty. And while the word processor may continue writing, there is no machine—at least not yet—that can think through these issues in the way Abe did, and carry on where he left off. Now that engrossing task falls to Abe's readers and interpreters: it falls to us.

Reference Matter

Notes

Introduction

1. The scene described appears in the first part of the documentary *Abe Kōbō ga sagashiateta jidai* (Abe Kōbō in search of an era). A good deal of material from the documentary is reproduced in a special issue of the journal *Eureka* titled *Abe Kōbō: nichijō no naka no chōgenjitsu* (The everyday supernatural of Abe Kōbō).

2. The film and novel share the same title in Japanese—*Suna no onna*—but the customary English titles differ slightly: the film title omits the initial definite article and is rendered simply as *Woman in the Dunes*.

3. The term "slipstream" was coined by science fiction writer and critic Bruce Sterling in the late 1980s. Tatsumi Takayuki has applied the word to contemporary Japanese fiction and to Abe specifically. See Sterling, "Slipstream"; Tatsumi, "History" E-037; and Tatsumi, "Hakobunejō muishiki." In 2007, the World Science Fiction Convention was held in Japan for the first time, and featured several English and Japanese panels devoted to slipstream writing.

4. A useful overview of the issue of identity in Abe's work, written from a biographical perspective, is found in Takano Toshimi's "Hyōden Abe Kōbō" (Critical biography of Abe Kōbō) in the Abe volume of *Shinchō Nihon bungaku arubamu* (Shinchō album of Japanese literature). Edited by Takano, this volume also documents many of Abe's technical interests and hobbies that are discussed above, using photographs and material exhibits from throughout the author's life.

5. See Foster, "Creating Monsters" 9. Foster elaborates this argument in *Pandemonium and Parade*, which discusses the mixing between what Foster terms the "encyclopedic" and "ludic" modes in writing about these creatures (30–76).

Chapter One

1. For more on the significance of Hokkaidō for Abe, see Shields 32–33. Much of the biographical material in this and the following paragraphs is based on the chronology of Abe's early life in Tani 7–27.

2. On the mix of idealism and brutal colonialism that formed the atmosphere of Abe's youth, see Keene, *Five Novelists* 67, 73.

3. Nancy Shields published this interview under the name Nancy Hardin. On the frightening possibilities of Manchuria, see also the discussion in Shields's *Fake Fish* (27–34), which is based on this and other interviews, as well as on Abe's own essays.

4. The reader will notice other parallels to Kafka in the stories described below, but beyond the surface similarities are some important differences between these two authors. These are largely outside the scope of this book, but for a summary of Abe's efforts to locate his own work in relation to Kafka and contemporary Western writers, see Schnellbächer, *Strategist* 296–306. For an early comparison of Abe with Kafka and Samuel Beckett, see William Currie's *Metaphors of Alienation*. Both Currie's text and Shield's *Fake Fish* were subsequently published in Japanese, something that may hint at the prominent role Western scholars have taken in work on Abe. For a detailed catalog of Abe criticism in Japanese, see Tani 189–256 and Kuwahara.

5. Timothy Iles approaches this old problem from a new direction, by comparing the dilemma of community in Abe's novels not with his early life but with his later activities directing the Abe Kōbō Studio. Iles argues that Abe's experimental theater troupe was a social and dramatic experiment that tried to supply an ideal balance of freedom and community that is never achieved in the worlds of his novels.

6. In the course of a celebrated dialogue titled "Nijū seiki no bungaku" (Twentieth-century literature, 1966), Mishima once asked Abe if there were any traditions he respected. Abe replied "the traditions of science," i.e. "method." Abe contrasted reliance on process with faith in truth or facts, saying "In science, facts are extremely brittle things. That's what I love about it" (*AZ* 20:74).

7. In a summary of this period in *Dawn to the West*, Donald Keene dismisses many of these debates with a statement that "The factional disputes among various left-wing literary organizations do not make for edifying or even interesting reading. . . ." (973), but in a reminiscence of Abe's life in *Five Modern Japanese Writers*, Keene spends a considerable part of the short essay trying to contextualize and ultimately downplay Abe's party involvement. Between Keene's thumbnail sketch and Schnellbächer's detailed survey, Okaniwa Noboru gives a helpful summary that tries to locate Abe within the various currents that constituted the postwar Japanese avant-garde (9–28).

8. Here Abe turns the gaze of science and medicine that is so often harnessed in colonization back at the colonizer. The way he disavows the importance of biographical or bodily experience (*taiken*) while emphasizing empiricism (*keikenteki na urazuke*), however, amounts to a rather precarious distinction. Nancy Shields (32) and Timothy Iles (24–25) cite this same conversation, which is from *Han gekiteki ningen* (The anti-dramatic human, 1973).

9. For a detailed theory of the interrelationship between a transformed environment and a transforming self, see Okaniwa 49–69.

10. One oft-repeated anecdote had it that after devoting so much of his energies to literature in the final years of his medical education, Abe was allowed to graduate only on the condition that he never treat patients (Tsutsumi Seiji, qtd. in Tani 25).

11. For details, see the biographical timeline in Tani 19–22. For an in-depth narrative account of Abe's activities in 1948, see Schnellbächer, *Strategist* 114–50.

12. For an in-depth exploration of these transitions, see Schnellbächer, *Strategist* 131–50 and 399–407, and Watanabe, *Abe Kōbō*.

13. Another interesting perspective is provided by Abe's reception in communist countries. Abe was popular in the Soviet Union as well as the Eastern Bloc, but his Czech and Polish translators report that for many readers, Abe's work on the restrictions of community represented a criticism of the state, and translation and teaching of his work were not always tolerated by the government. (For an overview, see Saeki, "Kokusaika" 101–3.) This is another example of how widening the context in which we regard Abe's work generates both new ambiguities and new meanings.

14. All four of these critics characterize Common's transformation as a divided symbol, but they differ on whether the story is finally optimistic or pessimistic. Okaniwa concurs with Takano that the metamorphosis defeats essentialism, but also says that this alienation from the body represents postwar poverty, a state from which society and the individual must recover (26–28). On the other side of the aisle are critics such as Watanabe, who sees a hope for a positive kind of community emerging from the negativity of "Dendrocacalia": "By moving the terms from the left to the right side of the equation," he says, "Abe made plusses out of minuses" (*Abe Kōbō* 64). Despite the scientific vocabulary borrowed from Abe's style, Watanabe's argument, like those of Takano, Nakamura, and Okaniwa, contains its share of reversals and ambiguities.

15. This recalls a similar scene in Akutagawa Ryūnosuke's autobiographical story "Spinning Gears" ("Haguruma," 1927), in which the narrator imagines himself transformed into Tantalus in the *Inferno*. In Akutagawa's story the narrator's deteriorating mental state is expressed in a series of delusions and a recurring hallucination, a pattern of rotating gears that floats in his field of vision.

The stress the narrator feels is clearly linked to the cultural changes accompanying modernization, and the gear image makes it tempting to assign technology most of the blame for his insanity. But the narrator's anxieties actually center equally on these imagined coincidences between the events of his own life and literary fiction. He sees himself consigned to the fictional worlds created by Dante, then Dostoevsky, Shiga Naoya, Gustave Flaubert. "I picked up Madame Bovary," he says ". . . only to sense that I myself was the bourgeois Monsieur Bovary" (217). The title image is not only an image of technology, but an image of synchronicity between life and language, which (as in "Dendrocacalia") mesh like gears with one another.

16. The first few pages of *S. Karuma-shi no hanzai* are translated by Juliet Winters Carpenter in *Beyond the Curve*. For a summary of the entire story, see Yamamoto Fumiko, whose discussion of narrow rationality and metamorphosis in the text could serve as a point of departure for my reading. Yamamoto also discusses "Dendrocacalia" and other early works.

17. For more on the significance of Rilke and naming in Abe's early work, see Watanabe, *Abe Kōbō* 11–19.

18. Even Schnellbächer's fine book, which is very careful about the way it relates Abe's political activities to his writing, sometimes feels a bit limited by its intent to reconstruct the attitudes and intents of Abe as an authorial subject. This is in some tension with Schnellbächer's own conclusion that for Abe, even an essay's meaning must be constructed on the fly by each new reading, which is also a kind of synthesis, rewriting, or critique (391, 472).

19. As the quote above suggests, some of Abe's statements about his own past are probably made up. Keene writes that "Abe, a writer of fiction, may have had trouble at times distinguishing between what had actually happened and what might have happened if other people were more like himself. . . . But, there were enough improbable occurrences in Abe's life to make almost any story he told seem plausible" (*Five Novelists* 72).

Chapter Two

1. The *Abe Kōbō zenshū* contains all the original *Nami* essays in order of publication. For the contents of the *Warau tsuki* collection, see the notes to the title essay (*AZ* 25:362n). In general, these notes in the back of each *zenshū* volume provide the most detailed available publication history for Abe's works.

2. Even when the focus is science- or technology-related postwar protest movements, Nakayama Shigeru concludes that such protests (from the Japanese Communist Party's criticism of government science policy to grassroots environmental activism) may have criticized the implementation of new tech-

nologies and policies, but that they have rarely questioned the fundamental ideas and values that have underlain science since the Meiji period.

3. On phenomenology, Schnellbächer writes: "What sets Abe apart from the other Night Society members, is his scientific approach, which finds expression in his concern both with mathematical precision and with the phenomenological method" (*Strategist* 280). For Schnellbächer's reconstruction of Abe's psychological model, see the final section of the present chapter.

4. As for the calculus in "Bungaku to jikan," Schnellbächer concludes that it is neither rigorous nor radically transformed, but simply metonymic.

5. Murphy's analysis seems to embody this kind of creativity, though he appears reluctant to take credit for it. For example, when he reads Karatani Kōjin and Edogawa Ranpo in one chapter, the arguments in the Japanese texts do not look very rigorously scientific at all, until Murphy adds some creative math of his own, resulting in a breathtaking reading of both texts. Here and elsewhere in the book, the impressive ability to bridge literature and science that Murphy claims for these two Japanese figures (and Japanese authors in general) seems to belong more specifically to Murphy himself. In this I hope to follow the example of *Metaphorical Circuit*, if not its stated intent.

6. For example, the "Christianity" that Karatani links with scientific causes and effects is something that he rarely treats in a concrete way; it serves as a *deus ex machina* in his presentation, able to embody any and all features of American and European thought and to knit them together into the unified epistemological framework that *Origins* requires. (Murphy, on the other hand, sees the discussion as being unified and made mathematically rigorous by Karatani's discussion of Western linear perspective, in which God becomes an ultimate vantage and vanishing point [Murphy 116–21].)

7. The phrase is David Lindberg's (4). On the disciplinary boundaries of early science, see also Wightman 80–86 and Schmitt 35–51.

8. Bernard Weinberg's encyclopedic survey of Renaissance Italian literary theory exhaustively traces the influence of Plato, Aristotle, and Horace. For a summary of Plato's role, see particularly 250–52, 293–96, 345–48, and 800–802.

9. Mazzoni concurs that although poetry may treat subjects "pertaining to the sciences," it should not employ the language and methods of science because they are not readily understandable. "The poet must speak to the people, among whom are many vulgar and ill-educated men, and therefore if he should present knowledge in a fashion suited to the sciences, they would not understand him" (169).

10. On Locke's influence on eighteenth-century literature, see MacLean 1–17.

11. Schnellbächer (*Strategist* 273–81, 286–96, 382–407, 427–40) traces these ideas from Abe's debut lecture to the Yoru no Kai and his early "Shūruriari-

zumu hihan," (A critique of surrealism, 1949); then through his essays developing the idea of reportage in the 1950s, "Mazu kaibōtō o" (First the dissecting knife, 1955/57), "Kiroku seishin ni tsuite" (On the spirit of documentation, 1958) and "Shin kiroku shugi no teishō" (A case for neo-documentarism, 1958); and finally to his capstone essay "Geijutsu kakumei: geijutsu undō no riron" (Artistic revolution: a theory of art movements, 1960). Title translations are Schnellbächer's.

12. For example, Murphy's reading of Sōseki focuses on the latter's model of attention. Murphy emphasizes that the science underlying Sōseki's model is "quite solid and surprisingly current. . . . The soundness of Sōseki's intuition that the phenomenon of literature could be located in the second by second analysis of [a] waveform of consciousness is echoed by neurophysiologist William Calvin" in 1999 (41). Murphy also advances his own experimental model of "non-reductive creativity" to characterize the work of Terada Torahiko (55–104).

13. Schnellbächer himself identifies a transition over the course of Abe's essays, from early efforts to construct a rigorously mathematical model of literary experience to the later use of science as a kind of metonym. Schnellbächer writes that by 1962, "Abe has evidently become more skeptical of theories since 'The moment of creativity' [1948–49], when he had expressed the hope that he would be able to formulate his problems in precise mathematical terms, but his love of theory, and of technology, at no point declined. . . ." (*Strategist* 464). Schnellbächer also distinguishes between science as metonym and science as metaphor—the latter a more radically creative manipulation of science that appears only sporadically in Abe's essays up to 1962 (*Strategist* 27–28, 254–56, 306). I would argue, though, that the later essay "Warau tsuki" and certainly Abe's novels are metaphorical in Schnellbächer's sense.

14. Another example appears in *Principles of Literary Criticism*, where Richards illustrates his detailed model of perception with a diagram titled "The Analysis of a Poem" that shows light rays reflected off the words of the poem entering the eye and producing sensations that progress through a realistic-looking forest of neurons ("references") before spiraling through a series of "emotions" that resemble nothing so much as laboratory glassware, as if the process of distilling emotions hinted at in the text were carried out literally here by tiny condensers. Finally, the "attitudes" that are Richards's final result are tracked at the bottom of the diagram on something like an EEG trace. This mixed bag of imagery is avowedly schematic or metaphoric, but seems to aspire rather desperately to a place in the laboratory (116).

15. We have already seen hints of this violence in Abe's fiction, and it will emerge even more clearly in Chapter 3. However, in the original psychological

model related by Schnellbächer, the contact between unconscious and higher consciousness is already a site of "friction": both the censorship of the higher consciousness (in part the effect of social coercion) and the creative impulse that destabilizes that censorship are described as sources of psychological discomfort (*Strategist* 290, 481).

16. On Abe's early encounters with German philosophy, see Tani 11–12. The quotation is from the epilogue to the revised edition of *Owarishi michi no shirube ni* (*AZ* 19:476). The translation is Schnellbächer's. For this and other references to Nietzsche in Abe's early work, see Schnellbächer, *Strategist* 268, 274–77, 312.

Chapter Three

1. The Japanese terms are *kurōrupuromajin, fukugō fidobakku, arata-tai, inshoku-tai no baika, naihaiyō, shinkei bunpitsu saibō*, and *kotei hassei wa keitō hassei o kurikae-su mono desu* (*AZ* 9:58, 95). Some of these translations are my own. Others appear on pages 117–18 of the English version.

2. Translations of passages from *Inter Ice Age 4* are mostly taken from the published English translation by E. Dale Saunders, with page numbers indicating the translation. In a few cases, Saunders's translation does not quite capture the vocabulary or logic of the technical language, so I have substituted my own English version and cited the Japanese text.

3. This kind of textbook language can be taken as typical of basic scientific style in Japanese. As evidence of this, the same passage from the biology text appears with minor alterations in a language textbook for English-speaking scientists studying technical Japanese (Daub, Bird, and Inoue 355).

4. See Okuno, "Hito" 484–85; Kusaka 150; Ishikawa Kōji 173. Naitō Yoshitada and Tomoda Hiroyuki brought the Ginga Shobō collection to my attention.

5. Okuno Takeo (in "Hito to sakuhin"), Yamano Kōichi (in "*Daiyon kanpyō-ki*"), and Sukegawa Noriyuki all see Katsumi as a man unable to transcend his present. For a treatment of the problem in broader terms, as a problem of humans' inability ever to transcend their own subjectivity, see Shindo Masaaki and Isoda Kōichi (Kaisetsu).

6. The identity of the narrator is never taken for granted in Abe's works. Kumamoto Mariko argues plausibly (if not conclusively) that the machine narrates not just this final section but the whole novel.

7. Hariu Ichirō and Sukegawa Noriyuki also praise the final section in similar terms.

8. The quotes from Taki and Kusaka are cited by Kumamoto Mariko, who divides the novel's interpreters broadly into those who accept Abe's postscript and those who reject it. But even critics who condemn Katsumi, like Okuno

Takeo (in "Hito to sakuhin"), Isoda Kōichi, and Yamada Kazuko, still find some way to rehabilitate science in the ways described.

9. What is translated as discourse in Bakhtin's texts is *slovo*. In a note in *The Dialogic Imagination*, the translators associate this term both with "an individual word and a method of using words . . . that presumes a type of authority" (427). This is the same range and connection I want to imply.

10. Sterling argues for the internationalism of cyberpunk by noting that the first magazine to publish a cyberpunk special issue was Japan's *SF magajin* (*Mirrorshades* xii). Ironically, while Abe's novel borrowed the exoticism of Western technology and an associated *katakana* technical vocabulary, Gibson's novels rely on Japan as the source of technology, future culture, and even language. In *Inter Ice Age 4*, the role of the alien Other is fulfilled not only by the aquans but by the opposing technological powers of the United States and Russia, with their rival prediction machines. But in several of Gibson's novels, the role of America's other is played by Japan.

11. See the essays in Miyoshi and Harootunian for a range of opinions.

12. See Jameson 64 and Azuma's essay "The Animalization of Otaku Culture," along with Thomas Lamarre's introduction to the latter. "Animalization" refers to the way that affective responses are now reduced to involuntary reactions that can be manipulated by the media. Azuma observes this in the *otaku* of the essay's title—nominally fans of animation, comics, and computer games, but arguably a stand-in for a more general postmodern Japanese subject. Unlike Jameson, Azuma identifies a series of productive responses to this situation, including fan activities that appropriate, remix, and reedit pop culture texts: by spreading the resulting stories, images, and video online, fans can effectively feed their own narratives back into the media.

13. Even writing at a time when the concept of a computer language was an unfamiliar one, Abe is careful to point out that the computer simulation of Katsumi does not simply use language; it *is* language. At the outset, the novel explains correctly that a computer program is itself a linguistic entity, composed of lines of computer language originally printed on the "programming cards" from which two sections of the novel take their titles (7–8). When the computer has Katsumi killed, the novel arrives at the point Hayles describes, where technology permits us to equate information with life itself. In a twist on Hayles's examples—artillery coordinates and missile guidance—the information that constitutes the program becomes a lethal weapon aimed back at its creator. Hayles investigates the historical context for this technological fantasy of converting the human into data in *How We Became Posthuman*.

14. Here Joseph Murphy is quick to complete the Lyotard quote: ". . . a scientist is before anything else a person who 'tells stories.' The only difference is

that he is duty bound to verify them" (Lyotard 60). Murphy decries the "caricature" of Lyotard used by some critics to argue that science and literature are both equally fictional, and he sees Japanese critics as more careful, and more informed (178–83). Science, Murphy reminds us, is still internally consistent and verifiable (at least, Lyotard would add, within its individual subdisciplines). At times Murphy seems to take this criticism too literally, reading it as if it were scientific prose, rather than as an inevitable admixture of rigor and hyperbole; this point is examined more thoroughly in Chapter 6. But Murphy does remind us that if we are to remain faithful to the rigorous side of arguments such as those by Lyotard or Hayles, we must distinguish carefully how certain terms are used, and not slide too easily between different senses of a single word. Science is in some sense arbitrary, in the sense of being a closed system, but not random; it is chaotic in the sense of being unpredictable to us, but not in the sense of being utterly incoherent; and it is narrative or fictional in the sense Lyotard describes, but not necessarily false.

15. Hayles also focuses on chaos theory as a non-totalizing system that might unite science and literature. See her *Chaos Bound* and *Chaos and Order*.

16. For an opposing reading, see Murphy's view of Sōseki's language in this essay and *Bungakuron* (Theory of literature, 1907). Murphy argues that when Sōseki defines literature as "F+f" (a concept/impression F, or an emotional response f, or both), the rigor of his mathematical notation makes us conscious of a fourth possibility, a literature devoid of concepts or impressions and emotions. Overstating Murphy's case slightly for emphasis, this very rigor suggests the possibility of an escape from Western literature, as well as from Western science, Western modernity, and (almost) Western history—the very things that trouble "The Civilization of Modern-Day Japan" (24–54).

17. Responses to Baudrillard's essay from Ballard, Hayles, and others can be found in *Science Fiction Studies* 18.3 (1991).

18. Abe himself praised an earlier apocalyptic novel by Komatsu, *Fukkatsu no hi* (Day of resurrection, 1964), calling it "a masterpiece whose unbridled fantasy has a reality beyond the real." But he also suggested that it transcended the limitations of the genre by adding, "Komatsu Sakyō no longer needs the label science fiction writer" (*AZ* 19:23). My own discussion of *Japan Sinks* is based on the abridged English version of the novel. For a more detailed reading that compares Abe and Komatsu, see Thomas Schnellbächer's essay "Has the Empire Sunk Yet?"

19. As it turned out, Abe himself never did produce a teleplay for "R62 gō no hatsumei," but a radio version was broadcast on NHK in 1987 and even sold on cassette. For an example of this kind of adaptation by Abe himself (and a precursor to *Inter Ice Age 4*), see his story and teleplay "Namari no tamago"

(The leaden egg, 1957), about a man awakened after 800,000 years in suspended animation (*AZ* 7:411–33; *AZ* 8:21–35). The prose and radio texts consist almost entirely of conversations between the man and the plant-like aliens into which humans have evolved.

Chapter Four

1. Abe scholar Julie Brock informed me that Abe's descriptions of the mask's construction are not only painstakingly described but technically plausible as well. Brock interviewed doctors and theatrical mask makers in her research on the novel.

2. "Thinking to remind the mask of my own position," the narrator says at one point near the end of the white notebook, "I brought up a crucial problem from the laboratory." He goes on to give the technical details of an experiment on "the functional relationship between pressure- and temperature-related changes in the elasticity of certain polymers." But the scientific language is unable to exorcise the mask, which "merely furrowed its brow slightly in annoyance" (*AZ* 18:412–13).

3. For example, Shirai Kenzaburō's early review article places responsibility for these failed relationships at least partly with the narrator himself. Muramatsu Takeshi sees the problem as endemic to modern society, while Morikawa Tatsuya discusses it in the context of human sexuality and human nature.

4. See the interpretation by Satō Yasumasa, for example.

5. See the discussion of Schnellbächer's *Literary Strategist* in Chapter 1. For other interpretations like Ōe's, see Napier (104) and Hirano Hidehisa's Marxist reading of the novel. Hirano also begins from the need for social action and outreach, but sees the narrator as a failure, his final violent decision an overcompensation for his fundamental inability to act.

6. See for example Napier 127, 209–14 and Suter 12–13, 177.

7. Condemning the very thing that Zola praises, Nietzsche disapproves of the novel for its realism, justification, and psychology, which he traces back to the Socratic impulse and the Socratic dialogue, where "philosophic thought overgrows art and compels it to cling close to the trunk of dialectic" (91). But in the dialogic format of Plato's texts, Bakhtin sees a productive uncertainty that may characterize both literature and science: Plato's dialogues constitute "a remarkable document that reflects the simultaneous birth of scientific thinking and of a new artistic prose model for the novel" (*Dialogic* 24). This difference of opinion is repeated by other writers, such as the New Critics. In "Poetry: A Note on Ontology," John Crowe Ransom criticizes what he calls "Platonic" poets who succumb to the "predatory" urge of science, the urge to reduce the world to abstract ideas. But while R. P. Blackmur also champions

the role of an unscientific uncertainty in literary criticism, he nevertheless approves of Plato, whose style has a breadth and an irony that "always holds conflicting ideas in shifting balance, presenting them in contest and evolution, with victory only the last shift" (273).

8. Hirano Hidehisa (in "Kamen no tsumi") and Okuno Takeo (in "Jigoku meguri") both suggest that the narrative escapes Abe's control.

9. Komori has shown that the work of the Meiji novelist Futabatei Shimei can be read in Bakhtinian terms, connecting the worlds inside and outside the text by dealing with the social identity of Futabatei's readership and the literary style of his contemporaries alongside problems of character identity and narrative voice. Komori concludes that Futabatei is able to access the "internal dialogue of self-consciousness" in his protagonists by cutting off the hero's dialogue with anyone outside himself, in the same way that Abe's narrator turns inward when he is unable to reach the other ("Buntai" 41–56; "Kattōtai" 114–21).

10. For example, Takano Toshimi's *Abe Kōbō ron* (176–82), Morikawa Tatsuya, and Satō Yasumasa all treat the novel as an examination of the human condition. Shirai Kenzaburō and Hirano Hidehisa see it as a critique of society. Fukushima Akira, Muramatsu Takeshi, and the afterword by Ōe Kenzaburō combine the two perspectives.

Chapter Five

1. Translations of the novel through 1997 are listed in *AZ* 16:115*n*. For more recent translations, see the Japan Foundation's online database *Japanese Literature in Translation*.

2. Translations from *The Woman in the Dunes* in this chapter are mine. This novel makes such frequent and significant use of ellipses that it may be worth restating an editorial convention introduced earlier: ellipses in quotations from Abe correspond to ellipses in the original Japanese or the published translation, while omitted material is indicated using bracketed ellipses [. . .].

3. The protagonist's given name, written with the characters for "orderly" and "even," is romanized alternately as "Jumpei" in the published translation and some English criticism of the novel.

4. A few critics have seen the ending negatively: Earl Miner, for example, identifies the man's final surrender as ironic and pessimistic: the woman's "strange appeal is partly that of enslavement, partly of femininity. . . . What happens seems intolerable precisely because it is so grotesquely credible" (32).

5. Of the protagonist's transformation, Pollack says, "Jumpei makes an about face and simply accepts this new world and its logic built on shifting sand. . . . The logic of Jumpei's insight is that of all accommodation in general: a logic

of reversal, of the topsy-turvy" (129–30). Pollack suggests that at best the ending can become an ironic relativization that allows the novel and the reader to call into question both ideologies. At worst, it is a naive substitution of one ideology for another. In other words, Pollack seems undecided about whether it is just Niki or Abe himself who is captured by this false hope for a kind of community tied to traditional values. At one point, he suggests that Abe moved beyond this lingering attachment after "the ambiguous results of the experiment" that was *The Woman in the Dunes* (135).

6. We can trace this line of criticism from the time of the novel's publication onward, starting with influential early essays by Isoda and Sasaki, "Mukokuseki-sha no shiten" (A nationless perspective, 1962) and "Dasshutsu to chōkoku" (Escape and conquer, 1966), and continuing in later book-length studies of Abe and his circle by Nakamura (5–129) and Watanabe (*Abe Kōbō* 74–103). A similar interpretation appears in Takano Toshimi's excellent retrospective article for the Abe volume of the *Shinchō bungaku arubamu* series ("Hyōden" 38–68).

7. For example, in his book *Abe Kōbō*, Watanabe Hiroshi frames his reading of *The Woman in the Dunes* and Abe's other work using a phrase we encountered in Chapter 1, Abe's claim in 1957 that he had passed from existentialism to surrealism and then to communism (*AZ* 7:476). Some critics argue that *The Woman in the Dunes* draws to varying degrees on all these elements: as in existentialism, a kind of concrete materialism displaces received realities and concepts; as in surrealism, a new more imaginative reality replaces the old; and from Abe's progressive politics, the work gains an optimistic engagement with social reality. In addition to Watanabe, see Okaniwa, Nakamura, and especially Takano ("Hyōden" 38–68). For a discussion in English of *The Woman in the Dunes* in the context of Abe's involvement with the Japanese Communist Party, see Motoyama.

8. For comparison, the full passage in Saunders's translation reads: "The theory had been advanced that the man, tired of life, had committed suicide. One of his colleagues, who was an amateur psychoanalyst, held to this view. He claimed that in a grown man enthusiasm for such a useless pastime as collecting insects was evidence enough of a mental quirk. Even in children, unusual preoccupation with insect collecting frequently indicates an Oedipus complex. [. . .] Indeed, the man had not once confided his interests to anyone, and this would seem to be proof that he realized they were rather dubious" (4–6).

9. Critics such as Komori Yōichi, James Fujii, and Naoki Sakai have argued that the ambiguous demarcation between voices is a feature of Japanese literature going back to the Meiji *shōsetsu*, to Edo *gesaku*, or to Heian *monogatari*. One

could argue about how much of this ambiguity is produced by the traditions of literary style and how much by the broader structure of the Japanese language, which routinely omits explicit subjects and objects. Analogously, one could ask whether Abe's use of these effects is a deliberate gesture or the inevitable outgrowth of writing in Japanese. Conversely, the strong narrative presence in Saunders's translation could be motivated by the translator's desire to order the narrative, or more subtly, by the requirements of English literary style and its reluctance to omit pronouns and subjects. The source of these differences is almost certainly a complex combination of all these factors, but here I will focus on the style that results, and on its implications for interpreting the novel.

10. There is some ambiguity about how to identify this second woman. In the film she is not identified: the context suggests she is someone back in the city with whom the man has a relationship. In the novel, the narration identifies her as "*otoko no tsuma*," normally "the man's wife," though he refers to her as "*aitsū*" (that one, her). Notes to the novel in *Abe Kōbō zenshū* point us to the fact that Abe's radio script changed this to "*otoko ga shitashiku shite ita aru josei*" (a woman he was close to) in the narration (*AZ* 16:115*n*, 17:121). E. Dale Saunders may have borrowed this description for his translation of the novel, which refers to this woman as "his wife, or at least the woman he lived with" (4).

11. This is my own translation of the dialogue from the film. The original film script appears in *AZ* 18:195–233, but differs from the finished film.

12. Keiko McDonald cites the possibility of communication as a source of tentative optimism in the film as well. She writes, "His eagerness to tell the villagers about the water reveals his desire for congenial human relationships, which might add some positive value to a life always aware of alienation. This potential is emphasized by the radio Niki is holding in his hands" (47).

13. One thing Niki Junpei does not really do is write. These connections between the protagonists' inventions and the writer's art are more explicit in later novels such as *The Face of Another* or *The Box Man*, where the inventor characters are called upon to express themselves in writing, and in the process to reconcile different voices or styles. In *The Woman in the Dunes*, there is just a hint that Niki Junpei's newfound urge to communicate is linked with an ability to write: after he invents the water trap, he begins to take down experimental data related to the functioning of the device. This act of writing is highlighted both in the novel and the film script: in the script, Abe actually supplies detailed versions of the table and diagram which the man draws, and Teshigahara's camera lingers on these figures as the man draws them (*AZ* 18:229).

14. In the film *The Face of Another*, these three leaders of the avant-garde were joined by a fourth, the noted modernist architect Isozaki Arata, who designed some of the otherworldly sets.

15. For an opposing view, see Dissanayake, who suggests that the camera reproduces the male gaze of the novel.

16. In *Critique of Judgment*, Kant used "disinterest" to describe the standpoint from which we experience beauty, a standpoint purified of worldly interest or physical desire. The link between beauty and disinterest thus moves beauty one step closer to the ideal world of reason. We could trace this same movement in Kant's definition of the sublime, which describes a physical experience of such magnitude (a landscape so overwhelming, for example), that it accomplishes a similar purification: a sublime experience threatens to overwhelm physical sensation and imagination, but it can never overwhelm our reason, which can always posit something even greater. (Recall that this is how the Kantian sublime links universal reason with practical experience.) One might construct a reading that compares the beauty of the woman with the sublime quality of the dune landscape, and discusses the role of both for the man's self-definition. This might allow us to discuss the film together with the novels *Inter Ice Age 4* and *Secret Rendezvous*, where the sublime voices of the texts seem to disrupt or foil ready understanding. But the reading in Chapter 3 relates *Inter Ice Age 4* to later incarnations of the sublime, advanced by Jameson or Lyotard. If the experience of watching Teshigahara's film is sublime, I would associate it with the more optimistic Kantian version, which allows us to intuit a universal truth beyond the self. This brand of universalism and transcendence is still far removed from most of Abe's projects.

17. For another phenomenological analysis of the film that invokes Merleau-Ponty and Sobchack, see Akira Lippit's *Atomic Light*. I encountered Lippit's reading after completing this chapter, but his approach has similarities to my own, though his conclusions are different. Lippit sees the confusion and overlap between characters that I associated with the novel continued in the film. Citing not only the double exposure that superimposes the man and his wife early in the film, but also the high-contrast cinematography that foils clear vision, and the way the characters' bodies seem to visually melt into one another (in the love scenes) and into the landscape, Lippit argues that the film never distinguishes the characters clearly enough to portray Merleau-Ponty's separate independent subjectivities coming together in communication. Instead, Lippit characterizes the film as an "emulsion," a combination of unmixable elements suspended together in a semi-stable matrix, neither wholly separate nor completely combined. "One over the other, one inside and alongside another," writes Lippit in a style that seems intended to mimic this unstable equilibrium. "Two scenes that coexist uncomfortably, never mixing: sand and water, smooth and striated spaces, letters and sand, man and woman, the same man and another woman, this moment and that, this world and another. He is inside and outside her,

she of him" (129). Lippit's larger argument is that *Woman in the Dunes* is a post-nuclear film, in which crises of representation are linked to the nuclear through the metaphor of radiation, a monstrous species of writing or photography and at the same time something invisible, something that is impossible to picture or to write about. Chapter 7 applies Lippit's ideas to Abe's novel of nuclear technology, *The Ark Sakura*.

18. Abe published photo essays in the literary journals *Umi* and *Eureka* in 1978, and these and additional photos were later incorporated into a book of interviews, *Toshi e no kairo* (Circuit to the city, 1978). Abe's photographs also appeared in several issues of *Geijutsu shinchō* during 1980 and 1981. Several exhibitions of Abe's photographs were held in conjunction with related events, including a 1978 exhibit at the Abe Kōbō Studio and another at Milwaukee's Performing Arts Center (in conjunction with a performance of *Friends*) (*AZ* 26:161–92, 433–81, 161*n*, 433*n*). There was also an elaborate show at Columbia University on the occasion of the Abe Kōbō Symposium in 1996, and an Abe exhibit at the Setagaya Bungakukan in 2003 (documented in *Abe Kōbō ten*). On Abe's relative importance as a photographer, I have relied on Parker

19. For precursors to these plays, see the notes that accompany them in *Abe Kōbō zenshū* 20:425*n*, 22:357*n*. For the performance history of Abe's plays in the 1950s and 1960s, see Shields 44 and Tani 143–66. The latter contains a full list of performances of Abe's dramatic works, with technical details about each production.

20. On Abe's drama, see Shields; see also Iles, which focuses primarily on Abe's work for the stage.

21. The description here is based on *Fake Fish*, as well as material presented by Shields and other Studio members at the Abe Kobo Symposium at Columbia University in 1996. This material included a film of *Kozō wa shinda* that Abe produced from video footage shot after the final performance.

22. For example, see Abe's lecture "Kotoba to nikutai no aida" (Between words and flesh, 1978) and two interviews with Watanabe Hiroshi: "Kōzō-shugiteki na shikō keishiki" (The structuralist form of thought, 1978) and "Engeki no anarogu kankaku" (The analog sense of theater, 1979) (*AZ* 26:323–37, 146–59, 395–400).

Chapter Six

1. Donald Keene reports that at one point Abe's publisher Shinchōsha implored him to write an article on *Kangaroo Notebook*, apparently because no one else would (*Novelists* 82–83). For an exception, see the fine work of the novel's American translator, Maryellen Toman Mori, who echoes Keene's praise of the novel.

2. I would apply Napier's general remarks about the potential of Japanese fantasy to *Secret Rendezvous*, but Napier reads Abe's late novels as more "nihilistic" (134). *Secret Rendezvous*, for example, is said to be a pure dystopia, "a world where technology and human beings together collaborate to violate individuality and human integrity" (76). See also Napier 73–77, 198–206.

3. More than just a recycling of familiar tropes, *Secret Rendezvous* could be seen as an almost literal sequel to Abe's earlier works. *The Woman in the Dunes* ends with the woman being taken to the hospital. The last thing the box man hears is the sound of an approaching siren, which could be the ambulance that opens *Secret Rendezvous*. (And as *Secret Rendezvous* will end with the narrator crouching in an underground chamber, Abe's next novel *The Ark Sakura* opens with Mole hiding in his underground quarry.)

4. On the confusion the novel produced, see for example Satō Tadao's review in *Fujin kōron*, which begins with the words, "This is a strange novel" (338).

5. Carpenter told me this story in 1996. When I asked her what had become of the napkin, she told me it was lost—the only appropriate conclusion to an anecdote like this. Incomplete, uncertain, or damaged maps are another well-known trope in Abe's work, and the central image of one whole novel, *The Ruined Map*.

6. See also Morota Kazuharu, who writes: "The writer presents the world of his imagination as the reality of the novel. Then he applies the power of that imagined world to the task of tearing down the reality that exists in the reader's consciousness" (5).

7. Yamano Kōichi summarizes: "The problem is this—what can readers conclude after picking up this report tossed from the world of dreams?" (3).

8. Efforts to see the novel as a satire or parody of sexed society, for example, have generally foundered. See Saeki's review and Hiraoka Tokuyori's confused afterword. A reviewer for *Shūkan Asahi* is probably closer to the truth when he writes that the novel neither mocks nor shocks; instead, it portrays a society so jaded that nothing can shock any more ("Chiteki" 116).

9. Some critics, casting about for such a figure, look to the horse's speeches. See the articles by Serizawa and Satō Tadao, for example, or Hanawa Yoshihiko's questions for Abe in a 1978 interview published as "Toshi e no kairo" (Circuit to the city, *AZ* 26:193–230). Although the horse's comments about reverse evolution do provide some clues to reading the novel, they do not amount to anything like a coherent philosophy. Abe could articulate his own ideas behind a term such as "reverse evolution" (an idea advanced by the horse and discussed in more detail below), but the author still refers to this idea as a "paradox" and to the horse's thinking as "a parody" of it (*AZ* 26:195).

10. See the 1958 roundtable discussion "From Science to Fantasy" ("Kagaku kara kūsō e," *AZ* 8:190–211) and the "Toshi e no kairo" interview cited above (*AZ* 26:193–230). The similarity of these comments, made 20 years apart, emphasizes the link between these two novels.

11. Elsewhere, Bakhtin defines parody as one mode of novelistic heteroglossia (*Problems* 193–99), and identifies the novel as a genre that exists as a parody of the epic genres that preceded it (*Dialogic* 20–24, 51–68).

12. In Hutcheon's definition, any work of art may be a parody if it incorporates another work or a "coded discourse" and establishes a difference or distance between itself and the original (8). She defines parody as "repetition, but repetition that includes difference" (37). This difference is what distinguishes parody from more straightforward repetition (such as quotation or plagiarism), but it does not necessarily imply any judgment or mockery of the target. In fact, the lack of overt judgment is one of the hallmarks of modern parody. Judgment lies in the realm of those texts that incorporate and comment on a reality outside themselves, and she labels these texts satire. The distinction between satire and parody serves the same purpose as Jameson's distinction between parody and pastiche, or Bakhtin's between parody and stylization; but in separating the text's attitude toward language from its attitude toward reality, Hutcheon resists Bakhtin and Jameson's tendency to equate every language or style with a world view (49–68).

13. Conceding that the publication of one article in one journal does not really say much about the state of the field, Sokal later played down the significance of the hoax itself and turned from ridiculing his own straw-man article to critiquing other published work in science studies. (See, for example, "What the Social Text Affair Does and Does Not Prove.") These later critiques revolved around issues of language and style, and are taken up below. But these ideas (which did not require a hoax to put forth) had less force in the evolving debate than the initial parody and Sokal's suggestion in *Lingua Franca* that "some fashionable sectors of the American Academic Left have been getting intellectually lazy," that in these fields "the emperor has no clothes" (64).

14. See "Science Wars and the Need for Respect and Rigour"; Scott; Sokal's interview with Robert Siegel; and Switzer.

15. Paul Boghossian uses this term "revealed" in his defense of Sokal (14). Surprisingly, some literary critics bought into this contradictory argument and focused their discussions on the author: though Bruce Robbins tries halfheartedly to sever the article from Sokal's intent and to defend it on its own merits ("Anatomy" 58), even Stanley Fish argues that it is not ethical for the author to submit an article if his or her intent runs counter to the text's.

16. For arguments on the bankruptcy of literary critical language, see Erich Eichman's article on the hoax for *The New Criterion*, or Jay Rosen's comment in *Tikkun* that "it is precisely the slow creep of jargon that turns institutions dumb" (60). While this accusation may seem trite, it is perhaps just the flip side of fears we heard from Jean-François Lyotard and Fredric Jameson, that specialized technical vocabulary is eroding our common language.

17. One can see this asymmetry or double standard in Sokal's complaints about critics who appropriate scientific terms and principles without understanding them, or use them in places where they have no relevance. This argument about language is the heart of Sokal's position in his later writing on the hoax. But while this has the air of a plea for a clearer use of language in general, it allows that scientists might have a specialized vocabulary not accessible to outsiders, while denying that criticism might have its own analogous technical language or style (in which scientific terms might play a part). Put another way, Sokal argues that the way scientists understand these terms should be given priority over the way critics understand them. This is behind his complaints about the "confusion between the technical and everyday senses of English words" ("Afterword" 93) or his demand that scientific terms should not be used loosely or even figuratively. To critics who want to use specialized scientific vocabulary in everyday prose (taking advantage of its strangeness, for example, to defamiliarize an everyday idea), Sokal says that even as a metaphor, scientific language must preserve its specialized technical sense. Writing with Jean Bricmont, he says: "The role of metaphor is usually to clarify an unfamiliar concept by relating it to a more familiar one, not the reverse. . . . we fail to see the advantage of invoking, even metaphorically, scientific concepts that one oneself understands only shakily when addressing a non-specialist audience" (Bricmont and Sokal 17). This may sound familiar: it is almost exactly the argument Joseph Addison adduces in 1712 to support the separation of scientific and literary language. Adhering to the Renaissance idea that scientific language is too unfamiliar for use in poetry, Addison restricts the metaphors permitted in criticism and other abstract writing: "the chief Design of an Allusion being to illustrate and explain the Passages of an Author, it should be always borrowed from what is more known and common, than the Passages which are to be explained. . . . for the generality, the most entertaining ones lie in the Works of Nature, which are Obvious to all Capacities, and more delightful than what is to be found in Arts and Sciences" (578). Sokal's double standard thus traces back to the empiricists: both demand a technical precision from criticism while forbidding it any special or technical way of using language. On the implications of the parallels between Sokal and the empiricists, see the conclusion of this chapter. For an argument that most

scientists have a more sophisticated view of metaphor than Sokal and Bricmont, see Murphy 183–85.

18. See the articles by Dennis Overbye in the *New York Times*, Richard Monastersky in the *Chronicle of Higher Education*, and Declan Butler in *Nature*.

19. John Baez asked on his own web page why the brothers defended their work and their reputations so aggressively in the face of overwhelming criticism from physicists, and concluded "the brothers Bogdanoff may be managing to make money from their minor reputation as experts in France. That would explain a lot." Other suggested motivations involved a plagiarism trial the brothers were involved in, a case in which having published scientific research to their names might conceivably have bolstered their claims. The Bogdanoffs for their part also attributed ulterior motives to some of their critics, tracing to "a very ancient editorial conflict that had nothing to do with science" (qtd. in Orlowski).

20. The Wikipedia article is titled "The Bogdanov Affair," though the title is also subject to debate and change. The message from "not Igor" is part of the extensive discussion by contributors that parallels the article, and is archived at <http://en.wikipedia.org/wiki/Talk:Bogdanov_Affair/Archive_7>. Accessed 10 Dec. 2006.

21. Here Murphy criticizes Sokal as well as Gross and Levitt for having an unacknowledged metaphysics of their own: a faith in a rational reality that exists outside the rational system of science, and in a transparent connection between the two. Murphy's critique is like the Foucauldian one described below, but Murphy relates it to a philosophical tradition extending from George Berkeley onward, one he thinks most practicing scientists already take into account (191–97). Murphy criticizes science studies for aiming their critiques at naively positivist scientist figures who are no more than "straw targets," but Sokal seems to resemble this straw man, so Murphy has some stake in disassociating him from other scientists. I have doubts that Sokal's epistemology is such an anomaly among scientists, but my conclusions are admittedly speculative, and my evidence anecdotal. Whatever scientists believe, a naively utopian view of science is not at all rare among the public at large in postwar and contemporary Japan and North America; this broader view, and not the attitudes of scientists specifically, is what I would identify as the target of Abe's prose.

Chapter Seven

1. See the negative reviews by Louis Allen in the *Times Literary Supplement*, Ivan Gold in the *Washington Post*, Michiko Kakutani in the *New York Times*, and Robert Taylor in the *Boston Globe*. For less hostile reviews, see Kevin Keane

in the *Los Angeles Times*, Brad Leithauser in the *New Yorker*, Edmund White in the *New York Times Book Review*, and Jack D. Kirwan in the *Chicago Tribune*.

2. See also the review by Watanabe Hiroshi.

3. See comments in the documentary "Abe Kōbō ga sagashiateta jidai." For some of Abe's early comments on using a computer, see his 1983 dialogue with Tsutsumi Seiji, "Sōsaku ni okeru wāpuro" (Writing with a word processor, *AZ* 27:136–41).

4. Elsewhere in Abe's work, we see transparency used both as a metaphor for the unreality of everyday social conventions and as a figure for the nuclear threat. For example, the final scene of *The Ark Sakura* recalls the opening of the film version of Abe's novel *The Face of Another*, in which we see a full-motion x-ray of the narrator speaking. The x-ray prefigures references to nuclear war in the novel and later in the film. But in the novel *The Face of Another*, transparency is also a metaphor for the emptiness or constructedness of social conventions and interpersonal relations. In Chapter 4 we saw the narrator of that novel dream about overturning those conventions, so that "other people will become transparent ghosts; everything will be full of gaps—like a picture painted in faint shades on glass" (*AZ* 18:452).

5. See the brief discussion in Chapter 4, which follows Schnellbächer, *Strategist* 406–7.

6. Morimoto Takako comes closer to the sense of the novel by focusing on simulation and by making reference to Baudrillard's simulacrum. She argues that the ark represents an artificial world; but instead of constructing a utopian space, Mole recreates the problems of the collective (*kyōdōtai*) found in the world outside (hierarchy, authority), and he hopes for the nuclear war that will allow his own simulation/simulacrum to replace the real world. But since the original and the copy are both founded on the bankrupt logic of the *kyōdōtai*, Morimoto says, both lose their reality in the novel's conclusion. On the surface, Morimoto follows Baudrillard's outline, but her reading seems to lack Baudrillard's notion (and Abe's idea in "The Dark Side of the Cherry Blossoms") that the simulacrum is powerful precisely *because* it lacks a deeper meaning. And Morimoto's conclusion—that "despite the very real possibility that nuclear war will occur in the near future, it is not something we can extrapolate [*michibiki-dasu*] from our accumulated everyday present reality" (78)—seems opposite to Baudrillard's conclusion and my own reading of the novel here, namely that the apparent reality (the nuclear threat as it is perceived or advertised) is a decoy that authorizes and conceals the theft or surrender of political freedom.

7. The comedy also revolves around awful caricatures of the native villagers, though the narrative perspective shifts rapidly in a way that seems to present these racist images in one moment and then mock them in the next, as

the story veers between targeted satire and unbridled pastiche. For a discussion of Tsutsui that focuses on his more recent and more interesting work but that also touches on humor and stereotypes, see Gardner.

8. In Japanese Azuma uses the term *unmei* for "fate," *bōrei* for "ghost," and the loanword *fēku* for "fake" (269).

9. For some brief comments in English along similar lines, see Azuma's "SF as Hamlet." The argument described above centers on the plots of these stories, but elsewhere Azuma extends it to the formal structure of the narratives in a way that might be suggestive for reading *The Ark Sakura* and Abe's late fiction. Citing Ōtsuka Eiji's idea of "narrative consumption," Azuma says that even into the 1980s, some science fiction series replaced the lost cultural metanarratives with large-scale fictional narratives sustained by their sheer length and complexity; but by the 1990s these had been replaced by more disjointed, discontinuous narratives such as advertising campaigns or episodic video games. However, Azuma associates these abbreviated narratives with more and more efficient audience manipulation and gratification, rather than avant-garde disruption ("Animalizing" 183–84).

Works Cited

All the texts by Abe cited in this book are found in the 29-volume *Abe Kōbō zenshū* (Complete works of Abe Kōbō), abbreviated *AZ* in the text and below. Translated works by Abe are also cited separately. The Japanese term *kaisetsu* is left untranslated here; it refers to interpretive essays by critics that were included as afterwords in the *bunkobon* (paperback) editions of Abe's novels.

Abe Kōbō. *Abe Kōbō zenshū* [The complete works of Abe Kōbō]. 29 vols. To-kyo: Shinchōsha, 1997–2000.

———. *The Ark Sakura*. Trans. Juliet Winters Carpenter. New York: Knopf, 1988. Trans. of *Hakobune Sakura Maru*. *AZ* 27:247–469.

———. "The Boom in Science Fiction." Trans. Christopher Bolton. *Science Fiction Studies* 29.3 (2002): 342–49. Trans. of "SF no ryūkō ni tsuite." *AZ* 16:376–83.

———. *The Box Man*. Trans. E. Dale Saunders. New York: Knopf, 1974. Trans. of *Hako otoko*. *AZ* 24:9–141.

———. *The Crime of S. Karma*. Excerpted and trans. Juliet Winters Carpenter. *Beyond the Curve*. Tokyo: Kodansha International, 1991. 35–42. Trans. of *S. Karuma-shi no hanzai*. *AZ* 2:378–451.

———. "Dendrocacalia." Trans. Juliet Winters Carpenter. *Beyond the Curve*. To-kyo: Kodansha International, 1991. 43–64. Trans. of "Dendorokakariya" (1952 version). *AZ* 3:349–65.

———. "The Dark Side of the Cherry Blossoms." Trans. Donald Keene. *Washington Post* 1 Nov. 1981: Book World 15. Trans. of "Sakura wa itan shinmon-kan no monshō." *AZ* 27:91–93.

———. *The Face of Another*. Trans. E. Dale Saunders. New York: Perigee, 1980. Trans. of *Tanin no kao*. *AZ* 18:321–495.

————. *Friends.* Trans. Donald Keene. *Contemporary Japanese Literature: An Anthology of Fiction, Film, and Other Writing Since 1945.* Ed. Howard Hibbett. Tokyo: Tuttle, 1978. Trans. of *Tomodachi. AZ* 20:425–86.

————. *Inter Ice Age 4.* Trans. E. Dale Saunders. New York: Knopf, 1970. Trans. of *Daiyon kanpyōki* with the postscript "Nichijōsei e no senkoku." *AZ* 9:9–174, 11:141–42.

————. Interview with Nancy S. Hardin. *Contemporary Literature* 15.4 (1974): 439–56.

————. "Journey Through a Wormhole in the Earth." Trans. Donald Keene. *New York Times* 11 June 1975: 43. Trans. of "Chikyū no mushikui ana e no tabi." *AZ* 25:359–60.

————. *Kangaroo Notebook: A Novel.* Trans. Maryellen Toman Mori. New York: Knopf, 1996. Trans. of *Kangarū nōto. AZ* 29:81–190.

————, dir. *Kozō wa shinda* [The little elephant is dead]. Seibu Bijutsukan and Shinchō Bungei Shinkōkai, 1979. Video.

————. *The Man Who Turned into a Stick: Three Related Plays.* Trans. Donald Keene. Tokyo: University of Tokyo Press, 1975. 53–82. Trans. of *Bō ni natta otoko. AZ* 22:357–99.

————. "The Red Cocoon." *A Late Chrysanthemum: Twenty-One Stories from the Japanese.* Trans. Lane Dunlop. San Francisco, CA: North Point Press, 1986. 159–62. Trans. of "Akai mayu." *AZ* 2:492–94.

————. *Secret Rendezvous.* Trans. Juliet Winters Carpenter. New York: Knopf, 1979. Trans. of *Mikkai. AZ* 26:7–140.

————. "Science Fiction the Unnamable." Trans. Thomas Schnellbächer. *Science Fiction Studies* 29.3 (2002): 349–50. Trans. of "SF kono nazukegataki mono." *AZ* 20:52–54.

————. *The Woman in the Dunes.* Trans. E. Dale Saunders. New York: Knopf, 1964. Trans. of *Suna no onna. AZ* 16:115–250.

Abe Kōbō ga sagashiateta jidai [Abe Kōbō in search of an age]. 2 episodes. ETV. NHK. 13–14 April 1994. Television.

Abe Kōbō: nichijō no naka no chōgenjitsu [The everyday supernatural of Abe Kōbō]. Special issue of *Eureka* 26.8 (1994).

Abe Kōbō ten [Abe Kōbō exhibition]. Tokyo: Setagaya Bungakukan, 2003.

Addison, Joseph. *The Spectator.* Ed. Donald F. Bond. Vol. 3. Oxford, UK: Clarendon Press, 1965.

Akutagawa Ryūnosuke. "Spinning Gears." *Rashōmon and Other Stories.* Ed. and trans. Jay Rubin. New York: Penguin, 2006. Trans. of "Haguruma." *Akutagawa Ryūnosuke zenshū.* Vol. 6. Tokyo: Chikuma Shobō, 1987. 359–410.

Allen, Louis. "Piranesian Prospects." Rev. of *The Ark Sakura. Times Literary Supplement* 12 Aug. 1988: 892.

Aquinas, Thomas. *Summa Theologica*. Trans. Fathers of the English Dominican Province. Vol. 1. New York: Benziger Brothers, 1947.

Aristotle. *The Poetics. Aristotle's Theory of Poetry and Fine Art*. 4th ed. Trans. S. H. Butcher. London: Macmillan, 1911.

Azuma Hiroki. "Tantei shōsetsu no sekai, SF no sekai" [The age of the detective novel and the age of science fiction]. *Yūbinteki fuantachi#* [Postal anxieties#]. Tokyo: Asahi Bunko, 2002. 265–76.

———. "The Animalization of Otaku Culture." Trans. Yuriko Furuhata and Marc Steinberg. Introd. by Thomas Lamarre. *Mechademia 2: Networks of Desire*. Ed. Frenchy Lunning. Minneapolis, MN: University of Minnesota Press, 2007. 175–87.

———. "Super Flat Speculation." *Super Flat*. Tokyo: Madra, 2000. 139–51. Trans. of "Sūpā furatto de shibensuru" in the same volume. 138–50.

———. "SF as Hamlet." Trans. Miri Nakamura. Bolton, Csicsery-Ronay, Jr., and Tatsumi 75–82. Trans. of "Hamuretto to shite no SF: SF to tetsugaku." *Yūbinteki fuantachi#* [Postal anxieties#]. Tokyo: Asahi Bunko, 2002. 265–76.

Baez, John. "The Bogdanoff Affair." *John Baez's Stuff*. 21 June 2006. Web. Accessed 10 Nov. 2006. <http://math.ucr.edu/home/baez/bogdanoff/>.

———. "Physics bitten by reverse Alan Sokal hoax?" Posting to sci.physics. research email distribution list. 23 Oct. 2002. Accessed 10 Nov. 2006. <http://groups.google.com/group/sci.physics.research/msg/9f8fde48d7c3566>.

Bakhtin, M[ikhail] M. *Art and Answerability: Early Philosophical Essays by M. M. Bakhtin*. Ed. Michael Holquist and Vadim Liapunov. Trans. Vadim Liapunov. Austin, TX: University of Texas Press, 1990.

———. *The Dialogic Imagination: Four Essays by M. M. Bakhtin*. Ed. Michael Holquist. Trans. Caryl Emerson and Michael Holquist. Austin, TX: University of Texas Press, 1986.

———. *Problems of Dostoevsky's Poetics*. Ed. and trans. Caryl Emerson. Minneapolis, MN: University of Minnesota Press, 1984.

———. *Speech Genres & Other Late Essays*. Trans. Vern W. McGee. Ed. Caryl Emerson and Michael Holquist. Austin, TX: University of Texas Press, 1986.

Bartholomew, James R. *The Formation of Science in Japan: Building a Research Tradition*. New Haven, CT: Yale University Press, 1989.

Baudrillard, Jean. *Simulacra and Simulation*. Trans. Sheila Faria Glaser. Ann Arbor, MI: University of Michigan Press, 1994.

Berkowitz, Peter. "Science Fiction." *New Republic* 1 July 1996: 15–16.

Blackmur, R. P. "A Critic's Job of Work." *The Double Agent: Essays in Craft and Elucidation*. Gloucester, MA: Peter Smith, 1962. 269–302.

"The Bogdanov Affair." *Wikipedia.* Web. Accessed 10 Dec. 2006. <http://en.wikipedia.org/wiki/Bogdanov_Affair>.

Boghossian, Paul. "What the Sokal Hoax Ought to Teach Us." *Times Literary Supplement* 13 Dec. 1996: 14–15.

Bolton, Christopher, Istvan Csicsery-Ronay, Jr., and Takayuki Tatsumi. *Robot Ghosts and Wired Dreams: Japanese Science Fiction from Origins to Anime.* Minneapolis, MN: University of Minnesota Press, 2007.

Borges, Jorge Luis. "The Analytical Language of John Wilkins." *Other Inquisitions 1937–1952.* Trans. Ruth L. C. Simms. Austin, TX: University of Texas Press, 1964. 101–5.

———. "Tlön, Uqbar, Orbis Tertius." Trans. Alistair Reid. *Ficciones.* New York: Knopf-Everyman's Library, 1993. 5–21.

Bricmont, Jean, and Alan Sokal. "What Is All the Fuss About? How French Intellectuals Have Responded to Accusations of Science-Abuse." *Times Literary Supplement* 17 Oct. 1997: 17.

Burke, Edmund. *A Philosophical Inquiry Into the Origin of Our Ideas of the Sublime and Beautiful.* Ed. J. T. Boulton. London: Routledge and Kegan Paul, 1958.

Butler, Declan. "Theses Spark Twin Dilemma for Physicists." *Nature* 420.5 (2002): 5. Web. Accessed 19 Feb. 2007. <http://www.nature.com/nature/journal/v420/n6911/pdf/420005a.pdf>.

Carpenter, J[uliet] W[inters]. Kaisetsu. *Hakobune Sakura Maru.* Bunkobon ed. Tokyo: Shinchō Bunko, 1990. 377–78.

Castelvetro, Lodovico. *Castelvetro on the Art of Poetry: An Abridged Translation of Lodovico Castelvetro's* Poetica d'Aristotele Vulgarizzata et Sposta. Trans. Andrew Bongiorno. Binghamton, NY: Medieval & Renaissance Texts & Studies, 1984.

"Chiteki sekkei ga yunīku ni sugite" [An erudite design that is just too unusual]. Rev. of *Mikkai. Shūkan Asahi* 10 Feb. 1978: 115–16.

Cornyetz, Nina. "Technologies of Gazing in *Woman in the Dunes.*" *U.S.–Japan Women's Journal (English Supplement)* 26 (2004): 30–54.

Currie, William. "Abe Kōbō's Nightmare World of Sand." *Approaches to the Modern Japanese Novel.* Ed. Kinya Tsuruta and Thomas E. Swann. Tokyo: Sophia University, 1976. 1–18.

———. "Metaphors of Alienation: The Fiction of Abe, Beckett and Kafka." Ph.D. diss. University of Michigan, 1973. Ann Arbor: UMI, 1974. Trans. Anzai Tetsuo as *Sogai no kōzu: Abe Kōbō, Beketto, Kafuka no shōsetsu.* Tokyo: Shinchōsha, 1975.

Daub, Edward E., R. Byron Bird, and Nobuo Inoue. *Comprehending Technical Japanese.* Madison, WI: University of Wisconsin Press, 1975.

Dissanayake, Wimal. "Self, Place and Body in *The Woman in the Dunes*: A Comparative Study of the Novel and the Film." *Literary Relations East and West: Selected Essays*. Ed. Jean Toyama and Nobuko Ochner. Honolulu, HI: College of Languages, Linguistics, and Literature, University of Hawai'i at Mānoa and the East-West Center, 1990. 41–54.

Dworkin, Andrea. *Intercourse*. New York: Free Press Paperbacks, 1987.

Eichenbaum, Boris M. "The Theory of the Formal Method." *Russian Formalist Criticism: Four Essays*. Ed. and trans. Lee T. Lemon and Marion J. Reis. Lincoln, NE: University of Nebraska Press, 1965. 99–139.

Eichman, Erich. "The End of the Affair." *New Criterion* 15.4 (1996): 77–80.

Etō Jun. Rev. of *Daiyon kanpyōki*. *Tosho shinbun* 14 Feb 1959. *Zen bungei jihyō* [Complete reviews]. Vol. 1. Tokyo: Shinchōsha, 1989. 44–45.

The Face of Another. Dir. Teshigahara Hiroshi. Screenplay Abe Kōbō. Music Takemitsu Tōru. Sets Isozaki Arata. *Pitfall, Woman in the Dunes, The Face of Another: Three Films of Hiroshi Teshigahara*. Criterion-Janus, 2007. DVD.

Fish, Stanley. "Professor Sokal's Bad Joke." *New York Times* 21 May 1996, late ed.: A23.

Foster, Michael. "Creating Monsters: Toriyama Sekien and the Encyclopedic Imagination." *Minikomi* 64 (2002): 7–9.

———. *Pandemonium and Parade: Japanese Monsters and the Culture of Yōkai*. Berkeley, CA: University of California Press, 2008.

Foucault, Michel. *The Order of Things: An Archaeology of the Human Sciences. A Translation of* Les Mots et les choses. New York: Pantheon, 1970.

———. "The Discourse on Language." Trans. Rupert Swyer. *The Archaeology of Knowledge & The Discourse on Language*. New York: Pantheon. 215–37.

Fujii, James. *Complicit Fictions: The Subject in the Modern Japanese Prose Narrative*. Berkeley, CA: University of California Press, 1993.

Fukushima Akira. "*Tanin no kao* ni tsuite no sanbunteki memo" [A prose memo on *The Face of Another*]. *Eureka* 8.3 (1976): 110–13.

Gardner, William. "Tsutsui Yasutaka and the Multimedia Performance of Authorship." Bolton, Csicsery-Ronay, Jr., and Tatsumi 83–98.

Gold, Ivan. "Waiting for the End of the World." Rev. of *The Ark Sakura*. *Washington Post* 27 Mar. 1988, final ed.: Book World 10. *ProQuest National Newspapers Premier*. Web. Accessed 14 June 2008.

Gross, Paul R., and Norman Levitt. *Higher Superstition: The Academic Left and Its Quarrels with Science*. Baltimore, MD: Johns Hopkins University Press, 1994.

Hanada Yutaka. *Avan gyarudo geijutsu* [Avant-garde art]. Bunkobon ed. Tokyo: Kōdansha Bungei Bunko, 1994.

Hariu Ichirō. Rev. of *Daiyon kanpyōki*. *Nihon dokusho shinbun* 20 July 1959: 3.

Hayles, N. Katherine, ed. *Chaos and Order: Complex Dynamics in Literature and Science*. Chicago, IL: University of Chicago Press, 1991.

———. *Chaos Bound: Orderly Disorder in Contemporary Literature and Science*. Ithaca, NY: Cornell University Press, 1990.

———. *The Cosmic Web: Scientific Field Models and Literary Strategies in the 20th Century*. Ithaca, NY: Cornell University Press, 1984.

———. *How We Became Posthuman*. Chicago, IL: University of Chicago Press, 1999.

Hirano Hidehisa. "Kamen no tsumi: Abe Kōbō *Tanin no kao*" [The crimes of the mask: Abe Kōbō's *The Face of Another*]. *Kamen no tsumi: sengo sakka ron* [The crimes of the mask: studies of postwar authors]. Tokyo: Kindai Bungeisha, 1983. 9–33.

Hiraoka Tokuyori. Kaisetsu. *Mikkai*. Bunkobon ed. Tokyo: Shinchō Bunko, 1983. 248–54.

Hutcheon, Linda. *A Theory of Parody: The Teachings of Twentieth-Century Art Forms*. New York: Methuen, 1985.

Iles, Timothy. *Abe Kōbō: An Exploration of his Prose, Drama and Theater*. Fucecchio, Italy: European Press Academic Publishing, 2000.

Ishiguro Tatsuaki. *Heisei sannen gogatsu futsuka, kōtensei men'ekifuzen shōkōgun nite kyūsei sareta Akadera Nobuhiko-hakushi, oyobi ni. . .* [Dr. Akadera Nobuhiko, who passed away suddenly from acquired immune deficiency syndrome on May 2, 1994, and. . .]. Tokyo: Fukutake Shoten, 1994.

Ishikawa Kōji. "Keshigomu de kakareta SF" [Science fiction written with an eraser]. *SF magajin* 34.4 (1993): 172–73.

Ishikawa Takashi. "Abe Kōbō no bunshō: *S. Karuma-shi no hanzai* ni tsuite" [Abe Kōbō's prose style: *The Crime of S. Karma*]. *Gengo seikatsu* 49 (1955): 37–43.

Isoda Kōichi. Kaisetsu. *Daiyon kanpyōki*. Bunkobon ed. Tokyo: Shinchō Bunko, 1970.

———. "Mukokusekisha no shiten" [Perspective of a nationless person]. *Nihon bungaku kenkyū shiryō sōsho: Abe Kōbō, Ōe Kenzaburō* [Library of research materials in Japanese literature: Abe Kōbō and Ōe Kenzaburō]. Tokyo: Yūseidō, 1974. 30–39.

Jadczyk, Arkadiusz, and Laura Knight-Jadczyk. *The Bogdanov Affair*. Web. Accessed 10 Nov. 2006. <http://quantumfuture.net/quantum_future/bog-content.htm>.

Jameson, Fredric. *Postmodernism, or, the Cultural Logic of Late Capitalism*. Durham, NC: Duke University Press, 1991.

Japan Foundation. *Japanese Literature in Translation Search*. Web. Accessed 14 June 2008. <http://www.jpf.go.jp/e/db/index.html >.

Nihon chinbotsu [Japan sinks]. Dir. Higuchi Shinji. Screenplay Katō Masato. Jeneon, 2007. DVD.

Kafka, Franz. *The Metamorphosis*. Ed. and trans. Stanley Corngold. New York: W.W. Norton, 1996.

Kakutani, Michiko. "Half Boys' Clubhouse and Half Survivalist Bunker." Rev. of *The Ark Sakura*. *New York Times* 23 Mar. 1988: C24. *ProQuest Historical Newspapers New York Times*. Web. Accessed 14 June 2008.

Kant, Immanuel. *Critique of Judgment*. Trans. Werner S. Pluhar. Indianapolis, IN: Hackett, 1987.

Karatani Kōjin. *Origins of Japanese Literature*. Trans. Brett de Bary et al. Durham, NC: Duke University Press, 1993. Trans. of *Nihon kindai bungaku no kigen*. Tokyo: Kōdansha Bungei Bunko, 1988.

———. "One Spirit, Two Nineteenth Centuries." *Postmodernism and Japan*. Ed. Masao Miyoshi and H. D. Harootunian. Durham, NC: Duke University Press, 1989. 259–72.

Kawamata Chiaki. "Tsuitō Abe Kōbō" [Obituary for Abe Kōbō]. *SF magajin* 34.4 (1993): 172.

Keane, Kevin. "A Nuclear Noah Builds His *Ark*." Rev. of *The Ark Sakura*. *Los Angeles Times* 17 Apr. 1988, home ed.: Book Review 6. *ProQuest Newspapers Los Angeles Times*. Web. Accessed 14 June 2008.

Keene, Donald. *Dawn to the West: Japanese Literature in the Modern Era*. New York: Henry Holt, 1984.

———. *Five Modern Japanese Novelists*. New York: Columbia University Press, 2003.

Kirwan, Jack D. "Casting a Theater of the Absurd Deep Inside a Japanese Cavern." *Chicago Tribune* 24 Apr. 1988, Final ed.: Books 6. *ProQuest Newspapers Chicago Tribune*. Web. Accessed 14 June 2008.

Komatsu Sakyō. Interview with Susan Napier et al. Trans. Christopher Bolton. *Science Fiction Studies* 29.3 (2002): 323–39.

———. *Japan Sinks*. Abr. and trans. Michael Gallagher. 2nd. abr. ed. Tokyo: Kodansha International, 1995.

Komori Yōichi. "Buntai to shite no jiko ishiki: *Ukigumo* no shujinkō" [Self consciousness as style: the protagonist of *Floating Clouds*]. *Buntai to shite no monogatari* [Narrative as style]. Tokyo: Chikuma Shobō, 1988. 21–57.

———. "Kattōtai to shite no katari: *Ukigumo* no ji no bun" [Narrative as conflict: the language of *Floating Clouds*]. *Kōzō to shite no katari* [Narration as structure]. Tokyo: Shin'yōsha, 1988. 85–124.

Kumamoto Mariko. "Abe Kōbō *Daiyon kanpyōki* ni tsuite" [On Abe Kōbō's *Inter Ice Age 4*]. *Kokubungaku nenjibetsu ronbunshū: kindai* 4 (1983): 178–83.

Kusaka Hideaki. "By Way: *Daiyon kanpyōki* ni tsuite" [By Way: On Abe Kōbō's *Inter Ice Age 4*]. *Eureka* 8.3 (1976): 146–51.

Kuwahara Masaomi. *Abe Kōbō bungaku kenkyū sankō bunken mokuroku* [Bibliography of Abe Kōbō research materials]. Nara: self-published, 2000.

Law, Jules David. *The Rhetoric of Empiricism: Language and Perception from Locke to I. A. Richards.* Ithaca, NY: Cornell University Press, 1993.

Leithauser, Brad. "Severed Futures." Rev. of *The Ark Sakura. The New Yorker* 9 May 1988: 122–26.

Levy, Hideo and Shimada Masahiko. "Genkyō no Manshū" [Manchuria, the phantom homeland]. Taidan [discussion]. *Eureka* 26.8 (1994): 72–84.

Levy, Alan. "The Box Man Cometh." *New York Times Magazine* 17 Nov. 1974: 36+.

Lewell, John. *Modern Japanese Novelists: A Biographical Dictionary.* Tokyo: Kodansha International, 1993.

Lidin, Olof G. "Abe Kobo's Internationalism." *Rethinking Japan.* Ed. Adriana Boscaro, Franco Gatti, and Massimo Raveri. Vol. 1. New York: St. Martin's Press, 1991. 2–9.

Lindberg, David C. *The Beginnings of Western Science: The European Scientific Tradition in Philosophical, Religious, and Institutional Context, 600 B.C. to A.D. 1450.* Chicago, IL: University of Chicago Press, 1992.

The editors of *Lingua Franca*, eds. *The Sokal Hoax: The Sham That Shook the Academy.* Lincoln, NE: University of Nebraska Press, 2000.

Lippit, Akira Mizuta. *Atomic Light (Shadow Optics).* Minneapolis, MN: University of Minnesota Press, 2005.

Locke, John. *An Essay Concerning Human Understanding.* Ed. Roger Woolhouse. New York: Penguin, 1997.

Longinus on the Sublime. Ed. and trans. W. Rhys Roberts. Cambridge, UK: Cambridge University Press, 1935.

Lyotard, Jean-François. *The Postmodern Condition: A Report on Knowledge.* Trans. Geoff Bennington and Brian Massumi. Minneapolis, MN: University of Minnesota Press, 1984.

MacLean, Kenneth. *John Locke and English Literature of the Eighteenth Century.* New York: Russell & Russell, 1962.

Mazzoni, Jacopo. *On the Defense of the* Comedy *of Dante.* Abr. and trans. R. L. Montgomery. *Critical Theory Since Plato.* Ed. Hazard Adams. 2nd ed. Fort Worth, TX: Harcourt, 1971. 163–73.

McDonald, Keiko I. "Sand, Man, and Symbols: Teshigahara's *The Woman in the Dunes.*" *Cinema East.* Rutherford, NJ: Fairleigh Dickinson University Press, 1983. 36–50.

Miner, Earl. "Life Is a Sandpit." Rev. of *Woman in the Dunes. Saturday Review* 5 Sept. 1964: 32.

Miwa Tomoo and Oka Hidemichi. *Seibutsu I* [Biology I]. Tokyo: Sanshōdō, 1972.

Miyoshi, Masao, and H. D. Harootunian, eds. *Postmodernism and Japan.* Durham, NC: Duke University Press, 1989.

Monastersky, Richard. "French TV Stars Rock the World of Theoretical Physics." *Chronicle of Higher Education* 5 Nov. 2002. Web. Accessed 25 Feb. 2007. <http://chronicle.com/free/2002/11/2002110501n.htm>.

Monk, Samuel H. *The Sublime: A Study of Critical Theories in XVIII-Century England.* Ann Arbor, MI: University of Michigan Press, 1960.

Mori, Maryellen Toman. "Aware na koara to kisei no kaiware: Abe Kōbō no *Kangarū nōto* ni okeru musō kōzō" [Pitiful koalas and parasitic sprouts: the dream structure of Abe Kōbō's *Kangaroo Notebook*]. *Nihon ni okeru shūkyō to bungaku* [Religion and literature in Japan]. Tokyo: Kokusai Nihon Bunka Kenkyū Sentā, 1999. 170–79.

Morikawa Tatsuya. "Abe Kōbō: *Tanin no kao/Suna no onna.*" *Kokubungaku: kaishaku to kyōzai no kenkyū* 15.10 (1970): 172–73.

Morimoto Takako. "*Hakobune Sakura Maru* ron: futatsu no 'ana,' aruiwa shimyurākuru o koete" [*The Ark Sakura*: two "holes," or, beyond the simulacrum]. *Kokubungaku: kaishaku to kyōzai no kenkyū* 42.9 (1997): 73–79.

Morota Kazuharu. Rev. of *Mikkai. Nihon dokusho shinbun* 23 Jan. 1978: 5.

Motoyama Mutsuko. "The Literature and Politics of Abe Kōbō: Farewell to Communism in *Suna no Onna.*" *Monumenta Nipponica* 50.3 (1995): 305–23.

Murakami Haruki. *Hard-Boiled Wonderland and the End of the World.* Trans. Alfred Birnbaum. Tokyo: Kodansha International, 1991.

Murakami Ryū. *Coin Locker Babies.* Trans. Stephen Snyder. Tokyo: Kodansha International, 1998.

Muramatsu Takeshi. "*Tanin no kao* ni tsuite" [On *The Face of Another*]. *Kokubungaku: kaishaku to kanshō* 36.1 (1971): 163–65.

Murphy, Joseph A. *Metaphorical Circuit: Negotiations Between Literature and Science in Twentieth-Century Japan.* Ithaca, NY: Cornell University Press, 2004.

Nakamura Kiyoshi. *Kōbō to Yutaka no sekai* [The world of Abe Kōbō and Haniya Yutaka]. Tokyo: Kongen Shobō, 1983.

Nakayama Shigeru. *Science, Technology and Society in Postwar Japan.* London: Kegan Paul, 1991.

Napier, Susan J. *The Fantastic in Modern Japanese Literature: The Subversion of Modernity.* London and New York: Routledge, 1996.

Natsume Sōseki. "The Civilization of Modern-day Japan." Trans. Jay Rubin. *Kokoro, a Novel, and Selected Essays.* Lanham, MD: Madison Books, 1992. 257–

83. Trans. of "Gendai Nihon no kaika." *Sōseki zenshū.* Vol. 11. Tokyo: Iwanami Shoten, 1975. 319–43.

———. *The Wayfarer.* Trans. Beongcheon Yu. Detroit, MI: Wayne State University Press, 1967.

Nietzsche, Friedrich. *The Birth of Tragedy and The Case of Wagner.* Trans. Walter Kaufmann. New York: Vintage, 1964.

"Nōberu bungakushō Ōe Kenzaburō-shi ga jushō" [Ōe Kenzaburō wins Nobel prize]. *Asahi shinbun* 19 Oct. 1994, early ed.: 1.

Numano Mitsuyoshi. "Furoppī disuku no naka ni hakken sareta tegami" [Letter found on a floppy disk]. *Herumesu/Hermes* 46 (1993): 76.

Ōe Kenzaburō. Kaisetsu. *Tanin no kao.* Bunkobon ed. Tokyo: Shinchō Bunko, 1968. 285–90.

Okaniwa Noboru. *Hanada Kiyoteru to Abe Kōbō no sekai: avan garudo bungaku no saisei no tame ni* [The world of Hanada Kiyoteru and Abe Kōbō: for the sake of the avant-garde's rebirth]. Tokyo: Daisanbunmeisha, 1980.

Okuno Takeo. "Abe Kōbō no bungaku no kessaku: mugen no kanōsei to iu jigoku meguri" [Abe Kōbō's literary masterpiece: a hell of unlimited possibilities]. Kaisetsu. *Tanin no kao.* Tokyo: Horubu, 1975. 493–511.

———. "Abe Kōbō: sono hito to sakuhin" [Abe Kōbō and his works]. Kaisetsu. *Sekai SF zenshū.* Vol. 27. Tokyo: Hayakawa Shobō, 1974. 483–93.

———. "Kyōretsu na bungakuteki hishōsetsu taiken" [An anti-novel experience, literary and intense]. Rev. of *Mikkai. Sankei shinbun* 9 Jan. 1978: 7.

———. Rev. of *Hakobune Sakura Maru. Bungei jihyō* [Reviews]. Vol. 2. Tokyo: Kawade Shobō, 1993. 49.

Orlowski, Andrew. "Bogdanov Brothers Deny Bogosity." *The Register* 5 Nov. 2002. Web. Accessed 25 Feb. 2007. <http://www.theregister.co.uk/2002/11/05/bogdanov_brothers_deny_bogosity/>.

Overbye, Dennis. "Are They a) Geniuses or b) Jokers?; French Physicists' Cosmic Theory Creates a Big Bang of Its Own." *New York Times* 9 Nov. 2002, late ed.: B7.

Parker, William. "Enclosing the World in a Darkened Room: Ontological Aspects of Photography in *The Box Man.*" Abe Kōbō Commemorative Symposium. Columbia University. 20 Apr. 1996.

Plato. *The Dialogues of Plato.* Trans. B. Jowett. 3rd ed. Vol. 1. New York: Random House, 1937.

Poe, Edgar Allan. "Sonnet—To Science." *The Complete Works of Edgar Allan Poe.* Ed. James A. Harrison. Vol. 7. New York: AMS, 1965. 22.

Pollack, David. *Reading Against Culture: Ideology and Narrative in the Japanese Novel.* Ithaca, NY: Cornell University Press, 1992.

Ransom, John Crowe. "Poetry: A Note in Ontology" *The World's Body*. New York: Charles Scribner's Sons, 1938. 111–43.

Reynolds, Joshua. *Discourses on Art*. New York: Collier, 1961.

Richards, I. A. *Poetries and Sciences: A Reissue with a Commentary of* Science and Poetry *(1926, 1935)*. New York: W.W. Norton, 1970.

———. *Practical Criticism: A Study of Literary Judgment*. New York: Harcourt, Brace and Co., [1956?].

———. *Principles of Literary Criticism*. San Diego, CA: Harcourt, Brace and World, 1985.

Robbins, Bruce. "Anatomy of a Hoax." *Tikkun* 11.5 (1996): 58–59.

Rosen, Jay. "Swallow Hard: What *Social Text* Should Have Done. A Response to Bruce Robbins." *Tikkun* 11.5 (1996): 59–61.

Rubin, Jay. *Haruki Murakami and the Music of Words*. London: Harvill, 2002.

Saeki Shōichi. "Kokusaika no paradokkusu" [The paradox of internationalization]. *Abe Kōbō*. Ed. Takano Toshimi. *Shinchō bungaku arubamu* [Shinchō album of Japanese literature] 51. Tokyo: Shinchōsha, 1994. 97–103.

———. Rev. of *Mikkai*. *Shūkan dokushojin* 23 Jan. 1978: 2.

Sasaki Kiichi. "Dasshutsu to chōkoku: *Suna no onna* ron" [Escape and conquer: a study of *The Woman in the Dunes*]. *Shin Nihon bungaku* 17.9 (1962): 142–47.

Satō Tadao. Rev. of *Mikkai*. *Fujin kōron* 63.3 (1978): 338–39.

Satō Yasumasa. *"Tanin no kao."* *Kokubungaku: kaishaku to kanshō* 36.1 (1971): 105–10.

Schmitt, C. B. "Science in the Italian Universities in the Sixteenth and Early Seventeenth Centuries." *The Emergence of Science in Western Europe*. Ed. Maurice Crosland. London: Macmillan, 1975. 35–56.

Schnellbächer, Thomas. *Abe Kōbō, Literary Strategist: The Evolution of His Agenda and Rhetoric in the Context of the Postwar Japanese Avant-Garde and Communist Artists' Movements*. Munich: Iudicium, 2004.

———. "Has the Empire Sunk Yet?" Bolton, Csicsery-Ronay, Jr., and Tatsumi 35–43.

"Science Wars and the Need for Respect and Rigour." Editorial. *Nature* 385 (1997): 373.

Scott, Janny. "Postmodern Gravity Deconstructed, Slyly." *New York Times* 18 May 1996, late ed.: 1+.

Serizawa Shunsuke. "Tōsaku no ronri o teko ni sekai o tentō" [Perverse logic as a lever to overturn the world]. Rev. of *Mikkai*. *Tosho shinbun* 17 Dec. 1977: 1+.

Shelley, Percy Bysshe. *A Defence of Poetry*. *The Complete Works of Percy Bysshe Shelley*. Ed. Roger Ingpen and Walter E. Peck. Vol. 7. New York: Gordian Press, 1965. 109–40.

Shields, Nancy K. *Fake Fish: The Theater of Kobo Abe*. New York: Weatherhill, 1996. Trans. as *Abe Kōbō no gekijō*. Tokyo: Shinchōsha, 1997.

Shimada Masahiko. "Shinkei kabin na hodo te no konda shikake" [A mechanism intricate to the point of oversensitivity]. *Asahi Journal* 8 Feb. 1985: 65.

Shindo Masaaki. "*Daiyon kanpyōki* to mirai no owari" [*Inter Ice Age 4* and the end of the future]. *Eureka* 26.8 (1994): 112–17.

Shirai Kenzaburō. Rev. of *Tanin no kao*. *Asahi Journal* 1 Nov. 1964: 71–72.

Snyder, Stephen. "Extreme Imagination: The Fiction of Murakami Ryū." *Ōe and Beyond: Fiction in Contemporary Japan*. Ed. Stephen Snyder and Philip Gabriel. Honolulu, HI: University of Hawai'i Press, 1999. 199–218.

Sobchack, Vivian. *The Address of the Eye: A Phenomenology of Film Experience*. Princeton, NJ: Princeton University Press, 1992.

———. *Screening Space: The American Science Fiction Film*. 2nd ed. New York: Ungar, 1993.

———. "Toward a Phenomenology of Cinematic and Electronic Presence: The Scene of the Screen." *Post Script* 10.1 (1990): 50–59.

Sokal, Alan D. *Articles on the "Social Text" Affair*. Web. Accessed 7 July 1998. <http://www.physics.nyu.edu/faculty/sokal/index.html>.

———. "A Physicist Experiments with Cultural Studies." *Lingua Franca* 6.4 (1996): 62–64.

———. "Transgressing the Boundaries: An Afterword." *Dissent* 43.4 (1996): 93–99.

———. "Transgressing the Boundaries: Towards a Transformative Hermeneutics of Quantum Gravity." *Social Text* 14.1–2 (1996): 217–52.

———. "What the *Social Text* Affair Does and Does Not Prove." *A House Built on Sand: Exposing Postmodernist Myths about Science*. Ed. Noretta Koertge. Oxford, UK: Oxford University Press, 1998. 9–22.

———. Interview with Robert Siegel. *All Things Considered*. National Public Radio. 15 May 1996. Web. Accessed 25 Feb. 2007. <http://www.npr.org/ramarchives/nc6M1501-7.ram>.

Steiner, Peter. *Russian Formalism: A Metapoetics*. Ithaca, NY: Cornell University Press, 1984.

Sterling, Bruce, ed. *Mirrorshades: The Cyberpunk Anthology*. New York: Arbor House, 1986.

———. "Slipstream." *SF Eye* 5 (July 1989): 78–80. *Electronic Frontier Foundation Publications Archive*. Web. Accessed 14 June 2007. <http://w2.eff.org/Misc/Publications/>.

Sukegawa Noriyuki. "*Daiyon kanpyōki*." *Kokubungaku: kaishaku to kanshō* 36.1 (1971): 96–100.

Suter, Rebecca. *The Japanization of Modernity: Murakami Haruki Between Japan and the United States.* Cambridge, MA: Harvard University Asia Center, 2008.

Switzer, John. "Unofficial Summary of the Rush Limbaugh Show for Wednesday, May 22, 1996." Posting to group alt.rush-limbaugh. 25 May 1996. Web. Accessed 26 June 2008. <http://groups.google.com/group/alt.rush-limbaugh/msg/063c76bb478255cf>.

Takano Toshimi. *Abe Kōbō ron* [A study of Abe Kōbō]. Rev. ed. Tokyo: Kashinsha, 1979.

———. "Hyōden Abe Kōbō" [Critical biography of Abe Kōbō]. *Abe Kōbō.* Ed. Takano Toshimi. *Shinchō Nihon bungaku arubamu* [Shinchō album of Japanese literature] 51. Tokyo: Shinchōsha, 1994. 2–96.

Taki Shigeru. "Kaitei no Īkarusu: Abe Kōbō *Daiyon kanpyōki*" [An undersea Icarus: Abe Kōbō's *Inter Ice Age 4*]. *Shin Nihon bungaku* 14.9 (1959): 112–17.

Tani Shinsuke. *Abe Kōbō hyōden nenpyō* [Abe Kōbō critical biographical chronology]. Tokyo: Shinchōsha, 2002.

Tatsumi Takayuki. *Full Metal Apache: Transactions Between Cyberpunk Japan and Avant-Pop America.* Durham, NC: Duke University Press, 2006.

———. "Hakobunejō muishiki: surippusutorīmu josetsu" [Ark-shaped unconscious: an introduction to slipstream]. *Herumesu/Hermes* 46 (Nov. 1993): 71–75.

———. "The History of Japanese Science Fiction 'Prodom': Between Japanese Science Fiction and Science-Fictional Japan." Trans. Christopher Bolton et. al. *Souvenir Book* [conference program] for Nippon 2007: Joint World Science Fiction Convention and Japan Science Fiction Convention. Pacifico Yokohama. 30 Aug.–5 Sept. 2007. E33-E39. Trans. of "Nihon SF purodamu no rekishi: Nihon SF to SF-teki Nihon no hazama de" in the same volume. J28-J34.

Taylor, Robert. "Kobo Abe's Artistic Shipwreck." Rev. of *The Ark Sakura. Boston Globe* 6 Apr. 1988: Living 30.

Tsutsui Yasutaka. "The African Bomb." *The African Bomb and Other Stories.* Tokyo: Kodansha English Library, 1986. 7–62. Trans. of "Afurika no bakudan." *Afurika no bakudan.* Tokyo: Kadokawa Bunko, 1971. 224–69.

U.S. Department of Homeland Security. *Ready.gov.* Web. Accessed Mar. 1, 2004. <http://www.ready.gov>.

Van Wert, William F. "Levels of Sexuality in the Novels of Kobo Abe." *International Fiction Review* 6.2 (1979): 129–32.

Watanabe Hiroshi. *Abe Kōbō.* Tokyo: Shinbisha, 1976.

———. "Datsu 'shūmatsu' kūkan no kyokō" [A fictional space outside the end times]. Rev. of *Hakobune Sakura Maru. Waseda bungaku* 17.3 (1985): 102–3.

———. Kaisetsu. *R62 gō no hatsumei, Namari no tamago* [R62's invention and The leaden egg]. Tokyo: Shinchō Bunko, 1974. 287–92.

Weinberg, Bernard. *A History of Literary Criticism in the Italian Renaissance.* 2 vols. Chicago, IL: University of Chicago Press, 1961.

Weinberg, Steven. "Sokal's Hoax." *New York Review of Books* 43.13 (1996): 11–15.

White, Edmund. "Round and Round the Eupcaccia Goes." Rev. of *The Ark Sakura. New York Times* 10 Apr. 1988: Book Review 9.

Wightman, W. P. D. *Science and the Renaissance: An Introduction to the Study of the Emergence of the Sciences in the Sixteenth Century.* Vol. 1. New York: Hafner, 1962.

Wimsatt, William K., Jr. and Cleanth Brooks. *Literary Criticism: A Short History.* New York: Knopf, 1957.

Woman in the Dunes. Dir. Teshigahara Hiroshi. Screenplay Abe Kōbō. Music Takemitsu Tōru. Cinematography Segawa Hiroshi. *Pitfall, Woman in the Dunes, The Face of Another: Three Films of Hiroshi Teshigahara.* Criterion-Janus, 2007. DVD.

Wordsworth, William. "Preface to the Second Edition of the Lyrical Ballads." *The Poetical Works of William Wordsworth.* Ed. E. de Selincourt. 2nd. ed. Vol. 2. Oxford, UK: Clarendon Press, 1952. 384–404.

———. "The Prelude, or, Growth of a Poet's Mind." Ed. Ernest de Selincourt. 2nd. ed. Oxford, UK: Clarendon Press, 1959.

Yamada Kazuko. "Gendai bungaku: sono SF-teki zen'ei 'Abe Kōbō'" [Contemporary literature: the science fictional cutting edge Abe Kōbō]. *Kokubungaku: kaishaku to kyōzai no kenkyū* 27.11 (1982): 112–13.

Yamamoto Fumiko. "Metamorphosis in Abe Kōbō's Works." *Journal of the Association of Teachers of Japanese* 15.2 (1980): 171–94.

Yamano Kōichi. "*Daiyon kanpyōki.*" *Eureka* 8.3 (1976): 142–45.

———. Rev. of *Mikkai. Shūkan dokushojin* 23 Jan. 1978: 3.

Yokomitsu Riichi. "Machine." Trans. Edward Seidensticker. *Modern Japanese Stories.* Rutland, VT: Tuttle, 1962. 223–44. Trans. of "Kikai." *Yokomitsu Riichi zenshū* [Complete works of Yokomitsu Riichi]. Vol. 3. Tokyo: Kawade Shobō, 1956. 359–77.

Zola, Émile. *The Experimental Novel and Other Essays.* Trans. Belle M. Sherman. New York: Haskell House, 1964.

Index

Harvard East Asian Monographs

(*out-of-print)